Glynn E. Newman, Ph.D.

Sixth Edition | *Texas Edition*

American Government

AND PUBLIC POLICY TODAY

ORIGINS, INSTITUTIONS AND MODERN DEMOCRACIES

Kendall Hunt
publishing company

Cover images © Shutterstock, Inc.

THE WORKSHEETS IN THIS TEXT ARE INTENDED TO BE TORN
OUT OF THE TEXT AND USED BY STUDENTS IN CONJUNCTION
WITH CLASSROOM INSTRUCTION.

Kendall Hunt
publishing company

www.kendallhunt.com
Send all inquiries to:
4050 Westmark Drive
Dubuque, IA 52004-1840

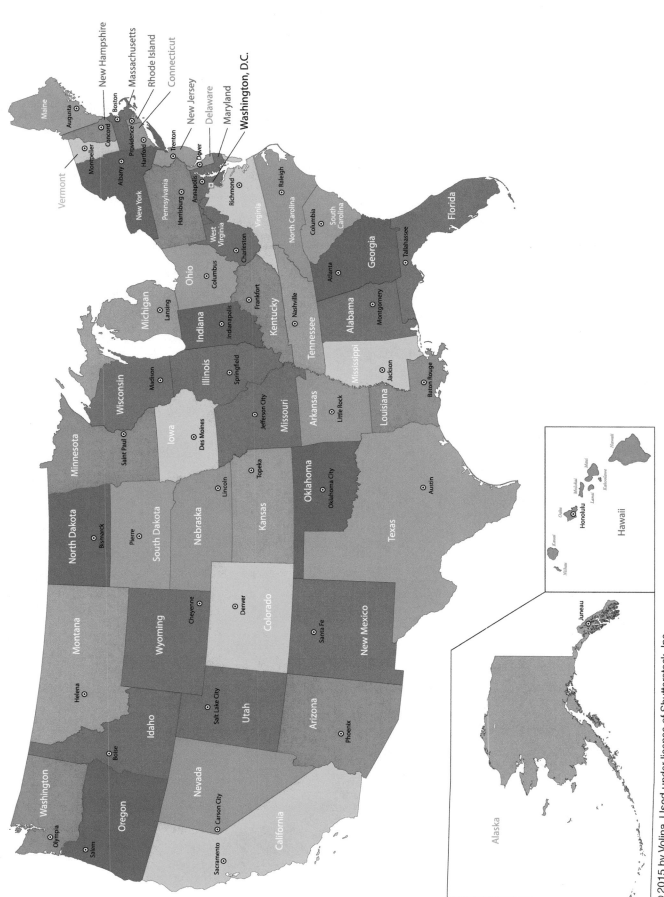

CONTENTS

ACKNOWLEDGMENTS

I have enjoyed the privilege of writing this book over the last year, but am glad to have completed it. It was always a dream of mine to one day write my own book and my students and department chair at Eastfield College in Mesquite, Texas inspired me to try once more to create new and innovative material.

In addition, I would like to thank the following:

- My God for giving me insight and faith so that I can always find encouragement and strength when things were moving slowly.
- Glynn Thomas Newman (GT), my son for giving me a new perspective on life.
- Brailey Newman, my beautiful daughter, whom I adore so much. Who is always keeping an eye on the calendar and encouraging me to finish the book so we can go out and play.
- Ruth Newman, my mother, whom I love and respect for all of her positive advice throughout the years.
- Sharon Newman, my wife, M.Ed., for her support and love of our family. I appreciate her constructive criticism and contributions as first stage editor during this arduous process.
- Finally, to the men and women who serve our country so that freedom can be a away of life for all of us in the United States.

ABOUT THE AUTHOR

Glynn E. Newman is part of the Government faculty for the Dallas County Community College, Eastfield Campus. He is the author of five books on American government and public policy. He has written articles on the leadership failures of Hurricane Katrina, e-government, and strategic management. He was appointed to serve as commissioner for the city of Dallas Automated Red Light Enforcement Commission in 2012, where his expertise was utilized as apart of the advisory body to the city manager and city council. He received several awards and accolades, including the Publisher Author Award in both 2009 and 2011. He has participated and moderated several political debates. Professor Newman received his undergraduate degree in political science from Saint Edwards University, a masters degree in public administration from St. Mary's University, further studies in political ecology from Virginia Tech and a doctorate in public policy from Walden University.

He is married and has a daughter and a son.

PART 1

American Government and Public Policy

CHAPTER 1
Democracy in America

EVOLUTION OF AMERICAN DEMOCRACY

Rawpixel/Shutterstock.com

America **democracy** is a system of government that gives power to the people, whether directly or through elected representatives. Many societies claim to have a democratic government; however, in order to have a true democracy a government must allow dignity of individuals, equal protection under the law, decisions made by majority rule, opportunity for each individual to participate in decision making, and one person having one vote. When any of the aforementioned concepts are removed, then democracy is incomplete. Let us examine for a moment where the notion of government comes from. During a period before Christ theorists began expressing such philosophies as **natural law,** a doctrine that says society should be governed by certain ethical principles that are a part of nature and can be understood by reason. It was Aristotle (384–322 BC) who was first to speak of natural law. By 1225, Thomas Aquinas added considerably to the theory of natural law by including a Christian framework. Aquinas argued that God created life and liberty from natural law. The king of England did not respect the theorist and continued to rule as a monarch, stating his rule came from a divine right directly from God. The king believed that if he was put in power, the citizens should not question God's will. The government reflected the will of God and people should not complain about it. During the Reformation period people began to reject Roman Catholicism and form a Protestant faith. It was this faith that promoted a belief that people could talk directly with God. The people did not believe they needed the priest and, as a result, they could also govern themselves. Additional ideas by philosophers and scientists would come during the period of Enlightenment.

Through the use of science, reason, and toleration Isaac Newton (1642–1727) expanded the notion of self-government. Together theorists were able to challenge the idea that fate controlled a person's destiny and kings ruled because God wanted them to. The belief that any person could talk directly with God caused the separatists to leave the Anglican Church. If you can talk to God one on one, why not govern yourself? They began to govern themselves and develop social compacts. The belief was very strong as noted from the early settlers arriving in America; they signed the Mayflower Compact while still aboard the ship. This compact was secular in nature; the Pilgrims called it a covenant because of the relationship with God. Other religions at the time were Baptist, Presbyterian, and Congregationalist.

It was not long before John Locke (1632–1704) and Thomas Hobbes (1588–1679), two English theorists of the seventeenth century, constructed a **social contract theory**. This theory says people are free and equal by God-given rights and that this, in turn, requires that all people give their consent to be governed, as expressed by John Locke. The two men believed that even with a God-destined government, people were free and equal by natural right. Because of this belief they argued that men should give their consent to be governed. It is very clear both theorists wanted some form of government. Hobbes argued that men were in fact brutish and by nature wanted war. If life was to exist Hobbes believed we needed the monarchy and without it life would be a state of nature in which men would destroy one another. In order for this not to happen, men would give the government rights over them. Hobbes said even a single ruler would be better than none at all. He said granting government authority over the individual is a small price in comparison to what life would be like without government. John Locke, on the other hand, was not as convinced as Hobbes about giving control to one ruler. Locke argued that the main responsibility of government was to preserve and protect private property of the citizen. It is very noticeable that Locke's work made its way into our Constitution. He also believed that the consent of the people is the fundamental basis for any sovereign's right to rule. With government, Locke says, we can preserve life, liberty, and property and ensure justice. Thomas Jefferson used much of Locke's work while writing the Declaration of Independence because of his explanation on life, liberty and property. This was the American colonies' justification for a split from England based on violations of the social contract.

POLITICS IN AMERICA

What is politics? **Politics** is the science or art of government, or the allocation of resources. Harold Lasswell defines it as "determining who gets what, when, where, and how in society."[1] What is it that we want out of society? Power, money, sex, cars, respect itself. When we come to the subject of politics, many people believe they have some general knowledge of the topic. Most people experience politics in some fashion in their lives. The political experience may have been in church, on a date, at the office, and on campus. The reason we study politics is specific to the government. Though politics do exist beyond government our focus is government. When we study political science it is the study of who gets what, when, where, and how. The reason we study political science is to understand our political environment or political atmosphere, who is in power, the president and Congress. It enables citizens to hold an intellectual conversation about government and politics and to know how government and politics operate in one's society. **Government** is an organization that extends to the entire society that legitimately uses force to carry out its decisions. When we think of politics as it extends to the whole society, it can only be in the form of government. Even though politics are a part of schools, churches, and businesses, those do not extend to the whole society. For example, Eastfield College has politics, but the politics are isolated to the members associated with the school; however, they can extend beyond the institution on matters of transportation and law enforcement.

A LAND OF LAW, NOT OF PEOPLE

America is a nation of laws, not of people. The Constitution of the United States is the basis for limiting the powers of government. It is the Constitution that allows people freedom and disallows government to interfere with your freedoms. When we read the First Amendment to the Bill of Rights we recognize "Congress will make no law" is simply letting the citizen know government will not interfere with certain rights. These rights are considered beyond the reach of government. The First Amendment guarantees the freedom of speech, press, and religion to be removed from the hands of government. Even if a majority of citizens decide to stop religious freedom the government could not do so because of the law. If a majority of citizens or the legislative branch vote to pass a law to halt religious freedom, the judiciary would step in and declare the law unconstitutional.

A FOREIGN EYE ON DEMOCRACY

In 1835 a French philosopher Alexis de Tocqueville, visited America and observed the workings of our system of self-government. He published a book called *Democracy in America* based on what he observed while visiting the country. He witnessed America and more, seeing a land of fear, character, hope, prejudice, and passion. He would later explain he saw America beyond a framework; his eyes saw a democracy.[2]

Many countries claim to have a democracy but are not true democracies. In America we try to set an example for the world of how democracy should work. We began that process over two hundred years ago. Our country has had its fair share of problems; given our level of diversity, rate of crimes and hostility, we still rank as the best there is compared to other democracies in the world. We must continue to make our system work better each day, realizing it is an ongoing process.

DIRECT AND REPRESENTATIVE DEMOCRACY

Democracy is a system where people rule, either directly or through elected representatives. We are a government of the people, by the people, for the people as stated by Abraham Lincoln in his Gettysburg Address years ago. America still holds on to that phrase today. It is an idea that has allowed people to share in government. Today America is spread across more than 4 million square miles with 275 million Americans. The possibility of Americans coming together to discuss issues of concern with public officials would be impossible today. The people would need more than 5,000 years just to be heard; many would turn gray or die waiting to speak.[3] Some countries allow the people direct political control; other countries allow indirect power. A system of **direct democracy** is a type of government where people govern themselves, vote on policies and laws, and live by majority rule. We no longer rely on direct democracy. The closest thing we have today is the New England town meeting, a type of government going back to the early 1700s. The town meeting was held by a vested board of public officials elected by the townspeople to make policies between town meetings and appointed administrators who carried out day-to-day operations. The citizens all participate and have an opportunity to express their views and cast their votes equally on issues that affect their lives each and every day. A town meeting could be held in a smaller town today, but generally it does not occur. We saw in the 2000 presidential campaign that U.S. Senator John McCain called a town meeting in New Hampshire's presidential primary. The purpose was to hear the concerns of the people directly for himself. The process of direct democracy was not favored by King George III and went against his principles of dictatorship. The method was useful for the time and still is being used in 80 percent of New England townships today.

Representative democracy recognizes the limits on the American people and realizes that not all people can come together to make decisions on every issue. This is the type of democracy we have in the United States. Elected representatives make decisions on behalf of the people. The elections must be competitive so all people have an opportunity to participate and give a chance to elect a candidate that best represents their own views. The election should be in an environment of free speech and press so both candidate and voters can express their views freely. The candidate elected will serve with terms so that if the people decide the views of the candidate no longer reflect their views then he or she can be removed from office. If a government is to be a representative democracy it must meet the following requirements: (1) all people have an opportunity to vote, (2) free expression will be allowed by candidate and voters, (3) elections will be competitive, and (4) votes select the representatives periodically. Saddam Hussein has called his government a democracy, but ask yourself why there was only one party running a candidate? Are candidates and voters free to express themselves? Are the leaders elected for life? If the answer is yes to any of these questions, then it is not a democracy.

THE MAJORITY OR POWER ELITE

The United States of America is generally perceived by a large number of people to be controlled by a majority of the citizens. The democracy is an ideal that allows Americans to feel empowered. In reality can millions of Americans really govern themselves, or have an equal say? Maybe it is a few people who govern because they have gained more power than others. Is it the majority or the elite governing? I suggest we take a close look at the power elite in America.

Online Connections

Use the Web to learn more about democracy.

The following Internet websites are ways that you can enhance your study of democracy. An Internet site is listed with a description of what you can find on the page.

This site highlights Alexis de Tocqueville's thoughts on American democracy. *http://www .tocqueville.org*

The U.S. State Department authors this website. Here you will find links to general government knowledge that describe the workings of the government. *http://usinfo.state.gov/ usa/infousa/politics/politics.htm*

This website highlights the CNN special, *Democracy in America*. It follows the 2000 presidential election and its impact on society. *http://www.cnn.com/SPECIALS/2000/ democracy*

Key Terms

Democracy   3

Natural law   3

Social contract theory   4

Politics   4

Government   5

Direct democracy   5

Representative democracy   6

Suggested Readings

Anthony V. Bouza, *The Decline and Fall of the American Empire: Corruption, Decadence, and the American Dream* (New York: Plenum Press, 1996).

David Easton, *The Political System* (New York: Knopf, 1953).

Edward Greenburg and Benjamin Page, *The Struggle for Democracy* (New York: Free Press, 1991).

Michael Sandel, *Democracy's Discontent: America in Search of a Public Philosophy* (Cambridge: Harvard University Press, 1996).

Notes

[1]Harold Lasswell, *Politics: Who Gets What, When and How* (New York: McGraw-Hill, 1936).

[2]Alexis de Tocqueville, *Democracy in America*, 2 vols., 1835 (New York: Vintage, 1955).

[3]E. E. Shattschneider, *Two Hundred Million Americans in Search of a Government* (New York: Holt, Rinehart, & Winston, 1969), p. 63.

NAME_____ COURSE_____ SECTION_____

1. Name and explain the five components of a democracy.

_____

_____

_____

_____

2. Define social contract theory and explain the implications of life without it.

_____

_____

_____

_____

_____

3. Why is America a "land of law, not of people"?

_____

_____

_____

_____

4. Compare and contrast direct democracy and representative democracy.

_____

_____

_____

_____

Directions: Write the word or phrase that completes the statement.

1. Natural law was proposed by _____.

2. _____ is a doctrine that society should be governed by certain ethical principles.

3. _____ and _____ proposed the social contract theory.

4. _____ is determining who gets what, when, where, and how in society.

5. _____ limits the powers of government.

Directions: Circle the correct answer to each of the following questions.

6. Which of the following is not a characteristic of a democracy?
   a. Equal protection under the law
   b. Decisions made by majority rule
   c. One person having one vote
   d. Decisions made by Congress

7. In 1700 New England, the people conducted town meetings to vote on policies and laws, and live by majority rule. The people in this town governed themselves. What type of democracy is this?
   a. Direct democracy
   b. Indirect democracy
   c. Constitutional democracy
   d. Representative democracy

8. Locke and Hobbes differed in their notion of _____.
   a. what rights should be given
   b. consent of the people
   c. control given to one ruler
   d. none of the above

CHAPTER 2
The U.S. Constitution

THE CONSTITUTION: DEFINED

The purpose of a constitution is to provide structures, functions, and limitations of a government. In the United States we have a **constitutional** government, a government of laws, not of people. The freedom of individuals goes far beyond the reach of government and majorities, thus our constitution must limit governmental authority. The document does so by establishing individual liberties that are not to be touched by government even with the consent of the majority.

Governmental authority is legally established by our Constitution. It establishes governmental bodies (House of Representatives, the Senate, the presidency, and the Supreme Court). It determines the rules by which decisions are made and it spells out how members are to be chosen. Governmental bodies cannot change a constitution by ordinary acts. In order to change the Constitution it comes by a process called **general popular consent**, which means the majority of the American people agree on the change. The U.S. Constitution is "the supreme law of the land."[1]

CONSTITUTIONAL BEGINNINGS

In the New World, the British Empire no longer was in control. The settlers knew that as the new government was formed there were two parts that needed to be included, individual security and the **rule of law**, laws that govern the land. Several different forms of government evolved. These early governments served as a model for what American government would become. The first form of government was a compact type. The New England colonies started their governments on the idea of a **compact**, a type of agreement that legally binds two or more parties to enforceable rules. Puritan religion theory directly developed compacts. For example, Pilgrims that settled Plymouth colony entered into a covenant with God to start a church and secure one's own salvation, to forge a covenant or compact among each other to protect those natural liberties granted by God.

The second type of government established was a charter company. Charter companies were created for the purpose of exploiting the natural resources of the new world. The English King chartered the Massachusetts Bay Company as a private business venture. Trading companies created other colonies by charter to exploit the natural resources in the new world. The charter created a governing body made up of a governor, a deputy governor and assistants. The governing body was made up of freemen of the company with property and wealth. A trading company in England owned the Massachusetts Bay Company, but by 1629 the Cambridge Agreement caused stockholders to transfer governing rights from England to the Massachusetts Bay Company in the colonies.

A third type of government was proprietary colonies. The king granted individuals rights to set up a colony. They became the sole proprietor. New York, New Jersey, Maryland, Delaware, Pennsylvania, Georgia, and Carolinas were developed from royal grants, not compacts. The king issued a warrant granting land as a way of discharging the Crown's debts as well as governing rights to the barons or lords. In 1632, Lord Baltimore was granted Maryland and the territory of New York was issued to the Duke of York. These early colonies enjoyed the power and authority of kings. These proprietary colonies played a role unofficially by contributing to early American government by using parliamentary systems. Proprietary colony legislatures borrowed their structure and procedures from England's parliament consisting of two houses (bicameral), the House of Lords and Commons. In the United States today, we have a **bicameral legislature**, consisting of two chambers or two houses, fashioned after this model.

FIVE PRECEDENTS TO THE CONSTITUTION

There were **five** important events before the U.S. Constitution. The **first** important precedent came in 1215 known as the **Magna Carta**. This was a written document that stated that the powers of the king of England were not absolute. It recognized **feudal**, or individual, rights and limited monarchial power. The document supported the idea of **natural rights** articulated by the English philosophers, the most recognized of whom was John Locke. He wrote that people were born free and society was formed to protect their rights. The people believed that it was important to protect their rights as Englishmen, because the colonial government had denied them freedom. With 150 years of self-government the colonies were familiar with government. This helped them in the development of a constitution.

A **second** precedent was the **Mayflower Compact** of 1620, a written social contract made by the Pilgrims prior to landing at Plymouth. The Pilgrims were so eager to write a contract they wrote it while aboard the ship. They believed in the consent of the community and did not want to jeopardize the idea in any manner.

Third was The Colonial Charters (1630–1732) which led to the Constitution. These charters were designed by royal decrees, which were either **proprietary** or royal colonies. The states of Maryland, Delaware, and Pennsylvania were proprietary or royal. There were two colonies that used self-government, Rhode Island and Connecticut.

Fourth, the Declaration of Independence of 1776 proclaimed the freedom and independence of the states to create a new nation separate from the British. In 1774 twelve of thirteen original colonies met to discuss the continual interference of the British in colonial business. The members made up the First Continental Congress. It was not long before the Revolutionary War began on April 19, 1775, which interfered with the Continental Congress protest. This would turn out to be a bitter fight, but would enhance the independence from Great Britain. It also allowed for a unity to develop between the states of America. By 1775 the Second Continental Congress met and appointed George Washington as commander of the colonial troops. He was to surround the city of Boston and restore order brought on by armed organized citizens trying to protect their towns. These organized citizens were known as **minutemen**. The goal was not to leave or separate from Britain but to bring about change. However, as time passed, the Continental Congress decided to declare its independence from Britain.

Thomas Jefferson would be given the task of writing the justification for separating, which he did and presented it on July 4, 1776. The first Continental Congress president John Hancock signed the Declaration of Independence. During the war the government was in the process of creating a new structure. When General Charles Cornwallis surrendered at Yorktown it marked the end of the war.

The **fifth** precedent to the Constitution was the Articles of Confederation (1781–1789), our first constitution. The purposes of the articles were to create a league of friendship, to provide full faith and credit, to return wanted fugitives and perpetuate unity among the states. Prior to the end of the war in 1781 the Second Continental Congress passed a constitution and the states ratified it. The Articles of Confederation formed a loose league of friendship among the states. It created a confederation allowing states to maintain sovereignty and independence. A confederation is a type of government where the national government derives its powers from the states, a league of independent states. The Articles of Confederation were at times called the "**articles of confusion**." People were confused not only about the articles, but were confused about their identity. For example, Edmund Randolph remarked, "I am not really an American, I am a Virginian."[2] It would not be long before Americans would face problems in the new nation.

PROBLEMS FACING THE NEW NATION

Americans had enjoyed many successes from winning the war to creating its own nation. However, it could not escape the problems facing the new nation. The first problem was that Americans were loyal to their states and did not think of themselves as Americans. This lack of national unity in the absence of a war to unite the citizens produced a reluctance to give any power to the Congress. Congress operated under strict limitations. Congress was created with one house giving each state one vote. In the development no executive or judicial branch of government was in place. When the colonists set up Congress it reflected the British Parliament. They did not want a king because they were in fear of their prior experience in England. The belief was that a central government would become too strong and distant to protect the individual rights. Although some of the colonists, especially the farmers, were satisfied with the articles, not all were. The upper classes were very frustrated with the articles. The bankers and manufacturers in particular were dissatisfied. They wanted a commercial expansion replacing the agricultural economy of the eighteenth century. Their idea was to expand trade beyond local communities to national and international communities. This would develop a new economy that could sustain economic growth, but without any cohesiveness internally, nor any international security, the climate was not conducive to support commercial expansionism. Now that the war was over, the country was back in a predicament, particularly with internal disagreement and a disbanded army.

The British were hopeful that the internal disagreements would grant them an opportunity to intervene in colonial business. The problems were many, from North African Barbary pirates capturing American ships and sailors to British troops occupying the midwestern territory then called Northwest Territory; they also had troops in Canada, both of which were in violation of an earlier peace treaty. Congress did not have any authority to draft so it could not start an army, nor could it afford one. The only option was to ask the states to assist with soldiers and money. How could the states have any compassion for a distant government? They did not. The country's debt was mounting and no one wanted to pay, particularly not the states. The national government could not tax, as it had no money.

Another problem was that states produced more laws than the national government. The states also held more elections to a point of excessive democracy and printed their own money. This became very problematic because of the large sums of money being printed. The states printed themselves into **inflation**, a rise in the general price levels of the economy. Also, state officials passed laws relieving debtors from paying creditors. The creditors were the wealthy who felt state legislatures were stopping them from being paid. Leaders questioned the new system and Shays' Rebellion in 1786–1787 in western Massachusetts scared many. The merchants who made loans during the war wanted to be repaid, but the legislature levied heavy taxes that the farmers could not repay. The merchants felt without repayment they could not trade with foreign merchants. A private army paid for by the wealthy stopped Shays' Rebellion. This event led to a change in thinking about a national government. It needed to become more centralized.

THE CONSTITUTIONAL CONVENTION

From May 25 to September 17, 1787, the Constitutional Convention met in Philadelphia. The purpose of the meeting was for revising the articles. The convention was to have seventy-four delegates; fifty-five attended. The meeting was at Independence Hall, then called Pennsylvania State House. This was the same place some of the delegates signed the Declaration of Independence some eleven years before. Most important, the delegates at Philadelphia had a worldview. The point of view of the delegates was unified economically, militarily, and politically. The colonists in 1787 had a narrow state view; the delegates' viewpoint was far reaching, and they had a national commitment.[3] Though Rhode Island did not attend, every other state did. Rhode Island's concern was the states would be weakened by the convention. Also, farmers and debtors controlled the legislature and felt the convention would take away the states' powers from granting relief to debtors. The delegates were distinguished gentlemen and well-educated men in America for the time. At eighty-one years of age Benjamin Franklin was the best-known American of the group, having been a printer, scientist, and diplomat. George Washington was the most respected man at the time. The stature and presence of these men granted legitimacy to the convention. The purpose was to revise the articles but instead they wrote a new Constitution. This was done in secret because it was a violation of the orders by state legislatures. The problem at the convention was that delegates discussed the notion of a weak government, but simultaneously discussed the problems of a government too strong. The question was would we have *anarchy*, absence of any form of political authority, or *tyranny*, a government in which a single ruler is vested with absolute power. It was even brought out that the country might just have a monarchy, giving the government too much power over the people. There was much fear at the time and delegates needed to find answers to tough questions. Some delegates like Alexander Hamilton were too forceful, calling for an executive for life and senate, while others were too weak, calling for a compromise. If the delegates could envision the same type of government the convention could move forward. One thing they finally agreed on was that the country needed a *republic* form of government, a political order in which the supreme power lay in a body of citizens who are entitled to vote for officers and representatives responsible to them. They agreed that the new government would have three branches and a separation of power. The branches were the legislative, executive, and judicial. The legislative and executive would be the strongest.

Additional disagreements came over trade, representation, and slavery. First, because America had a manufacturing economy, the northerners wanted a tax on manufacturing goods imported from Britain. They believed without a tax the goods imported from Britain would be cheaper than their goods, making them less competitive. The southerners believed this would hurt their economy, and they did not want a tax on agriculture because it made them less competitive in foreign markets. Congress made a compromise by allowing a tax on imported goods but not on exported ones.

Second, representation delegates were concerned because of the size of states. Some of the states were larger than others and large states wanted a large government they could control, while small states wanted a small government that could not control them. At the beginning of the convention two plans were presented. The first was the Virginia Plan, introduced by Edmund Randolph indicating a strong central government giving more power to the legislature, executive, and judiciary. The problem was that the three largest states at the time, Massachusetts, Pennsylvania, and Virginia would have more representatives and could control the legislature. The second plan, introduced by William Paterson was called the New Jersey Plan.

This plan called for a strong government though not as strong as the Virginia Plan. He said there would be one house with representation by states casting one vote each. This is a replica of the Articles of Confederation. To solve this problem they came up with the Great Compromise or Connecticut Compromise. They did not want to leave without a constitution so the compromise sufficed. Delegates constructed a plan that the legislature would have two houses. In one house representation would be based on population; members would be elected by voters. In the other representation would be by states, and members would be selected by state legislatures. The large and small states would split the two houses.

A third issue was slavery. It became a big issue particularly with the southerners; they wanted slaves to be counted for population purposes. The delegates came up with the Three Fifths Compromise, which stated that three fifths of slaves would be counted in apportioning seats.

THE SECOND CONSTITUTION: 1787

On September 17, 1787, thirty-nine of the fifty-five delegates signed the new constitution. Some delegates refused to sign and others left altogether, feeling the convention gave too much authority to the national government. The Constitution did have some problems, but for the most part it was a smooth process. The founding fathers had experience writing such documents; after all they were in Philadelphia working on the Declaration of Independence. These men were political philosophers and therefore understood the work of philosophers in the field, which helped in the development of the thought behind the Constitution. In addition these men were not as close to the Revolutionary War period, which allowed them to make decisions not tied to state loyalty. The founders were well-educated merchants and lawyers. The delegates wanted to go home, so the differences they held over the Constitution came to a compromise. By September 8, 1787, the committee in style and arrangement was to receive the document from the delegates. The chief architect would be Governor Morris. By September 12, 1787, the convention delegates looked over the Constitution by each section. It was from this time forward that the founders put their signatures and the convention wrapped up the meeting by 4 p.m. that afternoon. The Constitution was sent to Market Street printers to be worked on overnight and sent out of Philadelphia the next day. It was now time for a debate on a larger scale on the new form of government.

The delegates returned home and allowed Alexander Hamilton to assess the chances of the Constitution's ratification. There was favor by the supporters of George Washington, commercial interest, property owners, creditors, and Americans who felt the Articles of Confederation were inappropriate. Those who opposed were state politicians and prior convention members who feared they would lose power and Americans who felt that the central government would not represent local interest. It would not be long before the

Figure 2.1   Basic Principles Reflected in the U.S. Constitution.

Basic Principles	Description	Location in the Constitution
Limited Government	Powers of government are restricted by the Constitution.	Articles I, II, III
Republicanism	Voters hold the sovereign power and elect representatives to exercise power of them.	Preamble and Article I
Checks and Balances	Each of the three branches of government exercises some control over the others, sharing power among them.	Articles I, II, III
Federalism	Power is divided between the national and state governments, limiting central power.	10th Amendment
Separation of Powers	Each branch of government has its own responsibilities and limitations.	Articles I, II, III
Popular Sovereignty	Authority for government flows from the people and they rule through their representatives.	Amendment IX and Preamble
Individual Rights	Unalienable rights guaranteed to all citizens.	Preamble and Bill of Rights

Source: https://constitutioncenter.org/interactive-constitution/articles/article-i-7

Federalists, who supported the Constitution, and the **Anti-Federalists**, who were against the Constitution, would be at odds.

The U.S. Consitutional development was resolved with agreement upon the importance of the separation of powers between the branches of government and the ability of each branch of government to provide a check and a balance to the other. The U.S. Constitution Articles 1-7 outline the branches of government, powers of each, and detail rights of the states.

Online Connections

Use the Web to learn more about the Constitution.

The following Internet websites are ways that you can enhance your study of the Constitution. An Internet site is listed with a description of what you can find on the page.

Constitutionfacts.com is a site where you can get the full text of the Constitution, little-known facts about the Constitution, and information about the signers. There are also exams and crossword puzzles so you can test your knowledge of the document. *http://www.constitutionfacts.com*

This site contains analysis and interpretation of the Constitution of the United States. The author of the page is the Congressional Research Service of the Library of Congress. Detailed information on the history of the document can be found. *http://www.access.gpo.gov/congress/senate/constitution*

The National Archives and Records Administration, the federal government's record keeper, has a website that gives a multitude of supplementary information on the constitutional process. Images of the Constitution are also included. After the welcome page, click on the link The United States Constitution. *http://www.archives.gov/welcome/index.html*

Key Terms

Constitutional   13

General popular consent   13

Rule of law   14

Compact   14

Bicameral legislature   14

Magna Carta   14

Feudal   14

Natural rights   14

Mayflower Compact   14

Proprietary   15

Minutemen   15

"Articles of confusion"   15

Inflation   16

Federalists   19

Anti-Federalists   19

Selected Readings

Bailyn Bernard, Ed., *The Debate on the Constitution: Federalist and Antifederalist Speeches, Articles, and Letters During the Struggle over Ratification*, 2 vols. (New York: Library of America, 1993).

M. E. Bradford, *Founding Fathers: Brief Lives of the Framers of the United States Constitution* (Lawrence, KS: University Press of Kansas, 1994).

Thomas Dye, *American Federalism: Competition Among Government* (Lexington, MA: Lexington Books, 1997).

Robert D. Putnam, *Making Democracy Work: Civic Traditions in Modern Italy* (Princeton, NJ: Princeton University Press, 1993).

Alexis de Tocqueville, *Democracy in America*, 2 vols., 1835 (New York: Vintage, 1955).

Notes

[1]James Madison, *Federalist Papers*, No. 53.

[2]David Hawke, *A Transition of Freemen* (New York: Scribner's, 1964), p. 209.

[3]Edward Millican, *One United People: The Federalist Papers and the National Idea* (Lexington: University Press of Kentucky, 1990).

NAME_____ COURSE_____ SECTION_____

1. What is the purpose of a constitution?

_____

_____

_____

_____

_____

2. What were the five important events before the U.S. Constitution was written?

_____

_____

_____

_____

_____

3. What was the purpose of the Constitutional Convention of 1787?

_____

_____

_____

_____

_____

4. Why were the Federalists and Anti-Federalists at odds over the Constitution?

_____

_____

_____

_____

_____

CHAPTER 3
Federalism

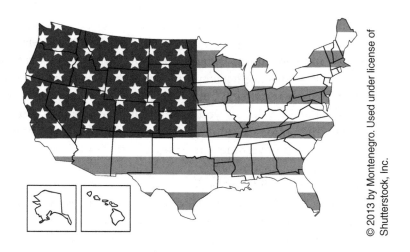

Federalism is defined as dividing power between two separate governments: national and subdivisional governments both exercise direct authority over individuals. In America, federalism has been and still is a controversial matter when it comes to the power struggle between the national government and the states. We know that federalism is a problem in the United States and in other foreign nations as well. Current day Russia formerly called the Soviet Union, which is a highly centralized government, ran into problems when it split into fifteen independent and separate nations. The Russian Federation today is faced with trying to redefine the federal relationship between twenty-one independent republics. "Nearly 40 percent of the people of the world now live in nations with a federal form of government. Another third live in countries that use some elements of federalism." [1] In this chapter we will focus on several aspects of federalism.

WHY FEDERALISM?

First we begin with why federalism? It was obvious that federalism would be the U.S. choice. In this system we are able to protect minorities from unjust and interested majorities. In our system of democracy majority rules, so we needed protections built into the system. In order to protect such things as liberty, dispersing power, and controlling faction, the founders used federalism. Liberty would be protected by putting in place opposite and rival power among governments and dividing power between national and state governments. The separation of power would be divided among the three branches of the national government. By creating this division of power, competition would come into play between governments and protection of liberty. The founding fathers did not believe in a single set of rulers; instead they believed in elections to select a large group of leaders who could offer more protection against **tyranny**. "In other parts of the world federal forms have not been notably successful from preventing tyranny and many unitary governments are democratic. Americans tend to associate freedom with federalism."[2] Also, when the national party loses an election the local or state can buffer, creating a base for a challenger to the incumbent. The local and state government thereby becomes a training ground for national political leaders.

Another reason for federalism is an increase in participation in the political process. We currently have more than 87,000 governments in the United States of America. These include school districts, county, special districts, municipalities, and states. Given the number of public institutions it grants more than a million people opportunities to serve in public office.

The government is filled with red tape, which is the collection or sequence of forms and procedures required to gain bureaucratic approval for something. Many times the forms are complex and time-consuming. Federalism reduces some of the red tape by again dividing responsibilities. It improves efficiency and makes the government more manageable. It would not be very wise to have all public needs met by a centralized government in Washington; for example, in order for you to get your road repaired you would have to call Washington D.C. The notion of centralized government in this example would not be productive. A decentralized government may serve better in this example. The local government would be better for road repair.

Federalism allows states to try different policies that may work best in a particular state. If a state can improve a service via experimentation, then other states can follow this lead, thereby creating cost savings for the government. If Texas, for example, can prove that a plural executive government serves the interest of the people best, then it becomes a pioneer in creating that system. If California becomes an expert in air-quality control, then that state becomes the leader for other governments and may even assist the national government in setting standards. So it is clear that federalism does encourage experimentation.

THE RECIPE FOR FEDERALISM

The founding fathers of the nation were unclear as to how they would solve the problem of dividing power between national and state governments. Federalism would divide the power, but they did not have an entire concept as to how it would all work. They were able to figure out a plan via trial and error. The Constitution of the United States was their road map to the process by indicating a strong national government; states could only have certain powers, with limitations on the national government. It was very clear the citizens wanted a strong national government, but the founders were uncertain as to how strong to make it. One thing the founders realized is that it would need to be stronger than the Articles of Confederation allowed. A federal government would need to have the power to tax, and to carry out foreign and domestic policies without asking the states. The new Constitution afforded specific powers to the Congress, taxation, and regulation of interstate commerce, which brings power to the national government. A clause allows Congress to pass all laws *"necessary and proper"* for carrying out its specific powers—this may also be called the implied powers clause.

The **necessary and proper clause** is found in article I, section 8 of the U.S. Constitution granting Congress the power to enact all laws that are "necessary and proper" for carrying out those responsibilities specifically delegated to it. We also call this the *implied power clause* derived from its enumerated powers to tax and spend.[3] These powers are not specifically mentioned in the Constitution but are inferred from the ones that are. The Constitution calls for states to not interfere with actions taken by the national government because their actions could cause conflict. The state is not allowed to coin money, enter into treaties, make war, create armies or navies, or levy taxes on imports and exports of goods. The national government is the superior being when it comes to foreign affairs and interstate commerce. Other limitations include ex post facto laws, which do not allow a state to pass a law then punish citizens after the passing of the law. This would be considered after the fact and is not applicable. The national government cannot create new states within a state or change the boundaries of a state without the approval of the state legislature that will be affected.

THE TENTH AMENDMENT AND THE STATES

The Tenth Amendment of the Constitution reserves certain powers to the states or the people. The reserve powers include states' rights to regulate marriage and divorce, to maintain control of property, criminal law, contract law, highways, byways, educational systems, and social welfare. So the states do have a substantial amount of power over the way they should operate. The states also enjoy concurrent power, which allows both state and national government to tax and spend money, establish a court system, and make and enforce laws. Finally, states have the right to control the way local governments will operate. Given the Tenth Amendment, local governments need to follow the laws of the State and Federal government.

It is important to understand that federalism brought many positive aspects to government. However, we must not fail to recognize that white separatists used the states' rights argument to deny African Americans equal protection of the law. So with the power reserved to the states, many believed it was the way to preserve a the white power structure within the states.

Due to many landmark cases we now begin to see the true nature of federalism. We know today that federalism does not mean racial segregation or inequality. Because of a better understanding we have a new opportunity to evaluate the meaning of a decentralized government.

THE FEDERAL SYSTEM EVOLVES

From the start of the American system of government some 200 years ago a battle ensued over state-centered federalism versus national-centered federalism. The power flow of the federal system has always flowed toward the national government. The states argued with the national government consistently over the division of power. It is important to keep in mind that political conflict between states and the nation has generally been decided in favor of the national government. Let's take a closer look at how federalism has evolved over the years.

State-Centered Federalism, 1787–1868

It is very clear that the states had more power as a subdivision of government. During the development of the Constitution of 1787 the American colonies used self-government and recognized themselves as independent, making it a difficult task to share power. The states provided more public services than the national government, and states resolved more policy questions. In addition states were also in control of the slave issue. Prior to 1860 slave states admitted into the union were as follows:

Delaware	December 7, 1787
Georgia	January 2, 1788
Mary land	April 28, 1788
South Carolina	May 23, 1788
Virginia	June 25, 1788
North Carolina	November 21, 1789
Kentucky	June 1, 1792
Tennessee	June 1, 1796
Louisiana	April 30, 1812
Mississippi	December 10, 1817
Alabama	December 14, 1819
Missouri	August 10, 1821
Arkansas	June 15, 1836
Florida	March 3, 1845
Texas	December 29, 1845

Dual Federalism, 1868–1913

The faith of the national government would be determined during the Civil War. How much supremacy would the national government have? The delegated power of the government would not be as effective as one could have imagined after the war. The states still conducted themselves as the ultimate policy makers. The government system is called **dual federalism** because of the separation of powers, in which the national government and state powers were clearly distinguished and functionally separate. The national government focused on national defense, tariffs, foreign affairs, interstate commerce, admission of new states, and coinage of money, post roads and post office. These were delegated powers. The state, on the other hand, focused on more domestic policies such as criminal justice, health, education, and welfare. We could call this type of separation a multiple-tier policy. The tiers feature the local governments on the bottom, the state governments in the middle, and the national government on top. Another analogy for dual federalism is viewing it as a layer cake with the same structure, the local on the bottom, state governments in the middle, and the national government on top.[4]

Cooperative Federalism, 1913–1964

By 1913 the federal government had developed a federal income tax. The country had experienced two world wars and the Industrial Revolution was in effect. The type of changes mentioned help create a national economy giving the federal government more power over the states. Franklin D. Roosevelt's New Deal programs were welcomed by state governors in the 1930s during the Great Depression. These were major federal spending programs to assist in the areas of agriculture, business, labor, and economic affairs. The national government goes one step further—it cooperates with the state on education, highways, public housing, urban renewal, and employment. Because of the cooperation between the state and the national government, the term **cooperative federalism** was coined. This is a relationship between two governments working to solve policy problems. We could call this "goulash" federalism. Just as you would mix several foods in a dish, so does the American federal system. It can also be compared to a marble cake.[5] The U.S. Congress made it clear that safety and health concerns were state matters and not national responsibility. However, with a cooperative relationship tax money would be shared to help the state and local governments achieve their goals. It is very uncommon to see the national government legislate local governments, given the relationship between the state government and local government.

Cooperative Federalism - FEMA

An example of cooperative federalism in action is the Federal Emergency Management Agency (FEMA) supporting states and local governments. When there are natural disasters such as hurricanes, tornadoes, brush fires, and flooding, the Federal government steps in to support families and victims as they recover. These disasters are more than the local or state government can handle and the support of FEMA is needed.[6]

Centralized Federalism, 1964–1980

The relationship between the national government and state government would soon lose its zest. By 1964 the Great Society program would be in effect clearly indicating that the national government had its own vision and goals. President Lyndon B. Johnson appeared to be in control of many of the problems facing America—air quality, solid waste, and consumer safety all seemed to be national problems. What had begun as a national and state relationship turned out to be **centralized federalism**, a system in which the national government assumes primary responsibility for determining national goals in all major policy areas and directs state and local government activity through conditions attached to money grants. One commentator observed that centralized federalism is like a pineapple upside-down cake: The frosting has moved to the top."

Representational Federalism, 1985–1995

Prior to 1985 it was still assumed that Congress could not legislate state and local governments because of centralizing tendencies. However, in 1985, in the decision to *Garcia v. San Antonio Metropolitan Transit Authority*, the U.S. Supreme Court said it would remove all obstacles to direct congressional legislation in Tenth Amendment matters, or power reserved to the states. The case developed after Congress forced the state and local governments to pay minimum wages to their employees. The result of the Court decision was that it dismissed the reserve powers clause and the Tenth Amendment, stopping Congress from legislating in state affairs. The Court instructed the states that the only way to protect themselves was through their roles in electing public officials, U.S. Senators, U.S. House members, and the President. What the Court was telling the states was that the way to protect their powers was through **representational federalism**. That is an assertion that no constitutional division of power exists between the nation and the states, but the states retain their constitutional role merely by selecting the President and members of Congress. Based on the Garcia case, if Congress should divide powers and not the Constitution, then the states are under legislative authority and not constitutional law.

FEDERALISM AND THE FEDERAL COURTS

Judges of Federalism

In 1819 the Court decided to look at the power between national and state governments. In *McCulloch v. Maryland* (1819), the state of Maryland levied a tax on the Baltimore branch bank of the United States, a branch established by Congress. The bank cashier, William James McCulloch, refused to pay arguing that the bank was an instrument of the national government. Does Congress have the power to incorporate a bank? According to Maryland's legal representative, Luther Martin, it is not a power delegated to the national government. He said the bank was not necessary, nor was it part of Congress. Delegated powers, therefore, should not have been established. Daniel Webster, a prominent lawyer of his time, represented the national government. He agreed with the fact that Congress creating a bank was not an implied power of the national government.

However, Congress may pass laws that are necessary and proper to exercise its enumerated powers that are specifically delegated to Congress. Based on this reasoning, Congress could incorporate a bank as a way of collecting taxes, protecting the property of the United States, and borrowing money. The Court was very clear in its decision and disregarded Maryland's case, declaring a conflict between a state and the national government, which is supreme. Chief Justice John Marshall set in motion the doctrine of **national supremacy**, indicating national law is superior to other laws passed by states or local governments.

The Court has looked at federalism as a political process and initially decided to stay out of the argument of which level of government should carry out various responsibilities. The legislative branch made the laws during the New Deal era while the Court stood by.

It was not until the 1980s that the Court decided to judge New Deal programs as constitutional. Some citizens argued that the courts needed to become more involved after New Deal legislation because some believed this legislation had changed the Constitution. The Supreme Court's decisions over federalism were in the areas of transportation, education, commerce, and elections. The federal government used grant money to help the states in many arenas. The state was encouraged to develop educational facilities such as colleges and universities. The universities were considered land grant schools because of the grants-in-aid programs dating back to the 1950s. The problem was that the states were in control of education under the Tenth Amendment granting it police powers. The Supreme Court decided to hear the case of **Brown v. Board of Education** (1954). The Court made it clear there was no place for segregation of any kind, not even state-mandated segregation in public school systems. In 1966 the court decided that state poll taxes would be invalid. This decision again took power from the state and transferred it to the national government. The purpose of the poll tax was to stop the poor in the South, who most often were black, from voting.

Federal Grants

Congress has established programs and given funds as early as 1790 to help pay off the debt incurred by the Revolutionary War. The Congress also determined the level of responsibility lower governments would have.

The major purposes of federal grants are: (1) to supply state and local governments with revenue, (2) to establish minimum national standards for highways and clean air and the like, (3) to equalize resources among the states by taking and transferring income from the wealthier citizens from income taxes and returning it, through grants to states with high poverty levels, and (4) to minimize the growth of federal agencies yet address national problems.

What makes Congress so important is that it funds programs for both state and local governments. The U.S. Congress does this through federal grants. There are several types of federal grants. We will examine them in the following sections.

Categorical Formula   **Categorical formula grants** are where funds are set aside for specific purposes such as welfare, school lunches, and transportation systems like light rail and airports Temporary Aid to Needy Families (TANF), Medicaid, and health care for the needy are federal- and state-funded programs.

Block Grant   **Block grants** are broad grants provided to states for prescribed activities in the area of education, social services, preventive health, and health services with only a few specific strings attached. The funds can be used by the states as needed with great flexibility. Once the funds are used for a fiscal year the federal government does not have any more matching funds.

Revenue Sharing (1972–1982)   **Revenue sharing grants** are grants given to the states and local government to be used at their discretion; they are subject only to very general conditions. Revenue sharing was terminated to the states in 1986 and to local government in 1987. Revenue sharing came to an end during budget deficits of the Reagan years. The states were cut first in 1986 and local governments in 1987.

Project Grants   Congress appropriates a certain sum for **project grants**, but the dollars are allocated to states and local units and sometimes to nongovernmental agencies based on applications from those who wish to participate. Examples are grants by the National Science Foundation to universities and research institutes to support the work of scientists. Project grants can also go to both states and cities to support training and employment programs.

TOMORROW'S FEDERALISM

In respect to the federalism of yesterday, those who predicted that states would lose to centralized powers proved to be wrong. Today federalism has proven to be more complex than in the past, but it also has gained momentum. Figure 3.1 shows the basic powers of federal and state government. The states have made tremendous changes over the years and have taken on greater responsibilities. States are better organized and have more structure, which allow them to be more efficient. It was perceived that the national government would do more for the people than states would do. The Civil Rights movement only strengthened the idea, particularly when the national government ordered states to integrate. Local governments at this time were looked on to do more than the national government. It is not that the federal government is more favorable to minorities, because many times federal laws will not intervene in marital privacy or gay rights, and the states and local governments have. Now that states have taken on greater roles and there are no signs that they will stop doing so in the near future, many businesses are asking for preemptive federal regulations to slow down strict state regulations, but also to prevent them from being subject to fifty different sets of state laws. **Preemption** is the right of a federal law to preclude enforcement of a state or local law or regulation. Many states would prefer a national standard to numerous inconsistencies. However, it is not very likely that the federal government will return given the large national agenda today. Americans are attached to the federal system possibly more than one would like to think, but the fact still remains that our state relationship has not declined either. In reality most Americans are concerned only with who can get the job done and for the least amount of money.

Figure 3.1   Powers of the Federal and State Government.

Federal Government	State Government
• Coin money	• Ratify amendments
• Declare war	• Manage public health and safety
• Conduct foreign relations	• Oversee trade within the state
• Oversee foreign and interstate trade	• Education

Source: https://www.thoughtco.com/federalism-powers-national-and-state-governments-3321841

Online Connections

Check out these websites for more about federalism.

A student designed this Internet website. It gives specific definitions of federalism, various perspectives on the topic, and links to other sites on the topic. *http://www.min.net/~kala/fed*

Temple University has a center devoted to the study of federalism. The website contains a report on federalism and new links to federalism. *http://www.temple.edu/federalism*

Try the Close-up Foundation's site for an in-depth look at federalism. *http://www.closeup .org/federal.htm*

Key Terms

Federalism   23

Tyranny   24

Necessary and proper clause   25

Dual federalism   26

Cooperative federalism   27

Centralized federalism   27

Representational federalism   27

National supremacy   28

Brown v. Board of Education   28

Categorical formula grant   29

Block grant   29

Revenue sharing grant   29

Project grants   29

Preemption   29

Suggested Readings

Center for the Study of Federalism, *The Federalism Report* (published quarterly by Temple University; one issue each year is an "Annual Review of the State of American Federalism").

Christopher Hamilton and Donald T. Wells, *Federalism, Power and Political Economy* (Upper Saddle River, NJ: Prentice Hall, 1990).

Paul E. Peterson, *The Price of Federalism* (Washington DC: Brookings Institution, 1995).

David B. Walker, *The Rebirth of Federalism* (Chatham, NJ: Chatham House, 1994).

Notes

[1]Daniel J. Elazar, *Exploring Federalism* (Tuscaloosa, AL: University of Alabama Press, 1987), p. 6.

[2]William H. Riker, *The Development of American Federalism* (New York: Springer Publishing, 1987), pp. 14–15.

[3]*McCulloch v. Maryland*, 4 Wheat. 316 (1819).

[4]Morton Grobzins, *The American System* (Chicago: Rand McNally, 1966), pp. 8–9.

[5]Ibid., p. 156.

[6]*Brown v. Board of Education of Topeka*, 349 U.S. 294 (1955).

NAME_____ COURSE_____ SECTION_____

1. Define the various models of federalism.

_____

_____

_____

_____

2. Name and explain the four types of federal funding grants.

_____

_____

_____

_____

3. Compare and contrast dual federalism and cooperative federalism.

_____

_____

_____

_____

4. Define the Tenth Amendment. What effect did it have on states' rights?

_____

_____

_____

_____

Directions: Write the word or phrase that completes the statement.

1. Federalism is _____.

2. Federalism encourages _____ in states.

3. The Great Society programs led to an era of federalism often called _____ federalism.

4. _____ federalism was in place during the development of the Constitution.

5. _____ federalism can be compared with goulash and a marble cake.

Directions: Circle the correct answer to each of the following questions.

6. The founding fathers created a federalist system in order to _____.
   a. preserve power for the elite in society
   b. prevent tyranny by dividing the powers of government
   c. establish a more democratic political system that was efficient
   d. establish a powerful central government to minimize the authority of local and state governments

7. A clause in the Constitution allows Congress to pass all laws "necessary and proper" for carrying out its specific powers. This clause is called the _____.
   a. enumerated powers clause
   b. elastic clause
   c. reserve powers clause
   d. implied powers clause

8. The Tenth Amendment provides for _____.
   a. states' reserve or police powers
   b. implied powers
   c. concurrent powers
   d. all of the above

Sample Test Questions

9. The Tenth Amendment was used to _____.
   a. make equal rights for all
   b. protect women
   c. deny African Americans equal rights
   d. deny equal rights to women

10. The Tenth Amendment allowed the states to have certain powers. Which of the following is not one of those powers?
   a. States are able to tax and spend money.
   b. States are able to make and enforce laws.
   c. States are able to maintain control of property.
   d. States are able to develop an educational system based on religion.

CHAPTER 4
Legislative Branch

© 2013 by Orhan Cam. Used under license of Shutterstock, Inc.

LEGISLATIVE BRANCH CONSTITUTIONAL ROOTS

When the founding fathers drafted the Constitution they made sure that they had provisions in it to prevent a monarchy. They set up a system where there were checks and balances on each of the three branches of government, so that no one branch could have control all government power. Article I of the U. S. Constitution states "All legislative Powers herein granted shall be vested in a Congress of the United States, which shall consist of a Senate and House of Representatives." created a **bicameral** legislature. This means that there are two chambers that make up the **legislature**, or **Congress**. There is a lower house, the **House of Representatives** and the upper house, the **Senate**. Each state elects two senators. The number of House members that each state receives depends on its population, so the large states have more members and the small states have fewer members. There are 435 members total in the House of Representatives and 100 members in the Senate.[1]

The Constitution has requirements for membership in both bodies. Senators must be at least thirty years of age, must have lived in the United States for at least nine years, and must be legal residents of the state they represent. A House member, on the other hand, has different requirements. House members must be twenty-five years old, must have lived in the United States for at least seven years, and must be a legal resident of the state they represent. These requirements are compared in Figure 4.1.

Figure 4.1   Comparison of the Congressional Body.

	U.S. House Of Representatives	U.S. Senate
Age requirement	25	30
Residence in United States	7	9
Residence of the state needed	Yes	Yes
Length of term	2 years	6 years
Total members	435	100
Constituencies	Districts	State
Leadership	Centralized, formal	Less centralized
Operation	Power less evenly distributed	Power evenly distributed
Emphasis	Tax and revenue policy	Foreign policy

The U.S. Constitution in Article I also spells out the length of the terms for both chambers. The purposes of the House and Senate are different; that is why the founders called for different term lengths. House members are elected every two years and therefore need to keep in close touch with their constituents. The House was seen as the more democratic of the two, because the membership would change more frequently. The constituent base of the members of the House is much smaller than that of the Senate. The constituent base is broken up into districts established by the state legislatures. **Redistricting** happens every ten years after a census is taken. The state legislatures look at the districts and make changes based on population shifts. Senators, on the other hand, have six-year terms and has more stature and more political influence, owing to the length of time in office. The Senate constituency is the entire state. Candidates running for the Senate need to have good name recognition and be able to reach the voters in all parts of the state (see comparison of the two houses in Figure 4.1).

THE POWERS OF CONGRESS

The Constitution also spells out the most important duty of the Congress—that is to make laws. A **bill**, proposed law, originates in the House or the Senate, but both the House and the Senate must pass the bill in order for it to become law. Congress has the power to impose taxes, regulate interstate commerce, establish a national bank, establish a post office, declare war, raise and support an army and navy, establish a court system, borrow and spend money, and propose amendments to the Constitution. The House of Representatives will select the president if the Electoral College does not produce a majority candidate and has the right to initiate impeachment. The Senate confirms the presidential candidates for the cabinet and the judiciary and can try an impeached official. (See Figure 4.2 for comparisons.)

CONGRESSIONAL DUTIES

The members of Congress have to make sure that their work pleases their constituencies, party leaders, and colleagues. This creates a lot of pressure. Members of Congress work twelve- to fifteen-hour days. Congressional members divide their time between Washington and their home states. In Washington they hold meetings with their staff, go to committee meetings, attend sessions in the chamber, and attend other conferences and events. In order to be able to keep in touch with all their constituents, members of Congress hold town meetings to discuss issues in their districts, send newsletters, and use full-time staff members to keep them abreast of all the happenings in their area.

Much of the work that congressional members need to do is called **casework**. This is helping their constituents deal with the problems they are experiencing with the bureaucratic systems. For example someone who is not receiving their Social Security check and veterans' benefits and needs assistance. Many members of Congress have large offices with draft legislation who are able to help constituents solve their problems. The average House office has seventeen full-time staff members and the Senators have forty-four full-time staff members. These people can help deal with the casework issues that could really become a problem if not dealt with by a friendly face.[2]

Figure 4.2   Congressional powers granted by Article 1, Section 8 of the Constitution.

Power	House	Senate
Impose and collect taxes	X	X
Borrow money	X	X
Regulate currency	X	X
Establish a post office	X	X
Regulate foreign commerce	X	X
Make patent and copyright law	X	X
Support an army and navy	X	X
Declare war	X	X
Create laws "necessary and proper" for the nation	X	X
Admit new states	X	X
Create lower courts	X	X
Propose amendments to the Constitution	X	X
Originate tax bills	X	
Bring impeachment charges	X	
Ratify governmental treaties		X
Confirm judicial and cabinet appointments by the President		X
Try impeachment offenses		X

Members of Congress get a salary of $174, 000 per year. They are not allowed to be paid for speeches and appearances. However, they are given many other perks, as you will see in the next section. Their salary does not need to be used for travel expenses or mailings.

INCUMBENCY ADVANTAGES

In 79% of elections **incumbents** usually win. Incumbents are the people who are holding office at the present time and running for reelection. In Congress the incumbents have an extreme edge on their opponents; in the U.S. Senate there is a 70 percent chance that the incumbent will win office. In the U.S. House of Representatives 90 percent of the incumbents win their office. The incumbents running for federal positions are able to use many resources that come with their jobs to help them stay in office.[3]

One of those resources is the **franking privilege**. This is the free use of the U.S. mail. This is to encourage members to communicate with their constituents. However, during election campaign this becomes increasingly more useful. The incumbent can send campaign literature through the postal service for no fee, whereas his or her opponent must pay for the same service.

Another resource available to the incumbent is the use of travel allowances at the tax payers' expense. When the incumbent travels across the country to make a campaign trip, the taxpayers pick up the bill. During a reelection bid this "free travel" benefits the incumbent who then can spend the travel money elsewhere. Opponents will need to use the money they raise in campaigning to pay for their travel expenses.

A third resource at the hands of the incumbents is name recognition. They have been in office over the years and their names become familiar to voters. Incumbents have communicated with their constituents, sometimes been on news programs to discuss an issue that is very important to them, or have had their name appear frequently in the newspaper. An incumbent's name is much more familiar than the name of a person running for office for the first time, unless the new candidate is a very well-known person in the media. When voters go to the ballot box and do not have much knowledge of the candidates they have a tendency to vote for the person who has the familiar name.

A fourth resource available to incumbents is the availability of campaign funding from interest groups and individuals. Many interest groups and individuals, if they contribute to the incumbent, have seen results and so will continue to contribute to the incumbent. The opponent most likely will not see these types of contributions because many of the interest groups and individuals are afraid that if they give their money to the opponent who does not win, they will no longer get the things that they need from the winning candidate. It is kind of like gambling; they go with the sure shot rather than the long shot winner.

MEMBERSHIP IN CONGRESS

"Congress is better educated, more white, more male, and richer than the rest of the United States."[4] In the 115th Congress the number of women in the House is eighty-eight and twenty-one in the Senate. The number of African Americans in the House hit a record number of forty-nine members; however there are only three African Americans in the Senate. The number of Hispanics in the House is forty. There are five Hispanics in the Senate at this time. There are fifteen Asian Americans serving in the House of Representatives and three in the Senate. There are two Native American in the House of Representatives. In the past there have been some of each in the Senate. This is why the Senate is often called the "Millionaires Club." These are people with influence and connections, and many times minorities are locked out of the system of privilege. Figure 4.3 lists the names and terms of the ethnic minorities serving in the Senate.

ORGANIZATION OF CONGRESS

Senate

The leader of the Senate is called the **majority leader**. The majority party elects their leader by a vote at the beginning of each new session. The Senate does not follow as many rules as the House due to the size of its membership—100 versus 435. Therefore, the majority leader of the Senate is not as powerful as the leader in the House of Representatives. In case of a tie in voting, the vice president will vote to break the tie.

House of Representatives

The leader of the House of Representatives is called the **Speaker of the House**. He or she presides over the House. The Speaker has many powers. He or she decides to which committees new bills will be assigned, appoints members to the Rules Committee, and controls the business on the floor of the House. The Speaker decides who will speak and can determine whether points made are relevant to the item being discussed. The Speaker is supposed to apply all the rules fairly and consistently to all members. The Speaker is elected by the full membership of the House. In the 115th Congress Paul Ryan, a Republican from Wisconsin, serves as Speaker of the House.

The House majority and minority members also choose other leaders—a party leader, a whip, and committee chairpersons. The majority leader's responsibilities are very similar to that of the House Speaker, but he or she cannot schedule legislation. The traditional primary role of the minority leader is to lead the minority party and counter the attempts of the majority to pass legislation. The current majority leader in the 112th Congress is Kevin McCarthy, a Republican from California and the minority leader is Nancy Pelosi, a Democrat from California. She is the first woman ever elected to this position. When the Democrats were in control of the House in 2008 Nancy Pelosi was the first woman to be the Speaker of the House. However, the Republicans took back control of the House during the midterm elections of 2010.

COMMITTEE SYSTEM

Committees in Congress were created as a way to divide up work and allow members to become experts in certain areas. Committees are formed for the purpose of screening and writing legislation. The real work of Congress is done in committees. These permanent committees that specialize in certain areas are called **standing committees**. House committees are made up of thirty to forty members and Senate committees have fifteen to twenty members. The ratio of Democrats to Republicans is the same as the makeup of the entire House or Senate. Every committee is chaired by a member of the majority party selected by the majority party of the House or Senate. In order for a bill to make it to the House or Senate floor it needs to pass through one of the standing committees. The committees may rewrite bills that come to them or write their own bills and submit them to the full House or Senate for review. Only a small number of bills make it to the floor of the House or Senate, fewer than 10 percent.

Figure 4.3 Historical Senate ethnic minorities.

African Americans
Hiram R. Revels (R-Mississippi), 1870–1871
Blanche K. Bruce (R-Mississippi), 1875–1881
Edward W. Brooke (R-Massachusetts), 1967–1979
Carol Moseley-Braun (D-Illinois), 1993–1999
Barack Obama (D-Illinois), 2005–2008
Roland Burris (D-Illinois), 2009–2010
Tim Scott (R-South Carolina), 2013–
William "Mo" Cowan (D-Massachusetts), 2013–
Cory A. Booker (D-New Jersey), 2013–
Kamala Harris (D-California), 2017–

Asian Americans
Hiram L. Fong (R-Hawaii), 1959–1977
Daniel K. Inouye (D-Hawaii), 1963–2012
Samuel I. Hayakawa (R-California), 1977–1983
Spark M. Matsunaga (D-Hawaii), 1977–1990
Daniel K. Akaka (D-Hawaii), 1990–2013
Mazie Hirono (D-Hawaii), 2013–
Tammy Duckworth (D-Illinois), 2017–
Kamala Harris (D-California), 2017–

Hispanic Americans
Octaviano Larrazolo (R-New Mexico), 1928–1929
Dennis Chavez (D-New Mexico), 1935–1962
Joseph M. Montoya (D-New Mexico), 1964–1977
Ken L. Salazar (D-Colorado), 2005–2009
Melquiades R. Martinez (R-Florida), 2005–2009
Robert Menendez (D-New Jersey), 2006–
Marco Rubio (R-Florida), 2011–
Ted Cruz (R-Texas), 2013–
Catherine Cortez Masto (D-NV), 2017–

Native American
Charles Curtis (R-Kansas), 1907–1913; 1915–1929 (Kaw)
Robert Owen (D-Oklahoma), 1907–1925 (Cherokee)
Ben Nighthorse Campbell (R-Colorado), 1993–2005 (Northern Cheyenne)

Source: U.S. Senate[5]

Subcommittees are also formed in each of the legislative areas. The House has about ninety subcommittees and the Senate has about seventy subcommittees. All of the subcommittees run separately from the standing committees. They have a small scope of operation and all bills that go through these committees must still pass through and receive approval from the standing committees in order to make it to the floor of the House or Senate. The committee and subcommittee system enables Congress to decentralize the business and weed out bills that are unimportant. It is a way to streamline the time that they are in full session.

When a candidate is asked to chair a committee or subcommittee it is an honor. It is an opportunity to be able to improve the member's chances of reelection by being able to attract media attention and exercise power. Party leaders choose committee assignments. However, the majority party chooses chairs for the committee. Many times the committee chairs are the longest-serving members of the majority party. This is called the **seniority system**. The members who have been there the longest basically get the more powerful positions and receive the committee appointments they want. They are seldom removed from a committee for a junior member to take their place.

A BILL BECOMES A LAW

There are three steps for a bill to become law. First one or more standing committees in both the House and Senate must approve it. Using parallel processes in both the House and the Senate usually means that the same bill is being introduced at the same time.

A member of Congress needs to introduce the bill. In order to gain even more support for a bill, many times a bill is sponsored by other members of the House or the Senate. This gives the bill more credibility and staying power, which is necessary because so many bills are introduced and only a few make it out onto the floor for a vote. After the bill is introduced it is given a number, copies are made, and it is distributed to the members of the committee. The Speaker or majority leader determines which bills will go to committee and which committee they will go to.

After the bill is sent to committee, the committee will refer it to one of their subcommittees to research. During the research process many times hearings are held, and the bill is revised. The hearings are open to the public and both sides of the issue are heard from. The subcommittee then votes to approve or veto the bill. If the bill is approved then it moves to the standing committee for review.

If the bill makes it out of committee it moves to the House or Senate floor. In the House the bill then goes to the rules committee to determine how long the bill can be debated and if amendments can be made; it then places the bill on the calendar. In the Senate, since there are no rules regarding how long a bill can be debated, bills are occasionally filibustered. A **filibuster** is when long speeches are made about bills or unlimited debate goes on and on about the bill. It causes inaction on the bill. This sometimes happens in the Senate.

After both chambers approve a bill but changes to the bill have been made in both the House and the Senate, a conference committee is selected to come to consensus on the changes. The bill then returns to the House and the Senate for a final vote. The bill is then passed to the president. The president has ten days to make a decision about a bill. He or she can sign it and make it law, veto it, wait the full ten days and if Congress is in session it will become law, or the president can pocket veto the bill. A pocket veto is when the president waits to sign the bill until the legislature goes to break, and the bill dies with the president in the president's "pocket."

The Congress is an instrumental part of our democracy. Their main function is to make and pass laws that are necessary for our country to run smoothly. Congress also is the only branch that can declare war. Congress places checks and balances on the other branches. As you will read in further chapters, though, the other two branches also check Congress.

Online Connections

Check out these websites to find more about Congress.

The U.S. Senate official web page. *http://www.senate.gov*

The U.S. House of Representatives official web page. *http://www.house.gov*

Go to the Legislative Resource to check on bills that have been proposed, passed, and rejected. *http://www.thomas.loc.gov*

Connect to the Library of Congress to conduct a search on a congressional topic of your interest. *http://www.loc.gov*

Key Terms

Bicameral   35

Legislature   35

Congress   35

House of Representatives   35

Senate   35

Redistricting   36

Bill   36

Casework   37

Incumbents   38

Franking privilege   38

Majority leader   39

Speaker of the House   39

Standing committees   39

Seniority system   41

Filibuster   41

Selected Readings

Timothy Cook, *Making Laws and Making News* (Washington DC: Brookings Institution, 1989).

Roger Davidson and Walter Oleszek, *Congress and Its Members*, 7th ed. (Washington DC: CQ Press, 1999).

Richard Fenno, *Home Style* (Boston: Little, Brown, 1978).

Linda Fowler, *Candidates, Congress, and the American Democracy* (Ann Arbor: University of Michigan Press, 1993).

Notes

[1]https://constitutioncenter.org/interactive-constitution/articles/article-i

[2]Norman Ornstein, Ed. *Vital Statistics on Congress* (Washington DC: CQ Press, 1998), p. 135.

[3]Thomas R. Dye, Tucker Gibson, and Clay Robison, *Politics in America*, 4th ed. (Upper Saddle River, NJ: Prentice Hall, 2001), p. 234.

[4]Karen O'Connor and Larry J. Sabato, *American Government: Continuity and Change* (New York: Addison Wesley Longman, 2002), p. 224.

[5]U.S. Senate, at *http://www.senate.gov/artandhistory/history/common/briefing/minority_senators.htm*

1. Compare and contrast the qualifications for the House of Representatives and the Senate.

_____

_____

_____

_____

_____

2. Compare and contrast the powers of the House and the Senate.

_____

_____

_____

_____

_____

3. List and describe the advantages of incumbency.

_____

_____

_____

_____

4. Explain how a bill becomes law.

_____

_____

_____

_____

Evaluation

Directions: Circle the correct answer to each of the following questions.

1. The process of solving the problems of constituents is called
   _____.
   a. incumbency
   b. red tape
   c. franking privilege
   d. casework

2. In the U.S. Senate there is a _____ percent chance that the incumbent will win office.
   a. 70
   b. 90
   c. 80
   d. 60

3. The advantages to incumbency are _____.
   a. travel allowances
   b. campaign funding availability
   c. name recognition
   d. all of the above

4. Incumbents have an extra perk, where they are able send mail for free. This is called _____.
   a. mailing privilege
   b. franking privilege
   c. red tape
   d. casework

5. In general, the members of Congress are _____ than the rest of the U.S. population.
   a. better educated
   b. whiter and richer
   c. more male
   d. all of the above

6. Permanent committees to which bills are screened and written are called _____ committees.
   a. sub
   b. bill approval
   c. ad hoc
   d. standing

7. Committee assignments are _____.
   a. selected by lottery
   b. a chance to improve reelection
   c. based on minority rights
   d. not based on seniority

8. In the House of Representatives the _____ determines when a bill can be debated, and if amendments can be made.
   a. Speaker of the House
   b. rules committee
   c. filibuster
   d. standing committee

9. Members of Congress earn _____ per year.
   a. $130,000
   b. $160,000
   c. $174,000
   d. $139,000

10. The U.S. Senate has the sole power to _____.
    a. declare war
    b. try impeachment offenses
    c. propose amendments to the Constitution
    d. originate tax bills

CHAPTER 5
Executive Branch

Source: www.whitehouse.gov

THE PRESIDENT

Today the President of the United States of America is among the most powerful people in the world. The idea of leadership derives from kings, queens, consuls, pharaohs, and prime ministers. There were numerous leaders governing, but no national government had a president. A **President** is an elected leader with authority equal to and independent of a national legislature. In the United States of America George Washington became the first elected leader. The purpose of the President is to serve as chief executive officer and check on bills passed by Congress and be the overseer of those laws enacted by Congress. The president is the commander in chief of the armed forces, chief diplomat, and head of state. The office of the presidency started out very weak: The office had very little power, few allies, and no standing army. In the thirteen original colonies executive power lay not in a president but instead in a **royal governor**. He was appointed by the king of England and given some appointment powers, military command, expenditures, limited pardoning, and law-making powers. The original colonists elected officials who were often at odds with the royal governor. Colonists thought the royal governor was too close to the king and therefore could not be trusted. During the period of seeking independence the colonists also wanted to reduce the power of the royal governor and make the office a symbolic one. The way the colonists took the rights away from the governor was by reducing this power in their state constitution.

Some states did not want a symbolic governor, but instead wanted a governor who was elected directly by the people. New York was a state that trusted the powers of its governor.

The idea of a chief executive as we know it today came from the Constitutional Convention when the new government was adopted. The new government was made up of three branches: the legislative, the executive, and the judiciary. The legislative branch would make the law, the executive would enforce or implement the law, and the judicial branch would interpret the laws. Some framers were concerned about vesting power in one person versus multiple people. The majority of the framers, however, agreed that vesting power in one person would be best. The second thing they agreed on was that George Washington would lead the new government. Some contemplated whether or not one of the eighteen presidents of the Continental Congress should become president, but these men had only been president in name only and really were not as prepared or as trusted as George Washington.

The name *President* comes from the Constitutions of Pennsylvania, Delaware, New Jersey, and New Hampshire where the founding fathers called the chief executive a president.

QUALIFICATIONS

The Constitution of the United States of America specifically spells out the qualifications to be the President of the United States. Article II gives the formal qualifications; one must be a natural-born citizen, at least thirty-five years old, and a resident of the United States for at least fourteen years before becoming president. It is important to point out some of the informal qualifications: white, male, wealthy, generally from small-town America, Protestant, German, or Scandinavian. It never hurts to be a good family man with a good family name who resides in a state with a large population. Today, obviously, the list of possible candidates for president has grown considerably as society has become more accepting of other ethnicities. Although U.S. society is becoming more accepting, some racial and gender barriers still remain.

TERM OF OFFICE

The amount of time a president would serve in office was initially very controversial. During the Constitutional Convention delegates considered allowing presidents to serve four, seven, and eleven years without any possibility of reelection. George Washington was appointed to serve as the nation's first president (1789–1797); he later sought reelection, but only once. After his presidency the framers decided on a four-year term with the eligibility for reelection. The founders did not want the presidency to become a monarchy. Ulysses S. Grant's bid for a third term created some fear, but the tradition of two, four year terms remained the norm for some 150 years.

The Great Depression would change the tradition of a two-term president when Franklin D. Roosevelt ran successfully in four elections while fighting off the Great Depression and World War II. Roosevelt was a popular president, but despite his mass appeal, a great concern was his tenure. The Congress in 1951 passed and ratified the Twenty-Second Amendment limiting a president to two four-year terms or a total of ten years, assuming the vice president served the second half of the past president's remaining term.

REMOVAL

The president is a powerful position, in the United States, but powers are limited. The president can be removed from office through the impeachment process. The Constitution of the United States, under article II, section 4, gives the Congress the ability to remove the president, vice president, federal judges, and other elected officials upon impeachment for and conviction of "Treason, bribery, or other high crimes and misdemeanors." The determination of any wrongdoing is a function of the House of Representatives, which acts as a grand jury governed by a majority vote. The Senate acts just as a trial jury would in a criminal trial, with the ability to convict and remove from office with a two-thirds vote of senators present. In 1868 President Andrew Johnson and most recently Bill Clinton in 1998 were impeached. The House of Representatives has impeached fourteen national officeholders; twelve were tried in the Senate and four were convicted. Richard Nixon would probably have been impeached, but he resigned first in 1974 to avoid removal from office. The power to impeach was placed in the hands of responsible officeholders in elected positions themselves, and in a politically responsible body of government, the House of Representatives. The people elected the president to office and a representative body of people would remove the president if necessary. The Constitution made these arrangements because they did not want the people's choice of a president to be easily overthrown. The fact that the country has used impeachment against two presidents shows that a president is not a king and should use good judgment; presidents are accountable for their actions and Congress will be the final judge of their decisions. Checks and balances ensure the balance of power.

BENEFITS

The President of the United States of America can be a rewarding job. The president does have a salary, which is determined by Congress as indicated by the Constitution. The **compensation** package received while in office cannot be increased or decreased during the term of office, according to the Constitution. A history of presidential raises is shown in Table 5.1.[1]

Table 5.1   Presidential Salary.

Date Established	Salary
September 24, 1789	$ 25,000
March 3, 1873	$ 50,000
March 4, 1909	$ 75,000
January 19, 1949	$100,000
January 20, 1969	$200,000
January 20, 2001	$400,000

Source: Adapted from https://www.presidentsusa.net/presidentsalaryhistory.html

In 1873 Ulysses Grant received the first presidential raise from $25,000 to $50,000. The other seventeen presidents prior to him received $25,000 in compensation. By 1974 Richard Nixon earned $200,000 as commander in chief. In 1999 the president's salary ranked 785 among the 800 highest-paid CEOs.[2] Many members of Congress argued that the pay of the president was too low and that, in turn, was holding down the pay for other top-level government recruitment. Congress agreed and in 2001 increased the president's pay to $400,000 per year and the vice president to $181,000. The president will also receive $50,000 for expenses and $100,000 for travel. In addition are the fringe benefits: living quarters in the historic White House, a vacation retreat in Maryland at Camp David, the best medical treatment available, cars, aircraft, pension after leaving office, security for the president and family, and financial assistance for an office and staff.

Succession   The Constitution explains that if the president dies, resigns, is removed from office, or becomes incapacitated the presidential powers shall devolve on the vice president. According to the Presidential Succession Act of 1792, the Senate president pro tempore was next in line after the vice president to succeed to the presidency, followed by the Speaker of the House. In 1886, however, Congress changed the order of presidential succession, replacing the president pro tempore and the Speaker with the cabinet officers. Proponents of this change argued that the congressional leaders lacked executive experience, and none had served as president, while six former secretaries of state had later been elected to that office.[3]

The Presidential Succession Act of 1947, signed by President Harry Truman, changed the order again to what it is today. The cabinet members are ordered in the line of succession according to the date their offices were established. Prior to the ratification of the Twenty-Fifth Amendment in 1967, there was no provision for filling a vacancy in the vice presidency. When a president died in office, the vice president was the successor, but the vice presidency seat then remained vacant. The first vice president to take office under the new procedure was Gerald Ford, who was nominated by Nixon on Oct. 12, 1973, and confirmed by Congress the following December 6.

The following is the order of succession to the presidency if the president is no longer able to serve:

- The Vice President
- Speaker of the House
- President pro tempore of the Senate
- Secretary of State
- Secretary of the Treasury
- Secretary of Defense
- Attorney General
- Secretary of the Interior
- Secretary of Agriculture
- Secretary of Commerce
- Secretary of Labor
- Secretary of Health and Human Services
- Secretary of Housing and Urban Development
- Secretary of Transportation
- Secretary of Energy
- Secretary of Education
- Secretary of Veterans Affairs
- Secretary of Homeland Security

DUTIES AND POWER OF THE PRESIDENT

The Constitution of the United States spells out the formal powers of the president. Unlike other articles in the Constitution, Article II is weak in comparison.

If we were to examine Article I, for instance, there would be a list of specifics. This is not the case in Article II. The chief executive was not given a list of powers because the founders were distrustful of a strong president. Given this distrust, in order to be effective the president must show leadership and style in order to rally the country. George Washington was considered an excellent president, but the founders were still not willing to grant too much power to the office. The powers of the president are enumerated in article II, which states, "The executive power shall be vested in a President of the United States of America." What is executive power? The founding fathers were very vague about the meaning. The president's power has changed over the years because of leadership styles. Some presidents are more involved in the political process than others. What makes the president most important is his or her ability to enter the policy-making process.

CHIEF EXECUTIVE

The Constitution states the enumeration of the formal duties of the president, by indicating an "Executive power shall be vested in a President." Congress was the policy-making body and the president would administer it according to the founders. The president can demand written reports from government officeholders, even though the Constitution does not spell out the administrative duties. The president also can control the bureaucracy with formal powers to appoint and the implied powers to remove members that were appointed and restructure agencies and make budget proposals. For example, President Bush reorganized the bureaucracy by putting **FBI** and **CIA** counter terrorism analysts under a single roof to strengthen efforts to detect and prevent terrorist attacks. The president increased the CIA headquarters from 30 to 300 employees.

APPOINTMENTS

The president has the power to appoint some 4,000 people to policy-making jobs, 1292 of these positions must be approved by the Senate. The purpose of appointing people is to help the president carry out the laws of Congress. All appointments must receive the advice and consent of the Senate: ambassadors, Supreme Court justices, U.S. Attorney General, and consuls.

The policy-making component is part of the president's authority, and many appointments made by the president can thwart substantial power. In reality, the president is more or less surrounded by policy makers, but, legally under article II, is limited in the policy arena him- or herself. All policy decisions are based on Congressional legislation.

The appointment process is very important to the president, particularly the federal judges and Supreme Court justices. The justices selected for the Supreme Court will be around much longer than the president's term in office, so it is vital for the president to select justices who are like-minded. Because of the length of time a judge may serve, these appointments are very important to the president. He or she selects people who are loyal, competent, and have integrity. George W. Bush selected five minorities for the first five available positions soon after taking office. In the evolution of presidential appointments, confirmation was sure to follow. Over the years, however, that has changed and the Senate has rejected some of the president's nominees. A problem arises when a nominee is not confirmed. This can be a major setback to the administration and can literally change its direction. For example, Robert Bork in 1987 was rejected by Senate Democrats in his nomination for the U.S. Supreme Court because of his conservative ideology and judicial philosophy, including his well-known positions against abortion, affirmative action, and First Amendment protection for nonpolitical speech.

REMOVING OFFICIALS

The Constitution does not mention anything about the president's ability to remove an appointee from office, even though presidents have done it. The people who are appointed are usually friends or prior colleagues of the president and can be trusted by the president. It is this relationship that allows the president to remove a person from office; this is not recognized under the law and sometimes Congress will not recognize the president's power to remove someone from office. The battle over removal from power came to a head in the Grover Cleveland administration. Cleveland became the twenty-second president in 1885 and decided to remove policy makers and appoint his own people. The Senate was not pleased with President Cleveland's decision and challenged him, although he won.

VETO AUTHORITY

Ulysses S. Grant in his State of the Union Address of 1873 discussed the idea of a line-item veto. During this period a line-item veto was enjoyed by state governors to disapprove certain items in a spending bill without having to veto the entire bill. Operationally, a line-item veto is the power to veto specific provisions of a bill without vetoing the bill in its entirety. After Grant's first call for this, many others would follow, including Presidents Eisenhower, Ford, Carter, Reagan, Bush, and Clinton.

Congress finally passed the line-item veto law, which took effect January 1, 1997; President Clinton became the first president empowered to veto specific spending or certain taxing provisions of legislation. The Constitution previously allowed a president only to veto an entire bill, perhaps containing many provisions of which he approved, in order to strike down one provision he opposed. On June 26, 1998, the Supreme Court, in a six to three decision, struck down the line-item veto law, declaring it unconstitutional. In the case of *Clinton v. City of New York*, the Court held the law unconstitutional on grounds that it violates the presentment clause; in order to grant the president a line-item veto, a constitutional amendment is needed (according to the majority opinion). On July 17, 1998, the Office of Management and Budget announced that funding would be released for the forty-plus cancellations made in 1997 under the Line Item Veto Act and not explicitly overturned previously. Measures seeking to provide a constitutional alternative to the Line Item Veto Act have been introduced in the 106th Congress.

Here is the way the line-item veto worked:

- Congress passes a piece of spending/tax legislation.
- The president signs the bill, as a whole, but then lines out the specific items he or she opposes.
- The president returns the lined-out items to Congress, which by a simple majority either approves or disapproves.

- If it disapproves, Congress sends a "bill of disapproval" containing the items back to the president.
- The president can then veto the disapproval bill; it would then require a two-thirds majority in Congress to override the president's veto.

BUDGET MAKING

The decision to prepare a budget for the United States has been the responsibility of Congress. The House of Representatives would prepare a budget each year. A **budget** is an itemized summary of estimated or intended expenditures for a given period along with proposals for financing them. The role of the president was minimal even when managing executive branch budgets. When an agency requested additional funding the White House did have a formal opportunity to make any changes. There had not been a strong budgeting office since the inception of government.

After World War I, the government realized it needed better management. The president would soon have a greater role once Congress decided to pass the Budget and Accounting Act of 1921, which would allow Congress to delegate priority setting and managerial responsibilities while giving the president a large presence in budgetary matters. The significance of the Budget and Accounting Act was that it required the president to estimate how much money it would take to run the government in a fiscal year. **Fiscal year** means a period of time relating to expenditures, revenues, and debt. The government **budget cycle** starts October 1 and ends September 30 the following year. The president was given power to determine the expenditure of departments, determining what would be cut and what would remain. This enables the executive branch to engage in the annual budget debate.

The Budget and Accounting Act also created the Bureau of Budget (BOB). The BOB was a part of the Treasury Department. In reality, the BOB was meant to help the president in developing budgetary policy. Because Congress has the exclusive power of the purse, the budget has created one the greatest sources of friction between the president and Congress. In 1939 the BOB became part of the executive office of the president. President Richard Nixon later changed the name from BOB to the **Office of Management and Budget** (OMB). Nixon wanted to show the importance of the budget in helping the president manage the executive branch.

Today OMB helps to formulate the president's spending plans, evaluating the effectiveness of agency programs, policies, and procedures, assessing competing funding demands among agencies, and setting funding priorities. OMB ensures that agency reports, rules, testimony, and proposed legislation are consistent with the president's budget and with administration policies. In addition, OMB oversees and coordinates the administration's procurement, financial management, information, and regulatory policies. In each of these areas, OMB's role is to help improve administrative management, to develop better performance measures and coordinating mechanisms, and to reduce any unnecessary burdens on the public.

PARDONING POWER

The president's ability to grant a reprieve or pardon is a check on the judiciary. A pardon means an executive grant providing all rights and privileges to citizenship to a specific individual charged or convicted of a federal crime. The president's pardon power is established under the U.S. Constitution, Article II, Section 2.

> *The President . . . shall have power to grant reprieves and pardons for offenses against the United States, except in cases of impeachment.*

Although the original versions of the New York and Virginia Plans that provided the frameworks for debate at the Constitutional Convention included no provisions for pardon, revisions to both plans eventually did. Scholars have suggested that the basic idea, when presented, was not controversial and therefore prompted little debate. The Virginia Plan pardon clause, inserted by John Rutledge, lodged the pardon power with the new executive branch. Alexander Hamilton supported this strategy in *Federalist* 74, writing,

> *It is not to be doubted, that a single man of prudence and good sense is better fitted, in delicate conjunctures, to balance the motives which may plead for and against the remission of the punishment, than any numerous body whatever.*

Reflecting on recent American experience, he added that, "in seasons of insurrection or rebellion, there are often critical moments, when a well-timed offer of pardon to the insurgents or rebels may restore the tranquility of the commonwealth."

But how, if at all, should such a power be limited? A proposal introduced by Connecticut's Roger Sherman to make presidential pardons subject to the consent of the Senate was considered but quickly rejected by the Convention (the Senate was deemed to be powerful enough already). So was Luther Martin's suggestion of confining pardons to convicted persons only; the framers concluded that preconviction pardons might be useful to further national interests—immediately pardoning a captured spy, for instance, might yield important military intelligence. The Constitutional Convention did, however, agree that pardons could *not* be issued "in cases of impeachment"; this may have been prompted by concerns arising from a seventeenth-century English constitutional crisis that had developed after King Charles II pardoned the Earl of Danby, Thomas Osborne, who had been impeached by Parliament. With the single exception of impeachment, then, the pardon power emerged from Philadelphia as exclusive, broad, and unfettered by the regular checks and balances of the governmental structure.

OFFICE OF THE VICE PRESIDENT

Today we think of the president and vice president as a team. The vice president has not always been a part of the presidential establishment. The common role of the vice president was to serve as president of the Senate. The vice president was never a significant part of the presidency, most times a tagalong. The evolution of the vice presidency has moved the office from a tagalong position to an important role. How do presidents choose their vice presidents? For the most part they use geographical, ideological, and demographical and any other reasons that might balance the ticket. If the presidential contender is from the South, the candidate may select a northerner to help balance the ticket. Some presidents have ignored this tradition and picked vice presidents from the same region of the country as they are from. George Bush did when he picked Dick Cheney, who had a long relationship with the Bush family and a conservative track record in politics. The vice president is the president's backup if something were to happen, but this is the second job of the vice president; helping the presidential candidate to get elected is first. The Carter administration helped redirect the path of the vice presidency when Jimmy Carter selected Walter Mondale as his running mate and granted him a significant role in the day-to-day operation of the presidency. This became known as the Mondale model.

Online Connections

View these sites to find out more about the presidency.

This is the official site for the White House. The website contains presidential speeches, news releases, and current events. *http://www.whitehouse.gov*

Use Find Law to look up important court cases as they refer to the executive branch. *http://www.findlaw.com*

Find the current federal budget and all fiscal responsibilities conducted by the Office of Management and Budget. *http://www.whitehouse.gov/omb*

The gateway to statistics from over 100 U.S. federal agencies. *http://www.fedstats.gov*

Key Terms

President   47

Royal governor   47

Compensation   49

FBI   51

CIA   51

Budget   53

Fiscal year   53

Budget cycle   53

Office of Management and Budget   53

Suggested Readings

Linda L. M. Bennett and Stephen E. Bennett, *Living with Leviathan: Americans Coming to Terms with Big Government* (Lawrence, KS: University of Kansas Press, 1990).

Paul Brace and Barbara Hinckley, *Follow the Leader: Opinion Polls and the Modern Presidents* (New York: Basic Books, 1992).

Theodore J. Lowi, *The Personal President Power Invested, Promise Unfulfilled* (New York: Cornell University Press 1985).

James Q. Wilson, *Bureaucracy: What Government Agencies Do and Why They Do It* (New York: Basic Books, 1991).

Notes

[1] http://www.pbs.org/newshour/character/essays/roosevelt.html

[2] David Stout, "Presidential Candidates seem Indifferent to a Salary Raise," *New York Times*, May 30, 1999.

[3] AP release, "Bush Announces Details on New Terrorism Center," CNN, February 14, 2003.

1. List the constitutional qualifications for the office of the president.

_____

_____

_____

_____

_____

2. Name and explain the powers of the president.

_____

_____

_____

_____

_____

3. Explain the benefits of the office of the president.

_____

_____

_____

_____

_____

4. Describe the development of the office of the presidency.

_____

_____

_____

_____

_____

NAME_____ COURSE_____ SECTION_____

Directions: Circle the correct answer to each of the following questions.

1. The president's term is _____ years.
   a. 2
   b. 6
   c. 4
   d. 8

2. The idea of the chief executive started with _____.
   a. the Constitutional Convention
   b. the Declaration of Independence
   c. the judicial branch
   d. none of the above

3. The first president of the United States was _____.
   a. James Madison
   b. John Adams
   c. Thomas Jefferson
   d. George Washington

4. In order to be elected to the presidency you need to _____.
   a. have resided in the United States for at least 25 years
   b. have resided in the United States for at least 15 years
   c. be at least 35 years old and a natural-born citizen
   d. all of the above

5. The president is limited to _____ terms or _____ years due to the ratification of the Twenty-Second Amendment.
   a. two, eight
   b. two, ten
   c. three, ten
   d. three, eight

6. The process of bringing charges against a public official is called

   _____.
   a. impeachment
   b. initiative
   c. removal
   d. recall

7. While in office the president receives _____.
   a. a salary of $400,000
   b. $50,000 for expenses
   c. free medical treatment
   d. all of the above

8. In order to remove the president from office, the House must impeach and then _____.
   a. 50 percent plus one of the Senate must vote for removal
   b. two-thirds of the Senate must vote for removal
   c. both houses must have a majority vote for removal
   d. both houses must have a two-thirds majority of removal

CHAPTER 6
The Federal Bureaucracy

© 2013 by Michael G Smith. Used under license of Shutterstock, Inc.

In the last chapter we discussed the executive branch, specifically the office of the President, which was created out of Article II of the Constitution. This chapter will focus on the federal **bureaucracy**. Bureaucracy means management or administration marked by hierarchical authority among numerous offices and nonelected officials. The bureaucracy is called the fourth branch of government. The focus of the bureaucracy is the structure of government that allows the system to be managed. In 1993 the President Clinton asked the Vice President Gore to reinvent the way the federal bureaucracy was being run. Al Gore accepted the task and began working with the frontline bureaucrats.[1]

Teams of people worked steadily through the summer of 1993 to come up with recommendations to help the government work more efficiently. More than 1,200 actions were developed in the process including the use of information technology. The recommendation was then passed on to the president for careful review. One of the most significant identifications was the realization that the federal bureaucracy was working on a factor system similar to the model issued by the German sociologist Max Weber many years ago. In this system there is a chain of command which has top management, middle management, and workers at the bottom. The factory system of government would be replaced with what has been described as **distributed intelligence**, which is a concept in computing. This new model distributes information and the tools to use that information throughout an organization. The idea is to let the frontline bureaucrats make the changes as problems occur in their day-to-day work environments. What was taking place was that citizens of the United States believed there was too much waste in the federal government and supported a waste basket theory. The waste basket theory allows for inefficient components of government to be thrown away. For example, Amtrak was created in 1970 to provide rail service across America and to be self-sufficient, but instead it has accumulated over $20 billion in operating losses in its thirty-two-year existence. Taxpayers have spent some $25 billion trying to keep the train in business. The waste basket theory would support getting rid of any area of Amtrak that is operating at a loss. According to the federal government routes that have the largest loss per passenger in 2001 are:

- Sunset Limited   −$342
- Pennsylvania   −$292
- Texas Eagle   −$258
- Three Rivers   −$245
- Southwest Chief   −$234
- Kentucky Cardinal   −$212

What we find from some of these losses is that it would be cheaper for the federal government to buy airfare for the person traveling to that destination.[2]

The purpose of government reinvention is for federal departments and agencies to improve the way they manage the government and to encourage common sense and accountability.

THE FEDERAL BUREAUCRACY

Our bureaucracy helps make up our large workforce in America. **Bureaucrats**, or career government employees, assist the president in the executive branch, which consists of the fifteen cabinet positions, fifty independent agencies embracing about 2,000 bureaus, divisions, branches, offices, services, and additional subunits of government. Some agencies are independent; others are responsible to the president. The Departments of the Army, Navy, and Air Force are among the big five agencies. These are all in the Department of Defense. The other two agencies are the Department of Veterans Affairs and U.S. Postal Service. Here is a list of the fifteen cabinet departments with dates of origin:

- Secretary of State, 1789
- Secretary of the Treasury, 1789
- Secretary of Defense, 1947
- Attorney General, 1870
- Secretary of the Interior, 1849
- Secretary of Agriculture, 1862
- Secretary of Commerce, 1903
- Secretary of Labor, 1913
- Secretary of Health and Human Services, 1953
- Secretary of Housing and Urban Development, 1965
- Secretary of Transportation, 1966
- Secretary of Energy, 1977
- Secretary of Education, 1979
- Secretary of Veterans Affairs, 1989
- Secretary of Homeland Security , 2003

Most of the members who serve in the president's cabinet have a number of years' experience with government affairs. Given the years of government service, we sometimes refer to these people as bureaucrats. The word *bureaucrat* comes from the French government in the eighteenth century. A bureau was a cloth covering the desk of government officials. Linking "bureau" and the suffix "ocracy" produces the word *bureaucracy*. *Bureaucracy* means rule conducted from a desk or office, that is, by the preparation and dispatch of written documents, or, these days, their electronic equivalent. In the area of postmodernism, bureaucracy can be referred to as a body of nonelected and nonappointed governmental officials in the executive branch who work for presidents and their political appointees. The term *bureaucrat* is usually not a popular name and is associated with negativity and inefficiency. A bureaucracy can be public or private, but it tends to be large—with a hierarchy. The bureaucracy has been considered part of the problem of government more than a solution to it. The federal bureaucracy is large (many believe too large), very powerful, and very wasteful, and a significant number of its employees are Democrats who are in control of policy implementation, but who tend to stall particularly when Republicans control the White House.

The German sociologist Max Weber argued that bureaucracies were necessary and provided a rational way for complex societies or organizations to organize themselves. He spoke of a model bureaucracy, which he said would have certain components, including:

1. A *chain of command* in which authority flows from top to bottom.
2. A *division of labor* whereby work is appointed among specialized workers to increase productivity.
3. A *specification of authority* where there are clear lines among workers and their superiors.
4. A *goal orientation* that determines structure, authority, and rules.
5. *Impersonality,* whereby all employees are treated fairly based on merit and all clients are served equally, without discrimination, according to established rules.
6. **Productivity,** whereby all workers and actions are evaluated according to established rules.[3]

THE EVOLUTION OF THE FEDERAL BUREAUCRACY

At the origin of the American system of government all federal responsibilities were discharged by white elites. **Elites** are a group or class of persons or a member of such a group or class, enjoying superior intellectual, social, or economic status. Given the environment at the time it should not be surprising that nonelite whites could not participate in the federal system of government.

The seventh president of the United States, Andrew Jackson, was concerned with the lack of inclusion of middle and lower classes. Jackson took corrective measures by calling for a **spoils system**, and was very successful with his idea up to 1890. A spoils system is a system of public employment based on rewarding party loyalists and friends. In earlier times elected officials felt party loyalists should be rewarded, and that government would be effective if friends of the president were in key federal positions.

The second idea was that government was not complicated and just about anybody could do the job. The result was a new federal bureaucracy with each new administration. It was once said by Senator William Learned Marcy "to the victor belongs the spoils."[5] The spoils system would become unacceptable in the late nineteenth century. The people began to see the abuse of power by government officials. A civil service movement started in New York in 1877, and although it developed considerable public support, the politicians refused to go along. Then came the assassination of President Garfield by Charles Guiteau, a disappointed office seeker, and the public clamor could no longer be ignored. The **Pendleton Act** classified certain jobs, removed them from the patronage ranks, and set up a Civil Service Commission to administer a system based on merit rather than political connections. As the classified list was expanded over the years, it provided the American people with a competent and permanent government bureaucracy. In 1883 fewer than 15,000 jobs were classified; by the time McKinley became president in 1897, 86,000, almost half, of all federal employees were in classified positions. Today, with the exception of a few thousand policy-level appointments, nearly all federal jobs are handled within the civil service system.

THE MERIT SYSTEM

Prior to the creation of the civil service system the United States relied on a **merit system** based on competence, neutrality, and protection from partisanship; all of these were introduced in the Pendleton Act of 1883. Pendleton Act intended to regulate and improve the civil service of the United States, in order to improve the way people were hired into the federal government. The president is authorized to appoint, by and with the advice and consent of the Senate, three persons, not more than two of whom shall be adherents of the same party, as civil service commissioners, and three commissioners shall constitute the U.S. Civil Service Commission. The commissioners shall hold no other official place in the government. The goal of the civil service is to hire government employees based on merit, which are determined by competitive examinations. From the outset 10 percent of workers would be considered civil service employees. Civil service coverage would increase, as more positions would be placed under the system. Also, presidential appointees are placed under the system to guarantee their position. Over time more than 90 percent of all federal employees would be covered by the civil service or a merit-based system. The system would create a general schedule (GS) of jobs from GS1 lowest to GS 15 highest including an executive schedule for government managers. Generally, to be under executive pay, a candidate needed a college degree and would be considered mid-level management. The government managers earned salaries from $50,000 to over $100,000 depending on years of service in the Dallas–Fort Worth job market. The numbers are shown in the salary table in Table 6.1.[6]

The implementation of pay grade has become a very powerful tool in the federal civil service system. It is a backbone for the bureaus and agencies and grants tenure to the employees; it also keeps politicians from controlling the bureaucrats. With 90 percent of government employees under a general schedule and secure in their positions, bureaucrats have rejected any change that could bring more efficiency to government. This lack of cooperation has made the bureaucracy the focal point of criticism by citizens. Also, trying to remove a civil service employee has proved to be very difficult, given the procedure under the civil service review board.

Table 6.1   Salary (2012.)

For the locality pay area of Dallas-Fort Worth, TX - Annual Rates by Grade and Step									
Grade	**Step 1**	**Step 2**	**Step 3**	**Step 4**	**Step 5**	**Step 6**	**Step 7**	**Step 8**	**Step 9**	**Step 10**
1	21483	22201	22915	23626	24340	24760	25466	26178	26206	26872
2	24155	24729	25528	26206	26500	27280	28059	28839	29618	30398
3	26354	27233	28111	28990	29868	30747	31625	32504	33382	34261
4	29586	30572	31558	32543	33529	34515	35501	36487	37473	38459
5	33101	34204	35307	36410	37513	38616	39719	40821	41924	43027
6	36897	38127	39357	40586	41816	43045	44275	45505	46734	47964
7	41002	42370	43737	45104	46471	47838	49206	50573	51940	53307
8	45409	46923	48436	49949	51462	52975	54489	56002	57515	59028
9	50154	51825	53497	55168	56839	58510	60182	61853	63524	65196
10	55232	57073	58915	60756	62598	64439	66280	68122	69963	71805
11	60681	62704	64726	66749	68771	70793	72816	74838	76861	78883
12	72733	75157	77581	80005	82430	84854	87278	89702	92127	94551
13	86489	89372	92255	95137	98020	100903	103786	106669	109551	112434
14	102204	105610	109017	112423	115830	119236	122643	126049	129456	132862
15	120221	124229	128236	132243	136251	140258	144266	148273	152281	155500

Source: United States Office of Personnel Management, General Schedule

POLICY IMPLEMENTATION

The Congress is the law-making body, the president enforces the law, and the bureaucracy must carry out the laws that are passed. Bureaucrats are the government employees who turn laws passed by Congress and signed by the president into rules and activities that have a real impact on people in their daily lives. This is **policy implementation**. When the Voters Rights Act was passed by Congress and signed into law by the president, it was turned over to the bureaucracy to put into action. Once clarity was brought forth rules were put in place and interpretation was made clear. All state and local government will be informed of the rules made by federal bureaucrats. They will provide assistance on any questions relating to the rules and watch implementation of rules by other governments. All policies must be monitored for revenue collection, dispute resolution, and oversight as to how the programs are working.

RED TAPE AND COMPLEXITY

Americans are cynical and skeptical about big government. Why are they concerned over big government? They associate bigness with distance, unresponsiveness, and incompetence. If government becomes too big, a question arises about how efficient is it. It becomes associated with wasteful spending and programs. The biggest criticism of the federal bureaucracy is its public employees who tend to have a job for life; once employed by the civil service system it seems not to matter what behavior or lack thereof the bureaucrat shows; it is very difficult to remove these people from their jobs. It seems they are the closest to having job security as a Supreme Court justice who is appointed for life. One of the major complaints is that the federal government does not have control of itself and should operate more like the business sector. When federal programs are not performing they should be cut, but in most cases they are spared. Cutting any government program will become a political fight because it was generally created to please some constituency. Programs are caught between party politics, which therefore makes any cut difficult. Furthermore, determining what is still good versus what is no longer good is hard to do. In addition to the problems just mentioned, once a program is developed, people become attached to it because of their interest in the cause. The Department of Homeland Security, for example, has people who are committed to protecting America's homeland and as time goes on they will push for more funding. Interest groups and other citizens outside of government will also request that the program go forward.

Online Connections

View these sites to find out more about the bureaucracy.

U.S. Government Bureaucracy. *http://www.questia.com*

Use Find Law to look up important court cases as they refer to bureaucracy. *http://www.findlaw.com*

View the White House website. *http://www.whitehouse.gov*

Key Terms

Bureaucracy 61	Spoils system 63
Distributed intelligence 61	Pendleton Act 64
Bureaucrats 62	Merit system 64
Elites 63	Policy implementation 65

Suggested Readings

Barry Bozeman, *Bureaucracy and Red Tape* (Upper Saddle River, NJ: Prentice Hall, 2000).

Anthony Downs, *Inside Bureaucracy* (Boston: Little, Brown, 1967).

Max Neiman, *Defending Government: Why Big Government Works* (Upper Saddle River, NJ: Prentice Hall, 2000)

Allen Schick, *The Federal Budget: Politics, Policy, Process* (Washington DC: Brookings Institution, 1995).

Notes

[1]National Partnership for Reinventing Government, Introduction by Vice President Al Gore (*http://govinfo .library.unt.edu/npr/library/announc/access/intro.html*).

[2]Office of Management and Budget, *Money Losing Train*, November 21, 2002 (*http://www.whitehouse.gov/omb/reform/index.html*).

[3]H. H. Gerth and C. Wright Mills, *From Max Weber* (New York: Oxford University Press, 1958).

[4]White House photo (*http://www.whitehouse.gov/history/presidents/aj7.html*).

[5]Quoted in U.S. Civil Service Commission, *Biography of an Ideal*: *A History of the Civil Service System* (Washington DC: Government Printing Office, 1973), p. 16.

[6]U.S. Office of Personnel Management, General Schedule and Locality Pay Table for effective January 1, 2003 (*http://www.opm.gov/oca/03tables/indexGS.asp*).

NAME_____ COURSE_____ SECTION_____

1. Max Weber taught certain characteristics of a bureaucracy. Name and explain these characteristics.

_____

_____

_____

_____

_____

2. Compare and contrast the spoils system with the merit system.

_____

_____

_____

_____

_____

3. Describe the evolution of bureaucracy.

_____

_____

_____

_____

_____

4. Explain the problems of a bureaucracy.

_____

_____

_____

_____

_____

Directions: Circle the correct answer to each of the following questions.

1. When federal governments and agencies change the way they run their organization, this is called _____ of government.
    a. distributed intelligence
    b. spoils system
    c. bureaucracy
    d. reinvention

2. The executive branch consists of _____.
    a. fifteen cabinet positions
    b. fifty independent agencies
    c. about 2,000 divisions and branches
    d. all of the above

3. According to Max Weber, a model bureaucracy consists of the following components: _____.
    a. Chain of command, division of labor, specification of authority, goal orientation, personality, no productivity
    b. Chain of command, division of labor, specification of authority, orientation, impersonality, productivity
    c. Chain of command, division of labor, specification of authority, goal orientation, impersonality, productivity
    d. None of the above

4. A way of rewarding party loyalists and friends by giving them employment is called _____.
    a. distributed intelligence
    b. spoils system
    c. bureaucracy
    d. reinvention

5. The Pendleton Act of 1883 classified certain jobs and created a federal government system based on merit. The group that would oversee the classification of jobs is called_____.
    a. the Office of Management and Budget
    b. the civil service commission
    c. the executive branch
    d. The merit commission

6. Which of the following is not one of the president's cabinet positions?
    a. Secretary of Labor
    b. Secretary of the Army
    c. Secretary of the Treasury
    d. Attorney General

7. The president appoints _____ members to the civil service commission.
    a. six
    b. four
    c. five
    d. three

8. _____ percent of the government employees are on a general pay schedule.
    a. Ninety
    b. Seventy
    c. Eighty
    d. Sixty

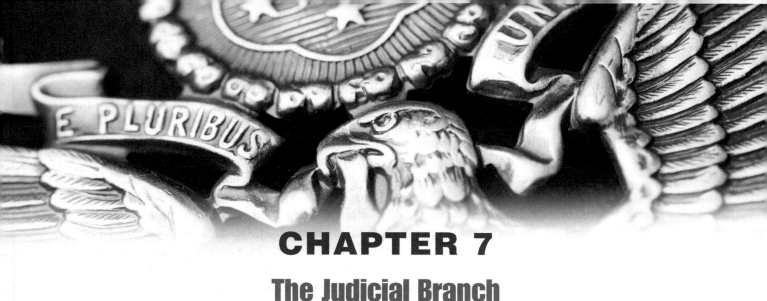

CHAPTER 7

The Judicial Branch

© 2013 by Matt Snodderly. Used under license of Shutterstock,Inc.

JUDICIAL POWER

The judicial branch must remain independent of a political party. Federal judges are appointed, not elected, and they hold their position for life, unless impeached. The judges have a responsibility to uphold the Constitution and determine which acts are and are not constitutional. The Constitution is the "supreme law of the land"[1] and it overrides any state law or local law that violates the Constitution. This power to review laws passed by state legislatures and local governments of local, state, and congressional laws to determine their constitutionality is called **judicial review**.

STRUCTURE OF THE COURTS

There are three levels within the federal court system. It consists of the Supreme Court, the Court of Appeals, and the district courts. The Supreme Court is established by the Constitution. As discussed in Chapter 15, Congress has the power to determine the number of appellate courts.

As you will see in Figure 7.1 the highest court is the U.S. Supreme Court. This court hears only a few cases each year., about 80. Cases that they hear most of the time have been appealed from lower courts, such as state courts or the U.S. Court of Appeals. This is called

appellate jurisdiction, where cases have already been ruled on in a lower court, but have been appealed to a higher court to hear the arguments. The Supreme Court determines the cases that they will hear. If there are disagreements between states or disagreements between the federal government and the states, then the Supreme Court may hear the case for the first time, which is called **original jurisdiction**., since 1869. Nine justices sit on the Supreme Court with one of them being the Chief Justice John Roberts. Currently there are five white men (Neil Gorsuch, John Roberts, Anthony Kennedy, Stephen Breyer, and Samuel Alito), three women (Ruth Bader Ginsburg, Sonia Sotomayor, and Elena Kagan) and one African American man (Clarence Thomas). The justices are appointed to their position by the president and approved by the Senate. Once appointed and confirmed by the Senate they serve lifetime terms. They are in session from October to June each year. Through this nine-month period, they schedule the cases that they determine are important to hear and reject other cases, many times giving no reason why.

The next level of court as seen on Figure 7.1 is the court of appeals or the circuit courts. There are twelve courts that make up this level. They only hear cases on appeal, so they are an appellate court. The court does not hold trials. It only will accept the briefs from the original case and no new evidence can be submitted. Just as with the Supreme Court the appellate judges are appointed by the president, confirmed by the Senate, and serve life appointments. Most of the cases that are sent to this level end here.

The third and final level of the federal court system is the district courts. The district courts are trial courts which hear cases and determine their outcome for the first time, called original jurisdiction. Every state has one court and large states have more, such as Texas, which has four district courts. As with the Supreme Court and the circuit court, district judges are appointed by the president and confirmed by the Senate for lifetime terms. They hear criminal cases and civil cases. The district courts are structured with first grand juries, used to hear the evidence and bring formal charges if determined by the evidence. After the **grand jury** has decided to hear the case then it is brought to a **jury trial**, which will determine guilt or innocence. Most of the work happens at this level of the system.

Figure 7.1   The United States Court System.

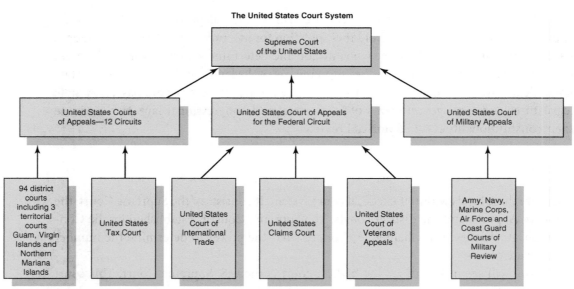

Source: The Federal Judiciary[2]

SUPREME COURT JUSTICE SELECTION CRITERIA

At each level of the court all federal judges are appointed by the president and confirmed by the Senate and serve lifetime terms. How are the judges chosen? Who is selected? Many of the justices, even though their thinking and beliefs about the Constitution are very different, hold common backgrounds in education and judicial experience.

Law Degree and Judicial Experience

Every person who has served on the Supreme Court has been trained in the law. Another commonality between many of the Supreme Court justices is that many have attended some of the most prestigious law schools, such as Stanford or Harvard. Most of the justices have also had previous federal-level judgeship experience.

Age

Most of the justices recently appointed to the Supreme Court have been in their fifties. Through their choice of justices the president can make a lasting statement; long after they are out of office, their appointments remain.

Race and Gender

The first female to be appointed to the U.S. Supreme Court was Sandra Day O'Connor. President Reagan appointed her in 1981. She had attended Stanford University with Justice William Rehnquist and was an Arizona State Judge. The second female appointed to the Supreme Court was Ruth Bader Ginsburg in 1993 by President Bill Clinton. She was an attorney for the American Civil Liberties Union, fighting gender discrimination and taught at the prestigious Columbia Law School.

The first African American appointed to the Supreme Court was by President Lyndon Johnson in 1967—Thurgood Marshall. Marshall had argued the *Brown* case in 1954 before the Supreme Court. He resigned his position on the bench in 1991 due to health reasons and died in 1993. President Bush in 1991 appointed another African American, Clarence Thomas, to keep the minority balance on the court, but made sure that the justice had conservative views.

The first Hispanic appointed to the Supreme Court was Sonia Sotomayor. She was appointed by President Barack Obama in 2009. She previously was a U.S. Circuit Court Judge.

Ideology or Policy Preference

Presidents seek to appoint members to the court who have policy views similar to their own. Most presidents also have goals in mind as they appoint a justice; they try to make the court as similar to their own beliefs as possible. Being of the same party affiliation is also something that presidents consider.

SUPREME COURT PROCESS

When the Supreme Court approves a case for review a number of steps will occur.

Step One—Filing Briefs

The attorneys for all sides submit briefs. These are written arguments to the Supreme Court that are hundreds of pages long, outlining the facts, legal and constitutional arguments, and answering all the opposing sides arguments. The legal briefs contain all the supporting evidence for the case.

Step Two—Oral Argument

After briefs are submitted, the Supreme Court sets the docket and oral arguments ensue. Each side is given thirty minutes to speak. Justices can interrupt during this time and ask questions.

It can cost up to $500,000 to take a case to the Supreme Court. The amount of time that it takes to craft the argument and research the case plus being able to present it in front of the justices, even while being interrupted, takes intense skill.

The Supreme Court conference room where justices meet to make decisions on cases.

Source: The Supreme Court[3]

Step Three—The Conference

Justices conduct meetings in complete secrecy, on Wednesday afternoons and all day Friday. At the meetings the justices give their opinions on the case and say how they are going to rule. This is their preliminary vote.

Step Four—Assignment of Opinions

After the conference has been conducted and the voting is over, it is time to determine who will write the **majority opinion**. The opinion is the court decision in written form. If the chief justice is in the majority he will assign the person who will write the opinion; if not, the senior justice from the majority will determine who will write the opinion. The assignment of the written opinion is decided based on the expertise of the members, their current caseload, their ability to reach consensus, and the speed at which they can write an opinion. If a justice is really opposed to the decision he or she might write the **dissenting opinion**, a written statement as to why he or she disagrees with the opinion.[4]

SUPREME COURT CHECKS AND BALANCES

Internal Checks

The courts do not have their own police force to enforce the laws that they hand down. They rely on the executive branch for support. However, the courts mostly rely on the fact that the decisions they render are seen as right, and even though you may not agree with them, you will abide by their decisions. This is called *legitimacy*.

During the civil rights era this was very difficult for many to follow. Many people did not agree with some of the decisions that the court made during this era. One case in particular was the decision to desegregate a Little Rock, Arkansas, school. The court needed to make sure that the laws were implemented so the National Guard was called in by President Eisenhower to control the peace so that the law could be followed.[5]

Presidential Influence

Through the power of appointment granted the president in the Constitution, the president can influence the balance of power on the Supreme Court. The Republicans tend to appoint conservatives to the court who show judicial restraint in decisions that they make. **Judicial restraint** is when decisions of lower courts are allowed to stand because they are in line with the Constitution rather than in line with the judge's own view of the situation.[6] Democrats tend to appoint more liberal judges who tend to use judicial activism. **Judicial activism** is when judges use their power to further justice, especially when it comes to equality and personal liberty.[7]

The balance on the court has shifted over the years. See Figure 7.2.

Congressional Checks

As discussed in Chapter 4, Congress can control the number of inferior courts that are established. President Jimmy Carter increased the number of federal judges when he was president because of the large numbers of cases. He used these new positions to appoint women and minorities to judgeships. Congress, however, cannot control the Supreme Court, but they can change the number of justices from nine to something else. This, however, is unlikely to change.

Congress cannot reverse a Supreme Court decision. The only way that the reversal could happen is by a constitutional amendment. In the *Dred Scott* (1857) decision slavery was considered protected by the Constitution. Congress, however, later (1865) passed the Thirteenth Amendment to the U.S. Constitution stating that slavery was unlawful, thus rendering the decision in the *Dred Scott* case invalid.[8]

Figure 7.2   Liberal and conservative court balance on the Supreme Court.

Chief Justice	Earl Warren (1968)	Warren Burger (1975)	William Rehnquist (2000)	John Roberts (2005)
Liberal	Earl Warren	William Douglas	John Paul Stevens	John Paul Stevens
	Hugo Black	Thurgood Marshall	Ruth Bader Ginsburg	Ruth Bader Ginsburg
	William Douglas	William Brennan	Stephen Breyer	Sonia Sotomayor
	William Brennan			Stephen Breyer
	Abe Fortas			Elena Kagen
Moderate	Potter Stewart	Potter Stewart	Anthony Kennedy	Anthony Kennedy
	Byron White	Byron White	Sandra Day O'Connor	
		Lewis Powell	David Souter	
		Harry Blackmun		
Conservative	John Marshall Harlan	Warren Burger	William Rehnquist	Neil Gorsuch
		William Rehnquist	Antonin Scalia	Clarence Thomas
			Clarence Thomas	Samuel Alito
				John Roberts

Figure 7.3   2017 U.S. Supreme Court Justices.

Justice	Date of Birth	Appointed by	Sworn in
Anthony Kennedy	7/23/1936	Ronald Reagan	2/18/1988
Clarence Thomas	6/23/1948	George H. W. Bush	10/23/1991
Ruth Bader Ginsburg	3/15/1933	Bill Clinton	8/19/1993
Stephen Breyer	8/15/1938	Bill Clinton	8/3/1994
John G. Roberts	1/27/1955	George W. Bush	9/29/2005
Samuel A. Alito, Jr.	4/1/1950	George W. Bush	1/31/2006
Sonia Sotomayor	6/25/1954	Barack Obama	8/8/2009
Elena Kagan	4/28/1960	Barack Obama	8/7/2010
Neil McGill Gorsuch	8/29/1967	Donald John Trump	4/10/2017

Source: http://www.thegreenpapers.com/Hx/SupremeCourt.html

Another way that Congress can disagree with the Supreme Court is to pass another version of the same law that was rendered unconstitutional by the Supreme Court. For instance in a 1990 case Native Americans were denied unemployment benefits for smoking peyote, a hallucinogenic drug, in a religious ceremony. The Supreme Court said the men were violating state antidrug laws.[9] The case was applied to many more cases to restrict the free exercise of religion. As a result, in 1993 Congress passed the Religious Freedom Restoration Act, which required the states to show a high level of proof before the state would interfere with religious rights. President Clinton signed the act into law.[10]

Congress can impeach federal judges, but only for committing crimes. Judges cannot be impeached for the decisions they make. Only five federal judges have ever been impeached.

CHECKS ON INFERIOR COURTS

As stated earlier the Supreme Court is the highest court in the land and decisions at this level affect every level below it in the federal and state system. When inferior state and federal courts rule on their own cases they need to comply with the Supreme Court's views, even when they do not agree. When the lower court judges do not agree with a decision, they may write their dissent into their opinion, but they still follow the law as interpreted by the Supreme Court. Federal judges oftentimes do not go against the grain in their interpretations because it might mean that the case could be overturned in the higher court. Judges do not want this to happen.

Online Connections

Check out these websites to find more about the judiciary.

The U.S. Supreme Court. Look to find out the cases they are hearing and learn about the history of the court. *http://www.supremecourtus.gov*

Read through to find out about your federal court system. *http://www.uscourts.gov*

Find out more about the Constitution and other areas of government. *http://www.archives.gov*

Key Terms

Judicial review 73	Majority opinion 77
Appellate jurisdiction 74	Dissenting opinion 77
Original jurisdiction 74	Judicial restraint 77
Grand jury 74	Judicial activism 77
Jury trial 74	

Selected Readings

Ethan Bronner, *Battle for Justice: How the Bork Nomination Shook America* (New York: Norton, 1989).

Kermit L. Hall, ed. *The Oxford Companion to the Supreme Court of the United States* (New York: Oxford University Press, 1992).

J. Woodford Howard Jr., *Courts of Appeals in the Federal Judicial System* (Princeton, NJ: Princeton University Press, 1981).

H. W. Perry, *Deciding to Decide: Agenda Setting in the United States Supreme Court* (Landham, MD: Rowman & Littlefield, 1996).

Notes

[1]Article VI of the U.S. Constitution.

[2]*http://www.uscourts.gov/understanding_courts/gifs/figure1.gif*

[3]*http://www.supremecourtus.gov/about/photo13.html*

[4]Larry Berman and Bruce Allen Murphy, *Approaching Democracy* (Upper Saddle River, NJ: Prentice Hall, 2001), 239–241.

[5]*Cooper v. Aaron*, 358 U.S. 1 (1958).

[6]Alexis de Tocqueville, *Democracy in America*, vol. 1, trans. Phillips Bradley (New York: Knopf, Vintage Books, 1945; org. published in 1835), 191.

[7]Elmer E. Schattschneider, *The Semi-Sovereign People*: A Realist's View of Democracy in America, 35.

[8]*Dred Scott v. Sanford*, 19 Howard 393 (1857).

[9]*Employment Division, Department of Human Resources of Oregon v. Smith*, 110 S. Ct. 1595 (1990).

[10]David E. Anderson, "Signing of Religious Freedom Act Culminates Three-Year Push," *Washington Post*, November 20, 1993, p. C6.

NAME_____ COURSE_____ SECTION_____

1. Describe the organization of the federal courts.

_____

_____

_____

_____

2. List and explain the process of the Supreme Court in deciding cases.

_____

_____

_____

_____

3. Name and explain the criteria for the Supreme Court judge selection.

_____

_____

_____

_____

4. Explain the checks on the Supreme Court.

_____

_____

_____

_____

Directions: Circle the correct answer to each of the following questions.

1. At which level of the federal court system are most cases determined?
   a. U.S. Court of Appeals
   b. U.S. District Courts
   c. U.S. Supreme Court
   d. All of the above

2. What are the "unwritten" selection criteria for Supreme Court judges?
   a. A law degree from a prestigious school.
   b. Views similar to that of the president.
   c. About 50 years of age.
   d. All of the above.

3. Which of the following displays the steps in the correct order of a Supreme Court case?
   a. Oral argument, conference, filing briefs, assigning of opinions
   b. Filing briefs, conference, assigning of opinions, oral argument
   c. Filing briefs, oral argument, conference, assigning of opinions
   d. Conference, filing briefs, assigning of opinions, oral argument

4. In order to prove the _____ of the Supreme Court's decision in Little Rock, Arkansas, the National Guard was called in to keep the peace.
   a. judicial restraint
   b. legitimacy
   c. judicial activism
   d. minority opinion

5. Congress can disagree with the opinion of the Supreme Court by _____.
   a. putting the law into place anyway
   b. passing another version of the same law
   c. impeaching the Supreme Court judges for their opinions
   d. none of the above

6. The current chief justice of the Supreme Court is _____.
   a. Warren Burger
   b. Clarence Thomas
   c. William Rehnquist
   d. Sandra Day O'Connor

7. _____ is when judges use their power to further justice.
    a. Judicial restraint
    b. Legitimacy
    c. Judicial activism
    d. Minority opinion

8. _____ is when decisions of lower courts are allowed to stand because they are in line with the Constitution.
    a. Judicial restraint
    b. Legitimacy
    c. Judicial activism
    d. Minority opinion

CHAPTER 8
Political Culture and Participation

Photo Courtesy Glynn Newman

POLITICAL CULTURE

In this chapter we are going to examine **political culture**, which is a widely shared belief concerning the relationship of citizens to government and to one another. When we think of right and wrong we use rationalization based on ideas. Values also become very important in American democracy. **Values** are shared ideas about what is good and desirable. Some of America's values include individualism, equality, liberty, justice, idealism, nationalism, and the rule of law. These values are widely shared and can come into conflict with one another. **Beliefs** are shared ideas about what is true. Can beliefs justify values? Since belief and values are often connected, yes, we can. If we believe in God as our creator, for example, then we will value God.

EIGHTEENTH-CENTURY CLASSICAL LIBERALISM

The values that are considered today as a part of the American fabric—individualism, equality, private property and liberty—were once limited. The Europeans were more concerned with values, given their historicity; a continent led by aristocracies that is a hereditary ruling class, the nobility. The ruling class created political and social inequality and had governments that did not disperse power fairly. It was political philosophers who argued against the system and called for classical liberalism. The argument was based on **natural rights**, the rights of all people to dignity and worth, also called human rights. If the government in any way interferes with these rights it must be stopped. Our founders would use some of the ideas of these Europeans in America to create our system of government. The idea of a free market economy and ownership of private property started during this period and is still a part of our society today. The Europeans used the same ideas to create change for themselves. If a person could own land that person could change his or her course in life. Our founders argued the same points in early colonial America.

INDIVIDUAL LIBERTY

Individual liberty in America has been the most widely held political value. This value has received a tremendous amount of attention since the early beginnings of our country. It was classical liberalism itself that asserted the worth of the individual and dignity. Under our system the individual is granted both rights and responsibilities. One concern was how much freedom of choice does an individual deserve; this tended to create political conflict. What we find is that individualism is just that—belonging to one person. If we were to place ideas, institutions, or practices over individualism, then we are putting boundaries on values, which takes away dignity.

Sometimes one's rights conflict with another's rights and when that occurs the government's responsibility is to keep order in society. The debate over legalized drugs has often been framed in these terms. There is one restriction placed on individualism and that is to not interfere with other peoples' liberty. Throughout our history people have chosen death if not **liberty**, which is the right and power to act, believe, or express oneself in a manner of one's own choosing. "Not the good man, but the free man has been the measure of all things in this sweet land of liberty; not national glory, but 'individual liberty' has been the object of political authority and the test of its worth."[1] When government has to intervene it is looked on as an evil, but an evil that is necessary. Another problem Americans face with liberty is deciding what type of liberty each person wants. Let's look at other liberties citizens may want.

POLITICAL LIBERTY

The idea of political liberty dates back to the Age of Reason and Enlightenment from the eighteenth century. Such philosophers as Thomas Jefferson, John Locke, Adam Smith, and Jean-Jacques Rousseau articulated belief in reason, virtue, and common sense. An attack on the monarchy, the privileged, and state established church is how classical liberalism developed. Asserting the self-worth and dignity of the individual led the founding fathers to write a Constitution of the United States and create our republic. The founders could use classical liberalism as a way to realize their dreams of a new nation. The argument by Locke was that, given the rights of the people, we would need a government to protect the people; that is why social compacts were formed. The notion was government will protect the people, but the activity by the government would be small.

ECONOMIC FREEDOM

Our economic system is **capitalist**, asserting the individual's right to own private property and to buy, sell, rent, and trade that property in a free market. It is an economic idea.

Economic freedom in America has allowed people to create a business, move from job to job, join professional groups, and negotiate for services. All of the choices given are the result of capitalism, which allows the individual to make economic choices without government intervention. Just as capitalism is an economic idea, political liberty is a political idea. When you look at the two you will notice freedom to choose is allowed in both. Classical Liberalism as a political idea allows you to vote, speak out, and develop a political party or not participate at all. Classical Liberal economics help individuals in finding a job, starting a business, spending money on what they believe is best for them. Government's responsibility then is to promote private enterprise and provide services that the private sector cannot afford. Our history has placed much emphasis on value in the area of politics and economics. The only value that stands in competition with liberty is equality in our American political culture.

THE PLIGHT OF EQUALITY

Thomas Jefferson wrote in the Declaration of Independence that "all men were created equal," ever since Americans have understood that no person is worth more than the next person. Given the year 1776, a period when slavery existed, the idea of individual dignity and equality was a hard sell. Nonetheless, it was the idea of equality that allowed members to vote who previously could not do so and ended slavery. The founders came to this country not for an opportunity, but for an equal opportunity. With this faith anyone could rise up no matter where he or she was born, gain status, own a business with a willingness to work hard and God's blessings. Americans agree no one is better than another; however we do know our notion of equality has been challenged by politics.

POLITICAL EQUALITY

Americans believe that no matter what status or economic condition, the laws of the land should apply equally. Our founders believed in a fundamental rule of law and that no one person was better than another. We had legal equality, which did not guarantee political equality in 1787 when the U.S. Constitution was written. The qualifications of voters were left to the states to decide, which proved to be problematic over the years to come. States required property, or one needed to be a taxpayer in order to vote. The battle over voting would extend over two centuries, but universal suffrage would be achieved. What we learned from the voting rights struggle was a lesson in contradiction. The people of the United States did value equality mostly in theory, not so much in practice.

EQUALITY OF OPPORTUNITY

When we speak of equality we can extend it to the **equality of opportunity**, which means to eliminate artificial barriers to success in life and the opportunity for everyone to strive for success. When a person attempts to become successful in life, create a business, get a professional career, be recognized for one's work, this is what we mean by equality of opportunity. The goal of the idea is that all people start the race in life at the same point and no one has a head start. When equality of opportunity has been followed Americans do not feel there is a need to feel angry with a successful person in life. Most Americans are not upset with a doctor, professor, or football player given that each had to put forth time and energy to achieve a skill that makes them more money and status than professions that require little skill or training. Many people take greater risk in America than do others. The people who take greater risk by investing in the market, creating a business, and developing products tend to earn more money than do people who work for others. The government ensures that people will have equality of opportunity and guarantees that every American has an opportunity to get an education, job, own a home, and is capable of doing so without the concern of race, religion, gender, or ethnicity preventing them from doing so. The idea of equality of opportunity is very much accepted in America, but when the government uses such remedies as affirmative action to achieve equality and to reverse past discrimination, then Americans run into differences.

EQUALITY OF RESULTS

The equal sharing of all income and material possessions, regardless of one's ability, talent, or life's work, is the **equality of results**. Theorists who argue on this basis believe that if we are all truly equal then we should all have the same living conditions. Inequalities should not be created between people, but people should be valued for their contributions to society. The government should act as the intermediary by transferring the income of the rich to the poor. This is a "Robin Hood model." In American society today this model is seen as morally wrong and socialist in nature. It is viewed that if there were absolute equality people would lose their incentive to work hard. This is often a complaint of the Texas school-funding model.[2] Americans believe more in the belief that there should be fairness for all, equality of opportunity, versus equality of results. Most people would argue that having the same goods and services as their neighbor would not be satisfying if they had not worked for it.

FAIRNESS

It is hard to agree on the definition of fairness, but most Americans believe in fairness. Americans believe that there should be a bottom income level that no family should be able to drop below. The amount of income that Americans feel is appropriate differs, but no Americans want to see families denied an equal opportunity. However, when it comes to an amount of income that should be the upper income, Americans do not want to set an amount. Americans are not very favorable when government determines what income we should be allowed to earn. Americans do believe that the government should have a floor, a base income, to help prevent poverty. It grants each American the equality of opportunity. Poverty denies children the opportunity to compete in life. The American people are a fair group, particularly with federal revenues for the elderly, children, and the poor.[3]

POLITICAL INFLUENCE

Income and Wealth

American society is very concerned with the distribution of income. Within the scope of American politics, economics have become a major issue. Conflict occurs when it is believed that one group is benefiting more than another. The wealthy as well as the poor are concerned with income distribution. Distribution of wealth affects the standard of living of any group if the redistribution does not flow in their direction. It is strange that the America people are so concerned with measurable income in society, given the fact that as a whole we are measured by mortality, income per capita, life expectancy, and gross domestic product.[4]

Figure 8.1   U.S. Average Income, 2014.

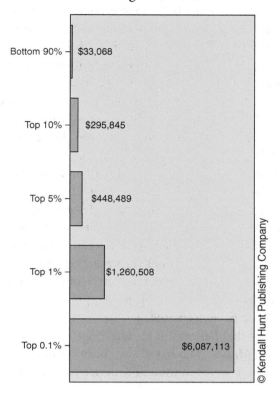

NEW INEQUALITY

In the United States income differences have declined over the years, but inequality has massively increased in recent years. The reason for the increase is the unprecedented abysmal earnings experience of low-paid Americans, stagnation covering about 80 percent of all families, and an increase in upper-end incomes. Given the rise in inequality the United States, more than other developed countries, has reversed the equalization in income and wealth, placing itself as the leader in inequality among advanced countries. Income in the poorest households declined while income in the highest households increased. Something is certainly wrong when the United States has become a country of working poor. The forces contributing to wage losses at the bottom, foreign competition, immigration of low-skilled labor, technological changes, shifts from manufacturing to service industries, declining union density, subcontracting, and so on are unlikely to reverse themselves anytime soon.

First, what are the causes of the new inequality? The short answer is that analysts disagree. Pat Buchanan and Ross Perot put immigration and trade at the top of the list of reasons. The Clinton Administration blamed technology. Republicans blame taxes and government regulations. The AFL-CIO stresses declining unionism and the fall in the real value of the minimum wage.

WHAT DOES SOCIAL MOBILITY MEAN?

Social mobility is used by social scientists to refer to movements by specific entities between periods in social economic status indicators. *Social mobility* means the extent to which people move upward or downward in income and status over a lifetime.

When there is social mobility in a country people have a good opportunity to get ahead if they go to school or work hard, save money, and invest wisely. People tend to withstand inequalities if they believe that in a lifetime there are chances of moving up, or at least of seeing their children do better than they. The United States calls itself the land of opportunity. But does America allow for people to improve their life relative to others? Our system allows people to move both upward and downward. Many Americans have experienced *total mobility* where life has moved from one specific place to another for example (1, 2, 3) to (2, 4, 6) in that manner. If the opposite happens (1, 2, 3) to (3, 2, 1) this is considered *relative mobility*. There is mobility even though total income and income distribution both are the same across the two periods.

Over a lifetime moving from one point in life to another may be the key to political scientists' understanding of *class conflict*. *Class conflict* occurs between upper and lower social classes over wealth and power. Many countries endure a large amount of conflict over class and power among society. The United States does not endure such widespread conflict. American's belief in *social mobility* reduces the amount of *class consciousness*. *Class consciousness* is an awareness of one's class position and a feeling of political solidarity with others within the same class in opposition to other classes. If people begin to feel that they had no real chance of moving up in life, political conflict would increase and class consciousness would have risen as well.

America is a country that believes in middle-class values. Most politicians campaign on middle-class values. *Middle class* has always been a more acceptable term than *rich*, and no one likes the term *poor*, even though America has a growing underclass.

PUBLIC OPINION

If someone were to ask you a series of questions concerning the way President Obama is handling the economy you would get any number of responses. Depending on the way the questions are asked will determine the way you answer them. The way a polling question is asked makes a difference in the response people give. This is a *hypothetical situation*. We collect data about the funding of Reverend Jesse Jackson's Rainbow Coalition, a professional survey research. The questions were published in a magazine and people were asked to mail in their answers.

1. Should the Rainbow Coalition be able receive contributions or does the law need to stop this type of special interest?   Yes 99%
2. Should the Rainbow Coalition be able receive funds, given the hundreds of seniors it helps, or should the contribution go directly to Jesse Jackson?   Yes 60%   No 40%
3. Do you favor the Rainbow Coalition receiving funds, or should the contribution go directly to Jesse Jackson since he is the founder and president?   Favor 70%   Oppose 29%

These questions are skewed to give answers that are more favorable to the organization. As you look at opinion polls it is important to examine the questions carefully. In this chapter we will look at political participation, agents of political socialization, voter decisions, and race and opinion.

Governments of all nations are concerned with public opinion because citizen unrest and protest can change the course of government. Public opinion in America is vital given that we are a constitutional democracy. The opinions of citizens are expressed in numerous ways from protest, to voting in an election, running for office, writing letters, and conducting demonstrations. Politicians seek the pulse of the people and their decisions are made around them. In a democracy one must have public opinion.

WHAT IS PUBLIC OPINION?

The operational definition of **public opinion** is the distribution of individual preferences or evaluations of a given issue, candidate, or institution within a population.

The word *distribution* means the proportion of the population that holds a particular opinion, as compared to people with opposing opinions or those with no opinion at all. During a U.S. presidential race preelection polls are monitored to determine who will win the office of the presidency. These polls help to determine what the results will be. However, in 2016 the polls were incorrect, polls were predicting that Clinton was going to be the victor, however this changed due to the margin of error in key swing states such as Pennsylvania, Michigan, and Wisconsin. The actual 2016 results for the presidency were Donald Trump with a 46.4 percent of the popular vote, followed Hillary Clinton with 48.5 percent. Clinton won the popular vote, however Trump won the Electoral College votes by winning in key states.[5]

HOW DO PEOPLE FEEL?

To better understand how people feel *random choice* is used. This means that every individual has an equal chance at being selected. For example, a survey of African Americans in college should not be conducted solely at black colleges since only 20 percent of African Americans attend black colleges. The way a question is asked is very important to survey research. The answer is dependent on the words chosen. How does one know if it is a good question? Good questions have been pretested and are written by trained professional interviewers. Some questions are intended to measure factual knowledge, views on hypothetical situations, opinions, and intensity of opinion. The order of the questions also determines the response. Polls are scientific so we can use a sample size, a margin of error, and the time that the poll was taken. All of this information can be reported to the public. It is very important to remember that polls change very rapidly and once taken, the data is good only for a short period of time. Sometimes public opinion is measured on individual, not group, preference. Groups can be elected officials, special interests, or news personnel. The universe or population is the relevant group. Suppose a large number of people agree on the same issue—for example, that same-sex marriage is wrong—there is a *consensus*. This is not always the case; most times issues are divided among people in various proportions. When a large portion of the voter population is divided over an issue we say they are *polarized*, for example, should there be bilingual education?

MEASURING PUBLIC OPINION

Public opinion has always been around, but it was not until recently that reliable ways were developed to measure it. The straw poll was one of the first attempts at measuring public opinion in the mid-1800s. A **straw poll** is a nonscientific method of measuring public opinion. The concept came from farmers throwing straw into the air to gauge the direction of the wind flow. The goal was to see the strength of the political breeze and in which direction it is blowing. A straw poll is filled with problems, most importantly is its inability to obtain a representative sample of the public. In order to conduct valid research a sample must be representative; it must represent the most important characteristics of the population. A sample of Americans that includes no men, for example, would be obviously invalid. The public demanded a more accurate way of polling after the 1936 poor presidential election poll. The poll was conducted by a paper called the *Literary Digest*, which predicted Republican Alfred M. Landon would beat incumbent President Franklin D. Roosevelt by a margin of 57 percent to 43 percent of the popular vote. The poll was wrong; Roosevelt beat Landon by receiving 62.5 percent of the vote carrying all but two states.[6]

WHAT HAPPENED?

The goal of the *Literary Digest* was to poll as many respondents as possible. They disregarded modern sampling techniques and used cross-sectional representation and selected or sampled as many people as possible according to a strict rule developed. Because there was no method to the way people were selected, it was as if they were grabbing straws in the wind. Three problems were faced by the *Literary Digest's* sample.

First, the sample was taken from phone books and automobile owners. By using this sample the pollsters were selecting only the upper middle class and the wealthy, which tend to be very strong Republicans. In addition to that in 1936 class lines were very close, which polarized voting. Thus the oversampling of the wealthy proved to be problematic because it severely underestimated the Democratic vote.

Second, the problem was timing. The *Digest* decided to mail the questionnaires in early September. Because they conducted the polls so early many people were still undecided and as events took place some voters switched candidates.

Third, the *Digest* faced a problem called self-selection. The cards they received back in the mail were from highly motivated individuals, 22 percent of whom responded. Researchers found that those who responded to the surveys were wealthy and better educated than the general electorate. Also, the *Digest* allowed the respondents to select themselves into the sample. Only one pollster got the election of 1936 correct and that was George Gallup.[7]

POLLING PERFECTED

By late 1940 polling techniques had become much more reliable than in the past. Businessmen and politicians were relying on polls for just about everything. They used polls for marketing goods and campaigns. Even though the process of polling had advanced it still ran into some problems now and then, particularly when Gallup predicted Thomas E. Dewey would defeat President Harry S. Truman in 1948.

AGENTS OF POLITICAL SOCIALIZATION

Over the years political scientists have come to believe that our attitudes are shaped in our political values. Our values are learned through **political socialization**, which is a process through which an individual acquires particular political orientations—the learning process by which people acquire their political beliefs and values. Three important agents are family, mass media, schools, and peers. For example, try to think about your earliest memory of an American president. It probably was Ronald Reagan or George Bush, but some of you may remember even earlier presidents. What did you think of the candidate? Was he a Republican or Democrat? Most of what you know about each candidate is knowledge you acquired from your parents. Just as your parents helped form your opinion about presidents or party politics, they also helped shape your beliefs about the flag, the police, and the military. Some additional factors in determining how your political views were formed include your social status, church, race, gender, age, and geographic location.

The Family

The family is said to be a child's first social agent. The family influences children in two ways: communication and receptivity. The parents pass on their views to their children, which help shape political values. For example, studies have shown the most important visible public figures for children under ten were police officers and the president of the United States.[8] Because parents tell children that the police are there to protect and the president is to be respected both are viewed as helpful. As children grow and become more exposed to the world their views become more selective. If a child is raised in a Republican household and the president is a Democrat, the children will tend to be more critical of the president than the Republican children. For example, if you were born during Reagan's presidency, you are more likely to align with Republicans today.

Schools

Respect for our nation and its symbols are taught to schoolchildren at an early age. Elementary schools are key when it comes down to teaching patriotism, beginning the day with the Pledge of Allegiance, which is a regular component of the school curricula. Children are taught to be proud of the flag and the United States. By creating such unity across the country for these two icons we can maintain national allegiance. When our country became involved in the Persian Gulf War, children across the country were encouraged to write the servicemen and women in support of the war.

High school plays a key role in building good citizens. It tries to reinforce what was taught in elementary school. High schools are a very important part of the political socialization process. Research shows that the more education one receives the more likely one will vote. So teaching civic responsibility in high schools is very important.

College tends to disrupt the thinking process of the student. College courses are designed to help students think critically about political issues. It is college where a student is called on and asked to question a political action or policy. Because of the styles many professors use in college it brings on a liberalizing effect on students. It is believed that for every year a student spends in college the more liberal he or she becomes. More Republican students entered college after the Reagan era. Clinton and Gore in 1996 may have softened the number of Republican freshman in college because of their outward reach toward young voters. This contributed to the liberal ideological identification of first-year freshmen.

The Mass Media

Since the invention of television Americans spend an enormous amount of time watching it. Studies have shown that the average adult watches at least thirty hours a week of television and children watch even more. Television has a major role in helping shape the way we view politics, government, and politicians. Where does our source of news come from? The sources are TV talk shows, talk radio, Internet newsletters, and magazines. All of these are important sources of news, but the problem is that a majority of the information is skewed. When more than 20 percent of the population learn of presidential candidates from late-night TV, how serious could the information be? The goal of late-night TV show hosts like Letterman are to make people laugh, not to become oversensitive. The younger the crowd that is less than thirty years old, the more likely their information comes from some form of comedy or talk show. Television has become a major part of the campaign process.[9] In the 2000 presidential election all candidates used some form of media to inform or sway voters. Even the Internet was used, though it was considered very new for the time. Candidates had set up websites to make themselves known to the public. Most sites would allow a supporter to contribute money to the campaign over the Internet. The number of people logging onto the Internet has steadily increased from the 1996 election to the presidential election of 2000.

The Internet completely changed the landscape of running for political office with the election of 2008, with Barack Obama and John McCain. Barack Obama's bid for the office of president would not have been won had it not been for the Internet. It was used as an interactive tool in order to advertise, communicate, organize, and fund-raise. Obama also used YouTube, which was a way to use free advertising versus paying for television time. The YouTube videos logged 14.5 million hours of viewing time, which would have cost the campaign $47 million on television. The introduction of social media to the political process has held elected officials more accountable and accessible to voters. Advertising can be done without paying for it, public opinion can be gained immediately, messages can be tailored to fit any group, and young people are more involved in the process because it is a "hip" way to keep connected.[10]

SOCIAL VARIABLES AND OPINION INFLUENCE

In politics we are all subject to some overall influences that shape the thought processes of society. Norms and values are learned behaviors from our families. We share the same political and economic events, we attend the same schools, and watch the same TV shows. It would be fair to say we are bound by a set of forces that mold our behavior. Even though we are very similar in many ways, however, people still differ in many ways, too. Our class and income, race and ethnicity, religion and region, and gender produce different life experiences that are bound to cause differences in the way we reflect our political differences.

Class and Income

Social and political values are shaped in society according to where we stand in society. According to social scientists, the way we are molded rests heavily on class or social status. How do we define class? Class is very complex and difficult to measure. Because of the complexity we resort to income because it is easier to define. Depending on one's income determines the political views they are more likely to hold. A potential mitigating factor between class and income is education. Those that are more wealthy and have more education tend to vote more than the less educated. A rule of thumb is the less income one has, the more one favors liberal economic policies that provide more security to people with less in society. These policies are in favor of Social Security, minimum wage laws, unemployment benefits, and welfare payments to the disadvantaged. If one's income is very high, one would tend to oppose these types of programs. Economic policies of the rich or the poor are both self-interested. Each category has its exceptions; some wealthy people are liberal and some poor are conservative. No matter how we dice it, income patterns still impact voter patterns in the United States. It would be fair to say poor people usually vote Democratic (liberal) and rich people usually vote Republican (conservative). The middle-class income people tend to split their vote depending on a number of circumstances.

Race and Ethnicity

The race and ethnicity of a person plays a key role in producing different perspectives on politics. The background and race of a person will strongly affect the attitude a person is likely to have. If you were born of a race different from what you are, would that affect the way you are politically? My guess is yes because of the different encounters each race endures. Many minorities in most cultures are discriminated against. For that reason they grow up feeling distrustful of and left out of their society and its public officeholders. African Americans are much more distrustful of government than whites. The result of this is that African Americans vote more Democratic generally, in support of economic benefits for those less well off. Race is America's greatest divider; it produces the most visible social delineation between two major political parties. Blacks are considered to be the bulk of the Democratic Party, while whites are seen as the heart of the Republican Party.

Hispanics are also considered strong liberal Democrats on economic issues. Hispanic groups where there is a large population density tend to have a voting influence. In the election of 2012 there was a 71 percent Hispanic Democratic vote for Obama where only 27 percent supported Mitt Romney, the Republican nominee for President. On the other hand in the election of 2016 Donald Trump maintained the low Hispanic support at just 28% of the Hispanic vote, but still won the election.

Cuban Americans are wealthier than average and were strong supporters of a conservative agenda at least until 1996. The rule for minorities is the more they rise in social status the more conservative they become.[11]

Religion

In the United States religious differences can produce strong political differences, as in many other countries. We will look at three principles that will help explain the effects of religion on political attitudes.

First, the less religious you are, the more liberal you tend to be. Democrats tend to take more liberal stands on social and economic issues because of their lack of religious affiliations. It is important that we understand that the number of people who feel this way are few, because most people profess to have some kind of religious belief.

Second, people of the United States who are religious tend to be more conservative. It would only make sense, since these people have invested more in the status quo. In the United States minority religious groups tend to be more liberal because of the level of oppression they face. Other groups like Protestants have long been the majority group. Roman Catholics, on the other hand, were a part of a smaller group like Judaism who have been discriminated against since they first came to this country. Given what we have read thus far it would be fair to say Protestants are the most conservative group and Catholics will most likely vote for Democrats. It is also important to point out that many of the smaller religious groups have moved into the conservative arena as their financial conditions have improved.

Third, the Republican Party is moving more to the right as a result of a large influx of evangelical white Protestants and right-to-life supporters joining the party. These churchgoers tend to weigh in on the right side of the political spectrum.

Online Connections

View these sites to find out more about political socialization and culture.

To find more information on political culture and the makeup of American society check out this website. *http://www.socialstudieshelp.com/APGOV_Political%20Culture.htm*

Take a political culture quiz online and help a university professor from the University of Pennsylvania. It will only take you a few minutes. *http://www.pitt.edu/~redsox/polcul.html*

This site helps you to examine your own political views. *http://www.thisnation.com/socialization.html*

This site gives a listing of articles and books on political socialization. *http://polisci.wisc.edu/users/sapiro/ps477_935/socz_bib.htm*

This nonpartisan site shares public polling information with the public. *http://www.pollingreport.com*

Key Terms

Political culture   85

Values   85

Beliefs   85

Natural rights   86

Liberty   86

Capitalist   86

Equality of opportunity   87

Equality of results   88

Public opinion   91

Straw poll   91

Political socialization   92

Suggested Readings

Herbet Asher, *Polling and the Public: What Every Citizen Should Know*, 4th ed. (Washington: CQ Press, 1998).

Irving Crespi, *Public Opinion, Polls and Democracy* (Colorado: Westview Press, 1989).

Edward S. Greenburg, *Capitalism and the American Political Ideal* (New York: Sharpe Publishers, 1985).

Kathleen Hall Jamieson, *Dirty Politics: Deception, Distraction, and Democracy* (New York: Oxford University Press, 1992).

V. O. Key Jr., *Public Opinion and American Democracy* (New York: Knopf, 1961).

Theodore Lowi, *The End of Liberalism* (New York: Norton, 1979).

Sondra Rubenstein, *Surveying Public Opinion* (California: Wadsworth Publishing, 1994).

Paul Ryscavage, *Income Inequality in America* (New York: Sharpe, 1999).

Notes

[1]Clinton Rossiter, *Conservatism in America* (New York: Vintage, 1962), p. 72.

[2]Marc Levin, District Achieves Legal Victory against Robin Hood Plan, *Houston Review*, August 13, 1999 at *http://www.houstonreview.com/articles/49.html*

[3]Stanley Feldman and John Zaller, "The Political Culture of Ambivalence: Ideological Responses to the Welfare State" *American Political Science Review 80* (June 1986): 383–402.

[4]Edward N. Wolff, "Recent Trends in Wealth Ownership, 1983–1998," April 2000. Table 2. Available on the website of the Jerome Levy Economics Institute at www.levy.org/docs/wrkpap/papers/300.html

[5]https://www.voanews.com/a/election-experts-puzzled-over-donald-trump-surprisevictory/3589558.html

[6]*Literary Digest* 125 (August 22, 1936).

[7]Ibid.

[8]Robert D. Hess and David Easton, "The Child's Changing Image of the President," *Public Opinion Quarterly* 14 (Winter 1960): 632–42.

[9]Sandor Polster, "Bad News for Much TV News," *Bangor Daily News*, May 18, 1996.

[10]https://www.thoughtco.com/how-social-media-has-changed-politics-3367534

[11]Claire Cain Miller, "How Obama's Internet Campaign Changed Politics," *The New York Times*, November 7, 2008, and http://www.reuters.com/article/us-usa-trump-polarization-analysis-idUSKBN13I10B

[12]Mark Hugo Lopez & Paul Taylor, "Latino Voters in the 2012 Election", Pew Research Hispanic Center, November 7, 2012.

1. Name and explain the values that are a part of the American fabric which were once limited.

_____

_____

_____

_____

_____

2. Compare and contrast values and beliefs.

_____

_____

_____

_____

_____

3. What impact has the Internet had on presidential elections?

_____

_____

_____

_____

4. Name and explain the agents of political socialization.

_____

_____

_____

_____

NAME_____ COURSE_____ SECTION_____

Directions: Write the word or phrase that completes the statement.

1. America has a _____ economic system.

2. _____ is when artificial barriers are removed for success in life.

3. Governments responsibility is to promote _____ enterprise and provide services that the private sector cannot provide.

4. The process through which an individual acquires particular political orientations is called _____.

5. _____ is when the laws of the land apply equally to all people.

Directions: Circle the correct answer to each of the following questions.

6. Political liberty was articulated by _____.
   a. Thomas Jefferson
   b. John Locke
   c. Jean-Jacques Rousseau
   d. all of the above

7. Polling techniques started to become more reliable in the
   _____.
   a. 1950s
   b. 1940s
   c. 1930s
   d. 1960s

8. The *Literary Digest*'s polling sample had a number of fatal errors, including
   _____.
   a. the wealthy were oversampled, leading to an oversampling of Republican voters
   b. polls were taken early in September and voters changed their minds by November
   c. postcards were sent out, so the samples ended up being self-selected— only 22 percent responded
   d. all of the above

9. The reason for the inequality of incomes over the past few years is
   _____.
   a. the increase in numbers of low-income Americans and the increase in the middle-class income
   b. the increase in numbers of low-income Americans and the increase in the upper-class income
   c. the increase in numbers of middle-class Americans and the increase in the upper-class income
   d. the increase in numbers of upper-class Americans and the increase in the middle-class income

10. Which of the following is not a force that has contributed to the wage losses?
    a. Foreign competition
    b. Technological changes
    c. Subcontracting
    d. High-skilled labor

CHAPTER 9
Campaigns and Voting

© 2013 by Frontpage. Used under license of Shutterstock, Inc.

Elections in a democracy bring about change. People are able to decide between various candidates and parties who they want in the position. Elections are a time when the people get to decide if they like the direction the country is taking, the laws that have been passed and put in place, and the economy's direction. One problem in today's society is that not enough people understand the actual campaign process and problems that candidates face. We will examine in this chapter the campaign process and problems that face the candidates and how this impacts voter turnout.

THE ART OF CAMPAIGNING

Being a politician is an art. No one politician is like the other; they all have unique qualities. In this section we will first examine the requirements for holding federal office and then we look at three unique qualities that most politicians have.

Requirements for Office

In order to run for a federal office you need to meet certain requirements. These requirements are found in the Constitution. They are as follows:

President   If you are running for the president of the United States you need to be a natural-born citizen of the United States, a resident of the country for at least fourteen years, and be at least thirty-five years old.[1]

United States House of Representatives   There are several of these from each state. Representation is based on the population of each state. California has the most with fifty-two. If you want to run for the U.S. House of Representatives you need to be a resident of the state from which you are elected, a citizen of the United States for at least seven years, and at least twenty-five years old.[2]

United States Senate   There are only two U.S. senators from each state, which makes a total of 100 U.S. senators in all. If you want to run for the U.S. Senate you must be a resident of the state from which you are elected, a citizen of the United States for at least nine years, and at least thirty years of age.[3]

Political Salesperson

In order to run for office you need to be able to sell yourself to others. People need to be able to believe in you enough to where they will be willing to give money to your campaign. Your job as a politician would be to raise money and be able to organize people to work for you. As a politician you would need to begin to reach the media and interest groups that would support your issues. You would need to be able to sell your ideas to others and make them believe in you as a legitimate candidate.

Communication Skills

Without communication skills you will not be able to get your message out. You will not be able to be your own "political salesperson," as you need to be. Politicians need to know how to communicate in many different settings such as press conferences and phone interviews, and with many different audiences from large auditoriums to one on one. Politicians need to be able to know their audience and what is appropriate to say to that audience. It is most important that politicians communicate to audiences with sincerity and compassion. The ability to debate and answer questions in interviews is also very important.

Politics in the Blood

When you are a politician you know it. Politics and everything associated with it will become your passion. Candidates need to have this passion. They need to love politics and everything associated with it, such as the handshaking, meetings, speeches, interviews, collaborating with others, and finding consensus on issues. The most successful politicians love politics.

CAMPAIGN STRUCTURE

For most state and federal offices this is the process that is followed for determining who the candidates will be.

The first step is the primary election or caucus. In the **primary election** it is decided who the candidate will be for each party. Each party on the primary election has its own ballot where you choose which candidate in the party that you want to be the one on the ticket in the general election. For example, in the 2012 presidential election before Mitt Romney was determined the Republican Party nominee, Mitt Romney was on a ballot with all the Republican nominees for president such as Herman Cain, Newt Gingrich, Rick Santorum, Rick Perry, and Michelle Bachmann. After primaries or caucuses were held in all states Mitt Romney ended up the winner for the Republican Party and he was the one who ran against the Democratic choice, Barack Obama. A **caucus** differs from a primary in that each party gathers at a different place and, instead of just voting, they spend time in meetings about the election and issues, and then they vote on the candidate for their party after the meeting.

After the primary election has been held, each party decides on a candidate for the **general election**. A general election is where there is a contest between two parties or more on the ballot and the outcome fills a political office. The largest and most popular of all general elections is the presidential election. This happens every four years on the first Tuesday in November. Americans can come and vote for the candidates on the ballot.

Presidential Elections

The presidential elections follow the same process as above, but have one more main focus, the party's convention and platform. After the primary and caucuses are over and the candidate for president has been chosen in each respective party, the national party conventions convene. Delegates from all 50 states meet to ratify the party's nominations for president and vice president and build the party's platform. The platform will outline the issues the party will focus on for the next four years. The candidates for president take this opportunity to build their core support for the upcoming election. After the convention convenes the general election follows in November.

The presidential election also does not end with the general election or the popular vote; as in the other elections, the person with the most votes wins. The presidential election goes one step further after this, and that is the person who wins the election is the person who wins the most votes in the *Electoral College.* The Electoral College was put in place by the framers of the Constitution to ensure that the president was chosen with intelligent input from all the states. It was a direct compromise between those who wanted Congress to choose the president and those who wanted a popular vote to choose the president.

The number of electors that each state has is the number of members they have in the U.S. Congress. For example, in Texas we have thirty-six U.S. Representatives and two U.S. Senators; therefore we have thirty-eight Electoral College votes. California has the most Electoral College votes with fifty-five. Texas is second with thirty-eight, followed by New York with twenty-nine. There are a total of 538 total Electoral College votes; 270 votes wins the presidency. We saw the result of the Electoral College votes in the 2000 election with George Bush and Al Gore. Al Gore won the popular vote by 544,683 votes, but he did not have enough electoral votes to win the office. Florida was the deciding state. Bush was declared the winner in Florida by 537 votes, and he gained the twenty-five Electoral College votes needed to win the Electoral College. Figure 9.1 shows which Electoral College votes went to each candidate. It is not how many popular votes one gets as a presidential candidate, but which states one gets the wins in and how many Electoral College votes they are worth. To win California, Texas, and New York as a candidate you are well on your way, but you need to make sure that you pick up some of the smaller states, too.[4]

The 2012 Presidential election between President Barack Obama, Democrat, and Mitt Romney, Republican, was another close battle. There were a few key battleground states in

Figure 9.1 Electoral College Votes.

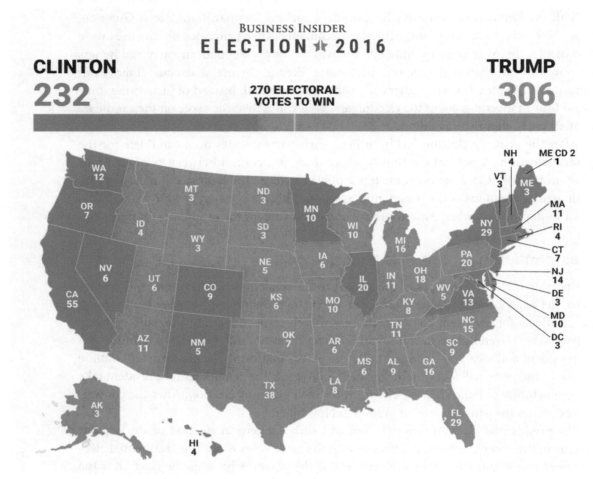

Sources: Associated Press, Fox News, CNN, NBC News, CBS News, ABC News

which the candidates spent much of their time and money campaigning. The battleground states were Pennsylvania, Ohio, Colorado, Florida, Wisconsin, and Virginia. President Obama won the election with 332 electoral votes. He also won the popular vote 51.2 percent to 47.16 percent for Mitt Romney. Figure 9.2 shows the Electoral College votes that went to each candidate.

CAMPAIGN INCUMBENTS

In all elections **incumbents** for the most part win. Incumbents are the people who are holding the office at the present time and running for reelection. The incumbents running for reelection are able to use many resources; these resources are perks that are a part of their current office.[5]

SOURCES OF FUNDING

Money is the name of the game when you are running for office. Candidates need to make sure that they have supporters who will help fund their campaigns. Money can come from a variety of sources, described in the following sections.

Figure 9.2

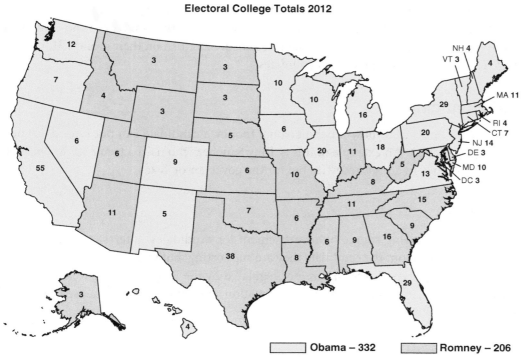

Electoral College Totals 2012

☐ Obama – 332   ▨ Romney – 206

Source: Federal Election Commission and http://corporatejusticeblog.blogspot
.com/2012_11_01_archive.html

Public Money

On your income tax forms you have the option of donating $3 of your tax money to the Presidential Election Campaign Fund. This fund is designed to help parties fund their conventions. The money is split equally between the two parties. In 2000 each party received $13.5 million from this fund.

Small Donations

Small donations are donations that are given directly to the candidate or given to political action committees that distribute money to the candidate by average everyday people. These are called *hard money* donations. They are subject to limits of $1,000 per individual donor.

Large Individual Donations

People who contribute $1,000 or more to the candidates are called large donors. The candidate will most likely know the contributors well and make sure that they are "taken care of."

Soft Money

This money is raised by the party the candidate is affiliated with. As of now there are no limits as to how much soft money can be used in an election.

Political Action Committees

Corporations and unions are not allowed to directly fund elections, but they may form political action committees (**PACs**) to solicit money from the workers in the company. Most PACs give their money to incumbents to ensure a return on their money. This is the most reliable source for money for candidates.

Self-Financing

There are no limits as to how much personal money a candidate can put into his or her campaign war chest. An example of this is Tony Sanchez who used a tremendous amount of his own money in an unsuccessful bid for the governor of Texas.

Issue Ads

Issue ads are a growing source of advertisement for candidates. Interest groups run the ads and do not spell out the candidate they are supporting, but most people can figure out whom the ad supports. These ads are not regulated by the Federal Election Commission and are a way the candidate can get out information about the issues without spending his or her own campaign money.

VOTER DECISIONS

Participation in election is based on many factors. About 40 percent of the adult population votes regularly. However, in the 2000 presidential race, 51.3 percent of the voting-age population voted.[6] Who votes and why do they vote? There are some key characteristics that define the people who vote. They are as follows.

Income

People with higher incomes tend to be highly educated. They vote more often than lower-income Americans who are less likely to believe that their vote will make a difference; they tend to be alienated from politics.

Age

Older Americans tend to vote often. They are most likely to believe that their vote makes a difference and are very familiar with what is going on in politics. The lowest group of voters is the age group from eighteen to twenty-four year olds. Many of these Americans are still trying to find their way in society and do not pay attention to politics.

Gender

Women were the final group to receive the right to vote in 1920 through the Nineteenth Amendment. Women in past elections of 1988, 1992, and 1996 had a greater turnout in voter participation than men.[7] Approximately 52 percent of voters are women. Women in the past also have had a tendency to vote for a Democrat over a Republican. In the 1996 presidential election, 54 percent of women voted for Clinton over 38 percent for Dole. In the 2000 presidential election Gore received 54 percent of the women's vote while Bush received 42. On the other hand Bush had 54 percent of the male vote over 43 percent for Gore. In the 2008 and 2012 election for president, women preferred the Democratic candidate, Barack Obama for president by margins of 10 to 12 percent.[8]

Political Affiliation

Many people vote for the candidate of their party, Democrat or Republican. It is one of the most powerful ways people choose their candidate. Over the past few years with the rebirth of third parties, however, this is not always the case. For example, in Minnesota in 1998 Jesse Ventura was elected to be the governor; he was an Independent.

Race

Race impacts the way in which voters select candidates. In terms of race, in general, African Americans are more likely to vote Democratic. Whites vote more regularly than African Americans. Hispanic Americans tend to vote Democratic, except those of Cuban descent who tend to vote Republican. Asian Americans are much more difficult to state in general terms as their voting record is much more diverse. In the 1996 presidential race, 50.6 percent of African Americans voted; this was down from 54 percent in the presidential election of 1992. The Hispanics' voting record remained the same with a change of 2 percent; in 1996, 26.7 percent of Hispanics voted and 28.9 percent voted in 1992.[9]

In the 2012 election for president, Barack Obama's win was secured in large part by the votes of Hispanics (10 percent of the electorate), Asians (3 percent of the electorate), and African Americans (13 percent of the electorate). However, his appeal among whites (72 percent of the electorate) plummeted. Mitt Romney secured 59 percent of white votes, the most of any presidential candidate; however, he failed to win the election. The overwhelming support of minorities in 2012 election helped Barack Obama win the election.[10]

Voter Turnout

Voter turnout in the United States trails others in the industrialized world. There are a number of causes for this voter apathy. In the 2016 Presidential Election 55.7% of the eligible voters cast their ballot. The reasons for this voter disengagement are as follows:

Voter Registration

Many will argue that voter registration discourages people to vote. In America, unlike in other countries, voters are required to register to vote before they vote. In other countries people are automatically registered to vote when they reach a certain age. In every state except North Dakota, first-time voters are required to fill out a form at least thirty days before the election takes place. This requires that people understand the process and know where they can register to vote. Many people are unaware that they need to register to vote in order to vote in the elections. This makes another responsibility for voters; not only do they need to be there on election day, but they also have to make sure they are registered. People who are not educated in the process would get lost very quickly.

In 1995 a new law went into effect whereby people will be able to register to vote at motor vehicle offices, public assistance agencies, or military recruitment offices. This should help people with the process of registering to vote.

Number of Elections

Americans are bombarded with news of elections. This not only happens in November, it happens year-round as special elections for mayor, city council, school board, and more are held. There are so many elections that Americans get burned out. It is hard to keep track of who is running for what, where you are supposed to vote, and on what day.

Absentee Voting

Absentee voting is used when you will be out of your local area for election day. Forms need to be filled out in order to be able to vote by absentee ballot. These forms need to be filled out in advance. Many states have strange laws about absentee ballots, such as you need to be there in person to fill out the form. Presumably, if you were in the area, you would not need an absentee ballot, so they are unable to retrieve one. U.S. military service people need to vote this way if they are overseas. For many, because of the hoops one needs to jump through in order to receive an absentee ballot, people just forget it and do not vote.

POLITICAL PARTIES

A **political party** is a group with a common vision that comes together to elect officials to public office. The focus of the party is to elect "the right" people to public office. Political parties were introduced back in 1796 at the beginning of our country because people had different views on how the country should be run. Forming a political party was a way to organize a group of people to fight for control of the offices. Today this struggle for power is still happening. In this chapter we will examine the various political parties that have been influential in the building of our nation. We will then examine the current state of our political parties in order for you to choose which party you align with.

As Washington left office he warned against the birth of political parties in his Farewell Address to the Nation. In 1796 the modern party system emerged as the Federalist Party, headed by Alexander Hamilton, and the **Anti-Federalist Party**, headed by Thomas Jefferson. The **Federalists** at this time supported the Constitution all the way through the ratification process and supported John Adams's candidacy for president. The Anti-Federalists, on the other hand, did not want the growth of a strong national government which would happen with the ratification of the Constitution. The candidate they supported in the 1796 election was Thomas Jefferson. In the 1796 election the mood in the country supported the Constitution and John Adams won. This election was the first time that political parties played a role in an election. There were two definitive sides, and people aligned themselves that way when they voted.

Birth of the Democratic Party

After losing the election of 1796, Jefferson began to rally the voters and pass out pamphlets about himself. He renamed the Anti-Federalist party the **Democratic-Republican Party**. This was the first organized get-out-the-vote campaign in history. During this time, though, remember that only white males could vote.

In the election of 1800, Thomas Jefferson won. The Electoral College in this instance voted a tie for Jefferson, presidential candidate and his running mate, Aaron Burr. The Electoral College voters were loyal to the party, but they each had to cast two votes and they did, one for president and one for vice president. The election was then put to the House of

Representatives to decide between Jefferson and Burr. The House **majority**, over 50 percent, voted for Jefferson. After this election the Twelfth Amendment was revised to state that the Electoral College members would vote separate ballots for president and vice president. Therefore it ended in a tie. This election was the first peaceful transfer of power exercised around the world; before this there would need to be a revolution or death of the current leader in order to transfer power. In this case, the loser, John Adams, left the post peacefully.

After this election the Democratic-Republican Party of Jefferson was so strong that the Federalist Party dissolved and the country was left with a one-party system for a period of years. This era in politics was a time where there were no divisive issues, and it lasted until 1824 with President James Monroe.

Birth of the Jacksonian Democrats

The election of 1824 marked the first time that the popular vote was to be counted. The candidate also needed to win a majority in the Electoral College to keep the House of Representatives out of the election. Andrew Jackson won more votes in the Electoral College than John Quincy Adams; however, Jackson did not win a majority of the Electoral College votes. The election then was brought to the House of Representatives where members were to make the decision. Jackson was popular with the American public, but not with the members of the House of Representatives where he was viewed as a political outsider. The House of Representatives voted for John Quincy Adams, and he became the tenth president of the United States in 1824.

As a result of the election of 1824, Jackson's followers organized to win the next election. Jackson brought back to life the Democratic-Republican Party, which was now called **Jacksonian-Democrats**. This party's support came from westerners, urban workers, and non-slaveholding southerners. The Jacksonian-Democrats won the election of 1828 and would remain in power for two terms.

The base of parties broadened with the electoral process. Congressional party leaders had previously nominated candidates, but after much debate the process was seen as elitist and undemocratic. This system gave way to at-large nomination conventions. The Democratic Party held the country's first major national presidential convention in 1832.[11]

During his terms in office Jackson wanted to abolish the national bank. As a result, business owners and slaveholders in the South formed the **Whig Party**, fashioned after the Hamilton Federalists. The Whigs wanted an active federal government. The two parties opposing one another during the period from 1830s–1850s were the Jeffersonian Democrats and the Whigs. Both parties campaigned fiercely, and they brought the United States the first nationally supported two-party system in the Western world. The Whigs managed to elect two presidents during this time period, Harrison in 1840 and Taylor in 1848. The advent of the Civil War and talk of the abolition of slavery led to the disintegration of the Whig Party.

Birth of the Republican Party

In the election of 1860 the Republicans emerged. This party represented the northern industrial base. The party was able to elect as their president Abraham Lincoln. The Democratic Party of this time represented the southern agricultural base. From 1860–1884 Republicans held the White House. They dominated national politics. In 1884 and 1892 Grover Cleveland, a Democrat, won the presidency. The Republicans gained back control in 1896 and held it until 1932, except for when Woodrow Wilson, a Democrat, was president (1913–1921 (see Table 9.1)

Table 9.1   Presidential Order.

Year	Presidential Nominees (Republican et al.)	Presidential Nominees (Democrat et al.)	Third Party
1789	Washington (appointed)		
1792	Washington		
1796	Adams (Federalist)	Jefferson (Anti-Federalist)	
1800	Pinckney (Federalist)	Jefferson (Democratic-Republican)	
1804	Pinckney (Federalist)	Jefferson (Democratic-Republican)	
1808	Pinckney (Federalist)	Madison (Democratic-Republican)	
1812	Clinton(Federalist)	Madison (Democratic-Republican)	
1816	King(Federalist)	Monroe (Democratic-Republican)	
1820	Adams (National Republican)	Monroe (Democratic-Republican)	
1824	Adams (National Republican)	Jackson (Democratic-Republican)	
1828	Adams (National Republican)	Jackson (Jacksonian Democrat)	
1832	Clay (National Republican)	Jackson (Jacksonian Democrat)	
1836	Harrison (National Republican)	**Van Buren** (Democrat)	
1840	**Harrison** (Whig)	Van Buren (Democrat)	
1844	Clay (Whig)	**Polk** (Democrat)	
1848	**Taylor** (Whig)	Cass (Democrat)	
1852	Scott (Whig)	**Pierce** (Democrat)	
1856	Fremont (Whig)	**Buchanan** (Democrat)	
1860	**Lincoln** (Republican)	Douglas (Democrat)	Breckenridge (Southern Democrat) Bell (Constitutional Unionist)
1864	**Lincoln** (Republican)	McClellan (Democrat)	
1868	**Grant**	Seymour	
1872	**Grant**	Greeley	

Year	Presidential Nominees (Republican et al.)	Presidential Nominees (Democrat et al.)	Third Party
1876	**Hayes**	Tilden	
1880	**Garfield**	Hancock	
1884	Blaine	**Cleveland**	
1888	**Harrison**	Cleveland	
1892	Harrison	Cleveland	
1896	**McKinley**	Bryan	
1900	**McKinley**	Bryan	
1904	T. R. Roosevelt	Parker	
1908	Taft	Bryan	
1912	Taft	**Wilson**	T.R. Roosevelt (Bull Moose Progressives)
1916	Hughes	Wilson	
1920	Harding	Cox	
1924	Coolidge	Davis	
1928	Hoover	Smith	
1932	Hoover	**F. D. Roosevelt**	
1936	Landon	**F. D. Roosevelt**	
1940	Willkie	**F. D. Roosevelt**	
1944	Dewey	**F. D. Roosevelt**	
1948	Dewey	**Truman**	Strom Thurmond (States Rights Democrat)
1952	**Eisenhower**	Stevenson	
1956	**Eisenhower**	Stevenson	
1960	Nixon	**Kennedy**	
1964	Goldwater	**Johnson**	
1968	**Nixon**	Humphrey	
1972	**Nixon**	McGovern	
1976	Ford	**Carter**	
1980	**Reagan**	Carter	Anderson (Independent)
1984	**Reagan**	Mondale	

Continued

Year	Presidential Nominees (Republican et al.)	Presidential Nominees (Democrat et al.)	Third Party
1988	**G. H. W. Bush**	Dukakis	
1992	G. H. W. Bush	**Clinton**	Perot (Reform Party)
1996	Dole	**Clinton**	Perot (Reform Party)
2000	**G. W. Bush**	Gore	Nader (Green Party)
2004	**G. W. Bush**	Kerry	
2008	McCain	**Obama**	
2012	Romney	**Obama**	
2016	Trump	Hillary Clinton	Johnson (Libertarian Party)

Source: *Information gathered from the Internet public library site: http://ipl.si.umich .edu/div/potus/*

The Pendulum Swings

In 1929 the Great Depression hit and the era of Republican domination in the presidency ended. Millions of people were out of work and had no source of money. The president during this time was Herbert Hoover, a Republican, and he was not going to give out anything to the American people. Then along came New York governor Franklin Delano Roosevelt, a Democrat, calling for "a New Deal" for the people of America.

In order to win the election Roosevelt knew that he needed to have a wide variety of voters on his side. He pulled together the urban working class, Catholics, Jews, the poor, southerners, and liberal intellectuals. This coalition was called the **New Deal Coalition**. With this broad base of support, Roosevelt won the election of 1932, carrying forty-two of forty-eight states. The Democrats held onto the White House between 1932 and 1968, losing to only one Republican during this period, Dwight Eisenhower in 1952 (see Table 9.1). The New Deal Coalition helped Democrats win elections until 1968, when the Democrats created many economic assistance programs under the leadership of Lyndon Johnson. During this time Johnson created programs that are still in place today, such as Medicare, Medicaid, and Head Start. Even though there would be a shift in control after Johnson's presidency, the Democratic programs are still in place today.

The Pendulum Swings Again

Since 1968 the Democrats have lost five of the last eight presidential elections (see Table 9.1). This change in partisan control has been gradual with Republicans slowly gaining more control in the U.S. House and the Senate until 2002, when the Republicans gained control in the U.S. House, Senate, and the presidency. There has been a conservative shift in America in the voting public, especially among the young voters. There has also been a growth in the number of independent voters in the public. However, the pendulum swings again with the demographic shift in the nation. After two terms with President George W. Bush, the public became distrustful of the Republicans. President Barack Obama was elected in 2008 and again in 2012. In Obama's first term (2008), the Senate and the House were both controlled by Democrats. In 2012 the Republicans pushed back again and won many seats in the House to regain back control in one of the three areas. As of 2013 the Democrats still control the Senate and the presidency.

POLITICAL PARTY STRUCTURE

National Committees

Both the Democrats and Republicans have large national parties that run the policy machines for their party. They are called, respectively, the **Democratic National Committee** (DNC) and the **Republican National Committee** (RNC). National chairs are selected for each party by the president for the party in power. The chair is an important spokesperson for party interests. Each party holds national conventions every four years where a party agenda is established and a presidential candidate is selected. Committees for support are also established for congressional races. These committees are formed by election from the Senate or the House. The congressional committees have been powerful influences over recruitment and training of candidates, and providing them with money for their campaigns.[12]

State and Local Parties

Much of the work of the political parties is conducted at the local level. Political science research has shown that state and local parties have become significantly stronger over the past three decades by comparing parties in 1964 and 1980; political science research found tremendous increases in several important campaign activities: campaign events, fundraising, publicity of party and candidate activity, registration drives, and the distribution of campaign literature.[13] Many informal groups have been established to help support the parties, such as the National Federation of Democratic Women and the Young Republicans.

ROLE OF POLITICAL PARTIES

Political parties today are not as popular as they were at other times in history; however, they play an important role as a way to resolve political differences and are a vital agent to promote change. Political parties assist in paring down the amount of information and ideas. We will examine the specific roles that parties play in the election process.

Gather Power

The way an elected official gains power is to have more of the other elected officials of his or her party in the same organization. If a person is elected from a certain party, that party will most likely support the elected official. The number of supporters one has is typically determined by the number of officials of the same party who are in office.

Stability

Political parties are a way to promote stability in the electorate. They help to drive the election toward their candidate in order to win the election.

Services

Political parties organize elections. They provide resources to candidates during elections, such as money, staff, and other services.

Policy Formulation

Every four years the political parties write a document that explains their stances on issues. They create a **National Party Platform**.

POLITICAL PARTIES AFTER THE ELECTION

Parties are important in the election process, but even more important after the election when the real work begins. They are a central part in the operation of the federal government. We will examine the roles political parties play in each of the three branches of government.

Legislative Branch

The legislative branch is called Congress, of which there are two houses: the U.S. House and the U.S. Senate. In each congressional body each political party elects a leader, the majority leader, for the party that has the most representation, and the minority leader, for the party with the least representation in the body. The majority leader is the leader of the party that is in control of the U.S. Senate. The majority party in the U.S. House and U.S. Senate chairs all the committees.

Party leaders in the U.S. House and U.S. Senate choose leaders of committees and select office locations for members. These are some of the ways that leaders keep the party under check.

Parties are more the same in ideology than they used to be. The backing of a party is important during the election process and while working in Congress. The coalition building can assist in all steps of the political process, whether you want a bill introduced or need help campaigning on the road. The coalitions that are built can help a person running for office or as you try to get things done on Capitol Hill.

Executive Branch

The president is a powerful party leader. The president can assist in raising money for the party and by campaigning for members of the party. Previous presidents Bill Clinton, George W. Bush, and Barack Obama have been very involved raising money and building party coalitions. The failures and successes reflect dramatically on the party. Another important part of the president's position is making appointments in the bureaucracy in Washington. The party in control of the White House has more than 4,000 positions to fill, such as cabinet positions and ambassadors to foreign countries.[14] In order to be appointed to one of these many jobs, one's party alignment needs to be firmly in line with the president.

Judicial Branch

Judicial positions are supposed to be nonpartisan; however, many of them are elected positions and the party affiliation of the candidate is well known. Judges at the federal level are appointed by the president and confirmed by the U.S. Senate. The judges who are appointed to these positions often have the same views and same political party as the president. Judges in the highest court in the land, the U.S. Supreme Court, remain nonpartisan in public arenas. For example, when in January of each year the president makes a State of the Union address, all of the members of the Supreme Court are present. However, when listeners stand and clap for programs and comments they favor, the Supreme Court justices remain seated, showing nonpartisanship.

THIRD-PARTY ROLE

Third parties help major parties change. When voters are not happy with the views of the two major parties they can join one of the third-party groups. Over time these groups have not affected the outcome of many elections. As you can see in Table 9.1, no third-party group has won a presidential election. However, third parties have been able to create change among the major parties. The issues that are brought up by the third parties many times are blended into one party to create a wider voter perspective, such as the ideas of Ross Perot, a presidential candidate of the **Reform Party** in 1992 and 1996, of reducing the debt of the country. In 2000 Ralph Nader was a presidential candidate for the **Green Party;** he did not win any electoral votes; however, he was able to bring up issues that the major parties were not speaking about. The Green Party's focus is on environmental issues. In the 2016 election the Libertarian Party, with candidate Gary Johnson as the presidential nominee, was on the ballot in all 50 states. Dr. Jill Stein the Green Party candidate was on the ballot in 40 states. The impact on the election was minimal.

Online Connections

To find more information on presidents, presidential elections, and political parties, check out these websites.

Campaign Line. *http://www.campaignline.com*

Website promoting better campaigning. *http://www.bettercampaigns.org*

PBS Democracy Project. *http://www.pbs.org/democracy*

Rock the Vote. *http://www.rockthevote.org/index2.html*

Presidents and presidential elections. *http://ipl.si .umich.edu/div/potus/*

Republican National Committee. *http://www.rnc.org*

Democratic National Committee. *http://www.democrats.org*

Links to Third Party sites. *http://www.3pc.net*

Key Terms

Primary election 102	Democratic-Republican Party 108
Caucus 103	Majority 109
General election 103	Jacksonian Democrats 109
Electoral College 103	Whig Party 109
Incumbents 104	New Deal Coalition 112
PACs 106	Democratic National Committee 112
Absentee voting 108	Republican National Committee 113
Political party 108	National Party Platform 114
Anti-Federalist Party 108	Reform Party 115
Federalists 108	Green Party 115

Selected Readings

Larry Bartels, *Presidential Primaries and the Dynamics of Public Choice* (Princeton, NJ: Princeton University Press, 1988).

Walter Burnham, *Critical Elections and the Mainsprings of American Politics* (New York: Norton, 1970).

Morris P. Fiorina, *Divided Government* (Boston: Allyn and Bacon, 1996).

Gary C. Jacobson, *The Politics of Congressional Elections*, 4th ed. (New York: Longman, 1997).

David B Magleby and Candice J. Nelson, *The Money Chase: Congressional Campaign Finance Reform* (Washington, DC: Brookings Institution, 1990).

David R. Mayhew, *Placing Parties in American Politics* (Princeton, NJ : Princeton University Press, 1986).

David E. Price, *Bringing Back the Parties* (Washington, DC: CQ Press, 1984).

Stephen J. Wayne, *The Road to the White House, 1996: The Politics of Presidential Elections* (New York: St. Martin's Press, 1996).

Notes

[1] U.S. Constitution, article II, section 1.

[2] U.S. Constitution, article I, section 2.

[3] U.S. Constitution, article I, section 3.

[4] *www.fec.gov/pubrec/fe2000*

[5] Thomas R. Dye, Tucker Gibson, and Clay Robison, *Politics in America*, 4th ed. (Upper Saddle River, NJ: Prentice Hall, 2001), p. 234.

[6] *www.fec.gov/pages/2000turnout/reg3to00.htp*

[7] *www.fec.gov/pages/genderto.htm*

[8] Ibid.

[9] www.fec.gov

[10] Lydia Warren, "Record Number of Hispanic and Asian Voters Head to the Poll to Help Obama Secure a Second Term—as his Support Among Whites Plummets," November 7, 2012, Daily Mailonline.

[11] The National Republican (one forerunner of the Whig Party) and the Anti-Masonic parties each had held more limited conventions in 1831.

[12] Thomas B. Edsall, *The New Politics of Inequality* (New York: Norton, 1984).

[13] Cornelius P. Cotter, James L. Gibson, John F. Bibby, and Robert J. Huckshorn, *Party Organizations in American Politics* (Pittsburgh: University of Pittsburgh Press, 1989).

[14] Bob Nash, director, White House Office of Personnel, interview with David Magleby, October 1998.

1. List the advantages of incumbency.

_____

_____

_____

_____

2. Describe the process by which a candidate runs for president.

_____

_____

_____

_____

3. Explain how the modern party system emerged in 1796.

_____

_____

_____

_____

4. Describe the role of the political parties in each of the three branches of government.

_____

_____

_____

_____

Evaluation

Directions: Write the word or phrase that completes the statement.

1. An election held to determine who the candidate will be for each party is called _____.

2. A _____ is where issues are discussed and the candi-dates are voted on.

3. A _____ is where there are two parties on a ballot and the winner of the election will take the office.

Directions: Circle the correct answer to each of the following questions.

4. Elections allow _____.
    a. people to decide if they like the direction the country is taking
    b. people to create change
    c. people to weigh in on the economy
    d. all of the above

5. One of the major problems with elections today is _____.
    a. not enough people know the campaign process
    b. finding a place to vote
    c. not seeing political advertisements
    d. none of the above

6. In order to run for the presidency you need to _____.
    a. be a resident of the United States for ten years
    b. be born in the United States
    c. be at least thirty-two years of age
    d. all of the above

7. The number of U.S. Representatives is _____.
    a. a fixed number of two for each state
    b. based on the population of the state
    c. one member per state
    d. changing every year

8. In order to run for office as a U.S. Senator you would need to _____.
    a. be a resident of the state from which you are elected
    b. be a U.S. citizen for nine years
    c. be at least thirty years of age
    d. all of the above

Sample Test Questions

CHAPTER 10

The News Media

One of the key elements in a democracy is the **freedom of the press**, the freedom of the media to criticize the actions or inaction of the government without being closed down or placed in jail. The news media, in a democracy, needs to provide objective information on the actions of the government so the citizenry is able to make decisions based on the reporting. The political news is simplified greatly. The news media provides small pieces of information to the public about events in order not to overwhelm the public with too many details. In order for our democracy to work effectively the people need to be informed of political actions to become involved in the political process. In a democratic society we as Americans have a duty to listen to what the media tells us and think critically about the message.

In this chapter we will examine the forms of news media and how these forms have affected the politics of American society.

FORMS OF NEWS MEDIA

There are several forms of news media or **mass media**. Mass media is the way in which the information is distributed to the public, such as through the newspapers, magazines, radio, television, the internet, or social networking. The two major areas in which politics has transferred information to the public are through the newspapers and the television. American society has evolved in its use of the mass media to gain information. The media has biases and as consumers we need to be aware and be ready to compare versions of the same story from different sources. We now will look at each form of mass media and the role that it played in the American political scene.

Newspapers

Newspapers have been important to American history back to the Revolutionary War period. The first newspapers were printed in the 1690s. They were a means of informing and mobilizing the public to take action. In the early years, newspapers were used as a way to educate the public on the new form of government in the United States. Today's newspapers, however, are filled with advertisements and personal interest stories rather than political information. In the 1960s most Americans received their news from newspapers, but by the 1980s people were choosing television as their way to get news by a two to one margin over newspapers.[1]

Newspapers influenced the news-making business and determined what constituted news. In the nineteenth century, the style of journalism changed. Bribery was not an uncommon happening. Investigators for newspapers were paid off to stop investigating; editors were paid to make sure certain stories did not get into the paper. Included in the paper at these times were sensational stories that focused on local news. The news of the time brought about two types of journalistic styles, called yellow journalism and muckraking.

Yellow journalism is the focus on sensationalized stories not based on fact, but based on reaction. The stories were coupled with colorful, detailed illustrations with an emphasis on violence and sex. This tactic was used in many big-city newspapers of Joseph Pulitzer and Randolph Hearst. In today's papers these tactics have usually been reserved for the tabloids, but this trend is changing. More and more newspapers today are turning to yellow journalism to sell papers.

A second journalistic style is **muckraking**. Muckraking is investigative reporting to bring out injustices done to people. This kind of reporting began in the nineteenth century and still is evident today. Newspapers today are going through a period of transition to keep pace with the digital internet explosion. Newspapers are using digital subscriptions to reach readers rather than printed copies delivered to doorsteps.

Magazines

Magazines are another form of mass media. Magazines offer the widest variety of subjects and can vary the article to the purpose of the reader. The people who buy magazines are often people of particular groups and the editors know their target audience. Magazines offer their readership very specific information on all topic areas.

A most highly read magazine is *Time*. It has been one of the most influential and important political forces in the magazine industry. A journalist stated that *Time magazine* "spoke to the whole nation on national issues speaking with one voice, and reaching an entire country."[2]

Radio

Radio became widely used in the 1920s. From the 1930s until after World War II radio was the most widely used medium for political information in America. ABC, NBC, and CBS all got their start in the radio business. Radio broadcasts could be broadcast in real time, which created some very exciting moments in history.

President Franklin Roosevelt was the most successful user of the radio in politics. His programs were called "fireside chats." He used his broadcasts to improve the American confidence for the reforms that he was making. Roosevelt's popularity increased as a result of the broadcasts.

With the invention of the television in the 1940s, radio's popularity began to decrease dramatically. Today, radio is still host to many political talk shows that have a national audience, such as Rush Limbaugh, who has become an important player in American politics.

Television

Television was introduced in the late 1940s. The major networks are CBS, NBC, ABC, and FOX. Americans see television as a cheap leisure activity; however, it is the most influential form of mass media for disseminating political information. The ability of the television to bring to viewers instant news from around the nation and around the world helps it to be such a powerful tool. Cable news has also been a powerful outlet for political news with channels such as CNN, CNBC, and FOX viewers can keep connected to political news around the clock. Television has been designed as a tool to entertain people rather than just to inform people.

Internet

The advent of the portable media devices such as the iPad, iPhone, Android, and others have created a new means to access mass media instantly. These devices all enable constant connection with information. Push technologies keep people informed by sending texts or alerts to digital devices wherever you are in the world.

Social Networking

Social networking is individuals coming together with common goals. Social networking sites such as Twitter, Facebook, and Instagram are mediums for political conversations between people. These mediums have been ways for people to share their views, read about others' views, and find out information that they did not know. One of the drawbacks to using social media is the lack of fact checking. Other media sources have professional standards that they need to follow before they write anything. When using social network sites and posting information, there is not a standard that needs to be followed. People using social networking sites as their only medium for political information need to be wary and use the information they read with caution.

Social network users also tend to share and read information that is posted by people only with likeminded views. The following characterizes social network users:

- Seventy-four percent are liberal, a higher percentage than the overall liberal population at 60 percent.
- Seventy percent are moderate, as compared with the moderate population overall at 61 percent.
- Sixty percent of social network users are conservative as compared with 49 percent of the conservative population overall.[3]

As this medium evolves it could create greater factions within the democracy because social network users become stronger in their convictions as they continue to have conversations and realize that they are not alone in their beliefs. It could create a strong political base for many.

THE NEWS MEDIA'S SOURCES OF POWER

The media can influence any aspect of American life. We will focus on four sources of the media's power in society. They are agenda setting, interpreting, persuading, and socialization.

The media plays a role in **agenda setting**, which is the power to create the national focus for the country. The news media plays an important role here because it has the power to say what is important and what is not. Have you heard the phrase "out of sight out of mind"? Well this can refer to political news. If we do not see it we will forget about it. The media has the power to decide what should be reported and how long the segment should be about the topic. People that do not have opinions about certain topics can be easily swayed to the opinion viewed from the media. Also when news media reports about topics that do not relate to our everyday life, it is easier for the media to control and change thinking.

A second source of power for the news media is *interpreting* the news. The news media can take a story and provide the viewer with only sections of the story. They interpret the important parts of the story, providing views with certain sound bites that are controlled by another. The viewer may not receive the whole story.

The news media is also out to change our frame of mind, to *persuade* us to think a certain way; this is the third source of media power. Paid advertisements, through all forms of news media, are used by companies to entice our spending and make us feel like we cannot live without the product or the service. Politicians, to change our viewpoint on political issues, use the Sunday morning talk show circuit. Presidents use the media through weekly radio addresses and television sound bites to influence public opinion about their job performance and the direction the country is headed. Presidents have open access to the television and other media outlets so that they can communicate directly with the American people at a moment's notice.

The fourth source of the media's power is socialization. **Socialization** is the learning of culture and values. Through television programs and articles, our values and opinions about politics and elections are shaped. Early in childhood the socialization process begins and continues throughout adult life. Advertisements shape the opinions and values we place on products also.

MEDIA AND ELECTIONS

Politicians can use media to their advantage in elections. Media is the main link between the candidates and the voters. The politicians can gain media coverage by attending certain events. Candidates need to be able to communicate with their audience and put people at ease. The advent of speechwriters and growth in the political consultant role in politics has been the result of this new look. In presidential races candidates spend over 50 percent of their money on television advertising.

Media is the place where voters get their information on candidates. If the media does not cover the person then the public is likely not to know about the candidate. The media focuses more on image making than it does on the issues. It focuses more on the race and the polling of voters than on the issues that surround the candidates. Negative campaigning has worked in elections. One candidate places a negative ad and the other needs to reply in some sort of way. Voters say that they do not like this tactic and it may have contributed to the decline in voter turnout.

GOVERNMENT REGULATION

The newspapers and magazines are not governmentally regulated. The Federal Communication Commission (FCC), however, oversees the electronic media market of radio and television. They must reapply for their broadcast licenses every six years. Airwaves are governmental property and leased to the radio and television stations. The regulation helps to ensure that the channels do not overlap and jam each other.

The first regulation in place by the federal government was the **fairness doctrine**. This doctrine required different viewpoints to be presented on a radio program, including controversial issues or people. This doctrine was repealed in 1987 by the Reagan administration.

A second regulation is the requirement to have equal time allotted for each political party during an election. This is called the **equal-time rule**, where television and radio stations must provide equal-time to the opposing candidate for the same price. The television and radio stations must give political candidates the same amount of time for the same price. The equal-time rule does not apply to newscasts or to talk shows. When the president gives a national address and the networks provide the opposing party with a response, they are doing this because they do not want to seem biased, not because they are required to do so by law. If a candidate buys time on the radio or television, the network must offer the opposing party candidate the same time for the same price.

A third government regulation is the **right of rebuttal**. If a person is attacked on television or radio that person needs to get equal time on the television or radio to respond.

The government cannot censor stories that get to the media before they are published or broadcast. The government cannot place **prior restraint** on publications or broadcasts before they are published. The U.S. Supreme Court has decided that the First Amendment's guarantee of freedom of speech should be interpreted this way. The Supreme Court's stance is, if the government does not want information out in the public, then it needs to make sure the information does not get into the wrong hands.

LIBEL AND SLANDER

The media does not have the right to tell untruths about individuals to damage their credibility or livelihood. If a person is able to prove in court that the speech caused damage, the First Amendment does not protect this type of speech. If a person has been written about falsely, and malicious words have been written about them that damages them, this is called **libel**. When a person has been spoken about falsely and malicious words have been said about the person that damages her or him, this is called **slander**.

As for public officials and libel and slander, the law goes one step further. In the court case *New York Times v. Sullivan* (1964) the U.S. Supreme Court found that the media couldn't have known that the libel was real. If the media places a falsehood about the public official in print or on television the only way that the public official has to collect damages is to prove that the media published or broadcast the piece knowing that the statements were incorrect. They had "malicious intent" when they broadcast the piece. This gives greater control to the media as to what they publish about public officials.[4]

The media plays an important role in the everyday lives of people. It helps to form our ideas about politics from an early age. In elections the media plays an important role by introducing the candidates to us and bringing them into our homes. Americans then can make more informed choices from the information received. Because the First Amendment gives us freedom of speech, the government does not have much control over what goes over our airwaves, except when that information is false and damages a person.

THE BLACK PRESS

The *Freedom's Journal* printed its first newspaper in 1827 and published through 1829. Both John Russwurm and Samuel Cornish were the paper's editors and believed their paper needed to challenge the racist views of the mainstream white press. There was also an international and national audience. This was a weekly paper that circulated in New York City and in eleven other states including the District of Columbia, Haiti, Europe, and Canada. The paper covered current events revealing the poor conditions of African American including slavery, lynching, and other injustices. A second purpose of the *Freedom's Journal* was to write biographies of well-established African Americans and to publish births, marriages, and deaths of African Americans.[5]

Freedom's Journal stopped its circulation in 1830 because of limited readership. Frederick Douglass founded the *North Star,* which was another antislavery newspaper that suffered the same problem as the *Freedom's Journal*—limited readership.[6]

Online Connections

Check out these websites to learn more about the news media.

The News Media & The Law is a quarterly magazine on all aspects of media law, covering cases, laws, and other events that may affect how journalists can cover the news. *http://www.rcfp.org/news/mag*

Up-to-date information from around the world. *http://www.reuters.com*

Washington Post—a top newspaper. *http://www.washingtonpost.com*

Key Terms

Freedom of the press 121	Fairness doctrine 125
Mass media 121	Equal-time rule 125
Yellow journalism 122	Right of rebuttal 125
Muckraking 122	Prior restraint 125
Agenda setting 124	Libel 125
Socialization 124	Slander 125

Selected Readings

Stephen Bates, *If No News, Send Rumors* (New York: St. Martin's Press, 1989).

Doris A. Graber, *Mass Media and American Politics,* 5th ed (Washington DC: CQ Press, 1996).

Richard Rubin, *Press, Party, and Presidency* (New York: Norton, 1981).

Mitchell Stephens, *A History of News: From the Drum to the Satellite* (New York: Viking Publisher, 1989).

Notes

[1]Harold W. Stanley and Richard G. Niemi, *Vital Statistics on American Politics* (Washington DC: CQ Press, 1988), p. 58.

[2]David Halberstam, The Powers That Be (New York: Dell, 1979), p. 72.

[3]Lee Rainie & Aaron Smith, "Social Networking Sites and Politics," March 12, 2012, www.pewinternet.org.

[4]*New York Times v. Sullivan*, 376 U.S. 254 (1964).

[5]*http://www.wisconsinhistory.org/libraryarchives/aanp/freedom/*

[6]*http://www2.vcdh.virginia.edu/afam/reflector/newspaper.html*

Evaluation

1. Name and explain the various forms of news media.

_____

_____

_____

_____

_____

2. Discuss the media role in the election process.

_____

_____

_____

_____

_____

3. List and explain how radio and television are regulated by government.

_____

_____

_____

_____

_____

4. Describe the four sources of media power.

_____

_____

_____

_____

_____

Directions: Write the word or phrase that completes the statement.

1. The news media contains the power to shape our values and beliefs on many subjects. This power is called _____.

2. A regulation that was brought about to require different viewpoints in programs was _____. It was repealed in 1987.

3. The media has the power to determine the national focus for the country. This is called _____.

Directions: Circle the correct answer to each of the following questions.

4. The most read magazine in the country is _____.
   a. *Newsweek*
   b. *People*
   c. *Good Housekeeping*
   d. *Time*

5. Television was introduced in the _____.
   a. 1940s
   b. 1930s
   c. 1950s
   d. 1920s

6. Which president successfully used the radio in politics, in his famous "fireside chats"?
   a. Woodrow Wilson
   b. John F. Kennedy
   c. Herbert Hoover
   d. Franklin Roosevelt

7. When the news media uses advertisements to encourage us to spend in a certain way they are using _____.
   a. interpretation
   b. agenda setting
   c. persuasion
   d. socialization

8. The Supreme Court ruled that the media could not have known the libel was real in the case of _____.
   a. *Wright v. United States*
   b. *New York Times v. United States*
   c. *Washington Post v. Mitchell*
   d. *New York Times v. Sullivan*

Sample Test Questions

CHAPTER 11
Civil Liberties and Civil Rights

IN THIS TEMPLE
AS IN THE HEARTS OF THE PEOPLE
FOR WHOM HE SAVED THE UNION
THE MEMORY OF ABRAHAM LINCOLN
IS ENSHRINED FOREVER

CIVIL LIBERTIES

Civil liberties are the individual rights and freedoms that are guaranteed by the federal government. The Bill of Rights specifically delineates the civil liberties that are to be protected. These rights cannot be violated in any way. Civil liberties give people freedom from the government, individuals, or groups dictating how you should act. Civil liberties violations are in most cases handled in court, where judges determine the outcome.

THE BILL OF RIGHTS

Civil liberties are guaranteed in the **Bill of Rights**, the first ten amendments to the U.S. Constitution. The Bill of Rights was passed by Congress and approved by the states in 1791. The Bill of Rights was added to the Constitution because people were afraid that the national government might interfere with the rights of people. Each state still had its own constitution that limited the involvement of the state government in individual liberties. In the early years of the Bill of Rights, it did not provide much protection against violations of personal liberties. It was not until the Supreme Court started to rule on cases that the states began to apply the Bill of Rights to protect individual freedoms.

In the case of *Barron v. Baltimore* (1833) John Barron wanted the state of Maryland to pay for monetary damages due to the loss of the use of a wharf he owned. He stated that under the Fifth Amendment that guarantees the seizing of private property for public use results in compensation from the state. The Supreme Court in this case refused to grant the Bill of Rights extensions to the states and denied Barron his monetary damages. It was not until the 1960s that the entire Bill of Rights would be applied equally to the states.[1]

Figure 11.1   Summary of Bill of Rights.

Amendment	Protection
First	Freedom of religion, speech, press, assembly, petition
Second	Right of people to bear arms
Third	Soldiers shall not be quartered in private homes
Fourth	Right to be secure in their persons, houses, papers, etc., and against unreasonable searches
Fifth	Right to notice of charges, protection from double jeopardy, testifying against oneself, and punishment without due process of the law
Sixth	Right to speedy trial by jury, to confront witnesses, to counsel
Seventh	Right to trial by jury
Eighth	Protection against excessive bail, and cruel and unusual punishment
Ninth	These stated tights do not mean that people could not have other rights as well
Tenth	Powers not given to the United States in the Constitutions are reserved for the States

Incorporation Doctrine

The wording in the Bill of Rights states that "Congress shall make no law . . .", was intended to limit the powers of the federal government. After the Civil War, and the addition of the Fourteenth Amendment to the Constitution the outlook of the Bill of Rights changed. The Fourteenth Amendment states, "No State shall make or enforce any law . . ." and with this statement people thought that the Barron (1833) rule would be overturned and the Bill of Rights limitations would apply to the states, but this was not immediately true. The Fourteenth Amendment was designed to give equality for newly freed slaves, but it also contained provisions that no one could be denied "due process" or "equal protection of the law." By 1920 the Supreme Court ruled on many cases that gradually brought **incorporation** of almost all the protection of the Bill of Rights to the states.[2]

THE FIRST AMENDMENT

Freedom of Speech and Press

American democracy has been built on the premise that all people are entitled to their own opinion and entitled to speak their mind. The First Amendment states "Congress shall make no law . . . abridging the freedom of speech, or of the press." The government has some regulation over this aspect; it is not a carte blanche, where you can say or do anything. The Supreme Court has ruled on several cases and as a rule the government cannot regulate what you think, what you say can be somewhat regulated, and what you do can be regulated. We will discuss several cases in which the government has attempted to limit the exercise of free speech and the outcome of each.

Alien and Sedition Acts   In 1798 Congress enacted the Alien and Sedition Acts. The acts made the publication of any antigovernment writing a criminal offense. These acts were in response to the criticism of the government by the Democratic-Republicans. At least ten Democratic-Republicans were fined and some even were given jail terms. In the presidential campaign of 1800 the acts became a critical issue as Jefferson was elected. Congress allowed the acts to expire before the Supreme Court heard the case.

Anti-Government Speech   In the early 1900s, with the advent of World War I, the government was looking for ways to control the antiwartime sentiment. In 1919 the Supreme Court heard the case of *Schenck v. United States*. Schenck was convicted of handing out pamphlets against the draft. The Supreme Court found that Schenck was guilty because the state could restrict speech "when the words used are in such a nature as to create a clear and present danger that they will bring out the substantive evils that Congress has a right to prevent."[3] The antiwar pamphlets were too much of a danger for wartime. The *clear and present danger test* was born from this case. Speech can be banned if it causes a clear and present danger to society.

In 1969 the Supreme Court developed a new test to determine whether the government could regulate certain kinds of speech. The new test makes it more difficult for the government to prove whether or not the speech is protected. The test was called the *direct incitement test*. This test states that the government can only punish the acts that produce "imminent lawless action."

Obscenity and Pornography   The challenge with obscenity and pornography is that the courts needed to define what these terms meant. The First Amendment did not protect obscenity, but there was not a clear definition of what it was. Many landmark court decisions led up to the current view of obscenity.[4]

The first landmark case was *Chaplinsky v. New Hampshire* (1942). The Supreme Court determined a standard by which they would determine protected speech and unprotected speech. The court ruled that obscenity, lewdness, libel, and fighting words are not protected by the First Amendment because "such expressions are not an essential part of any exposition of ideas, and are of such slight social value as a step to truth that any benefit that may be derived from them is clearly outweighed by the social interest in order and mortality."[5]

The second landmark case was *Roth v. United States* (1957). In this case the Court developed the *Roth test* to define what is obscene material. The question to ask was is the material "utterly without redeeming social importance?" Does the material "as a whole appeal to prurient interests?"[6] This definition over time became hard to define and the test hard to apply. What are "prurient interests?" It became difficult to determine whether a book or movie was "utterly without redeeming social importance." The Roth test was determined weak, allowing many sexually oriented books, magazines and videos to be sold to the public.

In 1973 the Supreme Court redefined *obscenity* with *Miller v. California*. In this case the Supreme Court gave power back to the local area. They stated that the way to decide whether the material was unacceptable or not was to ask, "does the work depict or describe, in a patently offensive way, sexual conduct specifically defined by state law?" And "does the work, taken as a whole, lack serious literary, artistic, political, or scientific value?"[7] The community standards spoken about in the Roth test were confined to the local area versus the national arena, so that different areas could develop their own standards as to what is obscene material.

The Supreme Court is more liberal as it refers to adult obscene and pornographic material; however, it has been proven to be very strictly against child pornography. The Court has permitted several convictions of people possessing child pornography.[8]

Freedom of Religion

Due to the distrust of the colonists of an established state religion, such as King George had in England, they did not want the same problem to happen in their new country of America. The colonists had left England to be able to practice their own religion and they wanted to keep that right. Therefore, the founders made sure that there was a spelled-out separation of church and state.

The First Amendment states, "Congress shall make no law respecting an establishment of religion, or prohibiting the free exercise thereof." There are two parts to this statement. The first, "Congress shall make no law respecting an establishment of religion," states that the government cannot establish a state religion, that there needs to be a separation between church and state. This part is called the **establishment clause**. The second part of the statement says that government cannot prohibit the exercise of religion. This is called the **free exercise clause**. However, both of these clauses have undergone much scrutiny by the Supreme Court and we will examine the outcomes below.

The Establishment Clause   The establishment clause has caused much controversy in the Supreme Court. The main question is how much separation should there be? Where should the balance be struck?

In 1962, a teacher led a nondenominational prayer in a public school. This act was determined by the Supreme Court in *Engel v. Vitale* (1962) to be unconstitutional. The court upheld a strict standard for separation of church and state. They believed that the founders' intent was to ensure that any student who did not believe should not be made to comply if he or she did not believe.[9]

In 1971 another case brought up the question of state aid to parochial schools. In *Lemon v. Kurtzman* (1971) the question was raised: Can the state give money to private schools for nonreligious classes? The Supreme Court developed the **Lemon test** in response to this case. The Lemon test determines the amount of money that states can give to private schools. This set the boundaries for state intervention.[10] In order for a law or practice to be constitutional, it must pass this three-pronged test:

1. The law or practice must have a secular purpose.
2. The law or practice must have a primary effect that neither advances nor prohibits religion.
3. The law or practice must not foster excessive government entanglement.

Applying the test in the Lemon case, the paying of teacher salaries at private schools failed the test and was ruled unconstitutional. Since 1980 the court has begun to interpret law and there have been several cases to test the viability of the Lemon test.[11]

The Free Exercise Clause

The right to practice your own religion without interference from the government is granted in the free exercise clause of the First Amendment. However, just as with the establishment clause, there have been exceptions to the rule. When the religious practice breaks a secular law, many times the secular law will prevail. In 1990 the Supreme Court outlawed the use of an illegal hallucinogenic drug by Native Americans due to the illegal nature of the drug.[12]

THE SECOND AMENDMENT

The second amendment was written by the founders to ensure that citizens could defend their property. It states that citizens have the "right to keep and bear arms." In 1934, with the increase in organized crime, the Congress passed a law that imposed taxes on machine guns and sawed-off shotguns. Following the spirit of the time, the Supreme Court in *United States v. Miller* (1939) stated that the Second Amendment protected only ordinary militia weapons and not unregistered sawed-off shotguns. The Supreme Court did not hear any other cases directly related to the Second Amendment after Miller.[13]

After the shooting of James Brady in 1981 and the attempted assassination of Ronald Reagan, many lawmakers called for a change in legislation. James Brady was badly wounded and left partially disabled. Sarah Brady, James's wife, led the way to a change in legislation. In 1993 the Brady Bill was enacted, which gave a mandatory waiting period of five days on the purchase of all handguns. In 1994, the Supreme Court ruled that the part of the Brady Bill that required states to conduct background checks violated state sovereignty.[14]

In addition in 1994, under the Clinton administration, Congress passed the Violent Crime Control and Law Enforcement Act. This act banned the sale, manufacturing, transporting, or possession of nineteen different semi-automatic weapons.

The right to bear arms was questioned in the *Heller v DC* (2008) case. Heller was a Washington DC special police officer who could carry a handgun while on duty. He registered to be able to have a handgun while not on duty at home and was denied the right. This case made it to the U.S. Supreme Court level with a 5-4 decision stating that Heller had the right to have a functional handgun in the home. The court's decision stated banning handguns, an entire class of arms that is commonly used for protection purposes, and prohibiting firearms from being kept functional in the home, the area traditionally in need of protection, violates the Second Amendment.[15]

DUE PROCESS RIGHTS

The due process rights are derived from the Fourth, Fifth, and Sixth Amendments. The founders felt it important that they protect citizens from government oppression. The Fourth Amendment gives the right to be left alone in your home, the Fifth Amendment grants the right to remain silent in a courtroom, and the Sixth Amendment grants the right to legal council.

Search and Seizure—Fourth Amendment

The Fourth Amendment guarantees "the right of the people to be secure in their persons, houses, papers, and effects, against unreasonable searches and seizures, shall not be violated, and no warrants shall be issued, but upon probable cause, supported by oath or affirmation, and particularly describing the place to be searched, and the person or things to be seized."[16] A proper search is one in which a warrant has been issued after the police have demonstrated to a judge that there is enough evidence to perform the search. Police need to demonstrate to the judge **probable cause**.

There are certain cases in which the police can conduct warrantless searches. They are as follows:

- **Automobile Cases**
  When police officers believe that a vehicle is being used to commit a crime or contains evidence of crimes or contraband, they may detain the car and search it. The police officer can lawfully order a driver out of his car without a violation of his Fourth Amendment rights. Police officers can also conduct pat-down searches of people they suspect are carrying weapons or contraband that can aid in committing a crime. The police officer has the right to search a car and frisk the person.[17]

- **Things in Plain View**
  Officers can seize evidence if they can see the evidence from a lawful position. If the officer can tell that the items are from a crime or are contraband from where they are standing, and if they have probable cause that the property is evidence of a crime or contraband, they can seize the evidence.[18]

- **Consent**
  Police can search with the consent of the person or a roommate.

- **Under a Valid Arrest**
  When a person is under arrest the officer can make a warrantless search of the person.

Self-Incrimination (Fifth Amendment) and Right to Counsel (Sixth Amendment)

The burden is placed on the government to prove guilt with the Fifth Amendment. *Miranda v. Arizona* (1966) protected against the police taking confessions from people without their awareness of even being arrested.[19] This is still in place today. The **Miranda warning** is as follows:

> *You have the right to remain silent. Anything you say can and will be used against you. You have the right to an attorney. If you cannot afford one, one will be provided for you. Do you understand these rights and are you willing to speak with us?*

Figure 11.2   Death Penalty Executions.

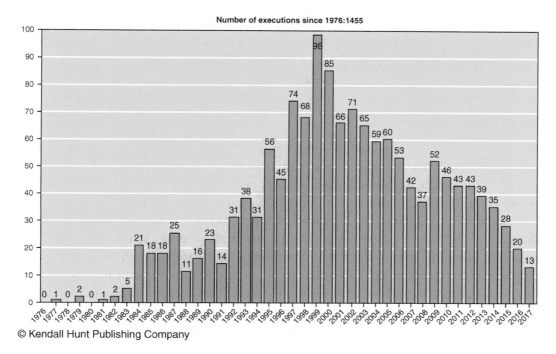

© Kendall Hunt Publishing Company

Cruel and Unusual Punishment—Eighth Amendment

The Eighth Amendment prohibits cruel and unusual punishment. The founders wanted to ensure that people who were arrested were not tortured and physically hurt, like they were in England. In England when people were convicted of a crime they were sent to the rack to die or other even more tortuous acts were performed.

All colonies had the death penalty during the time of the Constitution, and there was no question about its use. The use of the death penalty did not come into question until the 1960s when the National Association for the Advancement of Colored People (NAACP) Legal Defense Fund started to question the application of the death penalty in relation to African Americans. They stated that the death penalty was applied more frequently to African Americans than to others.

In 1972 in *Furman v. Georgia* the Supreme Court ruled that the death penalty is being applied in an inconsistent manner, which resulted in cruel and unusual punishment in violation of the Eighth and Fourteenth Amendments. The Supreme Court overturned the death penalty.[20] However a few years later in 1976 in *Gregg v. Georgia*, the Georgia death penalty statute was ruled constitutional.[21] Executions have become commonplace in America today. There are only eleven states that do not have the death penalty—Alaska, North Dakota, Minnesota, Wisconsin, Michigan, West Virginia, Massachusetts, Rhode Island, Maine, Vermont, and Hawaii. In Figure 11.2 you will see the decline of executions during the 1970s due to the Supreme Court decision and the sentiment of the country at the time.

PUBLIC PRIVACY RIGHTS

There are some rights that the Supreme Court has granted through court cases that are not spoken clearly of in the Bill of Rights. The Court interprets the framers' intentions as being that there are rights that should not have any government intervention. The right to practice your own religion means that you can exercise your own beliefs. Protection from search and seizure ensures that people should be secure in their homes. There are some rights that the court ruled on and used the right to privacy as their justification. For example in the case of Griswold v. Connecticut (1965) a couple was receiving marital counseling from Planned Parenthood about contraception. The Connecticut law stated this counseling was illegal. The U.S. Supreme Court ruled that the First, Third, Fourth, and Ninth Amendments, create a new constitutional right, the right to privacy in marital relations.

Abortion

In the 1960s abortion was legal in some states. In 1973, the Supreme Court agreed to hear the case of *Roe v. Wade.* A Texas woman wanted to have an abortion, but in Texas a woman could only have an abortion if it was necessary to save the life of the mother. Henry Wade, the district attorney for Dallas County, was the enforcer of the Texas law. The Supreme Court divided a pregnancy into three stages. In the first trimester the woman had the absolute right to terminate her pregnancy, free from government interference. In the second trimester the state could regulate abortions, but only to protect the woman's health. However, in the third trimester abortions would not be legal, because the fetus is viable at this time, but they stated that if the life of the mother was at stake the abortion could be conducted. The ruling created much controversy.[22] There have been cases to define parental consent for abortions and a twenty-four-hour waiting period rule, but the Supreme Court has not overturned *Roe v. Wade* (1973).

In 2016, the U.S. Supreme Court heard arguments in the case of *Whole Women's Health v Hellerstedt* (2016). In 2013, the Texas legislature passed a law stating that doctors who perform abortion needed admitting privileges to a hospital within 30 miles from where the procedure is being held. The U.S. Supreme Court decision found that the law was unconstitutional, because the law placed an obstacle in front of women seeking an abortion.

Source: https://www.oyez.org/cases/2015/15-274

Homosexuality

As far as privacy rights and homosexuality, the Supreme Court has declined to rule on the constitutionality of homosexual acts. In 1986, the court heard the case *Bowers v. Hardwick.* This case brought into question the constitutionality of a Georgia law outlawing heterosexual or homosexual oral or anal sex. The officer went to Hardwick's house to arrest him on a failure to appear in court on another charge. His roommate led the officer into the room, which led to an arrest for sodomy. The prosecutor did not file charges on the sodomy charge, but Hardwick filed suit against the Georgia law. The court ruled five to four to uphold the Georgia law. If prosecuted, Hardwick could have served twenty years if convicted.[23] Another case *Lawrence v. Texas* (2003) Lawrence and Garner were caught in a private, consensual sexual act. Due to Texas law they were arrested for the deviate sexual intercourse. The U.S. Supreme Court held that the Texas statute making it a crime for two persons of the same sex to engage in certain intimate sexual conduct violates the Due Process Clause of the U.S. Constitution. The Court reasoned that Lawrence and Garner were free as adults to engage in the private conduct in the exercise of their liberty under the Due Process Clause.[24]

Right to Die

When we think of the right to die many of us think of Dr. Jack Kevorkian, who assisted in many suicides of people with terminal illnesses. The Supreme Court will continue to receive more cases referring to personal autonomy. In 1990, in *Cruzan by Cruzan v.*

Director, Missouri Department of Health, the parents of Nancy Cruzan sued to remove her feeding tube. Nancy was living in a comatose state with a brain injury. The Supreme Court ruled with the state against the privacy claims of the Cruzans.[25]

On the state level there have been several cases, such as that of Dr. Jack Kevorkian. In 1999, after being acquitted on similar charges in four other cases, Dr. Kevorkian was found guilty in the assisted suicide of a fifty-two-year-old man with Lou Gehrig's disease.

In 1997 the Supreme Court of the United States ruled unanimously that terminally ill people do not have the right to doctor-assisted suicide. However 61 percent of the public believes that doctors should be able to assist terminally ill patients in suicide.[26]

In the previous section we discussed civil liberties, which are rights that each person has. This section of the chapter will focus on **civil rights**. Civil rights are the positive acts that government has taken to protect people against discrimination on the basis of race, sex, national origin, age, or sexual orientation. The focus of civil rights is the governmental acts that are taken to protect individuals.[27]

SLAVERY

Article I of the U.S. Constitution in 1787 protected slavery in the United States. It stated that for taxation and representation purposes slaves were to be counted as three-fifths of a person. The article also mandated that there was to be no regulation of the slave trade. Article IV also guaranteed that slaves that escaped would be returned to their owners. The wording used in the Constitution is "person held in Service or Labour" instead of slave. Congress banned the slave trade in 1808. By 1820 African Americans made up 25 percent of the population of the United States.[28]

The mood of the country at the time toward slaves is evident in the Supreme Court's decision in 1857 on the *Dred Scott v. Sanford* case. Dred Scott, a slave, was taken by his master from Missouri into Illinois, a free state. His master died. Scott was returned to Missouri. Scott stated that he was a free man, because he had lived in free territory where slavery was illegal.[29]

The court ruled that Scott could not sue in Federal court because he was not a citizen of the United States. No slave or enslaved person could ever become a citizen of the United States. This ruling really established the rule for the nation for the time being and closed the door for slave or enslaved person legal action.

Source: National Jefferson Expansion Memorial (Missouri Slaves).

After this ruling many people in the United States were upset and began fighting slavery; these people were called the **abolitionists**. William Lloyd Garrison was one of these prominent abolitionists. He was a white man from New England who founded the American Anti-Slavery Society in 1833.

CIVIL WAR

The Civil War was brought about in large part by pressure to bring about an end to slavery. The North was against slavery and the South needed slavery to remain a vital economy. The South was an agrarian economy and the free labor of the slaves allowed their economy to flourish. The North was an industrialized center that did not need cheap manpower like the South. Another reason for the advent of the Civil War was the secession from the Union by several southern states. The North and the South had no other answer to their conflicts and war ensued. The Civil War was the most tragic of the wars that we have had to date. There were very few families at the time that did not feel the loss of a loved one in battle.

In 1863, President Lincoln issued the **Emancipation Proclamation**, which stated that all slaves who lived in the Confederacy would be freed. The North had to win the war in order to place this into effect. The North did win the war and Congress was a big part in helping equality be a reality for the slaves.

Civil War Amendments

The first of the three Civil War Amendments was the **Thirteenth Amendment ratified in 1865**. All forms of "slavery and involuntary servitude" were banned. In order for the southern states to be readmitted to the Union after the Civil War they had to accept the Thirteenth Amendment. As a result of the amendment the southern states erected laws to stop the full scope of the Thirteenth Amendment being realized by slaves or enslaved people. These laws were called the black codes. The black codes were different from state to state, but all police officers could arrest unemployed slaves or enslaved people, fine them for vagrancy, and hire them out to satisfy their fines. Black codes were the beginning roots to the later Jim Crow laws.

Another Civil War Amendment was the **Fourteenth Amendment ratified in 1868**. This amendment stated "No state shall make or enforce any law which shall abridge the privileges or immunities of citizens of the United States; nor shall any state deprive any person of life, liberty, or property, without due process of law; nor deny to any person within its jurisdiction the equal protection of the laws."[30]

The third Civil War Amendment to the Constitution was the **Fifteenth Amendment** in 1870. This is called the voting rights amendment. It guaranteed the "rights of citizens to vote regardless of their race color or previous condition of servitude." These amendments led to a time between 1865 and the 1880s where African Americans were voting and African Americans held federal and state offices. Life was different for African Americans, but the military occupation of the South was about to end, due to the end of Reconstruction in 1877.

Segregation

The Compromise of 1877 ended the Reconstruction period and the national government ended its occupation of the South. The South agreed to support the United States Union and accept national supremacy. However, in 1883 five cases were brought forth to the Supreme Court called the *Civil Rights cases*. These cases were convictions of private citizens that did not allow African Americans into their place of private business. The Supreme

Source: Anti-Slavery Almanac[31]

Court found that the state or federal government could not discriminate in its buildings, but the private citizen had the right to discriminate because it was a private business, not a public one. The Fourteenth Amendment's scope was severely limited with this move. Congress could not prohibit private discrimination. Segregation between African Americans and whites became the way of life in the South. Ninety percent of all African Americans lived in the South during this time period and this ruling affected their lives dramatically.

African Americans were now being subjected to the **Jim Crow laws**. These laws stressed the second-class citizenship of African Americans. All areas of life were separate, such as schools, jobs, and restaurants. African Americans were denied economic, social, and political equality throughout their lives. Most of the time areas for the "colored" were substandard and hardly livable. The "colored" schools did not have the money or materials of white schools.

Another tool to lock out African American men specifically from the political system was by developing ways to keep them from being able to vote. The southerners developed *poll taxes,* making people pay to vote and oftentimes came at the wrong time for the sharecropping African American. A second means of blocking the African American male from voting was the *literacy test,* which meant that a reading comprehension test could be given to potential voters. Poor whites who could not read or those who did not own property could still vote if their grandfather could vote in 1867—before reconstruction and the freeing of slaves. This was called the **grandfather clause**.

In the landmark ***Plessy v. Ferguson*** (1896) case the segregation laws of the South were being challenged. Plessy, a man who was one-eighth African American, went to ride in a railroad car that was meant for "whites only." He was arrested for not sitting in the colored section for the car. Plessy argued that this was a violation of the "equal protection" of the Fourteenth Amendment. The Supreme Court ruled that as long as people in each race received equal treatment the equal protection clause of the Fourteenth Amendment was not violated. The court ruled that "separate but equal" was the law. Segregation was upheld as constitutionally sound and would continue until another landmark Supreme Court case in 1954.[32]

EQUAL PROTECTION FIGHT

In 1909 W. E. B. Du Bois and a group of whites started the National Organization for the Advancement of Colored People (NAACP) to fight legal battles for black people. In 1954 they led one of the most important legal cases for African Americans, the ***Brown v. Board*** *of Education* (1954) case. Thurgood Marshall led a team of lawyers to fight for "equal" treatment in education through the *Brown* case. The white schools and the African American schools were far from equal. The physical conditions of the buildings, the curriculum, teacher salaries, and qualifications for African American schools were inferior and that was the basis of argument for Marshall.

The Supreme Court in a historic decision overturned *Plessy v. Ferguson* (1896) and stated that separate was not equal. They went on to conclude that:

> *Segregation of white and colored children in public school has a detrimental effect upon the colored children. The impact is greater when it has the sanction of law, for the policy of separating the races is usually interpreted as denoting the inferiority of the Negro group. A sense of inferiority affects the motivation of a child to educational and mental development of Negro children and to deprive them of some benefits they would receive in a racially integrated school system. . . . We conclude, unanimously, that in the field of public education the doctrine of "separate but equal" has no place.*[33]

After the decision was handed down by the Supreme Court, there was immediate reaction. The governor of South Carolina at the time said, "Ending segregation would mark the beginning of the end of civilization in the South as we know it."[34] The case gave hope to African Americans that change would come. However, it would take time for full equal protection to be realized. Twenty-one states would need to change their educational patterns. The Supreme Court, however, did not require the change to be immediate; they gave the states time to figure out their plans for desegregation. It took until 1969 to stop the delays from states to become in compliance, nearly fourteen years after the landmark *Brown* case. The *Brown* case sparked a movement throughout the country calling for change and the *civil rights movement* gained momentum.

CIVIL RIGHTS

One year after the *Brown* (1954) case ruling, an event not well publicized added fuel to the civil rights movement that kept on growing, was the killing of Emmett Till. Emmett was a fourteen-year-old boy from Chicago, Illinois. In the summer of 1955 he traveled to Money, Mississippi, to visit his uncle and make some money working part time in the cotton fields. Being from the North he was not "schooled" in the ways of the South, and as he went into a convenience store to buy candy he whistled at the white female store clerk. The woman became very upset and Emmett and his friends left the scene. Several days later at 2:00 a.m., two white men armed with guns came to Till's uncle's house, demanding the black boy who had whistled at the white store clerk. The two men snatched Till and drove off with him. His mangled remains were found in the Tallahatchie River several days later with a seventy-pound cotton-gin fan around his neck to weight the body down. The only way the boy could be identified was by the ring on his finger. Mamie Till shared her grief with the country by showing the remains of the body untouched by the undertaker to a national magazine and placing his body for view by the public in Chicago. She wanted everyone to know what had happened to her son.

An all-white jury found the men not guilty. A few days after the trial the two men confessed and gave graphic accounts of the murder of Till to *Look* magazine. After this confession interview they were paid $4,000 for the interview, but were still able to live freely. One hundred days after Till's body was found, Rosa Parks refused to give up her seat and the civil rights movement was in full swing.[35]

In 1955 Rosa Parks refused to give up her seat on the bus to a white person and was arrested. Dr. King was asked by the Montgomery Improvement Association (MTA) to lead a transportation boycott of the city. This was a **nonviolent** protest. The people of Montgomery, Alabama, decided that they were not going to ride any public transportation until the law was changed. African Americans carpooled, rode in taxis, and walked to get to work. The city began to lose money and the boycott became costly for the city. Almost a year after it began, in 1956 a federal court ruled a segregated bus system violated the Fourteenth Amendment Equal Protection Clause.

Many leadership groups began to emerge, such as the Southern Christian Leadership Council (SCLC) led by Martin Luther King Jr. in 1957. King focused on ending discrimination and segregation throughout all aspects of life. He was made famous in the African American community and around the nation after the Montgomery bus boycott. King led several other nonviolent demonstrations over the next few years.

One of the most important years for the nonviolent movement was 1963. King led thousands of demonstrators in peaceful demonstrations in Birmingham, Alabama. The event was publicized on television and people watched in horror as peaceful demonstrators were attacked by dogs and sprayed with fire hoses. Support for the movement from whites was becoming widespread.

On August 28, 1963, the most famous march was conducted. Over 200,000 African Americans and whites participated in the nonviolent *March on Washington*. It was at the culmination of this march that Martin Luther King Jr. gave his most famous speech, "I Have a Dream." People from all areas of the country were calling for an end to segregation, which led to the Civil Rights Act of 1964.

The Civil Rights Act of 1964 was an important step toward equality for African Americans. In the act it states that people cannot be segregated or discriminated against on the grounds of race, religion, or national origin in public places, federal programs needed to end discrimination in programs and activities, and employers may not discriminate on the basis of race, religion, sex, or national origin.

Fair housing was not contained in the civil rights movement of 1964, because this area had the greatest effect on the South. On April 4, 1968, Martin Luther King Jr. was assassinated, and Congress passed the Civil Rights Act of 1968 in his memory. In the 1968 Civil Rights Act there were provisions against the discrimination in the sale or lease of a residence to any person based on race, color, religion, or national origin.

Figure 11.3   Civil Rights Legislation Impact.

Civil Right Law	Provision
Civil Rights Act of 1957	Created the Civil Rights division in the Department of Justice
24th Amendment	Ended poll taxes
Voting Rights Act	Authorized the U.S. Attorney General to send federal examiners to register voters
Civil Rights Act of 1964	Gave the federal government including equal access in the workplace and public areas Federal funds withheld from programs that practiced discrimination
Civil Rights Act of 1968	Outlawed discrimination in the sale or lease of housing

Source: http://www.history.com/topics/black-history/civil-rights-act

GENDER EQUALITY

The civil rights movement opened up the door for other groups to gain equality. In the Civil Rights Acts not only race was mentioned, but also gender was mentioned. The first step for women's equality was the passage of the 19th Amendment (1920) to the U.S. Constitution, it guaranteed the women's right to vote.

Early women's rights organizations resulted from the inability of women to own property. After the Civil War women were able to change many laws that made them slaves to their husbands. In 1800 the bulk of the efforts were on the protection of women in the families. The threats to a woman's well-being were her husband's drinking, gambling, and being with prostitutes. The Anti-Saloon League, which was led by women, was successful at outlawing gambling and prostitution in every state except Nevada.

In the early 1900s women began to demand the same right to vote as men. There were parades, picketing, and some nonviolent protests. As a result of these efforts women received the right to vote in 1920 with the passing of the Nineteenth Amendment, fifty-one years after African American men received the right to vote (Fifteenth Amendment, 1869) and 131 years after white men began voting (1789).

As time passed, the Supreme Court began to question whether sex discrimination might violate the Fourteenth Amendment. In *Reed v. Reed* (1971) it found that sexual classifications in the law must be "reasonable and not arbitrary."[36] The court has also made other rulings on gender classification. They are as follows:

1. Men and women must have the same ages for becoming legal adults[37] and for the purchase of alcoholic beverages;[38]
2. Women cannot be locked out of police or fire-fighting jobs by making up height and weight requirements that are impossible to meet;[39]
3. Women's insurance and retirement plans must be the same as male monthly benefits;[40]
4. Schools must pay girls' coaches the same as boys' coaches.[41]

Steps have been made toward equality for women, but there still are areas that need to be worked on. President Bill Clinton appointed the first female secretary of state, Madeline Albright. A first lady has been elected as a senator from New York, Hillary Rodham Clinton. President George W. Bush appointed another female secretary of state, Condoleezza Rice. President Barack Obama then followed suit by appointing Hillary Rodham Clinton to Secretary of State. Hillary Rodham Clinton also became the first female Presidential Candidate in 2016.

AFFIRMATIVE ACTION

Today, people in America agree that there is still discrimination in America today, but people have differing viewpoints as to how to prevent it from happening. In the search for equality there have been programs that attempt to improve the chances of minority applicants. These programs are called **affirmative action**. Affirmative action began in 1965 with an executive order from President Johnson. The target area for the first program was in the construction industry. The goal was to increase the number of minorities in the construction industry. The businesses were supposed to give chances to minority applicants (African Americans and women) even if they were not equal to the nonminority applicant. The Office of Federal Contract Compliance Programs (OFCCP) was formed to monitor the industry and set up goals and timetables for full implementation. Seven years later Congress followed suit and passed the Equal Employment Opportunity Act, which established the Equal Employment Opportunity Commission (EEOC). The EEOC had the powers to take any employer to court if they were found to have discriminating hiring practices, not just in the construction industry, but across all industries. The EEOC is still in place today.

The opponents of affirmative action wanted nothing to do with the development of quotas, which would discriminate against the whites. The supporters of affirmative action thought the programs being set up would level the playing field for nonwhites and women. They thought that it was about time to respond to the real needs of the community. The tensions became so strong that eventually a court case made it to the Supreme Court.

In 1978 the Supreme Court heard the case of *Regents of the University of California v. Bakke.* At the University of California at Davis there were sixteen seats set aside for minority applicants. Bakke, a white male, claimed that even though he was more qualified than the minority candidates were, he was denied admission into the school. He claimed that it was reverse discrimination. There was a split in the court; four of the justices sided with the school and the other four justices sided with Bakke. The ninth justice, Powell made the decision in the case. The Supreme Court stated that the admissions policy of the school could consider race and ethnic origin as they make decisions. However, the court ruled that setting aside a certain number of seats for minorities violated the Equal Protection Law of the Fourteenth Amendment.[42]

In another Supreme Court case, *United Steelworkers v. Weber* (1979), a chemical corporation in Louisiana that used to discriminate against African Americans had a program that guaranteed half the jobs at the plant would go to African Americans. The quota would remain until the number of African Americans that worked at the plant matched the proportion to the local labor force. The Court ruled in favor of this plan because it was trying to right the wrongs done in the past.[43]

Through the years of Reagan and Bush, 1981–1990, the programs began to be examined closely. The administrations argued that the only employers that should have to implement affirmative action programs are those that have had a record of discrimination in the past. The Supreme Court throughout these administrations reflected this viewpoint in their decisions. The affirmative action programs should be designed to meet the level of problems in the past.[44]

On April 1, 2003, the Supreme Court heard the two most current cases on affirmative action, *Grutter v. Lee Bollinger, et al.* (2003) case and the *Gratz, et al. v. Lee Bollinger, et al.* (2003). Both of these cases question the use of racial preference in admission decisions at the University of Michigan. The *Grutter* case refers to admission to law school, and the *Gratz* case refers to admission to the undergraduate program.

President George W. Bush has spoken about his view on the University of Michigan admission policies. He stated that the University of Michigan policy that gives preference to black and Hispanic applicants is "divisive, unfair and impossible to square with the Constitution." He goes on to state that, "We must be vigilant in responding to prejudice wherever we find it," he told reporters in the White House. "As we work to address the wrongs of racial prejudice, we must not use means that create another wrong, and thus perpetuate our divisions."[45]

The Supreme Court ruled in the law school admissions case, *Grutter*, that race could be considered in the admissions process. In a 5–4 decision, Sandra Day O'Connor wrote in the majority decision, "Our conclusion that the law school has a compelling interest in a diverse student body is informed by our view that attaining a diverse student body is at the heart of the law school's proper institutional mission, that the 'good faith' on the part of a university is presumed absent 'a showing to the contrary.' "[46]

However, in the *Gratz* case the court found, in a 6–3 decision, that the undergraduate admissions applicant point system was unconstitutional. Justice Rehnquist stated that the admissions process needed to look at the applicant as an individual and the Michigan undergraduate process did not take this into account.[47] In the Fischer v. University of Texas (2016) case Fischer failed to meet the 10% rule in Texas and was placed into the next category of applicants. She was denied admission to the University based on race. The U.S. Supreme Courts decided that the use of race was aligned to the goals of the University and only used as one element within the scope of the whole admissions process. They voted 4-3 to uphold the Appellate Court decision in favor of the University of Texas.[48]

IMMIGRATION POLICY

The United States is made up of immigrants. Pride in immigrant heritage is a part of the American fabric. In today's society about 12.9 percent of the entire population is foreign born.[49]

The federal government is responsible for enforcing and enacting immigration policy. Immigration policy is the entry regulation of noncitizens into the country. In 1921 after World War I the first comprehensive immigration law was passed. It established maximum numbers for new immigrants each year and set a quota of immigrants from each foreign country. There was a sentiment in the country at that time against immigrants of Eastern Europe and Jewish immigrants. That is why the quotas from each country were established.

The latest federal law establishing new immigration reform was passed in 1986. It was called the Immigration Reform and Control Act. This law focused on employers and punishing employers for hiring illegal aliens, which are people living in America that are not citizens. This law however allowed many different forms of documentation that are easily forged. This did not help with the continued flow of illegal immigrants across the borders. For workers that had been here since 1982 and they could prove that they had been working at that time, they were granted immunity from the law.[50]

There has been no federal law since this law in 1986 that has stopped the flow of illegal immigrants. Each year it is estimated that there are 400,000 (US government figures) to 3 million (unofficial) illegal immigrants entering the country. Immigrants enter the country by crossing the borders on their own or using forged papers, others have been here on vacations, student or work visas, and they just stay. The federal enforcement agency charged with enforcement of immigration laws is the Immigration and Customs Enforcement Agency (ICE).[51]

However since the federal government has failed to act on immigration reform, the state of Arizona, a state with border access to Mexico, has implemented new state laws that are causing much controversy. Arizona enacted a law that states if there is "reasonable suspicion" then local police have the authority to conduct an investigation to see if the person is in the country illegally. Civil rights groups say that this may cause certain groups, such as Latinos to be racially profiled. Legal challenges to the law are being fielded and President Obama has asked for an investigation into the constitutionality of the law.[52]

Online Connections

The U.S Commission on civil rights is a government fact-finding agency where people can file charges and view charges. *http://www.uscr.gov*

The Southern Poverty Law Center is a nonprofit group combating hate through education and litigation. *http://www.splcenter.org*

National Association for the Advancement of Colored People (NAACP). *http://www.naacp.org*

The National Organization of Women. *http://www.now.org*

The American Civil Liberties Union (ACLU) has information on the Bill of Rights and how it is being applied today. *http://www.aclu.org*

Use Find Law to look up important court cases as they refer to civil liberties. *http://www.findlaw.com*

Key Terms

Civil liberties   133

Bill of Rights   134

Incorporation   135

Establishment clause   136

Free exercise clause   136

Lemon test   136

Probable cause   138

Miranda warning   138

Civil rights   141

Abolitionists   142

Emancipation Proclamation   142

Thirteenth Amendment   142

Fourteenth Amendment   142

Fifteenth Amendment   142

Jim Crow laws   143

Grandfather clause   143

Plessy v. Ferguson (1896)   143

Brown v. Board of Education (1954)   143

Nonviolent   145

Affirmative action   146

Selected Readings

Taylor Branch, *Parting the Waters: America in the King Years, 1954–1963* (New York: Simon & Schuster, 1988).

Steven L. Carter, *Reflection of an Affirmative Action Baby* (New York: Basic Books, 1991).

Jean Bethke Elshtain, *Democracy on Trial* (New York: Basic Books, 1995).

David Garrow, *Liberty and Sexuality: The Right to Privacy and the Making of Roe v. Wade* (New York: Macmillan, 1994).

David Halberstam, *The Children* (New York: Random House, 1998).

David M. O'Brien, *Constitutional Law and Politics. Vol. 2, Civil Rights and Civil Liberties* (New York: Norton, 1997).

Lloyd Weinreb, *Leading Constitutional Cases on Criminal Justice* (New York: Foundation Press, 1998).

Juan William, *Eyes on the Prize: America's Civil Rights Years, 1954–1964* (New York: Penguin, 1987).

Notes

[1]*Barron v. Baltimore*, 32 U.S. 243 (1833).

[2]Ibid.

[3]*Schenck v. United States*, 249 U.S. 47 (1919).

[4]*New York Times v. Sullivan*, 376 U.S. 254 (1964).

[5]*Chaplinsky v. New Hampshire*, 315 U.S. 568 (1942).

[6]*Roth v. United States*, 354 U.S. 476 (1957).

[7]*Miller v. California*, 413 U.S. 15 (1973).

[8]*Knox v. United States*, 114 S. Ct. 375 (1993).

[9]*Engel v. Vitale*, 370 U.S. 24 (1962).

[10]*Lemon v. Kurtzman*, 403 U.S. 602 (1971).

[11]See also *Wolman v. Walter*, 433 U.S. 229 (1977); *Roemer v. Board of Public Works of Maryland*, 426 U.S. 736 (1976); *Committee for Public Education v. Nyquist*, 413 U.S. 756 (1973).

[12]*Oregon Department of Human Resources v. Smith*, 294 U.S. 872 (1990).

[13]*United States v. Miller*, 307 U.S. 174 (1939).

[14]K. O'Connor and L. Sabato, *American Government: Continuity and Change* (New York: Longman, 2002), p. 155.

[15]https://www.oyez.org/cases/2007/07-290

[16]K. O'Connor and L. Sabato, American Government: Continuity and Change (New York: Longman, 2002), p. 155., p. 157.

[17]*United States v. Ross*, 456 U.S. 798 (1982); *Pennsylvania v. Minms*, 434 U.S. 110 (1977).

[18]*Coolidge v. New Hampshire*, 403 U.S. 443 (1971); *Texas v. Brown*, 460 U.S. 730 (1983).

[19]*Miranda v. Arizona*, 384 U.S. 436 (1966).

[20]*Furman v. Georgia*, 408 U.S. 238 (1972).

[21]*Gregg v. Georgia*, 428 U.S. 153 (1976).

[22]*Roe v. Wade*, 410 U.S. 113 (1973).

[23]*Bowers v. Hardwick*, 478 U.S. 186 (1986).

[24]*Lawrence v. Texas*, 539 U.S. 558 (2003).

[25]*Cruzan by Cruzan v. Director, Missouri Department of Health*, 110 S. Ct. 2841 (1990).

[26]*USA Today/CNN Poll* (November 22, 1999): 21A.

[27]Jefferson National Expansion Memorial, St. Louis, Missouri (http://www.nps.gov/jeff/ocv-dscottd.htm).

[28]Karen O'Connor and Larry Sabato, *American Government: Continuity and Change* (New York: Addison Wesley and Longman, 2002), 179.

[29]*Dred Scott v. Sanford*, 60 U.S. 393 (1857).

[30]U.S. Consitution, Fourteenth Amendment, Article 1.

[31]*The New England Anti-Slavery Almanac for 1839* (Boston, 1838).

[32]*Plessy v. Ferguson*, 163 U.S. 537 (1896)

[33]*Brown v. Board of Education of Topeka*, 347 U.S. 483 (1954).

[34]Quoted in Juan Williams, *Eyes on the Prize: America's Civil Rights Years 1954–1965.* (New York: Penguin, 1987), 37

[35]Adrian Maher, "AR at Sundance—The Art of the Documentary," *The American Reporter*, Vol. 9, No. 2037, February 11, 2003.

[36]*Reed v. Reed*, 404 U.S. 71 (1971).

[37]*Stanton v. Stanton*, 421 U.S. 7 (1975).

[38]*Craig v. Boren*, 429 U.S. 190 (1976).

[39]*Dothard v. Rawlinson*, 433 U.S. 321 (1977).

[40]*Arizona v. Norris*, 103 S. Ct. 3492 (1983).

[41]*EEOC v. Madison Community School District,* 55 U.S.L.W. 2644 (1987).

[42]*Regents of the University of California v. Bakke*, 438 U.S. 265 (1978).

[43]*United Steelworkers v. Weber*, 443 U.S. 312 (1974).

[44]*http://supreme.lp.findlaw.com/supreme_court/docket/2002/april.html*

[45]Patricia Wilson, "Bush Opposes College on Race in Supreme Court Case," Reuters, January 15, 2003, Washington viewed online at http://*news.findlaw.com/politics/s/20030116/bushcourtracedc.html*

[46]Linda K. Wertheimer and Christy Hoppe, "College Race Policy Upheld," *The Dallas Morning News*, June 24, 2003, pp. 1A, 16A.

[47]Ibid.

[48]*Fischer v. University of Texas*, 579 U.S. (2016)

[49]https://www.census.gov/newsroom/pdf/cspan_fb_slides.pdf

[50]T. R. Dye, B. H. Sparrow, L. T. Gibson, and C. Robison. *Politics in America* (New York: Longman, 2009).

[51]Ibid.

[52]*http://www.usatoday.com/news/nation/2010-05-02-immigration_N.htm*

NAME_____ COURSE_____ SECTION_____

1. Explain three ways the government has limited freedom of speech.

    _____

    _____

    _____

    _____

    _____

2. Name and explain both parts of the First Amendment that deal with free-
    dom of religion.

    _____

    _____

    _____

    _____

    _____

3. Describe the case of *Brown v. Board of Education* of 1954. What was the
    significance of the case and what happened after the case was decided?

    _____

    _____

    _____

    _____

    _____

4. Explain issues raised by *affirmative action*.

    _____

    _____

    _____

    _____

    _____

Directions: Write the word or phrase that completes the statement.

1. The _____ Amendment protects the freedom of religion.

2. A five-day waiting period was imposed by the _____.

3. The _____ Amendment allows police officers to search items in plain view.

4. The _____ Amendment prohibits cruel and unusual punishment.

5. In 1976 the Supreme Court ruled the death penalty was unconstitutional. The case was _____.

Directions: Circle the correct answer to each of the following questions.

6. In _____ the Supreme Court found that segregation of rail transportation was constitutional because "separate, but equal" did not violate the equal protection clause of the Fourteenth Amendment.
   a. the Civil Rights Cases
   b. *Plessy v. Ferguson*
   c. *Brown v. The Board of Education*
   d. *Reed v. Reed*

7. The Supreme Court case that overturned *Plessy* (1896) that ruled "separate was not equal" was _____.
   a. the Civil Rights Cases
   b. *Regents of California v. Bakke*
   c. *Brown v. The Board of Education*
   d. *Reed v. Reed*

8. The significance of the Emancipation Proclamation was _____.
   a. Confederate slaves would be free
   b. northern slaves would be free
   c. both a and b
   d. none of the above

9. Slavery was banned by the _____ Amendment.
   a. Twelfth
   b. Thirteenth
   c. Fourteenth
   d. Fifteenth

Sample Test Questions

10. In which case did the Supreme Court rule that Congress could ban certain types of speech in times of war if it constituted a clear and present danger to society?
   a. *Near v. Minnesota*
   b. *Barron v. Baltimore*
   c. *Schenck v. United States*
   d. *Roth v. United States*

11. The Supreme Court in the case of _____ refused to grant the Bill of Rights extensions to the state.
   a. *Near v. Minnesota*
   b. *Barron v. Baltimore*
   c. *Schenck v. United States*
   d. *Roth v. United States*

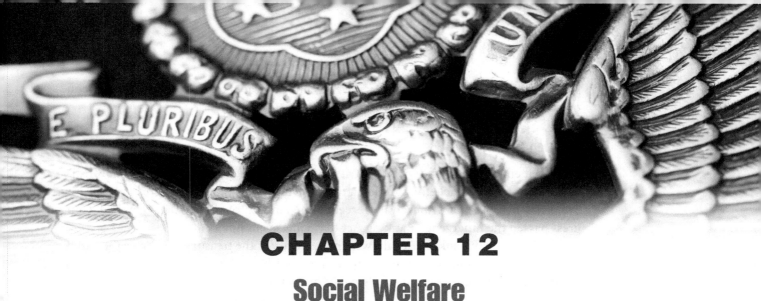

CHAPTER 12
Social Welfare

Social welfare policy is a government program designed to help people live more quality lives. **Entitlement programs** are rights granted to citizens and certain non-citizens by federal law. Some examples of these entitlement programs are Medicaid, Medicare, and Social Security. The programs may consist of educational opportunities, economic support, and health care support. The policies are designed to help the less fortunate segment in our society, the poor and elderly.

THE EVOLUTION OF SOCIAL WELFARE POLICY

Social welfare policy started as a reaction to the Great Depression of the 1930s with the **New Deal programs** of Franklin D. Roosevelt. During this time the government began to see that state resources and charitable resources were not enough to combat the poverty that was in our society. People who worked hard could not keep afloat, due to the tough economic times. Though left-wing critics demanded higher appropriations, most Americans were grateful for these measures. The relief programs of the New Deal gave hope to the have-nots, African Americans, and the unemployed, and restored confidence in the government.[1]

After the stock market crash of 1929, the economy in the country followed the crash. By 1933 the unemployment rate in the country was 25 percent, up from 3.2 percent in 1929. This was the darkest time.[2] As a result of these tough economic times the government began to take a more active role in helping the American people out of this struggle. Roosevelt developed many government programs to help the American economy through the hard times.

Bank Issues

Roosevelt entered into office on March 4, 1933. By March 9, 1933, he proposed new legislation to Congress to help the banking industry. During this time there were banks closing every day because the withdrawals exceeded the amount of money that they had. Congress passed the Emergency Banking Act that same evening.

The Emergency Banking Act allowed the secretary of the treasury to oversee the banks. Banks that were financially sound could open and banks that were not would remain closed until the accounting methods could be worked out. The president explained the banking act to the American people over the radio. The following day deposits were more than withdrawals and the banking problems were over. President Roosevelt's plan for the nation and explanation to the country of the plan to make banks more financially sound institutions put people at ease and helped the banking industry improve.

Unemployment Issues

With the vast number of people who were unemployed, Roosevelt brought forth new programs to help put people to work. He believed that the programs would help the morale and spiritual fabric of the country by giving people a sense of purpose. In November 1933 Roosevelt created the **Civil Works Administration** (CWA) to put people to work right away on public works projects. Wages for people averaged $15 a week, two times more money than relief payments given to citizens. By January 1934 more than 4 million people were employed in the program. Critics of the program said that there was too much corruption in the organization and that the wages were too high. By 1934 the program was ended by Roosevelt.

There was still a need for employment programs and by 1935 Roosevelt began another work program called the **Works Progress Administration** (WPA). The wages that people earned through this agency were less than the CWA, $55 a month, which was more than relief payments, but less than what a person would make in the private sector. The WPA workers worked on improving hospitals, airfields, and playgrounds. The program helped reduce the number of people unemployed by giving jobs to 30 percent of the unemployed.[3] The WPA handed out approximately $11 billion in work relief to about 3.2 million American people a month between 1935 and 1942.[4] It served the purpose of getting the American people through a tough time in the economy.

Social Security Evolves

Social Security, an insurance program for 65 and older Americans, was implemented with the passing of the Social Security Act of 1935, under Roosevelt's guidance. A payroll tax is placed on all Americans except government workers, farm workers, and domestic labor workers. This payroll tax helps pay for retirement benefits for older-aged people. Social Security is still in place today. There are many debates on the cost of this program for the future. The concern of the politicians is if we will be able to fund the program as it stands.

Unemployment Insurance and Compensation Evolves

The Social Security Act also included the development of an insurance fund for unemployed workers. This is called **unemployment**. Payroll taxes are deducted from workers' paychecks and placed into a fund for unemployed workers. When workers get laid off from their job they can collect money from the fund for a period of time while they are looking for another job. Workers are being protected in the event that they are laid off, which provides personal security. This is still in place today as a way to help support those who are laid off.

Aid to Families with Dependent Children

Another provision of the Social Security Act of 1935 is the **Aid to Families with Dependent Children** (AFDC). Another name for this is welfare. This is a relief fund that was set up by states to help widowed mothers or mothers with disabled husbands. The focus of this fund was on the mothers from nuclear families who needed assistance versus supporting unwed mothers. Since the states were administering this fund it was not provided equally in every state. In order for people to qualify for this program they needed to prove that their income was low enough to qualify.

The New Deal programs of Roosevelt began several social welfare programs that are still in place today, such as Social Security and Unemployment Insurance. The programs of the time, even though some were temporary, helped Americans get through a very tough economic time. The New Deal was the foundation for other programs to come.

THE GREAT SOCIETY

Another expansion of social policies came in the 1960s with President Lyndon Johnson calling for a Great Society where poverty and racial inequalities do not exist. The same tenet existed in the Great Society as in the New Deal; government can make life better for all Americans by taking action through programs.

Johnson proposed 115 programs to the Congress and 78 percent of them were passed. Some of the programs included expanding Social Security to include the health care

Figure 12.1 The Great Society Outcomes.

- Medicare—low cost medical and hospital insurance for the people of age 65 and older
- Medicaid—health insurance for poor
- Head Start—Federally funded preschool
- Food Stamps
- Elementary and Secondary Education Act—funds school materials
- Department of Housing and Urban Development created
- Higher Education Act
- Passed legislation to improve air and water quality
- Wilderness Protection Act—rescued 9.1 acres from industrial development
- Lifting immigration quotas through the Immigration and Nationality Act of 1965
- Public Broadcasting Act of 1967 produced National Public Radio (NPR), Public Broadcasting System (PBS)
- Voting Rights Act banned discriminatory acts to deny right to vote
- National Endowment for the Arts and Humanities—federal money used to fund galleries and artists
- Consumer Safety standards raised

Source: http://www.ushistory.org/us/56e.asp

programs of Medicare and Medicaid for poor and retired Americans, financing housing programs for the poor, job training through Job Corps, and preschool education through Head Start. Figure 12.1 illustrates the outcomes of the Great Society.[5]

SOCIAL WELFARE POLICIES EVOLVE

Welfare Reforms of 1996

The criticism of AFDC, better known as welfare, grew in the early 1990s. Welfare was offered to anyone who met the federal guidelines. Women who did work at a low-paying job were worse off than when they were on welfare alone. Many recipients of AFDC received payments for a short period of time; it was a temporary fix for them. However, 20 percent of the women stayed on the program for six to nine years and 25 percent of the women stayed on AFDC for more than ten years. The majority of the people who fell into this category were African American or Hispanic women with no high school diplomas who were teenage mothers. This was a problem and when President Clinton came to office in 1993 he called for a change in the program.[6]

In 1996 AFDC was ended and put in its place is the program called **Temporary Aid to Needy Families** (TANF). This program is not offered to all who meet the guidelines, as was AFDC. The goal of TANF is to keep the nuclear family intact. The three objectives of the program are —job preparation, work, or marriage. After being on the program for two years recipients are required to work. Working can include receiving training or going to school, but the lifetime maximum for the program is five years of assistance. States have the option of reducing this maximum. By the year 2000, single parents had to participate for at least thirty hours per week in work-related programs and two-parent families had to participate in work activities for at least thirty-five or fifty-five hours per week. However, states were allowed to adjust the rules for single parents with young children. The special benefits include not penalizing them for failing to meet work requirements if they cannot obtain child care or if the child is under one year of age, the parent does not have to meet the work requirement. After five years families can receive noncash child care support or transportation support.[7]

The new program has reduced the number of families that remain on assistance. Figure 12.2 shows the decline in the percentages of people receiving welfare since 1960. The figure shows that the peak number of welfare recipients was in 1994; after the passage of TANF the number has decreased each year. The economy was very good throughout the late 1990s, and this could have helped many of those go from welfare to work; however in the early part of 2000 our economic condition was not as certain and more people were being laid off of work. We will need to continue to watch the evolution of TANF to see if it will meet the needs of the poor working-class families in the current and future economic times.

Health Care

At the time of the New Deal, Congress discussed the possibility of nationalizing health care; however, the American Medical Association (AMA) opposed it, and therefore it was not included. It would be several years before any relief would be passed in Congress. In the 1960s under President Johnson's leadership Medicare and Medicaid were passed. This would provide hospital care for all Americans covered by Social Security.

Figure 12.2   Number of U.S. Population Receiving Food Stamps.

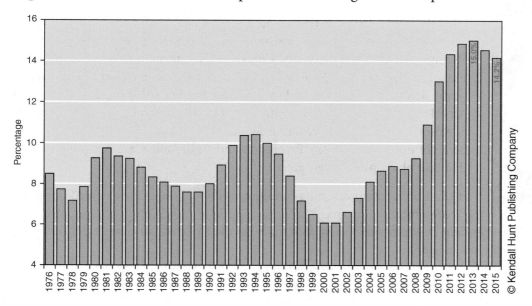

Medicare is the public health insurance program that is used by the elderly and disabled to fund health care costs. It pays for hospital visits and physicians visits. The hospital visits are paid for by the Social Security tax, but the physicians' visits are funded by the monthly premiums paid by participants. It has helped the general health of the elderly; however, Medicare is expensive and many who need the program have trouble paying the monthly premiums. Changes need to be made in this program in order to ensure that the fund will not go broke.

Medicaid, on the other hand, is a federal and state partnership program that helps the low income and elderly pay for their medical bills. States set the qualifying standards for Medicaid.

There are a number of problems with the health care system that is in place right now in the United States. One problem is the high cost of health care. Consumers and employers have had to foot the bill with rising health care costs. People are living longer, and there are greater demands on the health care system. With the demand for medical care increasing and the number of people needing care increasing, costs will only rise.

A second problem with the American system is the uninsured. There are about 40 million people who are not covered by any insurance. There are many people who work full time and make just above the poverty line and do not qualify for Medicaid. When the uninsured need care, they go to the emergency room for critical care. This critical care costs more money than preventive care done more regularly.

A third problem is the high cost of malpractice insurance for doctors. Malpractice insurance costs have doubled over ten years. Lawyers bring about cases against doctors that have caused huge payouts for families. These payouts from litigation have cost the entire community of doctors. President Bush proposed a cap be put on all malpractice litigation of $250,000 for pain and suffering incurred due to a medical mistake made, which he stated would help the problem. Many groups, however, opposed this measure. For example, a Wisconsin woman who had both breasts removed after she was wrongfully diagnosed with cancer protested the $250,000 cap.[9]

HEALTH CARE REFORM

On March 23, 2010, the first comprehensive health care reform since Medicare in 1965 was signed into law by President Obama. There have been many attempts since 1965 to implement health care reform, and 2010 was the first time it had passed. No Republican in either the House of Representatives or in the Senate voted for the bill. At the time the bill was passed 83 percent of Americans had health care; with the passing of the new reform up to 95 percent of Americans will have access to health care.[10]

Some of the features of the Protection and Affordable Care Act (Obamacare) that take place immediately are:

1. Children with preexisting conditions will not be able to be denied insurance coverage.
2. Dependent children will be able to remain on their parents' insurance until they are 26 years of age.[11]
3. Health coverage could not be dropped for those who suddenly become very sick.
4. Adults with preexisting conditions will be able to purchase affordable insurance.
5. Small busin3esses can get tax credits to help purchase insurance.[12]

By 2014, additional measures were be put in place:

1. Employers with 50 or more workers not offering health insurance will be fined.
2. People without health insurance will have to purchase it at work or on their own or they will be fined.
3. States will need to set up insurance exchanges where people and employers can purchase health insurance that meets federal standards.[13]

There are many skeptics to the bill; there was no Republican support for the bill. The argument against the bill is that it will leave the nation with unaffordable levels of debt, give the states expensive new obligations, and give the government a huge new role in the health care system. By 2016 there were 23 million more people with health insurance. With the 2016 election, one of the promises was to repeal and replace the bill. Only time will tell what the new reforms will bring for the American people.[14]

Education

Education is another form of social welfare that state and local governments for the most part oversee. State government provides most support for local districts. The balance between local districts and states is different in each state. The federal government's role in education today is relatively low. States and communities develop curricula and determine requirements for enrollment and graduation. The structure of education finance in America reflects this predominant state and local role. Of an estimated $1.5 trilion being spent nationwide on education at all levels for school year 2012–2013, about 92 percent comes from state, local, and private sources.[15] In Hawaii most of the burden of paying for education comes from the state. In Texas the state provides funding based on local property taxes, which is inherently an unequal system. The current Texas system of school funding is under scrutiny by the districts that have to give back large sums of local money raised by the property taxes; this is called the Robin Hood plan.

Figure 12.3   Percentage of First-Time, Full-Time Undergraduate Students Awarded Grants and Loans at 4-year Degree-Granting Post-secondary Institutions, by Type of Financial Aid and Control of Institution: Academic Year 2014–2015.

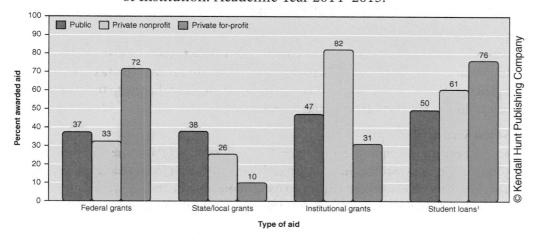

The federal government also provides low-interest loans to people who are attending college, and it also gives grants—gifts that the student does not need to pay back—to lower-income families. Figure 12.3 shows the distribution of how students received money in the 1999–2000 school years.

Social welfare policy has been a part of American life for many years. There are many programs that have been in existence for years that continue to evolve with the changing needs of the country. Social welfare policy needs to evolve so that the needy segment of our society, the poor and the elderly, do not live is substandard conditions.

ECONOMIC POLICY

Even though we have a free market economy, the federal government attempts to manage the economy in the country. The goal is to keep unemployment and inflation down and income on the rise. There are two ways the government controls the economy. The first is through **fiscal policy**, which is the government controlling taxing and spending. The second is through **monetary policy**, which is controlling the money supply and the interest rates. We will discuss both of these and the evolution of these measures.

FISCAL POLICY

As stated earlier fiscal policy is the taxing and spending authority of the federal government. In a time of big government, when the government is more involved in the investment of public programs, more money will be spent out of the federal budget. On average the federal government spends 34 percent of the gross domestic product.[16] The federal government receives money from collecting different types of taxes.

- **Individual Income Taxes**
  The federal government collects **income taxes** on a yearly basis. They are due by April 15 of every year for the past year's taxes. Taxes have gotten more complex due to the number of exemptions that people can take for certain items. Forty-six percent of the federal tax money comes from personal income taxes.

- **Corporate Income Taxes**

  Ten percent of the tax revenue comes from **corporate taxes**. These taxes are collected from large and small corporations on the income made by the company. The corporate tax rates range from 12%–35%. President Trump has continually called for a reduction of taxes on corporations and small businesses.

- **Excise Tax**

  Four percent of the federal revenue comes from **excise taxes** on items such as liquor, telephones, gasoline, tobacco, air travel, and other luxury items. This tax is sometimes called the "sin tax." The state also taxes many items such as tobacco, so they consumers pay a "double tax," of both state and federal taxes.

- **Social Security Receipts**

  Social Security receipts are the second largest source of income for the federal government. These are the monthly payroll deductions sent to the federal government. The lower-income workers end up paying more out of their paycheck for Social Security than higher-income workers. Therefore, it is called a **regressive tax**.

- **Duties and Tariffs**

  This is no longer a large source of income for the federal government, but it still collects a tax on people bringing items in from other countries.

FEDERAL SPENDING

The money that is raised is spent on many different programs, but a large percentage of the budget focuses on payment of benefits for entitlement programs such as Social Security. Entitlement programs are government programs that provide benefits to qualified citizens (Social Security, unemployment insurance). Fifteen percent goes to pay interest on the national debt, 15 percent goes to national defense, 15 percent goes to grants for states, 50 percent of the budget goes to Social Security payments (Medicare, Medicaid, etc.), and 5 percent goes to all other operations.[17]

The money that is set aside for Social Security and Medicare benefits is always growing automatically. With the cost-of-living increase and the cost of health care increasing, so do these payments. As the nation's population grows older those who have been paying into the system will begin to draw their retirement benefits. This part of the budget needs to be there for people as they grow older. Unless Congress and the president agree on changes to the system the payments will keep increasing.

Figure 12.4 Federal Government Spending.

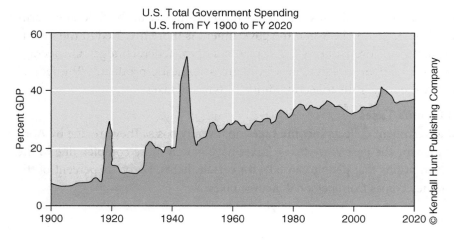

Figure 12.5   Federal Government Spending By Department.

Most Funds Paid Out by Agency—FY 2017		
Agency	**Funds Awarded**	**Number of Transactions**
Department of Health and Human Services	$706,321,190,510	135,667
Social Security Administration	$570,658,217,140	153,872
Department of Defense	$122,449,830,837	1,452,148
Department of Veterans Affairs	$112,249,445,773	667,434
Department of Education	$45,891,127,116	381,157
Department of Agriculture	$34,906,144,427	454,468
Department of Transportation	$29,385,800,663	130,018
Department of Housing and Urban Development	$26,261,350,899	102,435
Department of Energy	$16,887,918,324	12,313
Department of Homeland Security	$12,167,052,888	67,518
National Aeronautics and Space Administration	$11,677,362,665	28,900
U.S. Agency for International Development	$8,724,260,210	9,123
Department of State	$8,367,552,877	43,608
General Services Administration	$5,792,381,128	99,519
Department of Labor	$5,271,040,897	9,237
Department of the Interior	$4,358,405,470	50,168
Department of the Treasury	$4,149,050,155	14,268
Department of Justice	$4,125,261,812	80,740
Department of Commerce	$2,040,200,481	17,247
National Science Foundation	$2,031,893,849	10,169
Environmental Protection Agency	$1,233,645,971	10,969
Office of Personnel Management	$382,573,733	1,304
Small Business Administration	$312,315,288	100,852
Nuclear Regulatory Commission	$79,720,578	987
Railroad Retirement Board	$5,287,343,449	54,780
Export–Import Bank of the United States	$1,486,715,039	1,494
Overseas Private Investment Corporation	$950,506,938	222
Executive Office of the President	$216,203,787	1,590
Securities and Exchange Commission	$215,396,179	1,685
Broadcasting Board of Governors	$205,786,113	4,150

Continued

Most Funds Paid Out by Agency—FY 2017		
Agency	**Funds Awarded**	**Number of Transactions**
National Foundation on the Arts and the Humanities	$192,707,054	2,081
Corporation for National and Community Service	$133,014,505	1,419
Smithsonian Institution	$122,676,715	1,801
N/A	$118,140,642	604
National Archives and Records Administration	$72,488,534	762
Federal Communications Commission	$64,501,238	424
Consumer Financial Protection Bureau	$60,997,039	362
Commodity Futures Trading Commission	$35,582,566	433
Government Accountability Office	$33,150,321	624
Federal Trade Commission	$32,055,639	401
Gulf Coast Ecosystem Restoration Council (9533)	$26,448,207	10
Delta Regional Authority	$13,737,863	55
Consumer Product Safety Commission	$11,242,322	493
Denali Commission	$9,983,929	85
National Labor Relations Board	$9,358,018	207
Equal Employment Opportunity Commission	$7,707,061	296
Court Services and Offender Supervision Agency for the District of Columbia	$6,575,222	139
Federal Election Commission	$5,521,996	82
U.S. International Trade Commission	$3,147,156	109
National Transportation Safety Board	$2,749,395	144
National Credit Union Administration	$2,212,466	31
Pretrial Services Agency—CSOSA	$2,079,318	123
Federal Mine Safety and Health Review Commission	$1,851,092	147
Merit Systems Protection Board	$1,619,771	173
Federal Mediation and Conciliation Service	$1,397,598	41
The Council of the Inspectors General on Integrity And Efficiency	$935,975	49
Federal Labor Relations Authority	$457,098	15

Most Funds Paid Out by Agency—FY 2017		
Agency	Funds Awarded	Number of Transactions
Chemical Safety and Hazard Investigation Board	$368,075	52
Federal Maritime Commission	$285,964	38
Federal Housing Finance Agency	$225,000	1
Administrative Conference of the United States	$188,671	10
National Capital Planning Commission	$133,371	12
Defense Nuclear Facilities Safety Board	$116,823	30
Occupational Safety and Health Review Commission	$90,993	5
Library of Congress	$0	17
Selective Service System	$0	1

Source: https://www.usaspending.gov/Pages/TextView.aspx?data=AgenciesMostFundedBy
FiscalYear

Part of the budget that can change is defense spending. Many cuts have been made in this department since the end of the Cold War. However, since September 11, 2001, an increase in spending for defense occurred, and with the war against Iraq, there has been a further increase in spending.

THE BUDGET PROCESS

The **Office of Management and Budget** (OMB) located inside the Treasury Department of the executive branch is responsible for the creation of one budget that is sent to Congress. The Federal fiscal year is October 1–September 30, but the budget process begins long before then. The process will be explained below according to roles in the process.

Executive Branch Role

The office of the president prepares the budget for Congress to review. The Office of Management and Budget (OMB) is the workhorse behind the president. From February through December, departments and agencies within the government project their budget needs for example staffing, supplies, and office space. It is a detailed breakdown of the expected expenditures. After these reports are submitted to the OMB, the reports are taken and aligned with the president's vision for the country. Changes are made by the OMB based on the vision and the view of the entire budget. Throughout December this revision and alignment process takes place. The budget then is brought before a committee to justify the changes that were made.

The OMB director then delivers one document, comprising thousands of pages, to the president for approval. The president takes several days to review the document. The president then needs to submit to Congress the document and a statement about the vision for the country between the first Monday in January and the first Monday in February.

Legislative Branch Role

After the president submits the budget to Congress, the **Congressional Budget Office** (CBO), reports to the Senate and House budget committees are prepared by February 15. Congress has from March to September to determine the budget and approve spending and revenue bills. Remember that the Constitution states that Congress must appropriate funds and raise taxes. As Congress is reviewing the budget careful consideration is given to raising money in the form of new taxes, especially if the president will not support it, because the president can veto the budget, but Congress can override Presidential veto.

General Accounting Office Role

The *comptroller general*, who is appointed by the president with Senate approval to a fifteen-year term, heads the **General Accounting Office** (GAO). The GAO conducts audits of agencies and programs to ensure that money is being spent appropriately. The comptroller has the authority to approve spending and disapprove spending by agencies. The comptroller general from 1998–September 2010 was David M. Walker. He was appointed to the office in 1998 by President Clinton. The current comptroller general, appointed by President Obama, is Eugene Louis Dodaro.[18]

MONETARY POLICY

As stated in the beginning of the chapter, the second way the federal government can control the economy is by controlling monetary policy. The Federal Reserve's primary responsibility is controlling monetary policy.

The Federal Reserve

The Federal Reserve System's Open Market Committee determines monetary policy. They regulate interest rates on home mortgages and car loans. The president appoints the members of this committee, called the Board of Governors. In order to protect the members from the political wiles of the president and keep the body consistent, members serve fourteen-year terms. There are six members and a chairperson. The committee meets to discuss the buying and selling of securities, to regulate the twelve federal banks, and oversee foreign currency. The decisions they make determine interest rates and therefore impact all economic activity.

The president appoints the chairperson of the Board of Governors to a four-year term. The current chairperson is Janet Yellen. Dr. Yellen has been the chairman of the Federal Reserve since 2014. She appears before Congress four times a year to report on the state of the economy. At that time she indicates if interest rates will rise or fall, which has an automatic bearing on the stock market.

DEFICIT

Just as with your own budget, if you spend more than you bring in you are in a deficit with your money. The way the federal government determines its surplus is the difference between the revenues raised and the expenditures of the government. Since the 1980s the United States has had large annual budget **deficits**. The amount of money that the government has brought in from annual **revenues** has been less than the money it has spent, the **expenditures**.

Figure 12.6   Federal Reserve Structure and Functions.

Source: https://www.federalreserve.gov/aboutthefed/structure-federal-reserve-system.htm

In an attempt to reduce the deficit, the Gramm-Rudman-Hollings Act was passed in 1985. It created a gradual procedure for deficit reduction. The act sets a cap on the amount of money allowed in the deficit. If the deficit meets or exceeds that number then automatic cuts in spending are mandated. However, entitlement spending, the largest part of the budget, cannot be touched. These areas are Social Security, Medicare, veterans' benefits, student loans, and unemployment. People have paid into the various programs and have a right to reap what they have sown into the program. The cuts are made in other areas of the budget, such as defense.

DEBT

The **national debt** is estimated at about $14 trillion. The national debt is different from the deficit. The debt is the accumulation of all the budget deficits over the years.[19] The factors that have contributed to the nation's huge deficit are many—tax cuts without requiring spending cuts, health care costs rising for the elderly, and other unforeseen problems such as the money needed after September 11, 2001, to help get the economy going again. One way that the debt could be reduced is to require balanced budgets. Another way the debt could be reduced is by not allowing the Treasury Department to borrow any more money. However, when the government runs out of money it shuts down, which causes more problems. A third way that the debt could be reduced is by Congress printing more money. This is very problematic, however, and could cause large inflationary problems in the country.

The country needs to take a look at all the options and begin to dig out of debt before we dig ourselves into an even bigger hole.

TRADE POLICY

The first trade deficit was experienced in the United States in 1971. A **trade deficit** is when the value of the imports (items coming into the country) is greater than the value of the exports (items leaving the country).

Where one problem lies is that the United States is not producing enough goods to export to other countries. Another problem is that when goods are produced they may not be accepted by another country or such high taxes would need to be paid that it would not be worth it to trade the item. For example, the American car manufacturers are having a difficult time exporting them to Japan because of the unfair trade restrictions, specifying certain standards that are nearly impossible to meet. Counties are always looking for ways to benefit themselves and sometimes these trade barriers are developed to protect their market, not the consumer.

Barriers to Trade

America needs to balance free trade with protectionism. **Protectionism** is creating high tariffs on importing certain products, encouraging the selling of the product in another market. For example, if Americans begin buying more foreign computers than American-made computers, in order to protect the American computer companies, the government may increase tariffs on imported computers, therefore increasing their cost and reducing demand. However, in some cases, the increase in tariffs on goods here in America can also impact the American exports because countries may retaliate by increasing our tariffs on sales of our goods in their country. The protectionism policy needs to be used sparingly to reduce cases of retaliation by other countries.

GOVERNMENT REGULATIONS

The law of supply and demand, helping to regulate the American economy, is called a **competitive market economy**. Regulation of these markets is sometimes necessary by government. Regulation is the hand of government controlling the behavior of corporations and citizens. It helps to protect consumers against pollution, discrimination, or false advertising. The government can exercise its rights through the courts and through the use of its police powers.

Government uses two types of regulation. One is called **economic regulation**. This is when the government is controlling the behavior of businesses, mergers of businesses, the prices that are set by the companies, and the standards of service that the company provides. Some examples of regulated businesses are transportation and television. Today there are about eighty government regulation agencies. The Federal Communications Commission is an economic regulation agency.

A second type of government regulation is **social regulation**. This has to do with the concern for consumer and worker safety. Included in this area is also the regulation of discrimination in employment. The Equal Employment Opportunities Commission administers this. Another social regulatory agency is the Environmental Protection Agency (EPA). This agency is concerned with the harmful effects of a company's waste and emissions. The EPA ensures that companies pay fees for disposal of waste into the environment. The social regulation agency that is concerned with the health and safety of workers is the Occupational Safety and Health Administration (OSHA). This agency controls the safe practices for workers in many industries. OSHA's goal is to provide standards for safe practices that will reduce the number of injuries on the job.

The government has control over many areas of economic policy. The thought is that with their control at times and in certain areas the government can improve lives for all Americans. A large part of the federal government is dedicated to the social programs that Americans have become to depend on. One way that Americans can help to change economic policy that they feel is detrimental to the progress of the government is to be active and vote. The Congress and the president make most of the budget decisions. Make choices that you believe will benefit your area of the economy.

Online Connections

View these sites to find out more about Social Welfare and Economic Policy.

The Office of Management and Budget. *http://www.whitehouse.gov/omb*

This website is the national debt clock. It gives up-to-the-minute information on the national debt. *http://www.treasury.gov*

The Federal Reserve. *http://www.federalreserve.gov*

The Government Accounting Office. *http://www.gao.gov*

The United States Treasury. *http://www.ustreas.gov*

Department of Education. *http://www.ed.gov*

Social Security Administration. *http://www.ssa.gov*

Policy research. *http://www.policy.com*

Key Terms

Social welfare policy   157

Entitlement programs 157

New Deal programs   157

Civil Works Administration   158

Works Progress Administration   158

Social Security   158

Unemployment   159

Aid to Families with Dependent Children   159

Temporary Aid to Needy Families   160

Medicare   161

Medicaid   161

Fiscal policy   163

Monetary policy   163

Income taxes   163

Corporate taxes   164

Excise taxes   164

Regressive tax   164

Office of Management and Budget   167

Congressional Budget Office   168

General Accounting Office   168

Deficits   168

Revenues   168

Expenditures   168

National debt   169

Trade deficit   170

Protectionism   170

Competitive market economy   170

Economic regulation   170

Social regulation   170

Selected Readings

Gary C. Bryner, *Blue Skies, Green Politics: The Clean Air Act of 1990* (Washington, DC: CQ Press, 1993).

Marc Eisner, *Regulatory Politics in Transition* (Baltimore: John Hopkins University Press, 1993).

Joel Handler, *The Poverty of Welfare Reform* (New Haven, CT: Yale University Press, 1995).

Jonathan Harr, *A Civil Action* (New York: Random House, 1995).

Christopher Jenks, *Rethinking Social Policy: Race, Poverty, and the Underclass* (Cambridge, MA: Harvard University Press, 1992).

Paul Krugman, *The Age of Diminished Expectations* (New York: Cambridge University Press, 1984).

Charles Murray, *Losing Ground* (New York: Basic Books, 1984).

William Julius Wilson, *The Truly Disadvantaged* (Chicago: University of Chicago Press, 1987).

Notes

[1] Grolier, *The American Presidency Biographies* at http://gi.grolier.com/presidents/ea/bios/32proos.html

[2] Jeffery Cohen, *Politics and Economic Policy in the United States*, 2nd ed. (Boston: Houghton Mifflin, 2000), 49.

[3] Robert McElvaine, *The Great Depression: America 1929–1941* (New York: Times Books, 1984), 265.

[4] Grolier, *The American Presidency Biographies* at *http://gi.grolier.com/presidents/ea/bios/32proos.html*

[5] *Congress and the Nation, 1945–1964: A Review of Government and Politics I* (Washington: Congressional Quarterly Press, 1965) 1–13,625.

[6] Erik Eckholm "Solutions on Welfare: They All Cost Money," *New York Times*, July 26, 1992, p. 1FF.

[7] Fact Sheet on TANF, Department of Health and Human Services, September 2001 at *http://www.acf.hhs.gov/news/facts/tanf.html*

[8] U.S. Department of Health and Human Services, The Administration for Children and Families April 2001 at *http://www.acf.hhs.gov/news/stats/6090_ch2.htm*

[9] Julie Rovner, *Medical Malpractice 'Survivors' Protest Damage Caps, Reuters, Washington, February 11, 2003.*

[10] *http://www.time.com/time/politics/article/0,8599,1973989,00.html*

[11] *http://www.time.com/time/politics/article/0,8599,1973989,00.html*

[12] *http://www.nytimes.com/2010/03/22/health/policy/22health.html*

[13] *http://www.time.com/time/politics/article/0,8599,1973989,00.html*

[14] *http://www.nytimes.com/2010/03/22/health/policy/22health.html*

[15] U.S. Department of Education, The Federal Role in Education, at *http://www.ed.gov/offices/OUS/fedrole.html*

[16] Budget of the United States Government, Fiscal Year 2000 (Washington DC: Government Printing Office, 1999)

[17] Ibid.

[18] *www.gao.gov*

[19] *https://treasurydirect.gov/NP/debt/current*

1. Describe the impact of the New Deal programs on social welfare in America.

_____

_____

_____

_____

_____

2. Explain the purpose of the welfare reforms of 1996 and describe what changes have been implemented.

_____

_____

_____

_____

_____

3. Describe the budget process.

_____

_____

_____

_____

_____

4. Compare and contrast deficit and debt.

_____

_____

_____

_____

_____

Directions: Circle the correct answer to each of the following questions.

1. Which of the following is an example of a social welfare support?
   a. Education
   b. Economic support
   c. Health care support
   d. All of the above

2. Social welfare policy was started during the _____.
   a. 1920s
   b. 1930s
   c. 1940s
   d. 1950s

3. Under which president were the New Deal reforms created?
   a. Teddy Roosevelt
   b. John F. Kennedy
   c. Franklin D. Roosevelt
   d. Lyndon B. Johnson

4. Monetary policy is
   a. the government control of money and interest rates.
   b. the government control of inflation and interest.
   c. the government control of the economy.
   d. the government control of taxing and spending.

5. _____ percent of the federal government tax money comes from income taxes.
   a. Twenty-two
   b. Forty-eight
   c. Thirty-eight
   d. Fifty-eight

6. Which of the following is not true about the Works Progress Administration?
   a. Each worker was paid $55 a month to work.
   b. The workers were paid more than private-sector workers.
   c. The program reduced the number of unemployed people.
   d. One of the projects was to improve playgrounds.

Sample Test Questions

7. Social Security is _____.
   a. a security guard for all older Americans
   b. a payroll tax for all Americans
   c. car insurance for older Americans
   d. all of the above

8. When a worker is laid off from a job he or she can collect _____.
   a. social welfare
   b. Social Security
   c. payroll deductions
   d. unemployment

9. The education system in _____ is completely funded by the state.
   a. Texas
   b. Washington
   c. Minnesota
   d. Hawaii

10. Fiscal policy is _____.
    a. the government control of money and interest rates
    b. the government control of inflation and interest
    c. the government control of the economy
    d. the government control of taxing and spending

CHAPTER 13
Foreign and Military Policy

This chapter will focus on foreign policy, the evolution of the United Nations, the Cold War, and threats from the Middle Eastern countries. The foreign and military policies of the United States are very much a concern to other nations around the globe. U. S. Foreign policy makers focus attention on making sure resources are available to address terrorism and possession of weapons of mass destruction. Other important factors in the foreign policy are humanitarian issues, economic development, trade, and democratization. The United States may be the only superpower in the world, but we must remember there are rules we must follow to keep peace in the world. Some of the foreign policies by the United States have been failures, while other have been successful. Policy failure would include Vietnam, Soviet influence in Cuba, arms for hostages with Iran, and a weakened product market for American goods.

Despite our policy failures, we have had some successful policies including limitation of the nuclear arms race, the collapse of communism, easing tension with the People's Republic of China, and reducing the number of deaths due to starvation in Africa. In the eighteenth and nineteenth centuries foreign policies were used in creative ways to balance the power around the world. It would appear that the methods used were solid in stabilizing international relations by creating friendships to balance the power of one nation against another. The first goal of any foreign policy is to secure the homeland of the country. The United States has been fortunate that we have not had foreign armies on our soil since the War of 1812. Other nations cannot say the same due to the occupation of Germany, France, and the former Soviet Union in both the eighteenth and nineteenth centuries. U.S. foreign policies have been to deter war. We have been successful from the end of the Napoleonic War of 1815 until World War I in 1914. Today policy focus is on protecting our homeland. After the terrorist attack on America, September 11, 2001, homeland security became a major focus of the Bush administration. Finally, we must protect our electronic infrastructure to secure our economic stability in the world. Some of the latest types of attacks have been electronic, such as the possibility of Russia influencing the 2016 election.

THE EVOLUTION OF THE UNITED NATIONS

The world had become very unstable in the early 1900s. The Balkan nations called on the Allied Powers (England, France, Russia, and the United States) and just as these counties responded to the call, so did the Central Powers (Germany, Austria-Hungary, and Japan). The result of these powers coming against each other created one of the most destructive wars, killing at least 10 million between 1914 and 1918. The **balance of power** means to bring order to international relations by creating a system of friendship between nations where relative strength could balance that of the others. The balance of power would prove to be no longer successful. A new arrangement was implemented called *collective security*. **Collective security** means to bring all nations together to guarantee each other's territorial integrity and independence against external aggression. The forerunner of the United Nations was the League of Nations, established in 1919 under the Treaty of Versailles. Its purpose was to offer the same protection as collective security, but the United States refused to join because the Senate believed we would end up paying more than our fair share and engage in more conflicts than we would bargain for. President Franklin D. Roosevelt coined the name "United Nations." It was first used in the Declaration by United Nations of January 1, 1942, during World War II. The Axis powers were still in existence and twenty-six nations pledged their governments to continue fighting together against the Axis powers.[1] The United Nations Conference on International Organization met in 1945 to draw up the United Nations Charter and representatives of 50 countries were in attendance. The Charter of the United Nations was signed on June 26, 1945, in San Francisco, at the conclusion of the United Nations Conference on International Organization, and came into force on October 24, 1945.

These are established as the principal organs of the United Nations[2]:

- A General Assembly
- A Security Council
- An Economic and Social Council
- A Trusteeship Council
- An International Court of Justice
- A Secretariat

The General Assembly was created to handle any matters affecting world peace; the primary responsibility of the Security Council is to maintain international peace and security. No nation has a veto in the General Assembly, but every nation has one vote no matter its size or power. A majority vote can pass most resolutions.

WILL THE UN SURVIVE?

The role of the United Nations (UN) came into question by former President George W. Bush, over the use of force against Iraq. The president asked the UN for support to engage in battle to remove the leader of Iraq and eliminate weapons of mass destruction. The president asked the UN to "put up or shut up" and questioned the usefulness of the organization. The question of survival dates back to the end of the Cold War, 1991, which gave the UN new vigor. At this time the power struggle between the former Soviet Union and the United States was over, and Russia came to the UN as a cooperative force. The level of cooperation between the United States, Great Britain, France, Germany, and China helped move the world into a New World Order of international politics. The **New World Order** is a powerful and secret political movement aiming to place the world under a global totalitarian dictatorship called the New World Order or **One World Government**.[3]

The United Nations will survive, but it must have the United States on its side to do so. Without the United States the United Nations would decline quickly, given its huge bureaucratic operation in New York and the expense of its peacekeeping missions.

THE EVOLUTION OF THE COLD WAR

The **Cold War** was a political and military struggle between the United States and Soviet Union following the end of World War II and ending with the collapse of the Soviet Union's communist government in 1991. Nazi Germany posed a threat to the world, which caused the United States to join forces with the Soviet Union to stop the Nazi threat to the world. Stalin divided Germany into two parts—East and West. By 1948 he tried to remove the United States, France, and Britain with a blockade. Winston Churchill warned of the danger Stalin posed and called his division of Europe an *iron curtain*. President Harry S. Truman called for support of free people who are being pressured by armed minorities, which later became known as the Truman Doctrine. The **Truman Doctrine** was a pledge by the United States to support free people who are dissatisfied with pressure by minorities or by outside pressures.

CONTAINMENT

George Kennan, a diplomat and U.S. State Department adviser on Soviet affairs, introduced America's Policy of Containment in 1947. This policy had a few good points but many more bad points. Kennan's depiction of communism as a "malignant parasite" that had to be contained by all possible measures became the basis of the Truman Doctrine, Marshall Plan, and National Security Act in 1947. In his inaugural address of January 20, 1949, Truman made four points about his "program for peace and freedom": to support the UN, the European Recovery Program, the collective defense of the North Atlantic, and a "bold new program" for technical aid to poor nations. Because of his programs, "the future of mankind will be assured in a world of justice, harmony and peace." Containment was not just a policy. It was a way of life.

According to Kennan, the ultimate goal of U.S. foreign policy should not be the division of the world into Soviet and American spheres of influences. Rather, U.S. foreign policy should aid the establishment of independent centers of power in Europe and Asia and help encourage self-confidence in nations threatened by Soviet expansionism.

Containment was a strategy to oppose the expansion of Soviet Power, particularly in Western Europe and East Asia, with military power, economic assistance and political influence. The Soviet Union wanted to dominate Europe, and the only way to stop them was for the United States to use counterforce wherever the Soviet Union applied pressure.

MARSHALL PLAN

The **Marshall Plan** was a program to rebuild the nations of Western Europe in the aftermath of World War II in order to render them less susceptible to communist influence and takeover. In order for the policy of containment to be successful George C. Marshall indicated that the United States needed to rebuild the economies of Eastern European nations. Marshall reasoned that if the economy was strong then the European governments could resist the communist pressure (see Figure 13.1).

NORTH KOREA

In 1949, the Soviet Union aided the Chinese leader Mao Zedong in taking control of mainland China. When North Korean armies invaded South Korea in 1950 the *policy of containment* would be tested for the first time. The United States called on the Security Council to stop the invasion. The Soviets were upset with the Security Council for not making China a delegate and requesting that other nations send troops to stop the invasion. The problem the United States faced was a scaled-back military; President Truman decided to keep the American military in Europe. General Douglas MacArthur attacked behind Korean lines at Inchon and destroyed a large part of the Korean army. MacArthur struck with force and took the North Korean capital and moved toward China. The Chinese struck back in late 1950 with a million Chinese, inflicting many casualties, destroying entire units, and causing U.S. troops to back up. Truman decided to back off even though MacArthur urged Truman to retaliate, but the president wanted to keep the war small ending the Korean War in the bloody middle. MacArthur would be dismissed for speaking out against the president's decision. Did containment work? The war was settled with the election of Dwight Eisenhower—first with the threat of nuclear weapons and then the division of Korea along the original border lines. The United States lost many men, close to 40,000. Years later, the policy of containment was similarly used in the conflict in Vietnam.

THE VIETNAM WAR

The United States' involvement in the Vietnam War was incremental. The French were fighting the communist forces, the Vietminh Army. The United States provided aid to the French forces in 1950, in order to stop the spread of communism. At this time in America communism was viewed as anti-democracy, militarily aggressive, and a movement that needed to be stopped. The French, however, were not being successful in their war and pulled out of the war in 1954. It was at that point that President Eisenhower decided to

Figure 13.1 Marshall Plan Expenditures.

Economic Assistance, April 3, 1948 to June 30, 1952 (in millions)			
Country	Total	Grants	Loans
Total for all countries	$13,325.8	$11,820.7	$1,505.1
Austria	677.8	677.8	—
Belgium-Luxembourg	559.3	491.3	68.0[a]
Denmark	273.0	39.7	33.3
France	2,713.6	2,488.0	225.6
Germany, Federal Republic of	1,390.6	1,173.7	216.9[b]
Greece	706.7	706.7	—
Iceland	29.3	24.0	5.3
Ireland	147.5	19.3	128.2
Italy (including Trieste)	1,508.8	1,413.2	95.6
Netherlands (*East Indies)[c]	1,083.5	916.8	166.7
Norway	255.3	216.1	39.2
Portugal	51.2	15.1	36.1
Sweden	107.3	86.9	20.4
Turkey	225.1	140.1	85.0
United Kingdom	3,189.8	2,805.0	384.8
Regional	407.04[d]	407.0[d]	—

Source: George C. Marshall Foundation Statistics & Reports Division Agency for International Development November 17, 1975.

a. Loan total includes $65 million for Belgium and $3 million for Luxembourg: grant detail between the two countries cannot be identified.

b. Includes an original loan figure of $16.9 million, plus $200.0 million representing a pro-rated share of grants converted to loans under an agreement signed February 27, 1953.

c. Marshall Plan aid to the Netherlands East Indies (now Indonesia) was extended through the Netherlands prior to transfer of sovereignty on December 30, 1949. The aid totals for the Netherlands East Indies are as follows: Total $101.4 million, Grants $84.2 million, Loans $17.2 million.

d. Includes U.S. contribution to the European Payments Union (EPU) capital fund, $361.4 million; General Freight Account, $33.5 million; and European Technical Assistance Authorizations (multi-country or regional), $12.1 million.

intervene and train the South Vietnamese Army and send the Central Intelligence Agency in to begin gathering intelligence.

President Kennedy continued to send more troops to the war and at the time of his assassination in 1963, there were more than 16,000 U.S. military advisors and 400 special operations forces in Vietnam to train the South Vietnamese how to fight. By 1965

Figure 13.2   U.S. troop strength This graph shows the numbers of troops involved in the Vietnam war. As you can see the definitive troop surge that started in 1965 and increased to its highest levels in 1968.

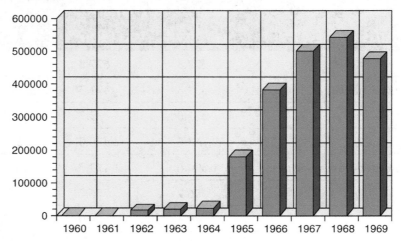

Source: The Vietnam War http://www.english.illinois.edu/maps/vietnam/timeline.htm

From http://www.historycentral.com/vietnam/troop.html. Copyright © by The Multimedia History Company. Reprinted by permission of Marc Schulman.

President Lyndon Johnson committed 3,000 forces to the area and ordered sustained bombing of targets in North Vietnam. Although the United States did not develop a successful war strategy for the Vietnam War, the war continued and troop levels continued to increase. President Johnson decided not to run for reelection in 1968 and Richard Nixon was elected president. During his administration he began to de-escalate the war and in 1972, troop levels were decreased by 70,000.

A cease-fire was signed in Paris in January of 1973. The impact of the war in the United States was multifaceted; the economic impact alone was estimated at $167 billion spent on the war. It also impacted the spirit of the American people. They became distrustful of government and very suspicious toward leaders in government. The human toll of the war effort was about 300,000 physically wounded, 2,387 listed as missing in action, and 58,000 who died in the war. As a result of the American feeling toward the war, the 2 million soldiers who returned home from the war were not welcomed home with parades; they were shunned.

NUCLEAR FREEZE

The idea of a nuclear freeze would not be an option for the United States, Britain, France and Germany. Instead the countries banned together to increase military buildup. President Jimmy Carter was in the forefront of defense spending. Congress would assist the executive branch in more than a decade in defense spending. While the United States had increased its spending, the Soviet Union was experiencing severe economic hardship and was not able to compete financially. President Ronald Reagan would continue to build our defense and increase spending in the area of technology. The focus was on conventional forces with additional attention given to ballistic missile defense systems. The Soviet Union would not be able to keep up with the United States and by 1985 Soviet President Mikhail Gorbachev would prepare the stage for his country to end to the Cold War. Gorbachev was instrumental in opening up the Soviet Union to decentralization in industry and less state control. The country was moving more toward a democratic system. One of the most significant contributions of the Gorbachev administration was his decision to not use the Soviet military to back communist governments in Eastern Europe.

REDUCING NUCLEAR WEAPONS

Once again, we the people of the United States of America are concerned about a possible nuclear attack. The two super powers of the cold war made the world secure and threatened the globe at the same time. The idea of nuclear weapons made the world more vulnerable, but it was the same idea that brought nations to the negotiating table.

During the Cold War period the United States reminded the Soviet of our second strike capability. The U.S. used **deterrence**, which was a way of deterring any nuclear attack from the Soviet Union by maintaining a second-strike capability. If the United States was hit by a surprise attack by our enemies we would fire back, destroying our enemies' nations. The second-strike capability is to survive an enemy attack and make an effective come back.

In the 1970s the idea of a nuclear attack was coming under strong opposition because of the destruction and retaliation it would cause. Given the capabilities of weaponry and destruction it would cause, nations realized they were being held hostage against a nuclear attack. Now that both superpowers had nuclear weapons and each could assure the other's destruction, the concept of **mutual assured destruction** (MAD) was coined. The only possible way for survival between nations was to engage in Strategic Arms Limitation Talks, better known as (SALT). This was the beginning of arms reduction talks. The **SALT I** treaty limited the number of antiballistic missiles (ABMs) and also placed caps on offensive missiles. This was step one in the arms reduction race. Step two would come in 1979 with SALT II. The agreement under the **SALT II** treaty was to limit the range of strategic nuclear launch vehicles. The limit would set long-range cruise missiles at 2,250 for each side on all intercontinental ballistic missiles (ICBMs) and submarine-launched ballistic missile (SLBMs). Additional talks would come when President Ronald Reagan moved from limited talks to reduction talks. President Reagan believed in Strategic Arms Reduction Talks (**START I**). The first treaty was signed in 1991 with then President George H. W. Bush in Moscow. This was the reduction in nuclear weapons. **START II** (January 1993) was most important because both President Bush and Russian President Boris Yeltsin agreed to eliminate first-strike capability on both sides. In 2016 President Obama led the Iran Nuclear Arms deal. Iran was placed under crippling economic sanctions as a result of the possibility of them producing a nuclear weapon. However, in 2016 the International Atomic Energy Association (IAEA) certified that the nuclear capacity has been limited. As a result Iran stands to gain access to more than $ 100 billion in assets frozen overseas, and will be able to resume selling oil on international markets and using the global financial system for trade. Inspections of the nuclear facilities will continue by the IAEA.

Figure 13.3   Post 911 image.

Source: U.S. Air Force photo by Gary Ell

OSAMA BIN LADEN

Osama bin Laden was the mastermind of the 9/11 terrorist attacks on America. In 1988 he started the organization of Al Qaeda. The mission of Al Qaeda was to support Islamic revolutions and protect against foreign intervention in the Middle East. The attacks of September 11, 2001, were by far the most coordinated and devastating of any of the Al Qaeda plots. On September 11, 2001, Al Qaeda operatives hijacked four planes. Two were flown into the World Trade Centers in New York, one into the Pentagon, and the fourth plane was crashed-landed into the countryside of Pennsylvania. The passengers onboard the hijacked plane heard about the other planes being flown into landmarks and they did not want the same result. They overtook the terrorists and crashed their plane. Nearly 3,000 people perished in the attacks combined.

After the attack on September 11, 2001, America used CIA operatives to search for Osama bin Laden. The Bush administration took a detour in trying to apprehend Osama bin Laden and focused their resources on an invasion of Iraq. As a result they captured Saddam Hussein. When President Obama entered office in 2008, the focus went back to the hunt for Osama bin Laden. It was not until April 2011 that the U.S. intelligence found his compound. Special forces were then sent into Pakistan under the command of President Obama to capture and kill bin Laden. Their mission was successful. Many in the country saw this as a way to bring closure to the 911 attacks.[4]

Terrorism

Terrorism is the use of violence to achieve political intimidation and instill fear. It is used as a means to achieve political, ideological, or religious goals. Terrorism can be government supported or not.

Terrorism has been in and out of the landscape of America and the world. The current wave of terrorism is largely based on religion, focused on advancing the Islamic beliefs and getting the United States out of the Middle East.

Combatting terrorism is very difficult due to the surprise attacks and the ability of groups to use methods that have never been used before.

Online Connections

View these sites to find out more about foreign and military policy.

Pentagon and Department of Defense. *http://www.defenselink.mil/pubs/pentagon*

The U.S. Air Force. *http://www.af.mil*

The Joint Chiefs of Staff. *http://www.dtic.mil*

National Center for policy analysis. *http://ncpa.org*

Key Terms

Balance of power   178

Collective security   178

New World Order   179

One World Government   179

Cold War   179

Truman Doctrine   179

Containment   180

Marshall Plan   180

Deterrence   183

Mutual Assured Destruction   183

SALT I   183

SALT II   183

START I   183

START II   183

Selected Readings

Stephen Ambrose, *Rise to Globalism*, rev. ed. (New York: Penguin Books, 1997).

Louis Fisher, *Presidential War Power* (Lawrence, KS: University of Kansas Press, 1995).

Robert S. McNamara, *In Retrospect: The Tragedy and Lessons of Vietnam* (New York: Times Books, 1995).

Kenneth Timmerman, *The Death Lobby: How the West Armed Iraq* (New York: Houghton Mifflin Co., 1992).

Notes

[1]Basic Facts About the United Nations 2000 (http://www.un.org/aboutun/index.html)

[2]Charter of the United Nations, 1945, chapter 3 article 7 (http://www.un.org/aboutun/charter/index.html)

[3]George C. Marshall Foundation (http://www.marshallfoundation.org/about_gcm/marshall_plan.htm#expenditures)

[4][S]Source: http://www.adl.org/terrorism_america/bin_l.asp

NAME_____ COURSE_____ SECTION_____

1. Describe the evolution of the United Nations.

_____

_____

_____

_____

_____

2. Explain the Marshall Plan.

_____

_____

_____

_____

_____

3. Describe the North Korean conflict.

_____

_____

_____

_____

_____

4. List the events in nuclear reduction.

_____

_____

_____

_____

_____

Directions: Circle the correct answer to each of the following questions.

1. The Truman Doctrine was a pledge made by the United States
_____.
   a. to support all nations
   b. to provide support to nations that are in financial trouble
   c. to provide support to nations being pressured by armed minorities
   d. all of the above

2. Containment was a strategy proposed by President Truman. Containment
is _____.
   a. a strategy to keep the United States as a world power
   b. a strategy to stop the Nazis from taking over in the world
   c. a strategy to stop the United Nations from becoming a world power
   d. a strategy to stop the Soviet Union from expanding

3. The Marshall Plan was _____.
   a. to arm the Eastern European countries with weapons
   b. to provide soldiers to protect Eastern European countries from occupation
   c. to assist in building new buildings for Eastern European countries
   d. to assist in the rebuilding of the economies in the Eastern European
   countries

4. Containment was tested for the first time in the _____ war.
   a. Vietnam
   b. Desert Storm
   c. Korean
   d. French-Indian

5. Which leaders brought a stop to the Cold War?
   a. Gorbachev and Carter
   b. Yeltsin and Reagan
   c. Yeltsin and Clinton
   d. Gorbachev and Reagan

6. The focus of the first Strategic Arms Limitation Talks (SALT I) was to
_____.
   a. limit antiballistic missiles and place caps on offensive missiles
   b. stop the production of all nuclear weapons
   c. limit cruise missile production
   d. all of the above

Sample Test Questions

189

7. The focus of SALT II was to _____.
   a. limit antiballistic missiles
   b. limit the range of strategic launch vehicles
   c. limit the number of people in each army
   d. all of the above

8. The law of supply and demand regulating the economy is called
   _____.
   a. a competitive market economy
   b. economic regulation
   c. social regulation
   d. all of the above

PART 2

A View of Texas Politics

CHAPTER 14

The Texas Constitution Yesterday and Today

© Junial Enterprises, 2013. Used under license from Shutterstock, Inc.

THE PURPOSE OF THE TEXAS CONSTITUTION

The constitution serves as a reminder that the country is made of laws not of people. From the evolution of the United States of America and the thirteen original colonies constitutions have set the framework as to how the government would operate. From 1789 to the present day the United States has followed a constitution. Our countrymen believed in a written charter ever since the Mayflower Compact or covenant. The covenant is in relationship to the religious life of the pilgrims. The idea of a written charter is not just likened to government, but also to businesses. Most of the corporations today operate under a charter. A constitution can be perceived as a legal document. On the other hand it can be seen as a complexity of ideas and a basis of political and governmental systems. The state of Texas also has a constitution serving as a reminder that our state is made of laws, not of people.

The constitution may appear to be a bunch of words on paper, but in reality they mean much more. The constitution is the basis of the law and provides for the general welfare of society, not for single rulers. Constitutions serve four purposes:

- Accommodate government with legitimacy.
- Create and organize government.
- Give government the necessary powers to operate.
- Restricts government.

LEGITIMACY

The Constitution of America is legitimate. If the document were not legitimate then it would be just a set of words as mentioned earlier. Since the people of the state of Texas value the constitution it is said to be legitimate. If the constitution is perceived as legitimate then the government is also seen in the same manner. The constitution is tied to the American creed and within the creed is democracy, therefore our constitution is a part of the democratic processes. Our government operates on the consent of the people, which means agreement as to opinion or a course of action. The approval of a constitution generally comes through a ratification process, which could create a problem if not all people had an opportunity to participate. A simple majority could control the outcome of an election, as did the Texas constitution of 1786, a document in good standing. The Texas constitution of 1876 is currently being followed today some one hundred years later. One thing to keep in mind is that those people who ratified the document are no longer alive. The constitution is still going strong and serving people who did not ratify it. The reason for it still serving people today is a concept called tacit consent. **Tacit consent** means implied by or inferred from actions or statements. For example, if the city passes a smoking ban in restaurants and you don't like it, but you do not leave the city, you tacitly consent to follow the law. Second if the people do like the law, changes can be made through constitutional amendments or constitutional conventions. The constitutional amendment allows people to change parts of the constitution they deem unacceptable. The constitutional convention allows people to rewrite the entire constitution to reflect the will of the people.

ESTABLISHMENT

The constitution of the state of Texas establishes and organizes the state government. The constitution established the state as the only legitimate government in the state. The people of the state of Texas have to answer only to one state government. The framework of the state is spelled out in the constitution, but structure and function is left up to the legislature to decide. This is known as ideal constitutions. Is the Texas constitution ideal? The Texas constitution is not as ideal as the U.S. Constitution given the functionality of a document that consists of 8,500 words and does not try to say what government can or cannot do. The Texas constitution, on the other hand, is just the opposite; it is lengthy and very specific as to what the state government can or cannot do. The constitution in Texas is so specific that we call it a statutory constitution. Whether a constitution is ideal or specific, it serves to establish and organize government.

POWER TO OPERATE

Social contract theory heavily influenced the Constitution of the United States and Texas. **Social contract theory** is a belief that people are free and equal by god-given right and that this, in turn, requires that all people give their consent to be governed—the work of John Locke. The constitution gives government the power to operate. The government of Texas has the rights of police powers and the power of taxation. The people of Texas understand they are engaged in a compact, which means there is a compact among the people. The state can enforce the laws to protect its people. Given the power to operate the government, the people turn to the state for protection. Before the concept of social contact theory, people in the state of Texas would have to defend themselves. For example, if you steal a car and the owner sees you prior to the social contract, the individual would be responsible for recovering their own car. Once the theory was in place the police would recover the car on the behalf of the owner. Hence a crime against one is a crime against the whole society. The social contract theory has proven effective, but it does not come without a price. The people of Texas will pay about 34 percent on a dollar to all levels of government, and 10 percent in Texas alone. Thirty-four percent of income going to government would make government the largest investment of a lifetime.

LIMITATIONS

In the histories of America and Texas a belief in limited government was imperative. Constitutions help by telling government what it cannot do. Both Texas and the United States have a Bill of Rights to limit government. The first ten amendments of the Constitution make up the Bill of Rights. The Bill of Rights in the U.S. Constitution came as a result of the Federalists arguing for ratification of the document and the Anti-federalist who were concerned over a lack of protection for the individual from the national government. Texans were just as concerned as the Anti-federalists and wanted to include a bill of rights in their constitution. The difference between the Texas and the U.S. Bill of Rights is that the national one provides minimum standards and the state provides maximums. The Texas constitution in article 1 calls for a bill of rights with thirty-one numbered sections. Below is an example of article 2.

> *Article 2—The Powers of Government*
> *Section 1—Division of Powers: Three Separate Departments; Exercise of Power Properly Attached to Other Departments*
> *The powers of the Government of the State of Texas shall be divided into three distinct departments, each of which shall be confined to a separate body of magistracy, to wit: Those which are Legislative to one, those which are Executive to another, and those which are Judicial to another; and no person, or collection of persons, being of one of these departments, shall exercise any power properly attached to either of the others, except in the instances herein expressly permitted.[1]*

There are seventeen articles in the Texas constitution explaining specifics about Texas state government.

Articles

1. Bill of Rights
2. The Powers of Government
3. Legislative Department
4. Executive Department
5. Judicial Department
6. Suffrage
7. Education
8. Taxation and Revenue
9. Counties
10. Railroads
11. Municipal Corporations

12. Private Corporations
13. Spanish and Mexican Land Titles (Repealed Aug. 5, 1969.)
14. Public Lands and Land Office
15. Impeachment
16. General Provisions
17. Mode of Amending the Constitution of This State[2]

TEXAS CONSTITUTION YESTERYEAR AND BEYOND

In the history of Texas there have been seven constitutions. The first Texas constitution was adopted in (1827); it recognized Texas when it was colonized by Anglo settlers under Stephen F. Austin as a Mexican state with Coahuila, its neighbor south of the Rio Grand (Constitution of Coahuila y Tejas). In 1821 Mexico declared its independence from Spain. Coahuila was a state within Mexico. Texas was a part of Coahuila, but prior to that it was a part of the Spanish Empire. In 1821 the new republic of Mexico adopted a constitution similar to that of the United States.

By 1836 Texas declared its independence from Mexico. In the constitution adopted during this time period the area was called the Republic of Texas. Texans adopted an ideal constitution that had a lasting effect on Texas government and politics. The constitution was specific in that it established the county as the basic unit of government. It also created three branches of government: the legislative, executive, and judicial functions of government.

The third constitution was written in 1845 when Texas was admitted back into the union. This constitution was regarded as the best one produced by the state. It was known as the Statehood Constitution. This was also an ideal constitution. A significance of this constitution is that it placed restrictions on the state's ability to incur indebtedness. Many scholars have called Texas the most democratic place on earth, given that Texas has the longest ballots in the country. The reason for such a long ballot is that Texas followed the Jacksonian democracy named after Andrew Jackson. This democracy consisted of two parts: (1) elect as many people as possible and (2) the spoils system. The citizens of Texas elect public servants to represent their interest, but because each officeholder is elected independently, Texas has a plural executive system of government. Judges are also elected in the state of Texas.

The second component Texas endorsed was the spoils system. The officeholders appointed people to work for them. Many of the people that made up the Texas bureaucracy were loyal to a particular party. Jobs were based on who you knew, not qualification or merit. Many people criticized the way people got their jobs in Texas. There was one major drawback to the spoils system and it was that individuals could be fired at will and replaced with a greater loyalist.

The constitution of 1845 also created the biennial session of the Texas state legislature. **Biennial** means that they meet once every two years. Finally, the 1845 constitution created a permanent school fund, where money would be distributed to schools. The creation of a permanent school fund was controversial in the origin and still is today. Next, the Homestead Act was created by the constitution. It stated that the only way a person's property could be taken is if they could no longer pay their taxes or had a lien on the property. Finally, the constitution created a community property provision similar to that of Mexican law. **Community property** is the notion that any property gained by one spouse during a marriage is equally the property of the other spouse.

Texans adopted the constitution of 1861 after the state seceded from the Union and joined the confederacy in 1861 (Civil War Constitution of 1861). The constitution of 1861 was very similar to the constitution of 1845. The difference between the constitutions of 1845 and 1861 was that Texas had membership in the confederacy. In addition, slavery was added to this constitution indicating Texas allowed it. Lastly, the constitution reflected the defeat of the south and the reentry into the United States. In order to be readmitted the state committed to three things:

- The abolition of slavery.
- The repudiation of secession from the union.
- The cancellation of debts and obligations incurred as a confederate state.

The 1866 constitution also gave Texas a line-item veto. This was especially important to the Texas governor. It allowed the governor to veto separate budget lines in any appropriations bill.

The constitution of 1869 was drafted to conform to the wishes of the Radical Reconstructionists.[3] This constitution contained many "modern" features such as annual legislative sessions, an appointed judiciary, and generous salaries for state officials. This was the constitution of E. J. Davis (Reconstruction Constitution of 1869).

Much of the 1866 constitution reflected the wishes of President Abraham Lincoln, particularly his view of the South. He wanted the southerners to return to their lifestyle; after all he had defeated the confederacy, abolished slavery, and restored the union.

After having achieved his measure of success Lincoln was assassinated in 1865. His assassination opened the presidency and Andrew Johnson moved up. He was a southern Democrat and became the first president to be impeached. He was not removed from office, but his presidency lost its power. The power he lost was replaced by a small segment of the Republican Party known as the Radical Republicans in their quest to punish the former confederate states because of the Civil War. It must be mentioned that the Radical Republicans were not alone in their behavior. The ex-confederates continued to talk about the south rising again and would not acknowledge their defeat. For example, the South segregated the school systems and blacks could not testify against whites, nor could a black policeman arrest a white person in the latter years.

It would not be appropriate to say the constitution of 1869 was wonderful, but it would be fair to say it was much different than the 1845 constitution. The Jacksonian democracy was reduced under this constitution, calling for the attorney general and state judges to be appointed. The Davis administration came to power under this constitution. Governor Edmund J. Davis used provisions in the constitution to his advantage. He was given full power over the Texas electorate. He could appoint governing bodies over towns and cities. Both the state police and militia were under his control. The **militia** is a voluntary force to protect the homeland. He was given the authority to declare martial law on districts he thought deserved it. The state police became his personal tools to be used as he pleased. His administration was so corrupt he would even ask his police to threaten any Texan who spoke out against him. Last, the constitution of 1869 did not have full consent of the people in the state, which questioned the legitimacy of the document.

The constitution of 1876 is our seventh and most current. It was adopted at the end of Reconstruction while Texas was still a rural frontier state. Amended many times more than any of the previous constitutions, it is a highly restrictive and antigovernmental document drafted by Texans reacting to the abuses of the reconstructionists' policies and the oppressive administration of Governor Davis. Tight restrictions were placed on the governorship, the legislature, and other state officials, which today inhibit the ability of the state government to respond to the complex needs of what is now a growing urban state.

Online Connections

Check out this website to learn more about the Texas constitution.

The site gives information with a link to the Texas constitution online. *http://www.texas-online.com*

Key Terms

Tacit consent   194

Social contract theory   194

Biennial   196

Community property   196

Militia   197

Suggested Readings

Harold H. Bruff, "Separation of Powers Under the Texas Constitution." *Texas Law Review* 68 (June 1990): 1337–1367.

Charles F. Cnudde and Robert E. Crew Jr., *Constitution Democracy in Texas* (St. Paul: West Publishers, 1989).

Donald S. Lutz, "The Texas Constitution." In *Perspectives on American and Texas Politics: A Collection of Essays* (Dubuque, IA: Kendall Hunt, 1987), pp. 193–211.

Seth Shepard McKay, *Seven Decades of the Texas Constitution of 1876* (Lubbock: Texas Technical College, 1943).

Lawrence Miller, "The Texas Constitution." In *Texas Politics Reader*, Anthony Champagne and Edward Harpham, eds. (New York: Norton, 1997), pp. 16–31.

Notes

[1]Texas State Constitution, article 1, section 2 (*http://www.capitol.state.tx.us/txconst/toc.html*)

[2]Texas State Constitution, article 1 (*http://www.capitol.state.tx.us/txconst/toc.html*)

[3]Braden, *Citizen's Guide,* 13–14; Seth McKay, *Seven Decades of the Texas Constitution of 1876.*

NAME_____ COURSE_____ SECTION_____

1. Explain the purpose of the Texas constitution.

_____

_____

_____

_____

2. Explain the limitations of the Texas constitution.

_____

_____

_____

_____

_____

3. Describe the history behind the first three Texas constitutions.

_____

_____

_____

_____

4. Explain the history behind the sixth change and the final Texas constitution change.

_____

_____

_____

_____

_____

Directions: Write the word or phrase that completes the statement.

1. The Texas constitution is a _____ constitution because it is so _____.

2. _____ is the belief that people are free and equal and that this requires that all people give their consent to be governed.

3. The first _____ amendments to the U.S. Constitution make up the Bill of Rights.

4. The first Texas constitution was drafted in _____.

Directions: Circle the correct answer to each of the following questions.

5. The U.S. Constitution provides _____ and the Texas constitution provides _____.
    a. minimum, maximum
    b. specifics, generalizations
    c. maximum, minimum
    d. generalizations, specifics

6. In the history of Texas there have been _____ constitutions.
    a. three
    b. seven
    c. five
    d. nine

7. The government of Texas has the right to _____.
    a. taxation
    b. police powers
    c. full military powers
    d. both a and c

8. The third Texas constitution brought about _____ for the state of Texas.
    a. statehood
    b. Mexican statehood
    c. independence from Mexico
    d. none of the above

Sample Test Questions

CHAPTER 15
Why Texas Politics?

© 2013 by Brandon Seidel. Used under license of Shutterstock, Inc.

UNDERSTANDING GOVERNMENT AND POLITICS IN TEXAS

Texas is a very special state. It has a history of individualism, moralism, and traditionalism. Given the strong characteristics of Texas, why are we studying it? The truth does not lie in the fact you are excited about the subject. The real reason is that the Texas state legislature requires each student to complete six semester hours of government or political science as a requirement to graduate. Does this sound fair to the student? Who decided to make this law? What was the purpose? The forty-first legislature in 1929 decided to pass a bill for sixth and seventh grades to study history and civics. If you were a high school or college student your options were different. These students were required to study the U.S. Constitution of 1789 and the Texas Constitution of 1876. Once these courses are taken the requirements for graduation are met. In addition to the legislatures' goal of political awareness, it is important to know your political sense will increase whenever you secure a career, have a family, get a home, and settle into a community.

The purpose of this chapter is to allow you the opportunity to understand and examine politics and government in Texas. Once you have developed a framework of the subject you will be able to articulate beyond the general barbershop politics. Without the proper knowledge of the subject your ability to comprehend will always be compromised.

TEXAS POLITICS AND GOVERNMENT

Many times we hear the words politics and government. Sometimes people assume the words are the same, but they are not. **Politics** is the art or science of government or governing, especially the governing of a political entity, such as a nation, and the administration and control of its internal and external affairs. It is also an authoritative allocation of resources.[1] In every society there are goods and services that people want and politics involves itself in the distribution of the things people value. For example, when the Boeing Corporation decided to relocate to Dallas or Chicago the executives of the company utilized politics at work. The politics were not government politics, but private politics. The Dallas mayor and the mayor of Chicago had politic dealings with company executives, using the resources of government. Government makes most of the allocation decisions about what is valued in society, although government does not make some decisions. **Government** is the act or process of governing, especially the control and administration of public policy in a political unit.

Public policy is any government decision. Governments consist of institutions such as the legislature, courts, and executive agencies that make those decisions. When the legislature makes a law requiring a cell phone user in an automobile to have a hands-free set, the legislature is making public policy. Once the law is passed and bureaucracies implement the law, which is also making public policy. We are now entering into processes, which include the way these decisions are made as well as the procedures whereby you and other Texans can influence those decisions. By now you should understand that politics and government are two different concepts.

IDEAS IN AMERICA AND TEXAS

America has held onto five basic ideas that have been rooted in the fabric of the country. These ideas are individualism, liberty, equality, constitutionalism, and democracy. These five ideas have received strong support from Americans since the late eighteenth or early nineteenth century and make up the *American creed*.[2] Although there were other ideas, none has received more support than the five mentioned. The reason is that they have consistently performed important functions for America. These ideas came with the Texas pioneers. These ideas are multipurpose; they serve as a national identity, limiting government authority and can be used to understand politics, government, and political change. When we discuss the ideas of individualism, liberty, and equality we are describing politics, and the other two, democracy and constitutionalism are used to examine government.

THREE IDEAS RELEVANT TO POLITICAL ANALYSIS

Individualism

The ideas of liberty and equality would not survive without its source—individualism. Individualism is the most important of the values for both Texans and Americans. From the evolution of American Government the idea of self-worth was very important. Individualism is a part of the American creed supporting the worth of human beings regardless of social status or income. The pursuit of life, liberty and property free from government intervention supports individualism as a political value. The idea means no authority over the individual's absolute freedom. However, we must understand limitations in order for society to survive. The individual is more valuable than the group or community. How do we know the intensity of individualism in Texas? The state decided to allow each individual the right to join a labor union if they wanted to by passing an open shop law. A high priority is placed on the individual.

Liberty

In Texas people are allowed to make their own choices whether good or bad and as often as possible. Unlike individualism that calls for complete freedom, liberty allows for interference in order to maintain control. There must be some restrictions in order for society to survive. If the protection goes beyond a certain point many will argue it is necessary to maintain traditional social values.

Equality

Equality has become the most problematic of the American creed, for both Texans and Americans. Why have such problems over equality? Equality to one person does not mean the same to another. To one person equality may mean **political equality**, which means each person's vote should count equally or the concept of one person, one vote. Political equality has been expanded in both the nineteenth and twentieth centuries to minorities and women. Others want economic equality, which means each person should have approximately the same wealth. Neither Americans nor Texans believe in this form of equality; they believe in the **equality of opportunity**, which means the elimination of artificial barriers to success in life and the opportunity for every one to strive for success. This does not guarantee the end result. Different people view government action in promoting ideas based on their relative importance of the idea.

Democracy

The idea of democracy comes from the ancient city-states of the Greeks. **Democracy** means the people rule. Democracy has a history of both stability and instability. Other problems facing democracy is its numerous forms, which are not all consistent with the principles of democracy. How will we determine what makes for a decent democracy? In Texas it is the right of all people to participate in governmental decisions and see that the people are treated equally. If democracy is to be respected it must meet certain conditions.

CONDITIONS OF DEMOCRACY

If a democracy is to be respected government institutions must meet four conditions: *political equality, participation, nontyranny,* and *deliberation* according to Samuel P. Huntington. These are conditions of democracy.[3]

- **Political equality** means no matter what my preference as a citizen, it is counted equally. In essence it amounts to one person, one vote. For example, each person's vote for a public office holder or bond package must be counted the same. If a country violates this principle then it would not be considered democratic.
- **Participation** means at least a majority of participants are engaged in the political process. When we discuss participation it means those who vote in elections and those

who protest in social movements. A true democracy will allow for various forms and allow its people to use them to bring about change to policies and procedures.

- **Nontyranny** means the fundamental rights of the citizens will not be infringed upon by governmental policy. In Texas, for example, the freedom of religion is a fundamental right to all citizens of the state. In order for democracy to be fair, all Texans must be afforded the right, no matter their ethnicity, income, or religion. There is no place for tyranny by majorities or minorities under this system and institutions of government must prevent it from occurring. A compact or constitution must be in place to prevent such acts.
- **Deliberation** means citizens have the ability to talk about issues or candidates and make certain all alternatives have been put forth before reaching a decision. Before electing someone for public office or voting on an issue, it should be discussed fully before making a decision.

FORMS OF DEMOCRACY: CLASSICAL, MAJORITARIANISM, AND PLURALIST

To meet all four conditions in a democracy would be ideal, but usually it is not reality. To have political equality, nontyranny, participation, and deliberation all working without compromise would be great. Given the nature of democracy that ideal is a utopia and compromise will occur; there will be trade-off so the most reliable condition of the moment can be used. Prior to each presidential election there is a primary election that promotes political equality and participation to all eligible voters. This process expands participation tremendously and counts each person's vote equally, but it does not allow for lengthy discussion at times, which citizen and candidates have criticized. The goal has always been to create a forum to achieve better conditions.[4]

Classical Democracy

The most important component of **classical democracy** is the individual. Before decisions are made, he individual must be given an opportunity to participate, because the decision will affect the individual. When the individual is valued and a commitment toward a political system is in place, then participation is valued as well. The system of democracy must not exclude anyone from participating no matter what background, social status, or income. Texas is considered a large state consisting of some 20 million people making participation all but impossible if working under direct democracy. The classical model supports the individual, but given the population of Texas or any large city this would be impossible. Two other forms of democracy may serve the people better: majoritarian democracy and pluralist democracy.

Majoritarian Democracy

Majoritarian means majority rule as a form of democracy. When you ask a person about forms of democracy they tend to most often think of majority rule. The reason for this is because people think of government as consent, therefore realizing any policy made will include the citizens. If policy is made by elected officials or a direct vote, the decision will come with the respect of the majority of the people. The majority is not always correct, so we must consider minority rights; if not, majoritarian democracy would pose a major problem. The idea of slavery is a good example. Suppose the majority called for a new form of slavery? Should the policy be considered since the majority requested such a policy? Political equality is a fundamental value and is supported by a majoritarian democracy. One person, one vote, everyone is counted equally, and it does not matter what race, income, how famous or lack of fame, educated or ignorant, well-known or unknown. It is this type of commitment that does not allow the majority to take away the rights of the minority.

If minorities choose to influence the majority that is a fundamental right, given the notion of political equality; but it does not support the majority trying to stop the rights of minorities. A **majoritarian democracy** must support a single leader such as the president. The president represents the broadest constituency and can bring political unity over issues surrounding the interest of majority minority rights.

Pluralist Democracy

The United States of America is very diverse. Because majoritarian democracy places such emphasis on representative government and minority rights, it sometimes appears excessive. The pluralist approach is to divide the power among many. The interest of the minority and the majority are protected. The key component is dividing power among the various levels of government. The purpose of dividing the political process is it affords citizens the opportunity to appeal to city, state, or national government. In Texas citizens have a bill of rights just like the U.S. Constitution; but the state sets the ceiling on rights and the national government sets the floor. The power in Texas is divided between different levels of government and representatives are elected to represent the citizens. The problem in Texas and other parts of the country is the elitist who challenges any form of democracy we accept.

ELITIST CHALLENGE

Who is in charge of government? According to Glynn Newman, the majority elects a representative to look after the interest of the city, state, or nation. However, in Texas and the nation, we have a small number of people who control the decisions that are being made. This is what the political scientist calls the elitist challenge. The elite are those who participate in the political process economically. If you were to run for public office, many times it is the elite who finance the campaign and therefore gain political influence through contributions. Masses can contribute by voting for a candidate, but if the person running for office cannot afford to run then the masses would have no one to vote for.

Online Connections

View these sites to find out more about Texas politics and government.

To find more information on Texas politics and government check out this website. *http://www.lonestarreport.org*

Texas Media Watch is a nonpartisan, independent media-monitoring project published in San Antonio. *http://www.texasmediawatchcom*

Texas online. *http://www.state.tx.us*

Key Terms

Suggested Readings

William Dornhoff, *The Power Elite and the State: How Policy Is Made In America* (New York: Aldine de Gruyter, 1990).

James S. Fishkin, *Democracy in the Fifty States* (Lincoln, NE: University of Nebraska Press, 1994).

Samuel P. Huntington, *American Politics: The Promise of Disharmony* (Cambridge, MA: Harvard University Press, 1981).

Daniel Yankelovich, *Coming to Public Judgment: Making Democracy Work in a Computer World* (New York: Syracuse University Press, 1991).

Notes

[1]David Easton, *A Framework for Political Analysis* (Englewood Cliffs, NJ: Prentice Hall, 1965), p. 50.

[2]Samuel P. Huntington, American Politics: *The Promise of Disharmony* (Cambridge, MA: Harvard University Press, 1981).

[3]Ibid., p. 10.

[4]Nelson W. Polsby, *The Consequences of Party Reform* (New York: Oxford University Press, 1983), pp. 8–9.

1. Compare and contrast politics and government and give an example of each.

_____

_____

_____

_____

_____

2. List and explain the conditions of democracy.

_____

_____

_____

_____

_____

3. Explain the difference between minority rights and majority rights.

_____

_____

_____

_____

_____

4. Which system works best for Texas—a majoritarian democracy or a pluralist democracy? Explain why you think it works best.

_____

_____

_____

_____

_____

Directions: Write the word or phrase that completes the statement.

1. The Texas legislature requires each student to complete_____ hours of government or political science to graduate.

2. _____ is the art or science of government.

3. _____ is any government decision.

4. _____ is the act or process of governing.

Directions: Circle the correct answer to each of the following questions.

5. The most important value to Americans and Texans alike is _____.
   a. liberty
   b. individualism
   c. equality
   d. democracy

6. People are allowed to make their own choices. There must be some interference from government to keep order in society. What value are these statements describing?
   a. Liberty
   b. Individualism
   c. Equality
   d. Democracy

7. _____ is when there is no authority over individual freedom.
   a. Liberty.
   b. Individualism.
   c. Equality.
   d. Democracy.

8. The right of all people to participate in governmental decisions is _____.
   a. liberty
   b. individualism
   c. equality
   d. democracy

Sample Test Questions

211

CHAPTER 16

Local Government: Texas Cities, Counties, and Special Districts

© 2013 by spirit of america. Used under license of Shutterstock, Inc.

LOCAL GOVERNMENTS IN TEXAS

Local governments in Texas are created by the state and follow the state constitution and the legislature. When we discuss local governments, we are including counties, cities, school districts, and cities. Most of these entities have found themselves struggling, given the demands placed on them by the citizens in their communities and the growing urban state. Another perspective is that the state government initiated local government to meet certain demands or improvement but did not provide them with any funding. The local governments must comply and pay for the improvements. The state of Texas has faced its own share of problems, particularly in the 1990s when the state requested that counties expand their jail facilities, but provided no money for improvements. The results were that local governments had to spend millions of taxpayers' dollars to meet the demands placed on them by the state. The K–12 system has also received orders from the state to improve the standards in the classroom, but they have not received any funding, which has caused the local property taxpayers to foot the bill. Local government is where the action takes place and is closest to home. No matter how we slice or dice the responsibilities, the burden of problem solving lies with the cities, not in Washington or Austin.

The local government is very important to the state because it can carry out many of the state's responsibilities. The Dillon rule is what allows states to have authority over local governments. It explains the relationship or theory of states and local government. The state of Texas granted cities' home rule status in 1912. Home rule allows cities to have authority over decisions and policies. The county could also have home rule status as of 1933, but no county ever exercised its right and by 1969 the amendment was repealed. Texas, like other states, has divided levels of responsibilities between governments. For example, local school districts are responsible for providing public education, leaving the roads, public welfare, and public health at the state level. The collection of garbage, recreation, libraries, and sanitation are responsibilities of cities. The counties share in the responsibilities of jails and courts.

TYPES OF CITIES

The image of Texas is no longer one of cowboys and cattle; instead, it is urban and consists of many ethnicities. It would be fair to mention that some parts of Texas are still rural. The diversity of the state is surprising to many visitors. When visitors arrive in Dallas the first thing they notice is the well-kept state-of-the-art international airport. If they travel by automobile from Houston to San Antonio they will see the diversity in our terrain and notice our exceptional universities and world-class sports facilities, highlighting our urban centers. In addition to the fabulous restaurants and hotels, the city of Austin is home to the state capitol and recognized by technology industry as silicon prairie.[1]

Looking back at Texas in the late 1800s it was a state that was very rural and agrarian. Fewer people called the city their home. According to census data, Galveston was the largest city followed by San Antonio and Dallas.[2] The population of Galveston was 22,248 on the high side and 10,358 was the population of Dallas in 1880. The urban dwellers have continued to populate the cities. The city of San Antonio is the second largest city in Texas, replacing Dallas with 1.3 million according to census data.

Table 16.1 Illustrates the number of governments from the National level to the local level.

Figure 16.1 shows the 10 largest Texas Cities.

Table 16.1 Governments in the United States and Texas (2012).

	United States	Texas
U.S. government	1	
State government	50	1
Counties	3,031	254
Municipalities	19,522	1,214
Townships and towns	16,364	N/A
School districts	12,884	1,079
Special districts	37,203	2,309
Total	89,004	4,856

Source: U.S. Department of Commerce, Bureau of the Census.[3]

Figure 16.1   Largest Ten Texas Cities (2013).

Texas City	Population
1. Houston	2,099,451
2. San Antonio	1,327,407
3. Dallas	1,197,816
4. Austin	790,390
5. Fort Worth	741,206
6. El Paso	649,121
7. Arlington	365,438
8. Corpus Christi	305,215
9. Plano	261,350
10. Laredo	236,091

Source: http://www.txdirectory.com/online/city/?top=true

Figure 16.2 shows predictions of where the population growth will be in Texas. The place with the greatest expected growth by 2020 is the Laredo area and the second-most growth area is McAllen. Both of these areas are border regions.

The Texas constitution of 1876 provides for two types of cities that can exist in the state. The first is known as a **general law city**, which means a city is only allowed to exercise those powers specifically granted to it by the legislature. General law cities have fewer than 5,000 residents. Under a general law charter a city has numerous restrictions.[4]

Figure 16.2   Texas Metropolitan Area population growth forecast (2000–2020).

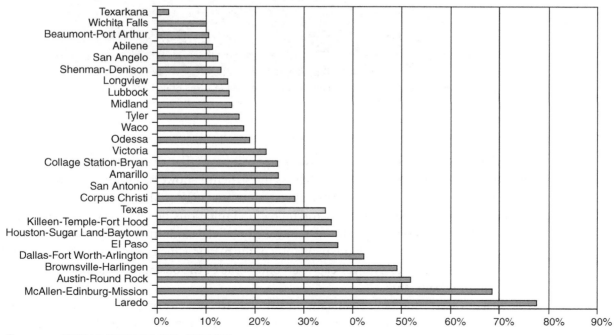

Source: TEXAS STATE DATA CENTER.

The second is known as a **home rule city**, which means a city has a population of 5,000 or more, and can adopt any form of government residents choose, provided it does not conflict with the state's constitution or statutes. The home rule city includes all its citizens. The citizens adopt a formal charter. The charter is the city's constitution creating the city's governing body, organizing the agencies and municipal courts, its taxing authority, and procedures for holding elections, annexing additional territory, and revising the charter.

FORMS OF CITY GOVERNMENTS IN TEXAS

In Texas there have been three different types of governments. The first was mayor council, followed by council-manager, and the commission. Today we have over 1,100 municipal governments in Texas and over 800 which are mayor-council form and 287 of which had council manager governments according to the 1990 census.

Mayor-Council

In the origin of local government the idea of a *mayor-council* form was taken from the English government. The goal was to allow the legislative function of the city to be vested in a council and a mayor would be assigned the executive functions. The fact that this model created a division in government shows it supports a separation of powers just as the state and federal governments. The mayor is elected by the people of the city and is the chief elected officer. There are two types of mayoral systems, the **weak mayor** and the **strong mayor**; the majority of Texas cities supports a weak mayor. All of the top ten cities above have a weak mayor system.[5]

Galveston, Texas Storm, reprinted by permission of the Texas State Library and Archives Commission.[6]

What determines the type of mayor a city will have? The city charter is a document, based on state authorization, which defines the structure, powers, and the responsibilities of a city government. The charter places restraints on a mayor. Many times the mayor has no authority over policy. Some of the following limitations on the mayor are that they do not have the power to appoint or remove city officials, minimal budget authority and other city officials are elected independently of the mayor, which results in a plural executive system. Sometimes a mayor can overcome some of the obstacles mentioned by using charisma and leadership.

Real power is vested in a strong mayor who can appoint city officials and remove them. If a mayor decides to appoint someone it will require the approval of the city council even though the official serves at the pleasure of the mayor. The strong mayor system divides the executive and legislative functions. El Paso and Houston are two cities in Texas that have adopted a strong mayor system, although this form is found primarily in larger cities. The strong mayor system has not been the most popular system because of its association with urban political machines, ward politics and political corruption. The fasting growing cities in Texas are weak mayor cities.

City Commission

The commission form of government in Texas can be traced back to Galveston, Texas, in the early 1900s. This form of government reflects reform, administration efficiency, and reduced partisan conflict and created a business environment to run the city government. In 1900 the great Galveston hurricane killed 8,000 people with a 15-foot storm surge, a barometer reading of 27.49 inches, and winds of 110 miles per hour; this was before the wall was built. Half of Galveston was destroyed with 2,600 buildings destroyed and 10,000 people left homeless. It is said that a one-inch-thick steel hull of an ocean-going freighter was pierced through with a piece of lumber.

After such a devastating natural disaster the city of Galveston was incapable of handling the catastrophe. The result was that a group of concerned citizens appealed to the Texas State Legislature to devise a more responsive government. The combining of city administrative and legislative functions into one office was the first step. Thus the city commission was formed. City commission is a form of government in which elected commissioners collectively serve a city's policy-making body and individually serve as administrative heads of different city departments. Other major cities in Texas would soon adopt this model, including Dallas, Houston, and San Antonio. The popularity of the commission form would not last very long with the development of the council-manager form of government. Even though there are current not any cities in Texas using a commission form of government, it is worth mentioning due to the impact it has had on Texas local governments. Houston, Dallas, and San Antonio have switched to council-manager governments. The commissioners are not administrators but instead are policy makers. The commission generally hires professional managers to run daily operations of the city.

Council-Manager

The **council-manager** form of government means policy is set by an elected city council, which hires a professional city manager to head the daily administration of the city government. This form of government became very popular both in Texas and nationally. The birth of the council-manager came from the commission. In 1913 the council-manager form of government was adopted by both the city of Terrell and Amarillo. Following the adoption by those cities other home rule cities opened up to this form of government. In this type of government there is a professional city manager; policy and administration are separate, and nonpartisan city elections are held. The mayor may be a figurehead who is selected by the council to represent the city at council meetings. Other cities elect their mayor citywide which gives the office more power than power vested in the office by a council. When the mayor is elected citywide there are a few powers like the ability to vote with the council, be a figurehead in the city, and promote ideas or create programs. Dallas mayor Ron Kirk was a prime example of excellent leadership; he was known as a history-making mayor being the first African American to hold a mayoral position. Ron Kirk was responsible for balancing the city's budget, which is a part of the Dallas city charter. The primary responsibilities of the city council is to set public policy, organize city departments, approve the city budget, enact city ordinances, set the tax rate, approve issuances of bonds, and investigate operations and ordinances of city agencies.

The council has the authority to hire a city manager, a professional who generally holds a degree in public administration. The job of city manager is to oversee the day-to-day operations of the city government. Other responsibilities include turning public policy into working applications, hiring assistant managers, creating the city budget and long-range planning. The council-manager government prides itself on professionalism. The best city managers tend to have excellent financial skills. A city manager's career tends to be three to five years long with an average salary of $183,000. The Dallas city manager in 2016 earned $400,000 and in a smaller city such as Mesquite the manager earned $166,354.

© 2013 by Khakimullin Aleksandr. Used under license of Shutterstock, Inc.

COUNTY GOVERNMENT IN TEXAS

The county is an administrative subunit of the state; its intial purpose was to serve the rural population. There are 3,066 counties in the United States. Counties vary greatly in size and population. They range in area from sixty-seven square kilometers (Arlington County, Va.) to 227,559 square kilometers (North Slope Borough, Alaska). The population of counties varies from Loving County, Texas, with 140 residents to Los Angeles County, California, which is home to 9.2 million people. Forty-eight of the fifty states have operational county governments. Connecticut and Rhode Island are divided into geographic regions called counties, but they do not have functioning governments. Alaska calls its counties boroughs and Louisiana calls them parishes. Above is a list of the largest counties by population.

In Texas there are 254 counties, more than any another state. A county has very few implied powers most of its authority comes from the state. The state wanted the counties to administer state law as a primary function. Legislation is not enacted in a county as in home-rule cities. The responsibilities are local in nature but are connected to the state, such as the collection of state taxes, enforcing state laws, and regulations. Counties are involved in the state's welfare programs and road programs. Each county serves different needs of the community, but must follow the basic principles of the state's constitution.

Table 16.2 provides details on the largest counties in the United States. As you can see Texas has two counties that are in the top 10.

Table 16.2   Largest Counties by Population.

Los Angeles, CA	9,213,533
Cook, IL	5,189,689
Harris, TX	3,206,063
Maricopa, AZ	2,784,075
San Diego, CA	2,780,592
Orange, CA	2,721,701
Dade, FL	2,152,437
Wayne, MI	2,118,129
Dallas, TX	2,050,865
Santa Clara, CA	1,641,215

Source: National Association of Counties, Largest Counties by Population 2002–2003.[7]

THE METROPOLITAN CHALLENGE

The **Metropolitan Statistical Area** (MSA) is the official designation of a metropolitan region in the United States, which consists of any county containing a city or contiguous cities of 50,000 people plus the surrounding counties that are economically integrated into the central county. The MSA is defined by the county; most will contain rural areas as well as urbanized areas. A problem of an MSA is when the rural areas cover more space than the urbanized areas. Once this occurs it is very difficult to make changes because no one is capable of becoming a spokesperson for the metropolitan area. The city has a mayor and the state has a governor as a spokesperson, but trying to create a sizeable metropolitan constituency with strong interests in metro problems can be very difficult. Most of the MSA is built around a central city, sprawls over into two or more counties and supports dozens of municipalities, school districts, and special districts. Some of the most vexing problems are air quality, crime control, housing, education, transportation, and racial discrimination. All of these cross into each other's governmental jurisdiction. Because of this growing problem attempts have been made to create a governmental structure that would address the metropolitan problems.

Online Connections

View these sites to find out more about local government.

To find more information on state and local government check out this website. *http://www.statesnews.org*

State and local governments on the web. *http://www.statelocalgov.net*

International City/County Managers Association. *http://www.icma.org*

National League of Cities. *http://www.nlc.org*

Key Terms

General law city   215

Home rule city   216

Weak mayor   216

Strong mayor   216

Council manager   217

City commission   217

Metropolitan Statistical Area   219

Suggested Readings

Thomas R. Dye, *Understanding Public Policy*, 8th ed. (Upper Saddle River, NJ, Prentice Hall, 1995).

Mike Greenburg, *The Poetics of Cities: Designing Neighborhoods that Work* (Columbus, OH: Ohio State University Press, 1995).

John J. Harrigan and David C. Nice, *Politics and Policy in States and Communities*, 2nd ed. (New York: Addison Wesley Longman, 2001).

E. W. Russell and Jay M. Shafritz, *Introducing Public Administration*, 2nd ed. (New York: Addison Wesley Longman, 2000).

Notes

[1]Roscoe C. Martin, *The Cities and the Federal System* (New York: Atherton Press, 1965), pp. 28–35.

[2]Char Miller and Haywood T. Sanders, *Urban Texas: Politics and Development* (College Station: Texas A&M University Press, 1990), pp. 3–29.

[3]U.S. Department of Commerce, Bureau of the Census, 2012 Census of Government, Vol. 1, Local Government by Type and State: 2012.

[4]North Central Texas Council of Governments, Top 10 Cities 2002–2003 Population Increase at *http://www.dfwinfo.com/ris/population/top10.gif*

[5]North Central Texas Council of Governments, Fastest Growing Cities 2002–2003 at *http://www.dfwinfo.com/ris/population/fastest02.gif*

[6]Texas State Library at *http://www.tsl.state.tx.us*

[7]National Association of Counties, Largest Counties by Population 2002–2003 at *http://www.naco.org/counties/general/chars.cfm*

1. Describe the difference between rural Texas and urban Texas. Would a visitor be surprised?

_____

_____

_____

_____

_____

2. List and explain the two types of cities that exist in Texas.

_____

_____

_____

_____

_____

3. What type of city government is in Dallas? Explain your answer.

_____

_____

_____

_____

_____

4. Explain the role of the city manager.

_____

_____

_____

_____

_____

Directions: Write the word or phrase that completes the statement.

1. A _____ city means that there are fewer than 5,000 people and that the city is only able to exercise the laws granted by the legislature.

2. A _____ city means that there are more than 5,000 people and that the city can adopt any form of government that does not conflict with the constitution.

3. The _____ determines the structure, powers, and the responsibilities of a city government.

4. There are _____ counties in Texas.

Directions: Circle the correct answer to each of the following questions.

5. _____ is where an elected group collectively serves as the city's policy-making body.
   a. Mayor-council system
   b. Council-manager system
   c. Strong mayor system
   d. City commission

6. All of the top ten cities have _____.
   a. a city commission
   b. a weak mayor
   c. a council-manager
   d. a strong mayor.

7. The largest county by population is _____.
   a. Maricopa, Arizona
   b. Los Angeles, California
   c. Cook, Illinois
   d. Harris, Texas

8. Which of the following is not a responsibility of counties?
   a. Collection of state taxes
   b. Enforcing state laws
   c. State welfare programs and roads
   d. Garbage programs

Sample Test Questions

CHAPTER 17
Texas Political Culture

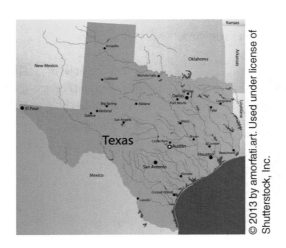

Texas is the second-most populous state in the nation, second only to California, and home to many diverse groups and cultures. Texas also is one of the fastest-growing states in the nation, with a 12.7 percent growth total, which is double that of the national total of 6.4 percent.[1] About 26 million people live in Texas, and the demographics of the state are very diverse.[2] With the second fastedest economic growth and third fastest job growth Texas is positioned a first for current economic climate. In addition, there are several companies based in Texas, including giants like AT&T, ExxonMobil and Dell.[3] Just as the demographics are diverse so is the terrain of Texas. We will now discuss the terrain of Texas and type of industry that each region is known for.

THE TEXAS TERRAIN

The Texas terrain is as diverse as the people. The terrain ranges from sea-level ocean views to the high mountains of Big Bend in West Texas. There are seven main areas of terrain described in Texas: Big Bend Country, Panhandle Plains, Hill Country, Prairies and Lakes, Piney Woods, South Texas Plains, and the Gulf Coastal Region (see Figure 17.1). Each of these areas will be discussed in more detail in the following section.

Big Bend Country

In far West Texas lies the mountains and basins region of Big Bend. The area is known for the extremes in temperature. The mountain ranges of Big Bend are cold with occasional snowfalls in the winter. The basins of the area are desert like where it is dry and hot at night and cool in the evening. Along the southern border of Big Bend the Rio Grande River flows. The river creates the Texas and Mexico border. The Rio Grande is the fifth-longest river in the United States.[4]

Big Bend National park is located in this region. The landmass of the park is larger than Rhode Island, 801,163 acres. It is home to several species of animals and plants that are found nowhere else in the world. The lands and species are protected. Many people, however, do not travel to the park each year because of the remoteness of the area. There are only five paved roads in the park. People who do visit the park come to hike and camp in primitive environments.[5]

Figure 17.1   Texas regions.

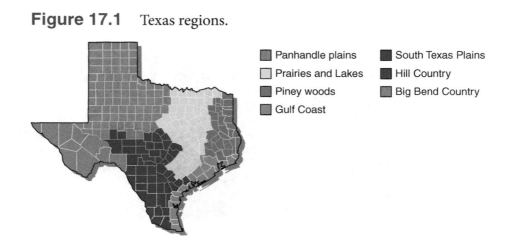

Some of the largest cities in the region are, Midland, Texas, at about 100,000 people. It was formed during the big West Texas oil boom on Texas and has been known for its vast petroleum deposits. Midland, Texas, is the birthplace of President George W. Bush. Odessa is the sister city to Midland. Its population is about 95,000. El Paso is the western-most point of Texas. It borders New Mexico and Mexico. The population of El Paso is about 600,000 people, which makes it the most populous city in the region.[6]

The voters in this rural region tend to be more conservative Republicans.

Panhandle Plains

The Panhandle plains of Texas are located at the northernmost tip of the state. The name is an analogy to the panhandle of a pan, due to the square nature of the handle, which then holds the rest of the state. The land is flat and grassy with the western region containing two major canyons, Caprock and Palo Duro. The largest cities in the Panhandle are Amarillo, Abilene, Wichita Falls, San Angelo, Lubbock, Amarillo.[7]

The economic engines of this area of the state are the crops, cotton, and grain, and livestock and the livestock production. The production of grain and cotton largely depend on the water from the Ogallala aquifer. Without the aquifer the area would not be able to produce the crops due to lack of rainfall and another water source.[8]

The voters in this rural region tend to be more conservative Republicans.

Hill Country

The Hill Country region is located in central Texas. The region is mostly rural. The area was founded by immigrants from Germany, Czechoslovakia, Poland, and Norway. The largest influence is German. The hill country is known as a place where people go to relax and enjoy the sites of springs, caves, and natural hills of the region.[9]

The area is home to the Edwards aquifer, which provides water to about 1.5 million people in and around the region. "An **aquifer** is an underground layer of rock or sand that captures and holds water."[10] This aquifer is critical to the survival of the region. The conservation and preservation of this natural resource is critical.

The majority of the political thinking in the area is conservative Republican; however, Austin is the liberal island of the state. The largest city in this region is Austin, the capital of Texas. It is often called the "Silicon Valley" of Texas due to the high technology influence in the city. Austin is known as the political and intellectual center of the state, due to the influx of well-educated people from the Northeast and West for the technology industry.[11]

© 2013 by Richard A McMillin. Used under license of Shutterstock, Inc.

The economy of the region has been largely mining for limestone, manufacturing such as plastics, Mars candy company, and Bluebell ice cream. The Killeen area is also home to Fort Hood, where the military is a strong force in the economic environment in the area.[12]

The area is also becoming a place where people from the urban areas such as San Antonio and Dallas like to come and retire.[13]

The Central Texas area is made up mostly of whites at 61.4 percent. This is a higher concentration of whites than compared with the population of Texas (see Table 17.1).

Table 17.1   Central Texas Region Compared to the State of Texas by Ethnicity (2008).

Ethnicity	Central Texas (%)	Texas
White	61.4	47.3
Hispanic	18.7	36.3
African American	15.2	11.4
Other	4.7	5.1

Information from Source: Window on State Government, Central Texas, http://www.window.state.tx.us/specialrpt/tif/central/exhibits/Ex11.php

Prairies and Lakes

The Prairies and Lakes region is home to rich soil, rolling hills, and even dinosaur fossils. In this region fossils of seventeen dinosaurs have been found. Dinosaur Valley State Park, located close to Glen Rose, is home to the highest number of footprint fossils of dinosaurs found in the state. Three state parks are located in this region: Lake Ray Roberts, Lake Fork, and Cedar Hill State Park. People go to these parks to fish in the lakes, which are nationally well-known for their fishing.[14]

This region encompasses north Texas, home to the Metroplex, the areas surrounding the major cities of Dallas and Fort Worth. The economic engines of the Metroplex are very diverse. The area is a mix of banking, defense, aerospace, and manufacturing. In the more rural areas of the region, farming and ranching are still mainstays.[15]

Piney Woods

Piney Woods of Texas is located in the east. The eastern landscape changes greatly from the plains, the dry areas of the west. The landscape is filled with pine trees and woodsy areas containing swamps and many large wetter regions. The Piney woods that begin in East Texas extend into Louisiana, Arkansas, and Oklahoma.

The economic engine that drives the region used to be cotton.[16] Many families in the region are well-established with long-time family industries based in retail, real estate, and construction.[17] The industries that have replaced cotton are manufacturing, lumber, and cattle.

South Texas Plains

The South Texas plains environment comprises brushy and grassy plains. The Rio Grande River flows through the southern portion of the region and is called the Lower Rio Grande Valley. The terrain in the Lower Rio Grande Valley changes into a subtropical environment, where palm trees and fruit trees grow in a very humid environment. The Rio Grande Valley region is also known for bird watching and is home to the World Bird Watching center.[18]

Figure 17.2 The graph in figure 17.2 illustrates the demographic background of the people that live in South Texas compared with the rest of the state of Texas.

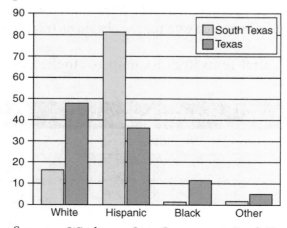

Source: Window on State Government, South Texas. http://www.window.state.tx.us/specialrpt/tif/southtexas/ demographics.html#exhibit24

Since this region is connected to the Mexican border, many cities in the region proudly display two cultures, Mexican and American. Eight-one percent of this region are people of Hispanic origin, the heaviest concentration in the state (see Figure 17.2).[19] The largest cities in this region are San Antonio and Laredo. The military have strong influences in this region with six bases located in this area. The economy of the area relies heavily on this influence. Due to the fertile nature of the soil around the Rio Grande basin, farming in this area is an economic source. However, the farms and large ranches are typically owned by one family that has owned it for several generations or by wealthy corporate ranchers

Table 17.2   Population by Ethnicity, Texas and Gulf Coast Region (2008).

Ethnicity	Texas (%)	Gulf Coast Region (%)
White	47.4	42.7
Hispanic	36.2	33.6
African American	11.3	16.5
Other	5.1	7.2

Source: U.S. Census Bureau Retrieved from http://www.window.state.tx.us/specialrpt/tif/population.html

who come in and purchase the land for use. The local people work the on the farms, they do not own them. The Mexican border region of Texas, the Rio Grande Valley, is one of the poorest regions of the United States.[20]

Gulf Coastal Region

The Gulf Coastal Plains is the region along the Gulf of Mexico. Along this region are marshes, islands, and a mostly flat plain.[21] The economic engines of this region are oil and chemical-related industries and international shipping. This region is home to the largest city in the state, Houston. Houston has become an international city with large ports and international banking industries.[22] Houston is home to the headquarters of these multi-national energy companies: Exxon-Mobil, Conoco-Phillips, Shell Oil, and BP. Houston is also home to the largest medical center in the world, The Texas Medical Center. On this campus are thirteen hospitals with academic institutions with the ability to employ, train, and take care of thousands for the future.[23]

The Texas Gulf Coast Region has a population very similar to that of the whole of Texas (see Table 17.2). The majority of the population is white at 47.4 percent, with Hispanics the next largest category at 36.2 percent.

DEMOGRAPHICS OF TEXAS

Texas is made up of many different types of ethnic groups. Texas is now a majority minority state. This means that when the minority groups are added together they outnumber the white population.[24]

The demographic breakdown in the state compared to the United States is as follows:

Table 17.3 Texas and United States Demographics. Illustrates a comparison of demographics in the state of Texas and the United States government.

Demographic Category	Texas (%)	United States
Black	12.2	13.1
American Indian and Alaska Native	1.0	1.2
Asian	4.0	5.0
Native Hawaiian and Other Pacific Islander	0.1	0.2
Persons reporting two or more races	1.7	2.3
Persons of Hispanic or Latino origin	38.1	16.7
White persons not Hispanic	44.8	63.4

Source: www.uscensus.gov, 2010.

From the figure you can see that the demographics of Texas are very diverse. The population is more diversely distributed across the categories than the national population. Texas is more heavily Hispanic in origin than the United States as a whole. There is about a 22 percent increase in the Texas numbers for Hispanic origin people. There is a large influence of all cultures across Texas. We will now discuss each group as a separate entity to view their contributions to the larger Texas culture.

The majority of Hispanics in Texas are people of Mexican descent. Hispanic people live in all areas of the state. Larger concentrations are in the border towns, cities, and in agricultural regions, such as the farms of the Panhandle or the Rio Grande Valley, as seen in the previous section.

Figure 17.3 Texas Population Growth (1980–2040).

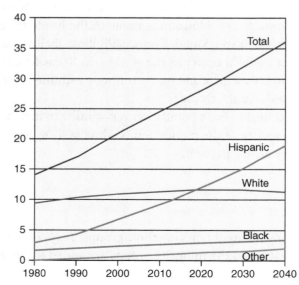

As the population continues to grow in Texas the Texas State demographer has predicted that the population of Hispanics by the year 2040 will be greater than all other groups. The demographer's predictions for the year 2040 are illustrated in Figure 17.3. The predictions are in millions.

POLITICAL CULTURE

Political culture is the political values and beliefs of a people about their political system. As described by Daniel Elazar (1972) three aspects of political culture are found across the United States. The three approaches are ways to frame government and politics and ways to describe values and beliefs more specifically.[25]

The **individualistic political culture** focuses on the individual without government interference. The objective of government in their culture is to foster private initiatives. The belief is strongly held that government should be used for the benefit of business interests. Government is seen as a means for individuals to develop their own interests. Areas of the country where this culture exist most prevalently are the Middle Atlantic States and areas to the west. The focus of this culture is on economic growth of the individual.[26]

The **moralistic political culture** focuses on government doing good for the people. Society is held as a more important value than the individual. This culture was born out of the deep religious beliefs in the New England colonies. The belief is that government should support the welfare of people and that citizens can better themselves by becoming involved in government and creates change. In this cultural frame, politicians should be servants of the people rather than gaining political or economic power from holding office. The region where this political culture is the most prevalent is New England, Northern Midwest and the Far West.[27]

Traditionalistic political culture is where the government is controlled by the society elite. Government is a means to maintain tradition and social order. This political culture reflects the values of the traditional South. This belief is in family connections and relationships between those that are connected and have powerful positions. The political structure is where the power is in the powerful small group of people that control the decisions. The political participation of the masses is limited.[28]

Of these three political cultural dimensions, Texas has traditionally been a combination of two of these types, the traditionalistic and the individual. There is a strong belief in Texas that there should be limited government involvement, such as that taxes are low. The business interests play a large part in the government role in Texas (individual). Businesses have a major role to play in the development of public policy. With the focus on the elite and businesses, the focus on the welfare of people and the social programs is low.[29]

Online Connections

View these sites to find out more about Texas political culture.

www.texasreason.net—A view of Texas Political Culture

www.ushistory.org/gov/4a.asp—Historical look at Political Culture

Key Terms

Aquifer   227

Political culture   231

Individualistic political culture   231

Moralistic political culture   231

Traditionalistic political culture   231

Suggested Readings

Champagne, A. & Harpham, E.J., (2013). *Governing Texas*. New York, NY: Norton.

Mora, S., Ruger, W., & Mihalkanim, E. (2013). *The State of Texas: Government, Politics, and Policy*. New York, NY: Mc Graw Hill.

Tannahill, N. (2013). *Texas Government: Policy and Politics*, 12th ed. Boston, MA: Pearson.

Notes

[1] http://www.window.state.tx.us/specialrpt/tif/population.html

[2] www.uscensus.gov, 2010.

[3] www.forbes/places/tx

[4] http://en.wikipedia.org/wiki/Big_Bend_National_Park

[5] Ibid.

[6] http://www.ehow.com/list_7282992_list-west-texas-cities.html#page=0

[7] http://www.tpwd.state.tx.us/kids/about_texas/regions/panhandle/big_kids/

[8] W. E. Maxwell, E. Crain, and A. Santos, *Tx.Gov.* (Boston: Wadsworth, 2014).

[9] Ibid.

[10] http://www.tpwd.state.tx.us/kids/about_texas/regions/hill_country/big_kids/

[11] W. E. Maxwell, E. Crain, and A. Santos, *Tx.Gov.* (Boston: Wadsworth, 2014).

[12] http://www.window.state.tx.us/specialrpt/tif/central/ecodevo.php

[13] Ibid.

[14] http://www.tpwd.state.tx.us/kids/about_texas/regions/prairies_and_lakes/big_kids/

[15] W. E. Maxwell, E. Crain, and A. Santos, *Tx.Gov.* (Boston: Wadsworth, 2014).

[16] A. Champagne and E. J. Harpham, *Governing Texas: An Introduction to Texas Politics* (New York: Norton, 2013).

[17] Ibid.

[18] http://www.tpwd.state.tx.us/kids/about_texas/regions/south_texas/big_kids/

[19] http://www.window.state.tx.us/specialrpt/tif/southtexas/demographics.html

[20] W. E. Maxwell, E. Crain, and A. Santos, *Tx.Gov.* (Boston: Wadsworth, 2014).

[21] http://www.tpwd.state.tx.us/kids/about_texas/regions/gulf_coast/big_kids/

[22] W. E. Maxwell, E. Crain, and A. Santos, *Tx.Gov.* (Boston: Wadsworth, 2014).

[23] https://www.window.state.tx.us/specialrpt/tif/gulf/ecodevo.php

[24] S. Mora, W. Ruger, and E. Mihalkanin, *The State of Texas: Government, Politics, and Policy* (New York: McGraw Hill, 2014).

[25] Daniel J. Elazar, *American Federalism: A View from the States,* 2nd ed. (New York: Thomas Y. Crowell, 1972).

[26] Ibid.

[27] Ibid.

[28] Ibid.

[29] A. Champagne, and E. J. Harpham, *Governing Texas: An Introduction to Texas Politics* (New York: Norton, 2013).

1. What is the ethnic and racial distribution of Texas's population? Which group has seen the most dramatic growth? What are the potential long-term political consequences?

_____

_____

_____

_____

_____

2. On average, where would you place Texans on the political culture spectrum? Why?

_____

_____

_____

_____

_____

3. In the region of South Texas name and explain the challenges that are faced.

_____

_____

_____

_____

_____

4. Explain why Texas is so unique.

_____

_____

_____

_____

NAME_____ COURSE_____ SECTION_____

Directions: Write the word or phrase that completes the statement.

1. The government that is controlled by an elite group of people is the
   _____.
   a. individualistic culture
   b. traditionalistic culture
   c. moralistic culture
   d. political culture

2. _____is the political values and beliefs of a people about
   their political system.
   a. Individualistic culture
   b. Traditionalistic culture
   c. Moralistic culture
   d. Political culture

3. The belief is strongly held that government should be used for the benefit
   of business interests. This belief is held by those in the _____.
   a. individualistic culture
   b. traditionalistic culture
   c. moralistic culture
   d. political culture

4. As the population continues to grow in Texas the Texas State demographer
   has predicted that the population of _____ by the year 2040 will
   be greater than all other groups.
   a. whites
   b. Hispanics
   c. African Americans
   d. all of the above

5. One of the poorest regions of the state is the_____.
   a. Gulf Coastal Plains
   b. Oakcliff
   c. Rio Grande Valley
   d. Panhandle

6. The region of Texas where dinosaur fossils have been found is_____.
   a. Gulf Coastal Plains
   b. Prairies and Lakes
   c. Rio Grande Valley
   d. Panhandle

CHAPTER 18
Texas Political Participation

© 2013 by Andresr. Used under license of Shutterstock, Inc.

Political participation is when you take an active part in influencing government decisions. Political participation activities are as basic as voting, signing a petition, or running for political office. Just as in the United States, in the state of Texas, the right to vote has not been granted equally to all groups. All groups have the right to vote but do not always exercise their right to vote. The state of Texas has a larger percentage of minorities than the non-Hispanic whites, however minorities are not the majority of the voters in the state. In this next section we will review the history behind the right to vote in Texas.

AFRICAN AMERICAN RIGHT TO VOTE IN TEXAS

Before the Civil War, African Americans did not have the right to vote or hold public office. African Americans comprised 30 percent of the population in 1860, due to slavery.[1] The Civil War ended in 1865. It took five years (1870) for the United States to draft a new amendment to the U.S. Constitution to grant the right to vote. The Fifteenth Amendment "prohibits each government in the United States from denying a citizen the right to vote based on that citizen's race, color, or previous condition of servitude."[2] By June 19, 1865, news reached Texas about freedom from slavery, or emancipation, or Juneteenth. However, in Texas, African Americans' right to vote did not come until later.[3]

In Texas the right to vote was viewed as a means to control groups of people. By not allowing minority groups to vote, it would mean continued control by whites. It was

© 2013 by Alan Bailey. Used under license of Shutterstock, Inc.

a means to keep oppression in place. The black codes were put in place by the white-controlled legislature to economically control freed slaves. Black codes prohibited freed slaves from holding office, marrying interracially, voting, and sitting on a jury.[4]

By 1870 African American males could legally vote in Texas. However, the white elite did not believe that they should have the right to vote. Polling places would be moved far away from population centers of minorities. If the polling place was close, bridges or roads would be blocked to prevent minorities from coming to the polls. Polling places would also be changed on the day of the election to prevent minorities from being able to vote. Other means to block the minority vote were comprehension tests, **poll taxes** (paying money to vote), or difficult-to-understand ballots.[5]

In 1895 Robert Lloyd Smith, the first African American was elected to the Texas House of Representatives. He was the principal in the city's training school for teachers (Oakland City, Texas). He served two terms in the twenty-fourth and twenty-fifth legislature. After he was elected it would not be until 1966 when three more minorities were elected into the Texas legislature. They were Barbara Jordan from Houston (Senate), Curtis M. Graves from Houston (House), and Joseph Lockridge from Dallas (House).

HISPANIC RIGHT TO VOTE

The Hispanic road to the vote was different from that of African Americans in Texas. Hispanics, called **Tejanos**, lived freely in Texas because this territory was Mexican. With the fall of Santa Anna at the Alamo, the 1836 Texas Declaration of Independence was signed

© 2013 by Diego Cervo. Used under license of Shutterstock, Inc.

by fifty-five men, three of whom were Hispanic: José Antonio Navarro, José Francisco Ruiz, and Lorenzo DeZavala. DeZavala served as the vice president of the interim government for three months until he died. During the Republic of Texas four Hispanics were elected from South Texas, Bexar County, to state offices: José Antonio Navarro, José Francisco Ruiz, Juan Seguín, and Rafael de la Garza.

After this time there were no Hispanics serving in federal offices until 1960. In state-wide races sixteen Hispanic candidates won seats in the State House of Representatives and three Hispanic candidates won seats in the Texas Senate between the years of 1846 and 1961. Much of the reason for this state of affairs between 1846 and 1961 for Hispanics was emphasis placed on minority status, land loss, language differences, and lack of educational and economic opportunities.[6]

In South Texas, where there was a heavy Hispanic minority, Hispanic persons were allowed to right to vote, but their vote was controlled by the ranch boss who would tell them how they needed to vote. The Hispanic ranch workers would fear losing their jobs and

© 2013 by Lisa F. Young. Used under license of Shutterstock, Inc.

would make sure they did as they were told. It was a way to stack the vote in favor of the ranch owner's choice of candidate. Most ranch owners were white.[7] In 1975 Congress reauthorized the Voting Rights Act to specifically embrace access for those that speak a different language. Voting stations would need to provide access for other languages if they made up 5% of the population in the area, such as Spanish speaking Americans. This meant elections would need to ensure voters that spoke Spanish had equal access to case their vote. Local offices, such as city council or alderman, have been held by Hispanics in South Texas.[8]

WOMEN'S RIGHT TO VOTE

The Fifteenth Amendment to the U.S. Constitution in 1870 granted the right to vote to African-American men due to their "previous condition of servitude"; however, the right of women to vote or run for office was not granted until 1920, forty-nine years after minority men were granted the right to vote. The Nineteenth Amendment to the U.S. Constitution states, "The right of citizens of the United States to vote shall not be denied or abridged by the United States or by any State on account of sex."[9] Of all the states in the South, Texas was the first to ratify the Nineteenth Amendment of the Constitution in 1918, which finally gave women the right to vote in Texas.[10]

Women in Texas have been an integral part of the political process and have become a big political force. Currently approximately 20 percent of state offices are held by women. Texas has had a female governor, Ann Richards, in 1990, a female senator, Kay Bailey Hutchinson, 1994–2012, which many states still have not had. Table 18.1 lists other "firsts" for females in Texas.

Table 18.1   The "Firsts" for Females in Texas.

1922	Edith Wilmans is first woman elected to the legislature (House)
1925	Miriam A. "Ma" Ferguson is elected governor
1971	Texas Women's Political Caucus founded to elect women
1991	Ann Richards (D) is elected governor
1993	Kay Bailey Hutchinson elected U.S. Senator from Texas
2003	For the first time, the House has more Republican (20) than Democratic (12) women

Source: Information from http://www.laits.utexas.edu/txp_media/html/leg/features/0304_01/gender.html

Women serving in elected office in Texas are close in number to keeping up with the numbers of elected women in other states. Table 18.2 shows the percentage of women in the Texas Senate is greater than the number of women in other states and more than the numbers of women in the House and Senate. Women are expected to continue to be a critical force in the electorate and as candidates in the future.

Table 18.2   Percentage of Women in the Texas House, Senate, and U.S. Congress (2013).

	House (%)	Senate (%)	Total (%)
Texas	20.7	22.6	21
All states	25.3	20.3	24
United States Congress	17.9	20	18.3

Source: Information from http://www.laits.utexas.edu/txp_media/html/leg/features/0304_01/gender.html

PARTICIPATION IN THE TEXAS VOTING PROCESS

In order to vote there are still requirements so that the government can ensure that everyone receives the opportunity to vote only one time. This process ensures that there are limited cases of voter fraud and tampering.

In Texas you are eligible to register to vote if:

- You are a United States citizen;
- You are a resident of the county where you submit the application;
- You are at least eighteen years old on election day;

- You are not a convicted felon (you may be eligible to vote if you have completed your sentence, probation, and parole); and
- You have not been declared by a court exercising probate jurisdiction to be either totally mentally incapacitated or partially mentally incapacitated without the right to vote.

If you meet the requirements to vote, you must make sure that thirty days before the election you register to vote. Registering to vote can be done at the U.S. Post Office with a form or online at voteTexas.gov.[11]

Online Connections

View these sites to find out more about voting in Texas.

www. voteTexas.gov

www.sos.state.tx.us

Key Terms

Political participation   237   Tejanos   238

Poll taxes   238

Suggested Readings

Champagne, A. & Harpham, E.J., (2013). *Governing Texas*. New York, NY: Norton.

Mora, S., Ruger, W., & Mihalkanim, E. (2013).*The State of Texas: Government, Politics, and Policy*. New York, NY: Mc Graw Hill.

Tannahill, N. (2013). *Texas Government: Policy and Politics*, 12th ed. Boston, MA: Pearson.

Notes

[1]http://www.tshaonline.org/handbook/online/articles/wmafr

[2]https://www.loc.gov/rr/program/bib/ourdocs/15thamendment.html

[3]http://www.tshaonline.org/handbook/online/articles/wmafr

[4]http://www.tshaonline.org/handbook/online/articles/wmafr

[5]https://www.tsl.state.tx.us/exhibits/forever/endofanera/page4.html

[6]http://www.tshaonline.org/handbook/online/articles/wmtkn

[7]N. Tannahill, *Texas Government* (New York: Pearson, 2013).

[8]http://www.tshaonline.org/handbook/online/articles/wmtkn

[9]http://law2.umkc.edu/faculty/projects/ftrials/conlaw/nineteentham.htm

[10]N. Tannahill, *Texas Government* (New York: Pearson, 2013).

[11]http://votetexas.gov/register-to-vote/register-to-vote/

NAME_____ COURSE_____ SECTION_____

1. What are the requirements to vote?

_____

_____

_____

_____

2. Explain the path to voting rights for African American males.

_____

_____

_____

_____

3. Explain the path to voting rights for Hispanic males.

_____

_____

_____

_____

4. What impact do women have on the political process?

_____

_____

_____

_____

1. Who was the first African American elected to the Texas House?
   a. José Antonio Navarro
   b. José Francisco Ruiz
   c. Robert Lloyd Smith
   d. Curtis Graves

2. Which of the following is not a requirement for voting?
   a. You are a resident of the county where you submit the application.
   b. You are at least twenty years old on Election Day.
   c. You are not a convicted felon (you may be eligible to vote if you have completed your sentence, probation, and parole).
   d. You have registered to vote.

3. What is the name of the man who was vice president of the Republic of Texas?
   a. José Antonio Navarro
   b. José Francisco Ruiz
   c. Robert Lloyd Smith
   d. Lorenzo de Zavala

Sample Test Questions

CHAPTER 19
Texas Elections and Voting

The previous chapter presented the historical nature of voting in Texas, how the various groups were granted access to voting at different times, and the requirements to vote in Texas. In this chapter the focus will be on the types of elections in Texas as well as the voting patterns of various groups in Texas.

In Texas **secretary of state** is the person in charge of all the of election activities. This person is appointed by the governor and serves in the position for as long as the governor decides, unless he or she resigns before that time. The current secretary of state is John Steen, who has been in office since November 2012.

The secretary of state ensures that all election laws are followed and administered fairly at all levels of the state. This office keeps election records and is responsible for paying for elections.[1]

TYPES OF ELECTIONS

In Texas there are three main types of elections: the **primary election**, the **general election**, and the **special election**. These processes are used as a way to find the one main candidate that the most people want to fill the elected post.

Primary Elections

The first step in the election process is the primary. The purpose of the primary election is to choose one Democratic candidate and one Republican candidate. Two primaries are

© 2013 by somartin. Used under license of Shutterstock, Inc.

held, one for the Republican Party and one for the Democratic Party. Primary elections are usually held on the first Tuesday in March of even-numbered years.[2]

The candidates for the Democratic or Republican position first state their intention for running for the elected post by paying a fee to the party and filling out necessary paperwork (see Table 19.1 for a list of filing fees for certain state offices).

Table 19.1   Filing Fees for Texas Statewide Office.

Democratic or Republican Party Nominee Public Office Sought in 2012	Filing Fee ($)
United States Senator	5,000
United States Representative	3,125
Railroad Commissioner	3,750
Justice, Supreme Court	3,750
Presiding Judge and Judge, Court of Criminal Appeals	3,750
State Senator	1,250
State Representative	750
Member, State Board of Education	300

Source: Texas Secretary of the State. http://www.sos.state.tx.us/elections/candidates/guide/demorrep.shtml

After their intentions are stated they begin campaigning for the post. If there is more than one candidate for the Democratic or Republican seat the candidates run against each other until a winner is chosen in the primary election. The purpose of the primary election is for the Democrats and Republicans each to select one candidate who then run against each other in a later election. If in the primary election a clear winner is not determined, meaning one candidate did not win a majority of the vote, a **runoff** primary election is conducted. This a primary where the two candidates with the highest votes in the primary run against each other again to determine which candidate will go on to the general election.

A voter has to choose which primary he or she will vote in, the Democratic or the Republican. A voter cannot vote in both primaries. Texas has an open primary system in which the voter does not have to declare a party before the primary, the voter can choose a party on primary day—Democrat or Republican. Texas and fifteen other states are open primary states.[3]

General Elections

General elections are held after the primary elections. The general election is where the Republican candidate for office runs against the Democratic candidate, generally. Candidates from third parties, such as the Green Party, or independents will also run in the general election. The elections are held on the Tuesday following the first Monday in November in even-numbered years.[4]

In order for independent candidates to run for statewide office in Texas they need to follow certain processes. First they need to collect a certain number of signatures from the voting constituents. For example, in the Texas House of Representatives races, candidates need to collect between 30,000 to 40,000 signatures. This number is based on 5 percent of the votes from the past election. The signatures have to be from people who are registered to vote and have not already voted in either primary election in the election cycle. Not many people have been elected to office from parties other than the mainstream Democratic or Republican parties.

In a landmark 2006 Governor General election in Texas, Governor Perry, the Republican candidate who had been in office for six years, ran against two independent candidates and a Democratic candidate. The independents were Kinky Friedman and Carole Keeyton Strayhorn and the Democratic candidate was Chris Bell. The results of the election are shown in Table 19.2.

Table 19.2   Texas Governor Election Results (2006).

Candidate	Percentage of Vote (%)
Rick Perry	38.1
Chris Bell	30.0
Carole Keeton Strayhorn	18.0
Kinky Friedman	12.6

In this general election the independent candidates seemed to take votes away from the Democratic Party candidate and assist the incumbent governor Rick Perry in winning reelection, with only 38 percent of the total vote.[5]

In another landmark governor election, 2014, it was a head to head challenge between the Democrats and Republicans, the incumbant could not run again, Rick Perry. Gregg Abbot, Republican and Wendy Davis, Democrat held a very contested election. The results of the election are shown in Table 19.3. Even though it was a contested race, Abbot was the clear victor with 59.8% of the vote.

Candidate	Percentage of the Vote(%)
Gregg Abbott	59.8%
Wendy Davis	38.9%

General elections for the main Texas state-level offices are held in off years from the presidential elections. Offices that have elections held in the off years include governor, lieutenant governor, comptroller, attorney general, land commissioner, and agricultural commissioner. This reason behind staggering these elections is so that the presidential elections do not control Texas state politics. Presidential election years have higher voter turnouts than in nonpresidential years.[6]

Special Elections

Special elections in Texas take place at various times throughout the year. A special election may take place if a candidate resigns his or her post before a term is over or if a candidate cannot complete the term due to personal reasons.

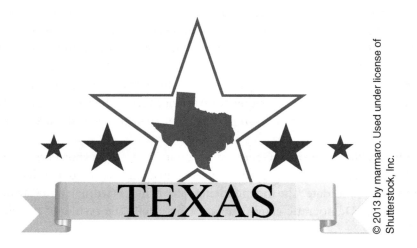

© 2013 by marmaro. Used under license of Shutterstock, Inc.

Another reason a special election may be held is to borrow money. If a school district wants to take out a bond for special projects the school district needs to have the voters vote on the bond. If a majority is in favor, the plan to borrow money through the bond is approved. If the voters do not vote in favor of the bond, the school district will not be able to borrow money through a bond. In all levels of the government the ability to borrow money has to be determined by the voters.

A third reason a special election may take place is to amend the Texas constitution. The Texas legislature would bring this type of special election to the attention of the voters. In 2011 there were ten proposed amendments to the constitution, of which seven were approved and adopted. One of the amendments, which was approved at 57 percent of the vote, was to increase the ability of the governor to pardon prisoners.[7]

TEXAS ELECTORATE

The average voter turnout across the United States is about 50 percent. However, Texas typically has even lower voter turnouts for elections. In the general election for the governor of Texas in 2006, Texas ranked forty-eighth among all states in voter turnout[8] with 26.4 percent of eligible voters participating.[9] In the general election of 2008 for president Texas ranked forty-seventh with 45.5 percent of the eligible voters participating. Then in the general election of 2010 Texas was ranked fiftieth for voting in its gubernatorial election with 27 percent of the eligible voters casting their ballots. In the 2012 presidential

© 2013 by Pressmaster. Used under license of Shutterstock, Inc.

election, 43.73 percent of the voting aged population in Texas voted, which was less than the national average of 53.6 percent. Texas in the 2012 race was forty-ninth in voter participation (Hawaii was fiftieth), with only 40 percent of eligible voters voting.[10] (See Table 19.3 for 2012 figures for Texas.)

Table 19.3   Texas Participation Rates for 2012 Presidential Race.

Registered Voters	13,646,226
Voting Age Population (VAP)	18,279,737
Percentage of VAP Registered	74.65
Turnout	7,993,851
Percent of Turnout to Registered Voters	58.58
Percent of Turnout to VAP	43.73

Source: Elections and voter information: http://www.sos.state.tx.us/elections/historical/70-92.shtml

Some of the states with the highest voter participation rates shown in Table 19.4.

The top three of the top six states with the highest voter registration are states in which voters can register on the same day that they vote (Minnesota, Wisconsin, and Maine). A total of nine states have this same law. In Texas you are required to register to vote 30 days before an election, so you cannot wake up on Election Day and go to vote if you have not already registered ahead of time. This could be one barrier to Texas voters.

A second factor that impacts the percentage of voters is education level. Texas ranks fifty-first in the percentage of people obtaining a high school diploma; this statistic even encompasses Washington DC. Texas has a large number of immigrants, many of whom do not finish school; they go to work instead. This is a major factor in voter participation.[11]

A third factor is income level. Texas ranks ninth from the top in people living below the poverty level; 16 percent of the population is living below the poverty level. California, which is a larger state, ranks twenty-third with 12 percent living below the poverty line. The numbers of people living at the lower levels of income also impact the voting percentage.[12]

Table 19.4   Six States with Highest Voter Participation.

State	2012 Voter Participation (%)	Average over Six Years (%)	Factors for High Voter Turnout
1. Minnesota	71.3	67.3	Same day registration History of third-party candidates winning office
2. Maine	66.9	62.1	Same day registration
3. Wisconsin	69.4	60.1	Same day registration
4. Alaska	55.1	60.42	Competitive races
5. South Dakota	57.7	60.1	Civic engagement Competitive races
6. Oregon	58.6	60.13	Vote by mail

Source: United States Elections Project. http://elections.gmu.edu/Turnout_2012G.html and Christian Science Monitor. http://www.csmonitor.com/USA/Elections/2012/1106/ Voter-turnout-the-6-states-that-rank-highest-and-why/Minnesota

Texas is a large state, with a large percentage of voters who are able to vote. In order to continue to empower citizens of Texas, changes are needed at all levels of the spectrum. The government needs to examine the types of structures that are in place to encourage voting; there need to be targeted efforts to enfranchise those who do not normally make it to the polls—the poor and uneducated.

Online Connections

View these sites to find out more about elections in Texas.

www. voteTexas.gov

www.sos.state.tx.us

Key Terms

Secretary of State   247

Primary elections   247

General election   247

Special election   247

Run off election   248

Suggested Readings

Champagne, A. & Harpham, E.J., (2013). *Governing Texas*. New York, NY: Norton.

Mora, S., Ruger, W., & Mihalkanim, E. (2013).*The State of Texas: Government, Politics, and Policy*. New York, NY: Mc Graw Hill.

Tannahill, N. (2013). *Texas Government: Policy and Politics*, 12th ed. Boston, MA: Pearson.

Notes

[1]http://ballotpedia.org/wiki/index.php/Texas_Secretary_of_State

[2]A. Champagne and E. J. Harpham, *Governing Texas: An Introduction to Texas Politics* (New York: Norton, 2013).

[3]W. E. Maxwell, E. Crain, and A. Santos, *Tx.Gov.* (Boston: Wadsworth, 2014).

[4]A. Champagne and E. J. Harpham, *Governing Texas: An Introduction to Texas Politics* (New York: Norton, 2013).

[5]S. Mora, W. Ruger, and E. Mihalkanin, *The State of Texas: Government, Politics, and Policy* (New York: McGraw-Hill, 2014).

[6]A. Champagne and E. J. Harpham, *Governing Texas: An Introduction to Texas Politics* (New York: Norton, 2013).

[7]http://www.tlc.state.tx.us/pubsconamend/constamend1876.pdf

[8]http://texas-politics.com/texas-politics/texas-voter-turnout/

[9]http://www.sos.state.tx.us/elections/historical/70-92.shtml

[10]http://elections.gmu.edu/Turnout_2012G.html

[11]http://www.texastribune.org/texas-education/public-education/why-does-texas-rank-last-in-high-school-diplomas/

[12]http://www.census.gov/statab/ranks/rank34.html

NAME_____ COURSE_____ SECTION_____

1. Name and explain the types of elections in Texas.

_____

_____

_____

_____

_____

2. Explain the role of the third party in Texas elections.

_____

_____

_____

_____

_____

3. What are some of the factors that have led to higher than average election results in Minnesota and Maine?

_____

_____

_____

_____

_____

4. Explain the barriers to voting percentages in Texas.

_____

_____

_____

_____

_____

1. The secretary of state in Texas is responsible for _____.
   a. elections
   b. filing fees
   c. election results
   d. all of the above

2. The _____ election is where the top candidate in the Democratic Party and Republican Party are chosen.
   a. Democrat
   b. primary
   c. general
   d. special

3. The _____ election takes place the Tuesday following the first Monday in November in even numbered years.
   a. Democrat
   b. Republican
   c. primary
   d. general

4. The top three states with same day voting are Minnesota, Maine, and _____.
   a. Wisconsin
   b. Oregon
   c. Alaska
   d. South Dakota

5. A _____ election takes place in Texas if a candidate cannot complete his or her term because of personal reasons.
   a. Democrat
   b. primary
   c. general
   d. special

Sample Test Questions

CHAPTER 20
Political Parties

Political parties are organizations that assist candidates in being elected to a government post. The political party helps voters identify the values of the candidates. It is difficult for voters to know lots of specific details about every candidate running for office, so the party affiliation helps them to be able to communicate to voters who they are quickly in line with the values of the party.

There are two main parties in the United States and that is also true in Texas. In Texas, however, the divisions of the political parties and the percentages of those who are a part of them are much more extreme. The two main political parties are the **Republicans** and **Democrats**.

REPUBLICAN PARTY

Republicans are symbolized by an elephant. The elephant is used to symbolize a strong and dignified party. Cartoonist Thomas Nast was the one who developed the symbols.[1]

The Texas Republicans have been in power in Texas since George W. Bush (later president) was elected governor in 1995. Before this time the Democrats were in control of the governorship (namely Ann Richards) and statewide offices. However, since 1998 the Republicans have been the majority in statewide offices and in the Texas House since 2002. This was the first time that no Democrat had been elected to statewide office.[2]

In presidential elections, the Republicans have won every race in Texas since 1976. In the 2012 election, Mitt Romney beat President Obama statewide 57 to 41 percent. All of the statewide races have also been won by Republican candidates, including, U.S. senator, lt. governor, governor, and attorney general.

DEMOCRATIC PARTY

The symbol for the Democratic Party is a donkey. The symbol was started in 1828 when the Democrat Andrew Jackson was called a "jackass" by his opponents. Jackson then started to use the symbol in his campaign literature. Cartoonist Thomas Nast also began to use this symbol in relationship to all Democrats. The donkey continues as a symbol for the Democrats being smart and brave.[3]

The state of Texas has not voted Democratic in a presidential race since Jimmy Carter won the state in 1976. In individual counties, however, the balance of power is a little different. Typically the urban areas are more supportive Democratic candidates. For instance, Dallas (Dallas area), Harris (Houston area), Travis (Austin Area), and counties along the Texas/ Mexico border were more supportive of Democrats. In the 2016 election results between Trump and Clinton, Trump was the victor in Texas. Texas remains largely Republican.

TEXAS PARTY PLATFORMS

Each election season the Texas Republicans and Democrats publish their platforms. A **party platform** expresses the values and beliefs that party believes in and will vote and fight for in their position. Table 20.1 shares the views of Republicans and Democrats. Texas leans toward Republican values as based on voting patterns. There are distinct differences with the way in which issues are viewed between the Republicans and Democrats. One of the areas of difference is education. The Republicans believe in school choice and support the use of

Figure 20.1 2017 Presidential Election in Texas.

D. Trump	Republican	52.4%
H. Clinton	Democrat	43.4%
G. Johnson	Libertarian	3.2%
J. Stein	Green Party	0.8%

Source: http://www.politico.com/2016-election/results/map/president/texas/

vouchers to enable students to enroll in any school. Democrats do not support vouchers; instead they believe in strengthening schools with strong teachers within neighborhoods to ensure equal opportunity for all students to be educated.

Another area in which they differ is on the role of government in the lives of people. Republicans believe that the role of government is to stay out of the way of businesses and citizens and allow them to live. In contrast, Democrats believe that the role of government is to ensure that all people have a fair chance to educated and have access to services. Government's role from these two perspectives looks very different.

© 2013 by patrimonio designs ltd. Used under license of Shutterstock, Inc.

In the area of marriage, the Republicans defend the Defense of Marriage Act, where marriage is permitted only between a man and a woman. In their state platform of 2012 Republicans wrote the following about homosexuality:

> *We affirm that the practice of homosexuality tears at the fabric of society and contributes to the breakdown of the family unit. Homosexual behavior is contrary to the fundamental, unchanging truths that have been ordained by God, recognized by our country's founders, and shared by the majority of Texans.[4]*

On the other hand, the Democrats believe that in Texas the government does not have any right to put limits on the rights of people to marry whom they please. The party supports the freedom of same-sex couples to marry.

The area of abortion is an area where many voters use the party stance as their choice for voting. The Democratic Party supports a woman's right to choose. In contrast, the Republican Party defines conception as the start of life and provides very detailed information on what types of laws are acceptable to their party. See Table 20.1 for an overview and a detailed description of abortion rights.

Table 20.1   Texas Republican Platform Versus the Democratic Platform (2012).

Topic	Republican Stance	Democratic Stance
Government power	Needs to be limited in all instances	Needs to be used for fair treatment of all
Education	Supports charter schools and vouchers No support for PreK or Kindergarten (responsibility of the parent) Bilingual education only for three years to transition a student No teaching of a multicultural curriculum, it is divisive	Opposes vouchers Access to all for PreK and kindergarten Free computer and Internet access Support bilingual education
Judiciary	Judicial restraint—maintaining strict accordance to the letter of the law	Judicial activism—adjusting the needs of law to meet the needs of society today
Marriage	Supports the Defense of Marriage Act No homosexual marriage	Supports the right of all to marry
Abortion	Against Life at conception Partial birth abortion banned Wants these laws into Texas law: 1. *Parental and informed consent;* 2. *Prohibition of abortion for gender selection;* 3. *Prohibition of abortion due to the results of genetic diagnosis* 4. *Licensing, liability, and malpractice insurance for abortionists and abortion facilities;* 5. *Prohibition of financial kickbacks for abortion referrals;* 6. *Prohibition of partial birth and lat term abortions; and* 7. *Enactment of any other laws which will advance the right to life for unborn children.*	Supports women's right to choose
Health care	Repeal "Obamacare"	Support access to health care to all

Source: Information obtained from the Texas Republican Platform 2012 (http://s3.amazonaws.com/texasgop_pre/assets/original/2012Platform_Final.pdf) and the Texas Democratic Platform 2012 (http://txdemocrats.org/2012/platform.pdf)

The two parties are philosophically so different sometimes they have a hard time coming to consensus on bills. At the local and state level there is more consensus between Democrats and Republicans than at the federal level.[6]

THE POLITICAL PARTY ORGANIZATION

Temporary Party Organization

In the general election years, even-numbered years, there is a temporary structure of each party so that party supporters can participate in and give input to the party's platform. This structure is called the **temporary party organization**, because it takes place only on the even-numbered years (see Figure 20.2). After the primary elections in March, supporters of the party who have voted in the primary form groups of people to elect party precinct delegates. The usual entry ticket is your stamped voter registration card to say that you voted. The precinct delegates will attend the next level of conventions, the county level.

County-level conventions are the next level. The county-level conventions are formal and more structured than the precinct level. Here delegates are chosen for the state convention and resolutions are passed to move forward to the state convention.

State conventions are held every two years. In the state convention the delegates adopt a platform, elect their chairperson, and pick an executive committee.[7]

Permanent Organization Structure

There are four levels to the **permanent organization structure** (see Figure 20.2): precinct level, county executive committee, state executive committee, and state chair level. Once elected to these positions they serve for two years until the next general election cycle. The conventions are the places where the positions are elected. The state executive committee establishes a party platform and raises money for the party. There are full-time

Figure 20.2   State Political Party Structure.

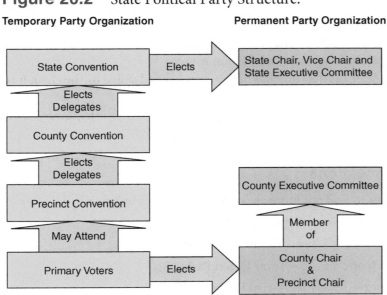

professional employees on both the Democratic and Republican side that handle the day-to-day operations of the party.[8]

Figure 20.2 illustrates the Texas political party structure for determining leadership at the state level.

Parliamentary Procedures

All government structures need to have ways to communicate. Using **parliamentary procedures** in meetings is a way to conduct meetings in an equitable and fair manner. There are specific rules of order that need to be followed as meetings are conducted. The Texas Senate, House, city council, and even your local PTA use parliamentary procedures to structure meetings. The *Robert's Rules of Order* followed for parliamentary procedures, states,

> *The application of parliamentary law is the best method yet devised to enable assemblies of any size, with due regard for every member's opinion, to arrive at the general will on the maximum number of questions of varying complexity in a minimum amount of time and under all kinds of internal climate ranging from total harmony to hardened or impassioned division of opinion.*[9]

The rules for assembly are as follows:

1. Introduction of business – A formal agenda is followed for every meeting.
2. What precedes debate – Motions need to be made before debate is allowed to occur. Another person must second the motion also.
3. Obtaining the floor – A member who has asked for the motion to speak, rises and asks the chairperson for the floor to speak and address the assembly.
4. Motions and resolutions – When something needs to be approved by the committee, someone makes a motion to approve, makes a motion to amend, or makes a motion for something else.
5. Seconding motions – All motions need a second, someone to back up the need for that discussion to take place.
6. Stating the question – After a motion has been motioned and seconded, the chair needs to restate it again before the committee.
7. Debate – After the question has been seconded and stated by the chair, it is debated by the committee.
8. Putting the question and announcing the vote – Chair asks, "Are you ready for the question?" then the item is up for vote.[10]

Online Connections

View these sites to find out more about political parties in Texas.

www. texasgop.org - Texas Republican Party

www.txdemocrats.org – Texas Democratic Party

www.greenpartyoftexas.org – Texas Green Party

www.lptexas.org – Texas Libertarian Party

Key Terms

Political parties   259

Republican   259

Democrat   259

Party platform   260

Temporary party organization   263

Permanent organization structure   263

Parliamentary procedures   264

Suggested Readings

Champagne, A. & Harpham, E.J., (2013). *Governing Texas*. New York, NY: Norton.

Mora, S., Ruger, W., & Mihalkanim, E. (2013).*The State of Texas: Government, Politics, and Policy*. New York, NY: Mc Graw Hill.

Tannahill, N. (2013). *Texas Government: Policy and Politics*, 12th ed. Boston, MA: Pearson.

Notes

[1] http://www.factmonster.com/ipka/A0881985.html

[2] W. E. Maxwell, E. Crain, and A. Santos, *Tx.Gov.* (Boston: Wadsworth, 2014).

[3] http://www.factmonster.com/ipka/A0881985.html

[4] Texas Republican Party Platform 2012, p. 8, http://s3.amazonaws.com/texasgop_pre/assets/original/2012Platform_Final.pdf

[5] Texas Republican Party Platform 2012, p. 8, http://s3.amazonaws.com/texasgop_pre/assets/original/2012Platform_Final.pdf

[6] A. Champagne and E. J. Harpham, *Governing Texas: An Introduction to Texas Politics* (New York: Norton, 2013).

[7] N. Tannahill, *Texas Government* (New York: Pearson, 2013).

[8] A. Champagne and E. J. Harpham, *Governing Texas: An Introduction to Texas Politics* (New York: Norton, 2013).

[9] http://www.rulesonline.com/index.html

[10] http://www.rulesonline.com/index.html

NAME_____ COURSE_____ SECTION_____

1. What are the core values of the Republican Party of Texas?

_____

_____

_____

_____

_____

2. What are the core values of the Democratic Party of Texas?

_____

_____

_____

_____

_____

3. Explain the temporary party structure.

_____

_____

_____

_____

4. What is the purpose of parliamentary procedures?

_____

_____

_____

_____

_____

1. The symbol for the Republicans is _____.
   a. a donkey
   b. an elephant
   c. a boat
   d. all of the above

2. The symbol for the Democrats is _____.
   a. a donkey
   b. an elephant
   c. a boat
   d. all of the above

3. In Texas the _____ are in control of all statewide offices.
   a. Democrats
   b. Independents
   c. Republicans
   d. none of the above

Sample Test Questions

CHAPTER 21

Interest Groups: Attaining Their Share and More

In the United States everything is organized from apples to fish. From fisherman to farmers every interest has an organization to represent it. Organizations are a part of our country; members of the American College of Obstetrics and Gynecology bring us into the world, and members of the National Funeral Directors Association escort us out. When these organizations try to achieve some of their goals with government assistance we call them interest groups. An **interest group** is an organized group that tries to influence public policy. Businesspeople want less government regulation so they can increase their profits, and farmers want subsidies so they are protected from foreign competition. Interest groups that try to influence government use lobbying. **Lobbying** is making contact with government officials, whether it's between a lobbyist, consultant, or lawyer, they are all the same. The lobbyist may use indirect attempts to smooth over public officials by using public opinion. The purpose of lobbying is to enhance your influence. Since politics is considered a contact sport, in order to be effective you need to be involved beyond the concept of one person, one vote, once a year. The truth is you need to be heard loudly. Our government is huge and we call it a bureaucracy made up of hundreds of agencies and commissions. In order to get things accomplished you need to participate, if not you will be run over.

© 2013 by Tribalium, Used under license of Shutterstock, Inc.

Our founders spoke of the selfishness of interest groups and warned of its evils. Because of the factions created by interest, Madison tried to correct this with the notion of the separation of powers, checks and balances, and federalism. Special interest has become problematic because it creates a system that forces government to favor a smaller segment of society rather than the larger. Are the people really represented in Washington? We know for certain everyone else is. In this chapter we will explore further to seek answers to some fundamental questions concerning interest groups. Do interest groups hurt or help the political process?

A NATION OF JOINERS

Alexis de Tocqueville, a French diplomat who traveled to America in the early 1830s, noticed American tendency to join groups. Even though he was speaking of the past it is certainly still true today that American citizens join more groups than people in other countries.[1] The reason is that America is open to the idea of the creation of groups. Our country is more diverse than many other countries, racially, religiously, and ethnically. Because these various views give rise to different opinions, people need a place to express their views.[2] Our Constitution allows for the formation of groups given our First Amendment guarantees to speak, assemble, and petition government. In other countries where these rights are not respected, it would make no sense to create a group unless you were willing to be punished or the government has given you a favorable charge. In order for your group to be powerful you must be organized at all levels of government. Our governmental system encourages the proliferation of groups. They are needed to counter the power of states and local governments.

WHY DEVELOP INTEREST GROUPS?

Interest groups develop in time. There are periods of rapid development and other times very little development. So why in shifts do we see development? First are social stresses and second is economics. During times of war people will develop groups for and against the war. The Vietnam War caused some people to support the war while others called for its end. During times of prosperity groups develop to protect citizen's rights. When businesses cut corners to increase profits while polluting the air, environmental groups form to protect our natural environment. The United States saw its greatest development of interest groups between 1900 and 1920. Immigration, urbanization, and industrialization caused our largest development of interest groups. Such groups as the National Association for the Advancement of Colored People (NAACP), Socialist and Communist parties, America Farm Bureau, United States Chamber of Commerce, and countless others developed.[3]

The national government expanded its power in the 1960s and 1970s. It was the post–World War II period, and Washington D.C. was the center of attention for creating favorable public policy. With the success of the civil rights movement and the war protests other groups were energized. Business lobbying increased because of the success of consumer and environmental groups' abilities to encourage government to increase safety in the workplace and improve environmental standards.

Another contributor to the expansion of groups was technology. The railroad and telegraph created a national network that contributed to an increase in group development in the early 1900s. WATS lines (wide-area telephone service) and computer-generated direct mail was used to solicit money and get people involved. Between 1960 and 1970 the number of groups increased by 60 percent and the number of lobbyists doubled.[4]

Interest groups have developed out of every corner of earth with the personal computer and the Internet. The Internet has allowed people with limited resources to develop groups with very little financial backing. The computer allows members to keep each other informed. The government often relies on groups to keep them informed. Group development can be to government advantage. Government will often provide funding to certain groups. Nonprofits tend to receive the most funding. The funding comes from grants and contracts that groups must apply for. The National Council for Senior Citizens, the National Governors Association, and the American Council of Education are just a few that receive federal funding. The organizers of groups are very experienced, generally from other established groups. In the 1950s and 1960s many people gained their talents while protesting the Vietnam War. Once one group has developed it opens the doors for the development of many more.

THE PURPOSE OF JOINING

In America most people join groups for economic and social reasons.[5] There could be a political goal or cause. Group members may receive a perk from being in a group. The discounts at drugstores, hotels, travel services, and investment counseling are often the benefits of belonging to the Association of Retired Persons (AARP). The services provided to the members bring millions of dollars to the group. Some members join groups for social reasons; their reason for joining is to make friends.

To maximize membership the group provides a mixture of benefits. Because members pay dues, it allows the organization to accomplish its goals and to enhance its influence with government. Why join the National Rifle Association (NRA)? It lobbies for gun regulations. Some members don't own a gun, but they receive other services such as their magazine, *The American Rifleman*, hunter's information guide, low-cost firearm insurance, and membership to local gun clubs. Some people join because they can't say no to pressure. Others join because they need to be a part of the organization to work. For example, Texas lawyers will join the Texas State Bar Association to practice law.

WHO JOINS?

Although we say America is a nation of joiners, not all people join organizations. The people who join the most are the wealthy and educated. They are the ones who can afford to pay the membership dues and have the free time to participate, with both the social and intellectual skills necessary to take part. Not only are groups looking for these types of people, the people are looking for groups to join. Whites are the largest group of people to join groups because of higher incomes and education.[6]

TYPES OF GROUPS

Many times we talk of interest groups as single-issue or multi-issue. Interest groups can be divided into categories, from economic groups, public interest groups, environmental groups, and good government groups. The AFL-CIO (1886) is an example of a multi-issue group even though it was founded around single issues. Groups tend to emerge over time and take on more issues. The NAACP began as a single interest group with a goal of advancing civil rights. Over time it evolved into a multi-issue group covering areas including legal, education, economic development, and prison population. Their education department seeks to accomplish their goals through policy development, training, collaboration, negotiation, legislation, litigation, and agitation. The NAACP Education Department's resources are strategically focused on three major objectives:[7]

1. Preventing racial discrimination in educational programs and services.
2. Advancing educational excellence.
3. Promoting an equal opportunity education agenda.

Other groups such as the National Organization for Women (NOW) are dedicated to making legal, political, social, and economic changes in our society in order to achieve their goals, which are to eliminate sexism and end all oppression. NOW was established on June 30, 1966, in Washington, D.C., by people attending the Third National Conference of the Commission on the Status of Women. Among NOW's twenty-eight founders was its first president, Betty Friedan, author of *The Feminine Mystique* (1963). Another founder, the late Rev. Pauli Murray, the first African American woman Episcopal priest, co-authored NOW's original Statement of Purpose which begins:

> *The purpose of NOW is to take action to bring women into full participation in the mainstream of American society now, exercising all privileges and responsibilities thereof in truly equal partnership with men.*

To be recognized as a multi-issue group, the organization must be prepared to operate on the local, state, and national levels to advance their interests.

Single-issue groups are different from multi-issue groups in both scope and range of their intensity. When a group's focus is concentrated in one area it can become more familiar with issues and can lead stronger lobbying efforts. The National Rifle Association is an excellent

example of a single-issue group aligned on its side of the gun control debate in America. Given the use of the Internet, people are creating all types of interest groups. Drunk driving or drug awareness groups, and gay rights groups, for example, can be classified as single-issue groups.

ECONOMIC INTEREST GROUPS

Interest groups need money to keep their daily operations going. The money received can be used to pay bills, staff, and other expenses. Members donate money so groups can perform certain functions for its members. Economic interest groups are concerned with the economic welfare of their members. Economic groups have a central focus, and that is the economic welfare of its members. There are many economic groups but the main three we consider here are business, organized labor, and farming. If a group decided to take on the task of representing economic interests, it must be fully organized more than some other types of interest groups. The only reason these groups exist is to make profits and increase the benefits of their members. These groups tend to have relationships with politicians who can help them achieve their goals through political means.

FUNCTION OF INTEREST GROUPS

Interest groups function as lobbyists. The bulk of what they do is provide money to members of Congress for their reelection campaign (see Table 21.1 for distributions). Washington D.C. has thousands of lobbyists working toward the same objective—to get more of whatever there is to get out of the government. Most lobbyists are very smooth talkers who may not be as unscrupulous as the media make them out to be. Most policy areas are split into several parts, and lobbyists tend to work these areas to their advantage. Let's examine transportation policy, which involves planes, trains, automobiles, suppliers, and consumers for state and local governments. When Congress votes on the basis of interest, are they really meeting the needs of constituents? Given the vast amount of work that is done by Congress, the idea of lobbyists functioning as a supplement to congressional representation could be problematic if the actions are not in line with the constituent base.

Table 21.1   Profile of Interest Groups.

Name	Single (S) or Multi (M) Issue	Members	PAC	2002 Election Cycle PAC Donation ($)
Economic Groups				
AFL-CIO	M	13 million	AFL-CIO	1,216,125
American Medical Association (1847)	M	300,000	AMA	2,479,885
Association of Trial Lawyers of America (1946)	M	60,000	Association of Trial Lawyers	2,796,753
National Association of Manufacturers (1895)	M	12,500	No	0
U.S. Chamber of Commerce	M	180,000	U.S. Chamber of Commerce	204,000

Continued

Name	Single (S) or Multi (M) Issue	Members	PAC	2002 Election Cycle PAC Donation ($)
Public Interest Groups				
American Association of Retired Persons (AARP) (1958)	M	32,000,000	No	0
Amnesty International U.S.A. (1961)	S	386,000	No	0
League of United Latin American Citizens (LULAC) (1929)	M	110,000	No	0
National Abortion and Reproduction Rights Action League (NARAL) (1969)	S		National Abortion and Reproduction Action League	444,663
National Association for the Advancement of Colored People (NAACP) (1909)	M	500,000	No	0
Human Rights Campaign Fund (1980)	S	17,000	Human Rights Campaign Fund	1,117,538
National Right to Life Committee (1973)	S	400,000	National Right to Life	43,000
Environmental Groups				
Environmental Defense Fund (EDF)(1967)	S	150,000	No	0
Green Peace (1971)	S	1,690,500	No	0
Sierra Club (1892)	S	550,000	Sierra Club	514,583
Good Government Groups				
Common Cause (1970)	S	270,000	No	0
Public Citizen, Inc. (1971)	M	100,000	No	0

Note: Figures are for the 2002 year. For up-to-date figures see www.opensecrets.org
From OPENSECRETS.ORG. Reprinted by permission.

Campaigns and elections are at the core of interest groups, but they also provide information both political and substantive. Congressional members are always concerned about who supports and who opposes legislation they are considering proposing. Lobbyists may conduct impact studies for members to see the effects of a proposed law. This is **substantive work**. It is very important that we not forget the technical work they provide such as drafting bills, selecting candidates to testify at legislative hearings, and writing questions that could be asked during the hearings.

INTEREST GROUP SUCCESS

The success of an interest group rests on its ability to raise money. The United States has seen more interest groups than any other country. If a group can help shape the public agenda it is well on the way to being successful. Interest groups want to shape public policy.

Groups feel successful when they win legislation in favor of their agenda or court cases. Another success for the interest group is when one of their members becomes an elected official or crafts policy. Finally, political scientists have studied additional factors that make for a successful interest group: leadership, patrons, funding, and a solid membership base.

Table 21.2 shows the top ten spending companies in Texas and the dollars they spent on lobbying the legislature in 2011.

Table 21.2   Top Spending Lobbying Clients.

Company	Value of Lobby Contracts ($)	Number of Contracts	Interest Group
AT&T	10,560,000	110	Communications
Energy Future Holdings Corp.	2,640,000	50	Energy/natural resources/waste
American Electric Power	1,950,000	13	Energy/natural resources/waste
Centerpoint Energy	1,805,000	22	Energy/natural resources/waste
McGinnis Lochridge & Kilgore	1,650,000	8	Lawyers/lobbyists
Global Gaming, LSP	1,600,000	9	Miscellaneous business
TX Assn for Home Care	1,565,000	11	Health
Oncor Electric Delivery Co.	1,525,000	26	Energy/natural resources/waste
TX Medical Assn.	1,480,000	25	Health
TX Assn of Realtors	1,420,000	14	Real estate

Source: Texans for Public Justice, Austin's Oldest Profession (2011).

Online Connections

Check out these websites to learn more about interest groups.

Texans for Public Justice. *http://www.tpj.org*

Interest group watchdog organization. *http://www.opensecrets.org*

National Organization of Women. *http://www.now.org*

ProChoice Website. *http://www.naral.org*

Right to Life Group. *http://www.nrlc.org/*

National Organization for the Advancement of Colored People. *http://www.naacp.org*

League of United Latin American Citizens (LULAC). *http://www.lulac.org*

American Medical Association. *http://www.ama-assn.org*

Association of Trial Lawyers of America. *http://www.atla.org*

AFL-CIO. *http://www.afl-cio.org*

Key Terms

Interest group   271

Lobbying   271

Substantive work   276

Suggested Readings

Jeffery M. Berry, The *Interest Group Society,* 2nd ed. (Boston: Little Brown, 1989).

Osha Gray Davidson, *The NRA and the Battle for Gun Control* (Ames: University of Iowa Press, 1998).

E.E. Schattschneider, *The Semi-Sovereign People* (New York: Holt, 1975).

David B. Truman, *The Governmental Process: Political Interest and Public Opinion* (New York: Knoff, 1951).

Notes

[1]G. Almond and S. Verba, Civil Culture (Boston: Little, Brown, 1965), pp. 266–306.

[2]D. Truman, *The Governmental Process* (New York: Knopf, 1945), pp. 25–26.

[3]J. Q. Wilson, *Political Organization* (New York: Basic Books, 1973), p. 198.

[4]K. L Schlozman and J. T. Tierney, "More of the Same: Washington Pressure Group Activity in a Decade of Change," *Journal of Politics* 45 (May 1983), pp. 335–356.

[5]Wilson, *Political Organization*, chapter 3.

[6]N. Babchuk and R. Thompson, "The Voluntary Associations of Negroes," *American Sociological Review* 27 (October 1962), pp. 662–665.

[7]National Organization for Women, By Laws, Article 3, Statement of Purpose, November 1999 at *http://www.now.org/organiza/bylaws.html#ArticleII*

1. Explain why interest groups are selfish and explain how one of the founding fathers tried to correct this.

_____

_____

_____

_____

_____

2. Why do American citizens join more groups than people in other countries?

_____

_____

_____

_____

_____

3. Compare and contrast the National Organization of Women (NOW) and the National Organization for the Advancement of Colored People (NAACP).

_____

_____

_____

_____

_____

4. What are the functions of interest groups?

_____

_____

_____

_____

NAME_____ COURSE_____ SECTION_____

Directions: Circle the correct answer to each of the following questions.

1. The AFL-CIO, National Organization of Women, and the National Association for the Advancement of Colored People are examples of _____ interest groups.
    a. multi-issue
    b. public
    c. single issue
    d. economic

2. The interest group with the largest membership is _____.
    a. Green Peace
    b. the AFL-CIO
    c. the National Rifle Association
    d. the American Association of Retired Persons

3. Which interest group donated the most money to the 2002 election?
    a. American Medical Association
    b. Association of Trial Lawyers of America
    c. Human Rights Campaign Fund
    d. AFL-CIO

4. In order for an interest group to be successful, they need to
    a. win legislation.
    b. be able to raise money.
    c. have a solid membership.
    d. all of the above.

5. Interest groups are mainly concerned with _____.
    a. providing money to Congress.
    b. providing impact studies to Congress.
    c. drafting bills.
    d. all of the above.

6. Which of the following interest groups is an example of a public interest group?
    a. League of Latin American Citizens (LULAC)
    b. American Medical Association (AMA)
    c. Green Peace
    d. Public Citizen, Inc.

7. Which of the following is an example of an economic interest group?
    a. National Right to Life Committee
    b. Sierra Club
    c. National Association of Manufacturers
    d. Common Cause

CHAPTER 22
The Texas Legislature

© Elena Yakusheva, 2013. Used under license from Shutterstock, Inc.

TEXAS LEGISLATIVE STRUCTURE

The Texas legislature, much like that of the United States legislature, is **bicameral;** it has two chambers. The Texas House of Representatives has one hundred fifty members and the Senate has thirty-one members.[1] Just like the federal level, each chamber must pass a bill for it to be enacted into law. The House of Representatives must act on raising money for the state. The Senate confirms appointments made by the governor to executive branch positions. Both chambers have a responsibility in the impeachment of public officials. The House can impeach an official and the Senate runs the trial and conviction if necessary of the official.

Sessions

The legislature meets regularly every two years; it is a **biennial legislature**. They meet for 140 days; this is called a regular session. The governor has the right to call a special session at any time for any purpose. A special session may last no longer than thirty days, but a governor can call an unlimited number of them. In 1991–1992 Governor Ann Richards called four special sessions.

Figure 22.1   Texas State seal.

© 2013 by Morphart Creation. Used under
license of Shutterstock, Inc.

Qualifications and Terms

House of Representatives   The qualifications to become a Texas State Representative are found in article III, section 7 of the Texas constitution. The qualifications for office are as follows:

- Must be a citizen of the United States.
- Must be a qualified voter.
- Must be at least twenty-one years old.
- Must have been a resident of this state for at least two years preceding the election.
- Must be a resident for at least one year of the district elected.

If elected to the position article III, section 4 of the Texas constitution states that they will serve two-year terms.

Senate   The Senate qualifications and terms of office are different. The length of term for a Texas senator is four years, two years longer than a House member; therefore the member can establish a greater rapport in the body. In article III, section 6 of the Texas constitution the qualifications to become a part of the Senate are stated as follows:

- Must be a citizen of the United States.
- Must be a qualified voter.
- Must have been a resident of this state for at least five years.
- Must be a one-year resident of the district being represented.
- Must be at least twenty-six years old.

Leaders

House of Representatives   The House of Representatives elects the leader called the **House Speaker** through a vote. The Speaker is elected to a two-year term. The Speaker has important powers, which are as follows:

- Appoints committee chairs (cannot remove).
- Appoints all members of committees.
- Recognizes members who want to speak on the house floor.
- Assigns bills to committees.

Senate   The Texas constitution states that the lieutenant governor presides over the Senate as the **Senate president**. The lieutenant governor is elected to the position by a statewide vote to a four-year term. In the absence of the lieutenant governor the Senate will elect a president **pro-tempore**, pro-tem in order to take over the job. Special powers that are granted to the lieutenant governor are as follows:

- Appoints all committee chairs (cannot remove).
- Appoints all committee members.
- Recognizes senators who want to speak on the floor.
- Votes to break a tie.
- Assigns bills to committees.

Committees

Just as the federal level works through a series of committees, so does the state level. Committees are used to help make the organization more efficient. Committees are formed by areas of specialty to foster better decision making. Committees work on drafting and revising bills, and holding public hearings to learn more about the issues surrounding the proposed bill.

Pay and Compensation

The members of the House and Senate have a base pay set by the Texas constitution, article III, section 24. It states that the members of the House and Senate should earn a salary of $600 per month, which adds up to $7,200 per year, unless a greater amount is recommended by the Texas Ethics Commission and approved by the voters. Each member shall also receive a per day allotment of $118 per day for personal expenses while the legislature is in session. The amount of the per day allotment can be changed by the Ethics Commission without approval of the voters. They also receive the same mileage rate as other state employees.[2]

PERSONAL CHARACTERISTICS

Occupation

The national trend with state legislatures is a shift from the traditional businessperson or lawyer running for office, to more teachers and preachers running for office. In Texas, however, this is not the case. One big possible reason for the trend not extending to Texas is the low pay of the state legislature and the flexibility needed in the job with the legislature meeting every two years for half of the year. The average teacher could not take off work for that long without losing her or his job or pay compensation. In the Texas legislature of 2017, large percentages of legislative members are businesspeople, lawyers, and members of nonprofit organizations where there is greater flexibility in the position.[3]

Gender and Party Affiliation

In 2017, the 85th Legislature, of the 150 members of the House of Representatives 81 percent of the members were male (121 members) and 19 percent of the members were female (29 members). As far as the party balances in the House 63 percent of the members were Republican (ninety-five members) and 37 percent were Democrats (fifty-five members).[4]

In the Senate, which has fewer members, the 2017 membership looks much different. Out of the thirty-one members, 25 percent were women (eight members) and 75 percent were men (23 members). As far as party the percentages are the same as the House, 63 percent of the members were Republican (twenty members) and 37 percent were Democrats (eleven members).[5]

LEGISLATIVE PROCESS

In order for bills to become law special processes are followed to ensure that all people have a right to speak out for and against the proposed law. The process that is followed in order for a bill to become law is called the **legislative process**.

A Bill Becomes a Law

For the state legislature to change a law or make a new law, a bill first needs to be drafted. Any person can write a bill; however, it needs to be sponsored and brought through the process by a member of the House or Senate. The Texas State constitution requires that a bill needs to be read on three separate days in the House and in the Senate. The bill must be read in the House and the Senate using the exact wording of the bill.

The first reading is conducted on the floor of the legislature; after this reading the bill is forwarded to a committee for review and revision. Committees must choose to hold public hearings or formal meetings on the bills. A public meeting requires that the committee posts notice five days in advance of the hearing on the bill. Public hearings also require open voting. The chair calls the meeting and then listens to testimony. In a formal meeting no expert witnesses are called. After the meetings, whether public or formal meetings, the committee determines what happens to the bill, approve it, amend it, send it to a subcommittee for review, take no action, or defeat it completely. If a bill reaches the next point and makes it out of committee, then it goes either to the House Calendars Committee if it is a house bill or to a procedural committee in the Senate.

House Calendar Committee

Once the bill has made it through a committee, it must next pass through another important juncture, the calendar committee, which sets the daily calendar for the House of Representatives. The calendar committee sends notice to all members of the House thirty-six hours before a bill will be heard in front of them. At the calendar committee hearing the committee must take a public vote on placing the bill on the House calendar within thirty days of receiving the bill.[6]

Senate Procedural Committee

The Senate has the Senate administration committee that sets a local and uncontested calendar for bills. If bills are to be considered out of the order there needs to be a two-thirds Senate majority vote in order to suspend the regular order of business.

Figure 22.2 Texas legislative process.

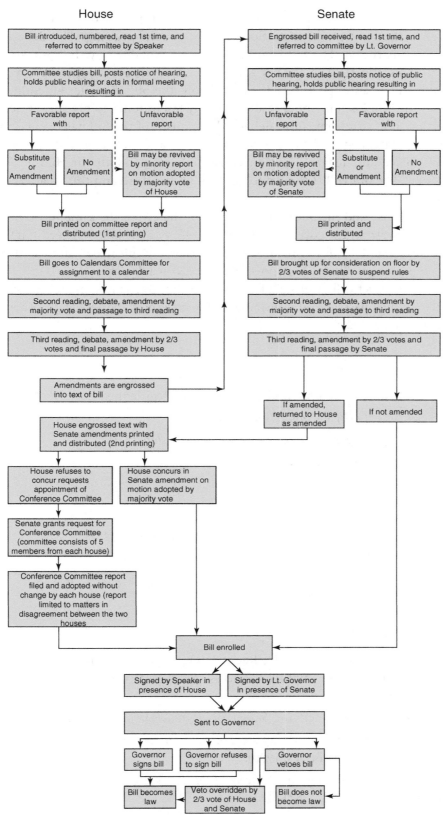

The Bill Reaches the House or Senate Floor

If the bill has passed through the committee and been placed on the calendar, then it will reach the House or Senate floor for the second reading. The debate really happens on this round. The bill is announced and explained by the sponsor within twenty minutes and then questions are asked. Then all House members and Senate members have an opportunity to speak about the bill and offer amendments or changes to the bill. Each member is allowed only ten minutes to give his or her opinion about the bill. After the entire debate, the sponsor of the bill has twenty minutes to close the debate. Just as in the U.S. Senate, the Texas Senate does not have any time constraints placed on debate. The time constraints refer to only the House. The vote is then taken. The bill will still need to go through the third and final reading during the next session.

After the House and the Senate have approved the bill in the same form, the bill is passed to the governor. The governor can sign the bill, veto the bill, or ignore it. If the governor ignores the bill it will automatically become law, but this makes an executive statement by not signing it. Figure 22.2 shows the process on a flowchart.

This figure shows the flow of a bill from the time it is introduced in the House of Representatives to final passage and transmittal to the governor. The Senate procedure is the same, but in reverse order.

Online Connections

Check out these websites to find more about the Texas legislature.

The Texas Senate. *http://www.capitol.state.tx.us*

The Texas House of Representatives. *http://www.house.state.tx.us*

Texas Resources. *http://www.texasonline.state.tx.us*

Key Terms

Bicameral 283	Biennial legislature 283
House Speaker 284	Senate president 285
Pro-tempore 285	Legislative process 286

Suggested Readings

Arthur J. Anderson, "Texas Legislative Redistricting: Proposed Constitutional and Statutory Amendments for an Improved Process," *Southwestern Law Journal 43* (October 1989): 719–757.

Gary Boulard, "Lobbyist as Outlaws" *State Legislature 22* (January 1996): 20–25.

Alan Rosenthal, *Governors and Legislatures: Contending Powers* (Washington, DC: Congressional Quarterly Books, 1990).

Texas Legislative Council, *Presiding Officers of the Texas Legislature, 1946–1984* (Austin: Texas Legislative Council, 1982).

Notes

[1]Texas Constitution article 3, section 2 at *http://www.capitol.state.tx.us/txconst*

[2]Texas Constitution article 3, section 24 at *http://www.capitol.state.tx.us/txconst*

[3]http://www.senate.state.tx.us/75r/Senate/facts.htm

[4]http://www.lrl.state.tx.us/sessions/memberStatistics.cfm

[5]http://www.lrl.state.tx.us/sessions/memberStatistics.cfm

[6]Texas Legislature Online, How to follow a bill through the legislature at *http://www.capitol. state.tx.us/tlo/help/legislative_process.htm*

[7]Available at *http://www.capitol.state.tx.us/capitol/legproc/diagram.htm*

1. Describe the structure of the Texas legislature.

_____

_____

_____

_____

_____

2. List the qualifications and terms of the members of the legislature.

_____

_____

_____

_____

_____

3. Explain some of the personal characteristics of the people in these offices.

_____

_____

_____

_____

_____

4. Explain how a bill becomes law in Texas.

_____

_____

_____

_____

_____

Directions: Circle the correct answer to each of the following questions.

1. The Texas legislature has two chambers, the House and the Senate. This is called a _____ legislature.
   a. biennial
   b. triennial
   c. bicameral
   d. tricameral

2. The Texas Senate has _____ members and the House has _____ members.
   a. 31; 150
   b. 35; 155
   c. 150; 31
   d. 155; 35

3. The _____ can raise money for the state.
   a. House of Representatives
   b. Senate
   c. both a and b
   d. none of the above

4. The _____ confirms appointments made by the governor for the executive branch positions.
   a. House of Representatives
   b. Senate
   c. both a and b
   d. none of the above

5. In order for a bill to become law the _____ must pass the bill.
   a. House of Representatives
   b. Senate
   c. both a and b
   d. none of the above

6. Which of the following is not a qualification to become a Texas State representative?
   a. Need to be a qualified voter.
   b. Need to be at least twenty-one years of age.
   c. Need to be a citizen of the United States.
   d. Need to be a resident of the district elected to for at least two years.

7. The legislature meets every two years for 140 days. It is a
   _____ legislature.
   a. biennial
   b. bicameral
   c. triennial
   d. tricameral

8. House of Representative members are elected to _____-year terms.
   a. two
   b. six
   c. four
   d. eight

CHAPTER 23
The Texas Executive Branch

© 2013 by spirit of America. Used under license of Shutterstock, Inc.

TEXAS EXECUTIVE STRUCTURE

Texas has a unique executive system of government, where no singular leader has control of the executive branch. In the federal system there is a leader, the president, who appoints his staff to positions in the executive branch. However, in Texas we have a **plural executive branch** where each of the members of the executive branch are elected to positions rather than appointed. The Texas constitution in article IV, section 1 states that, "The Executive Department of the State shall consist of a Governor, who shall be the Chief Executive Officer of the State, a Lieutenant Governor, Secretary of State, Comptroller of Public Accounts, Commissioner of the General Land Office, and Attorney General." Article IV, section 2 goes on to state that all the members of the executive branch should be elected to positions, except for the secretary of state who is appointed by the governor.[1]

The plural executive system that Texas has was created to ensure that no one person had control over everything. The actions of the government are controlled and checked even within the same branch. The conflict can be created when members of the executive branch are from different parties and have very different views on the way that things should be done. Many times this can create discordance of policies and a lack of getting things done. Other states have a cabinet system set up where the governor chooses his or her own cabinet. There are forty-three states with this system, where the governor can

© 2015 by f11photo / Shutterstock.com

choose the cabinet.[2] At press time in 2013, we have an executive branch that is all from the Republican Party, many of whom are newly elected to their positions.

THE GOVERNOR

The governor is the most recognized and highly publicized office in the state. The governor of Texas has many different roles in the function of the state. Many times it has depended on the personality of the officeholder as to how large of a role that governor played in influencing policy decisions.[3]

Qualifications

The Texas constitution spells out the qualifications and term of the governor. Article IV, section 4 states, "[T]he governor shall hold his office for the term of four years, or until his successor shall be duly installed. He shall be at least thirty years of age, a citizen of the United States, and shall have resided in this State at least five years immediately preceding his election."[4]

Most of the Texas governors have been Democrats, well-educated, wealthy, white males. There have been four Republican governors: Bill Clements (1979–1983 and 1987–1991), George W. Bush (1994–1999), Rick Perry (1999–2014), the longest serving governor, and currently Greg Abbott (2015–present). Texas has had two female governors: Miriam A. "Ma" Ferguson (1925–1927 and 1933–1935) and Ann Richards (1991–1995).

Powers

The governor of Texas has limited powers over the budget and appointments to a personal cabinet. The governor's specific powers are detailed in the following sections.

Appointment Powers   The governor cannot appoint his or her own cabinet, like the president. The governor can appoint members to his or her own staff without approval from the Senate. The governor can appoint people to about 150 boards and commissions. All of the board appointments need to come with the consent of two-thirds of the Senate. The members of the committees, however, serve six-year terms, which do not change-over all in the same year. Therefore, the governor does not have the power to do wholesale changeover on these committees, especially if the governor only serves one four-year term. The governor cannot remove a person from a committee just because another governor appointed him or her. The only way that an appointee can be removed is for the governor to show cause for the removal and then obtain two-thirds of the Senate approval.

Budgetary Powers   The Texas governor lacks budgetary control. The governor makes recommendations to the legislature, but they are solely responsible for creating and crafting a budget. The **Legislative Budget Board**, which consists of the lieutenant governor, the speaker of the house and eight other legislative members, creates a budget and submits it to the legislature.

The governor has been allowed since 1985 to act in emergency situations when the legislature is in recess to transfer funds to another agency.

The governor also has the responsibility to report to the state the budget situation at the beginning of each session. The governor needs to "address the Legislature every session to report on the condition of the state, status of public money controlled by the governor, recommend a biennial budget and money to be raised by taxation."[5]

Military Powers   The Texas constitution provides in article IV, section 7 for the governor

> *shall be Commander-in-Chief of the military forces of the State, except when they are called into actual service of the United States. He shall have power to call forth the militia to execute the laws of the State, to suppress insurrections, and to repel invasions.*[6]

The governor cannot declare war on another country, but when natural disasters occur or riots break out the governor can call on the National Guard, Texas Rangers, or the department of Public Safety to keep peace and protect citizens.

Clemency Power   The governor appoints a board of pardons and paroles. They oversee the release of prisoners into society. The board can make recommendations to the governor on pardons for criminals, change of a death penalty sentence to life in prison, or conditional pardons. The governor then has the final decision on the release or changing of the sentence. The governor can issue only a thirty-day stay of execution for a person on death row. The two entities serve as a check and balance system.

© 2013 by Dan Lee. Used under license of Shutterstock, Inc.

Veto Power   The governor has the power to veto legislation. All the bills that pass in the House and Senate must pass the governor's desk for approval. The governor has ten days to act on a bill if the legislature is in session and twenty days, if the legislature is not in session. If the governor signs the bill it becomes law. However, the governor may veto one item in a bill or the entire bill. This is a powerful tool for the governor. The legislature can overturn the veto with a two-thirds vote in both the House and Senate for the bill. The governor can also not sign the bill, ignoring it, whereby it automatically becomes law.

Special Session Power   The governor has the power to call special sessions of the legislature for thirty days at a time. There is no limit to how many the governor can call. During the special session the governor sets the agenda. The special session is a use of the governor's power that tests the rapport that he/she has with the legislature.

Compensation

The state provides the governor with this compensation package.

- Salary per year: $153,750
- Mansion to live in
- Travel expenses
- Security team
- Access to state-owned planes, cars, and helicopters

The governor of Texas is in the middle of the pack when it comes to salary. New York's governor earns $179,000 per year. The lowest salary for a state governor is Maine with $70,000 per year. Pensylvania's governor has the highest salary of $190,823 per year.[7]

The Texas constitution forbids the governor to work in another job. Article IV, section 6 states,

Table 23.1   Governor Compensation by State ($).

THE COUNCIL OF STATE GOVERNMENTS July 2016 Capitol Research: Governors' Salaries 2016	
2015/2016 Governors' Salaries	
	2016 Governor's Salary
	Current Dollars
Alabama*	$120,395
Alaska	$145,000
Arizona	$95,000
Arkansas	$141,000
California	$182,789
Colorado	$90,000
Connecticut	$150,000

THE COUNCIL OF STATE GOVERNMENTS
July 2016
Capitol Research: Governors' Salaries 2016

2015/2016 Governors' Salaries

2016 Governor's Salary

	Current Dollars
Delaware	$171,000
Florida*	$130,273
Georgia	$139,339
Hawaii	$149,556
Idaho	$122,597
Illinois*	$177,412
Indiana	$111,688
Iowa	$130,000
Kansas	$99,636
Kentucky	$140,070
Louisiana	$130,000
Maine	$70,000
Maryland	$170,000
Massachusetts	$151,800
Michigan	$159,300
Minnesota	$127,150
Mississippi	$122,160
Missouri	$133,821
Montana	$111,570
Nebraska	$105,000
Nevada	$149,573
New Hampshire	$129,992
New Jersey	$175,000
New Mexico	$110,000
New York	$179,000
North Carolina	$142,265

Continued

THE COUNCIL OF STATE GOVERNMENTS July 2016 Capitol Research: Governors' Salaries 2016	
2015/2016 Governors' Salaries	
	2016 Governor's Salary
	Current Dollars
North Dakota	$129,096
Ohio	$148,886
Oklahoma	$147,000
Oregon	$98,600
Pennsylvania	$190,823
Rhode Island	$132,710
South Carolina	$106,078
South Dakota	$109,264
Tennessee*	$187,500
Texas	$153,750
Utah	$109,900
Vermont	$145,538
Virginia	$175,000
Washington	$171,898
West Virginia	$150,000
Wisconsin	$147,328
Wyoming	$105,000
National Average	$137,415 . . .

Source: The Council of State Governments, The Book of the States. "Table 4.3: The Governors: Compensation, Staff, Travel and Residence." 2015, 2016.

*Alabama—Gov. Robert Bentley is not accepting his salary until the unemployment rate in Alabama drops.

*Florida—Gov. Rick Scott does not accept a salary.

*Illinois—Gov. Bruce Rauner returns all but $1.00 of his salary.

*Tennessee—Gov. Haslam returns his salary to the state.

> *During the time he holds the office of Governor, he shall not hold any other office: civil, military or corporate; nor shall he practice any profession, and receive compensation, reward, fee, or the promise thereof for the same; nor receive any salary, reward or compensation or the promise thereof from any person or corporation, for any service rendered or performed during the time he is Governor, or to be thereafter rendered or performed.*[8]

LIEUTENANT GOVERNOR

The lieutenant governor is said to be one of the most powerful officials in Texas State government. This position is filled primarily with legislative duties. The **lieutenant governor** is elected to the position and serves a four-year term. The legislative powers that the lieutenant governor has includes the power over the senate and influence over legislation. The lieutenant governor can also become governor if the governor becomes ill and has to leave office, dies, is removed from office, or leaves before his or her term is up. This occurred in 1999 when George W. Bush left the office of the governor to run for the presidency of the United States. The lieutenant governor at that time was Rick Perry, who then became the governor.

The lieutenant governor also has control over the budget because he or she is chair of the Legislative Budget Board. The current lieutenant governor is Dan Patrick, a Republican elected in 2014 and sworn in on January 20, 2015. He makes the same salary as the Texas legislative members, $7,200 per year. The power of the position outweighs the salary.

ATTORNEY GENERAL

The attorney general is the state's lawyer. The attorney general helps collect child support payments, enforces consumer protection laws, and defends state laws. This office generally deals with civil law cases. The criminal cases are left to the local areas to deal with. However, the office does provide for consultation on cases or in some cases will handle appeals. The attorney general in Texas has a salary of $150,000 per year and serves four-year terms. The current 51st attorney general is Ken Paxton.[9]

COMPTROLLER OF PUBLIC ACCOUNTS

The **comptroller** is the tax collector and chief accountant for the state. The comptroller must show that there is enough revenue in the budget to pass a bill. This is called a **pay as you go system**. The legislature cannot pass a bill unless the money has been proven to be there by the comptroller. The comptroller receives all the state revenues and administers deposits to the banks. The comptroller also has the authority to conduct audits of school districts and state agencies. The comptroller has a salary of $150,000 per year. The current Comptroller of Public Accounts is Republican Glenn Hegar.[10]

COMMISSIONER OF THE GENERAL LAND OFFICE

The **land commissioner** manages the state-held land and mineral rights. In Texas there are about 22 million acres of land that the state owns and collects mineral rights on. The land

commissioner is also responsible for providing veterans with low interest loans on land. The current land commissioner is Republican George P. Bush.

COMMISSIONER OF AGRICULTURE

The **agricultural commissioner** is responsible for ensuring there is support for agricultural research and education. The agricultural commissioner is responsible for making sure that the agricultural laws are followed and provides inspections of scales, pumps, and meters. This person is elected to a four-year term. The salary for the current agricultural commissioner, Republican Sid Miller, is $92,217 per year.[11]

SECRETARY OF STATE

The **secretary of state** is responsible for carrying out election laws and oversees election activities. This is the only appointed position that the governor has. The current secretary of state is Republican Rolando B. Pablos; he has a salary of $125,880.[12]

Online Connections

Check out these websites to learn more about the Texas executive branch.

Texas Overview. http://www.texasonline.com

Governor. http://www.governor.state.tx.us

Lieutenant governor. http://www.ltgov.state.tx.us

Attorney general. http://www.oag.state.tx.us

Key Terms

Plural executive branch 295	Legislative Budget Board 297
Lieutenant governor 301	Attorney general 301
Comptroller 301	Land commissioner 301
Agricultural commissioner 302	Secretary of state 302

Suggested Readings

John B. Connally, *In History's Shadow: An American Odyssey (New York: Hyperion, 1993)*.

Kenneth E. Hendrickson, *Chief Executives of Texas: From Stephen F. Austin to John B. Connally, Jr.* (College Station: Texas A&M University Press, 1995).

Mike Shropshire and Frank Schaefer, *The Thorny Rose of Texas* (New York: Carol Publishing, 1994).

Texas General Land Office, *The Land Commissioner of Texas* (Austin: Texas General Land Office, 1986).

Notes

[1]Texas State Constitution, article 4, sections 1 and 2, at *http://www.capitol.state.tx.us/txconst/sections*

[2]Council of State Governments, *The Book of States, Volume 33,* 2000, p. 27.

[3]James E. Anderson, Richard W. Murray, and Edward L. Farley, *Texas Politics,* 6th ed. (New York: HarperCollins, 1992), pp. 166–191.

[4]Texas State Constitution, article 4, section 4, at *http://www.capitol.state.tx.us/txconst/ sections/cn000400-000400.html*

[5]Texas Library and Archive Commission, Executive Branch, at *http://www.tsl.state.tx.us/ ld/pubs/govinfo/chap4.html*

[6]Texas State Constitution, article 4, section 7, at *http://www.capitol.state.tx.us/txconst/ sections/cn000400-000700.html*

[7]Council of State Governments, The Book of States, Vol. 33, 2000, p. 18.

[8]Texas State Constitution, article 4, section 6, at *http://www.capitol.state.tx.us/txconst/ sections/cn000400-000600.html*

[9]Council of State Governments, *The Book of States,* 2010.

[10]http://sunshinereview.org/index.php/Texas_state_government_salary

[11]http://sunshinereview.org/index.php/Texas_state_government_salary

[12]http://sunshinereview.org/index.php/Texas_state_government_salary

1. What compensation does the governor receive while in office?

_____

_____

_____

_____

2. List and explain the powers of the governor.

_____

_____

_____

_____

_____

3. List the qualifications to be governor.

_____

_____

_____

_____

4. Describe the role of the lieutenant governor in Texas government.

_____

_____

_____

_____

_____

Directions: Circle the correct answer to each of the following questions.

1. The Texas executive branch is elected to the position. This is called a
   _____ executive branch.
   a. singular
   b. powerless
   c. plural
   d. powerful

2. The one position in the executive branch that is appointed by the governor
   is the _____.
   a. attorney general
   b. secretary of state
   c. lieutenant governor
   d. comptroller of public accounts

3. _____ states have a cabinet system in the state government.
   a. Forty-five
   b. Forty-three
   c. Twenty-three
   d. Twenty-five

4. The cabinet system is where _____.
   a. the legislature elects the members to the executive branch
   b. the governor appoints members to the executive branch
   c. voters elect the members to the executive branch
   d. none of the above

5. In order to be the Texas governor you need to be at least _____ years old.
   a. twenty-five
   b. twenty-eight
   c. thirty
   d. thirty-five

6. Every _____ years there is an election for the Texas governorship.
   a. three
   b. six
   c. two
   d. four

Sample Test Questions

7. The governor must live in the state of Texas for at least _____ years before the election.
   a. three
   b. five
   c. four
   d. six

8. Texas has had _____ Republican governors.
   a. two
   b. four
   c. three
   d. five

CHAPTER 24
The Texas Judiciary

© 2013 by AlenKadr. Used under license of Shutterstock, Inc.

The laws that govern the Texas judicial system are based on the U.S. Constitution and the Texas constitution. There are two types of law in the Texas judicial system: the criminal and the civil. The punishments established for criminal activity are found in the Texas penal code. This is where punishments and crimes are listed. **Civil cases** are noncriminal legal disputes between entities. The Texas system is set up to handle both types of legal cases. Each court has special duties. The Texas Constitution article V, section 1 provides the Texas legislature with the responsibility to develop courts and jurisdictions of courts as they see necessary.

STRUCTURE OF THE JUDICIAL BRANCH

There are five levels in the Texas court system. Each level of the system has a different jurisdiction. One level of jurisdiction is **original jurisdiction**, where cases are heard for the first time. The second level of jurisdiction is **appellate jurisdiction**, where cases have been ruled on in a lower court and are sent to this level to determine if legal procedures were followed correctly. Texas courts have specific powers. Figure 24.1 shows the hierarchy of the system and the role that each plays in the entire Texas court system.

Municipal Courts and Justice of the Peace

The lowest-ranking courts are the municipal courts and the justice of the peace. The **municipal courts** have limited jurisdiction and they handle limited criminal cases, such as cases involving city ordinances and traffic tickets. The **justice of the peace** is another name for what other areas call small claims court. This court has limited jurisdiction over civil matters that involve less than $200 in damages and criminal matters that are punishable by fines only. Each of these lowest court judges has a constable who is elected to deliver warrants and perform other duties.

County Courts

The next level of court is the county court. The Texas constitution created these courts to assist in the rural areas. The constitution states only that there should be one county court. However, the Texas State legislature has designed two others to help relieve the burden of cases. There are three different courts at this level, and each is designed for a specific purpose.

The first at this level are the **constitutional county courts**. In each of the 254 counties of the state, one county court is presided over by a county judge. These courts have jurisdiction over civil cases in which the amount argued ranges from $200 to $5,000.[1] They have original jurisdiction over all Class A and Class B misdemeanor criminal cases, which are the more serious minor offenses. These courts have appellate jurisdiction in cases appealed from justice of the peace and municipal courts, except in counties where county courts at law have been established.

Figure 24.1

State Highest Appellate Courts	Texas Supreme Court	Court of Criminal Appeals	
	1 Court 9 Justices	1 Court 9 Justices	
	Civil Cases Only	Criminal Cases Only	
	Civil Appeals	**Criminal Appeals**	
State Intermediate Appellate Courts	**Court of Appeals** 14 Courts 80 Judges Cases on Appeal		
State Trial Courts of General and Special Jurisdiction	**District Courts** 409 Courts 409 Courts		
	Trial Courts Civil and Criminal Cases		
County Trial Courts of Limited Jurisdiction	**Constitutional County Courts** 254 Courts 254 Judges	**County Courts at Law** 187 Courts 187 Judges	**Statutory Probate Courts** 16 Courts 16 Judges
	Limited Civil and Criminal Cases	Limited Civil and Criminal Cases	Probate Cases
Local Trial Courts of Limited Jurisdiction	**Municipal Courts** 854 Cities 1,226 Judges Limited Criminal Cases	**Justice of Peace Courts** 838 Courts 838 Judges "Small Claims Court" Limited Civil and Criminal Cases	

Source: Texas Office of Court Administration

The county judge also serves as the administrative head of the county government. In the more populated counties, such as Dallas County, the administrative duties take up most of the time of the county judge, and the other courts at this level, mentioned above, take care of the judicial duties of that office.[2]

The second court, **statutory probate courts** of Texas, are located in the state's six largest metropolitan areas. These courts have original and exclusive jurisdiction over probate matters, guardianship cases, and mental health commitments of the county. In most counties, the constitutional county court has original probate jurisdiction.[3]

The third court at this level was created by the legislature to relieve the burden of the other county courts. These courts are called the **county courts at law**. The civil jurisdiction of most county courts at law varies, but is usually more than that of the justice of the peace courts and less than that of the **district courts**. County courts at law have appellate jurisdiction in cases appealed from justice of the peace and municipal courts.[4]

District Courts

The **district courts** are the trial courts of general jurisdiction of Texas. The area served by each court is established by the legislature. Each county must be served by at least one district court. District courts try both criminal and civil cases. They are responsible for any cases that are not handled in lower courts. Original jurisdiction is granted to all state district courts in these cases: felony criminal cases, cases involving title to land, divorce cases, election contest cases, and civil matters in which the amount of money is $200 or more. In more urban counties the courts may specialize in different areas such as civil, criminal, juvenile, or family law matters. In urban areas there is a large backlog of cases and many times in criminal cases this backlog results in plea bargains being made. A plea bargain is when a person charged with a crime negotiates a plea with prosecutors for a lesser sentence with out going to trial.[5]

Court of Appeals

The **court of appeals** hears only cases that have been ruled on by lower courts; it has appellate jurisdiction. Fourteen courts have been created by the Texas legislature. Figure 24.2 shows the location of the court of appeals in Texas. These courts hear both civil and criminal cases. Article V, section 6 of the Texas constitution states that the court of appeals must have a chief justice and at least two other justices. The legislature has increased the number in large areas of the fourteen courts; five of them have only three justices and the remaining have been granted more justices by the legislature. Dallas has thirteen justice positions. Currently there are a total of eighty justice positions across the state. Many times the court will meet in groups of three, but on the large cases the entire panel will hear the case.[6]

Court of Criminal Appeals

The **court of criminal appeals** is the highest state court in Texas when it comes to criminal cases. Article V, section 4 of the Texas constitution states that there will be eight judges and one presiding judge on this court. Cases that appear in this court that contain constitutional questions can be appealed to the U.S. Supreme Court after the court has heard the arguments.[7]

Figure 24.2 Location of Appellate Courts in Texas.

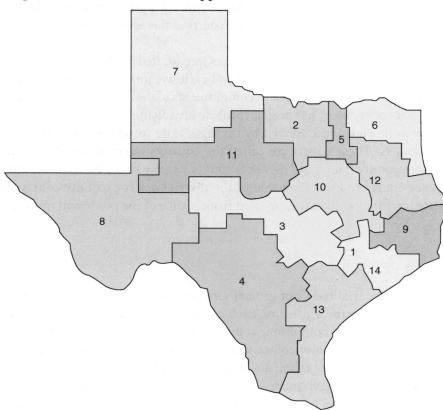

First Court of Appeals, **Houston**
Second Court of Appeals, **Fort Worth**
Third Court of Appeals, **Austin**
Fourth Court of Appeals, **San Antonio**
Fifth Court of Appeals, **Dallas**
Sixth Court of Appeals, **Texarkan**a
Seventh Court of Appeals, **Amarillo**
Source: Texas Judiciary Online[9]

Eighth Court of Appeals, **El Paso**
Ninth Court of Appeals, **Beaumont**
Tenth Court of Appeals, **Waco**
Eleventh Court of Appeals, **Eastland**
Twelfth Court of Appeals, **Tyler**
Thirteenth Court of Appeals, **Corpus Christi**
Fourteenth Court of Appeals, **Houston**

Texas Supreme Court

The Texas **Supreme Court** is the highest civil court in Texas. As provided by the Texas constitution, article V, section 2 the Supreme Court of Texas is made up of a chief justice and eight justices. The Texas Supreme Court has final appellate jurisdiction in all civil and juvenile cases. The Supreme Court also has many administrative duties. The court makes the rules of practice and procedure governing trials and appeals in civil and juvenile cases. It determines the rules of administration for the Texas judicial system and the rules for the operation of the state Office of Court Administration. The Supreme Court also appoints the Commission on Judicial Conduct and the Board of Law Examiners that oversees the state bar and the licensing of attorneys in the state. In order to help the court system run more smoothly and help in the distribution of cases in Texas, the Supreme Court also can transfer cases between the fourteen courts of appeals.[8]

HOW TO BECOME A JUDGE

The Texas constitution spells out the qualifications for becoming a judge and how judges are selected in Texas. Texas is one of only eight states still selecting its entire state judiciary by partisan ballot.[10] In the federal system, judges are appointed; however, in Texas all judges are elected, except for the municipal judges. Therefore, politics enters into the realm of the judicial system even more at the state level. The salary and qualifications gradually increase as one moves up in the hierarchy of the Texas court system. We will examine the qualifications and selections of judges at each level of the court system.

Municipal Judge and Justice of the Peace

Local municipalities determine criteria for selecting a municipal judge and most are appointed by the city council. On the other hand, the justice of the peace is an elected official and serves four-year terms. The salary for a justice of the peace is determined by the area in which they work. To be a justice of the peace you do not need to be a licensed attorney.

County Level Courts

Constitutional County Courts   The judges in this court are elected to a four-year term, countywide. A constitutional county judge is not required to be a lawyer. About 85 percent of county judges are not lawyers. However, they need to be well-informed about the law to ensure that they follow the correct procedures with evidence and legalities. The county judge is a state official who is paid $1,000 less than a district judge; the state minimum for a district judge is about $57, 300.

Statutory County Courts and Court at Law   The statutory courts and the court at law require that the judge have a law degree. The judges here are elected to four-year terms in countywide elections. These judges are also state officials who are paid $1,000 less than a district judge; the state minimum for a district judge is about $57, 300. Some statutory court judges have higher salaries than that of the chief justice of the Texas Supreme Court; the law does not set a maximum salary, and local counties determine their pay.[11]

District Courts   A district judge must be a citizen of the United States and of Texas, be licensed to practice law in Texas, and have been a practicing lawyer or a judge for four years before election. The judge has to have resided in the area in which he or she is campaigning for at least two years. District judges are elected to four-year terms and their salaries are fixed by the legislature. In order for district judges to get a raise the legislature needs to approve it. The current base salary for a district court judge is $57,000.[12]

Court of Appeals/Court of Criminal Appeals/Supreme Court

Court of appeals justices, court of criminal appeals justices, and Supreme Court justices all have the same qualification requirements. However, court of appeals justices are elected to four-year terms within the district that they represent and the other two are elected to six-year staggered terms in a statewide election. In order to become a justice of any of the three highest courts in Texas you would need to possess the following criteria:

- Licensed to practice law in Texas.
- Be a citizen of the United States and of Texas.
- Be thirty-five years old.
- Be a practicing attorney or judge for at least ten years.

The Texas constitution states that the salaries of the judges should be equal to one another and should "each receive such compensation as shall be provided by law." The state legislature again determines salaries for the justices.[13]

IS THE JUDICIARY FOR SALE?

As mentioned previously, Texas is one of only eight states still selecting its entire state judiciary by partisan ballot.[14] Politics enters into the realm of the judicial system even more at the state level. In the two highest courts, the Supreme Court and the court of criminal appeals, the candidates need to launch statewide elections, which require lots of money. With this need to raise campaign funds it has led many to wonder, can the justices be bought? Large campaign donations come from special interests, and many people are concerned if this is right. Reform of the judicial system, however, would require constitutional change.

The third branch of government is the judicial system. The Texas judicial system is based on the Texas constitution. The constitution spells out all the requirements of the justices and explains how the structure should function. The Supreme Court has the power to make changes in processes that they see will help the judiciary function better.

Online Connections

Check out these websites to find more about the Texas judicial system.

The court structure. *http://www.courts.state.tx.us*

The Supreme Court. *http://www.supreme.courts.state.tx.us*

The court of criminal appeals. *http://www.cca.courts.state.tx.us*

County courts. *http://www.county.org*

Municipal courts. *http://www.courts.state.tx.us/trial/municour.asp*

Key Terms

Civil cases   309

Appellate jurisdiction   309

Justice of the peace   310

Statutory probate courts   311

District courts   311

Court of criminal appeals   311

Original jurisdiction   309

Municipal courts   309

Constitutional county courts   310

County courts at law   311

Court of appeals   311

Supreme Court   312

Suggested Readings

Lawrence Baum, "Supreme Courts in the Policy Process," in *The State of the States*, ed. Carl E. Van Horn (Washington, DC: CQ Press, 1996), pp. 143–160.

Anthony Champagne, "Judicial Selection in Texas: Democracy's Deadlock." In *Texas Politics: A Reader*, eds. Anthony Champagne and Edward J. Harpham (New York: W. W. Norton, 1997), pp. 97–110.

John Hill, "Taking Texas Judges Out of Politics: An Argument for Merit Election," *Baylor Law Review 40* (Summer 1988): pp. 340–366.

Texas Judicial Council, *Office of Court Administration: Texas Judicial System, 69th Annual Report* (Austin: Texas Judicial Council, 1997).

Texas Research League, *Texas Courts: A Proposal for Structural-Functional Reform*. Report 2 (Austin: Texas Research League, 1991).

Notes

[1]Paul Womack, *Handbook of Texas Online: Judiciary, Texas State Historical Association*, January 2002 at *http://www.tsha.utexas.edu/handbook/online/articles/view/JJ/jzj1.html*

[2]Texas Judiciary Online, *Texas Constitutional County Courts* at *http://www.courts.state.tx.us/trial/constit.asp*

[3]Texas Judiciary Online, *Texas Statutory Probate Courts* at *http://www.courts.state.tx.us/trial/probate.asp*

[4]Texas Judiciary Online, *Courts at Law,* at *http://www.courts.state.tx.us/trial/catlaw.asp*

[5]Texas Judiciary Online, *District Courts* at *http://www.courts.state.tx.us/trial/courtlin.asp*

[6]Texas Judiciary Online, *Texas Courts of Appeals* at *http://www.courts.state.tx.us/appcourt.asp*

[7]*http://www.cca.courts.state.tx.us*

[8]*http://www.supreme.courts.state.tx.us/AboutCourt.htm*

[9]Texas Judiciary Online at *http://www.courts.state.tx.us/appcourt.asp*

[10]Chief Justice Thomas R. Phillip, *State of the Judiciary*, February 14, 1989, at *http://www.tomphillips.com/state5.htm*

[11]Paul Womack, *Handbook of Texas Online: Judiciary*, Texas State Historical Association, January 2002 at *http://www.tsha.utexas.edu/handbook/online/articles/view/JJ/jzj1.html*

[12]Texas Constitution, Article 5, Section 7 at *http://www.capitol.state.tx.us/txconst/sections/cn000500-000700.html*

[13]Texas State Constitution, Article 5, Section 2 at *http://www.capitol.state.tx.us/txconst/sections/cn000500-000200.html*

[14]Chief Justice Thomas R. Phillip, *State of the Judiciary*, February 14, 1989, at *http://www.tomphillips.com/state5.htm*

Evaluation

1. Contrast civil and criminal law.

_____

_____

_____

_____

_____

2. Describe the hierarchy of the Texas court system.

_____

_____

_____

_____

_____

3. Explain the role of the Texas Supreme Court.

_____

_____

_____

_____

_____

4. Explain the requirements to become judge at each level in the state system.

_____

_____

_____

_____

_____

NAME_____ COURSE_____ SECTION_____

Directions: Circle the correct answer to each of the following questions.

1. District courts are granted _____.
   a. only appellate jurisdiction.
   b. both appellate and original jurisdiction.
   c. only original jurisdiction.
   d. none of the above

2. The Court of Appeals hears _____ cases.
   a. appellate
   b. original jurisdiction
   c. probate
   d. none of the above

3. The Court of Appeals rules on _____ cases.
   a. civil
   b. criminal
   c. both a and b
   d. none of the above

4. There are _____ courts of appeals in Texas.
   a. ten
   b. twelve
   c. fourteen
   d. sixteen

5. The court of criminal appeals is the highest criminal state court in Texas. How many justices are there on the court?
   a. Five
   b. Nine
   c. Seven
   d. Eleven

6. After the court of criminal appeals where are cases appealed?
   a. The court of appeals
   b. U.S. Court of Appeals
   c. Texas Supreme Court
   d. U.S. Supreme Court

Sample Test Questions

Sample Test Questions

7. Which of the following duties does the Texas Supreme Court not conduct?

   a. Determines the rules for the state of Texas judicial system.

   b. Appoints people to the Board of Law Examiners.

   c. Final appellate jurisdiction in civil cases.

   d. Final appellate jurisdiction in criminal cases.

8. In Texas all judges are _____.

   a. appointed by the governor

   b. appointed by the Board of Law Examiners

   c. elected by the people of Texas

   d. elected by the legislature

APPENDIX A

The Declaration of Independence of the Thirteen Colonies In CONGRESS, July 4, 1776

THE UNANIMOUS DECLARATION OF THE THIRTEEN UNITED STATES OF AMERICA,

When in the Course of human Events, it becomes necessary for one People to dissolve the Political Bands which have connected them with another, and to assume among the Powers of the Earth, the separate and equal Station to which the Laws of Nature and of Nature's God entitle them, a decent Respect to the Opinions of mankind requires that they should declare the causes which impel them to the Separation.

We hold these Truths to be self-evident, that all Men are created equal, that they are endowed by their Creator with certain unalienable Rights, that among these are Life, Liberty and the Pursuit of Happiness—That to secure these rights, Governments are instituted among Men, deriving their just powers from the consent of the Governed—that whenever any Form of Government becomes destructive of these Ends, it is the Right of the People to alter or to abolish it, and to institute new Government, laying its Foundation on such principles and organizing its Powers in such Form, as to them shall seem most likely to effect their Safety and Happiness. Prudence, indeed, will dictate that Governments long established should not be changed for light and transient Causes; and accordingly all Experience hath shewn, that Mankind are more disposed to suffer, while Evils are sufferable, than to right themselves by abolishing the Forms to which they are accustomed. But when a long Train of Abuses and Usurpations, pursuing invariably the same Object evinces a Design to reduce them under absolute Despotism, it is their Right, it is their Duty, to throw off such Government, and to provide new Guards for their future Security. Such has been the patient Sufferance of these Colonies; and such is now the Necessity which constrains them to alter their former Systems of Government. The History of the present King of Great Britain is a History of repeated Injuries and Usurpations, all having in direct Object the Establishment of an absolute Tyranny over these States. To prove this, let Facts be submitted to a candid world.

He has refused his Assent to Laws, the most wholesome and necessary for the public good.

He has forbidden his Governors to pass Laws of immediate and pressing Importance, unless suspended in their Operation till his Assent should be obtained; and when so suspended, he has utterly neglected to attend to them.

He has refused to pass other Laws for the Accommodation of large Districts of People, unless those People would relinquish the Right of Representation in the Legislature, a Right inestimable to them and formidable to Tyrants only.

He has called together Legislative Bodies at Places unusual, uncomfortable, and distant from the Depository of their Public Records, for the sole Purpose of fatiguing them into Compliance with his Measures.

He has dissolved Representative Houses repeatedly, for opposing with manly Firmness his invasions on the Rights of the People.

He has refused for a long time, after such Dissolutions, to cause others to be elected; whereby the Legislative Powers, incapable of Annihilation, have returned to the People at large for their exercise; the State remaining in the mean time exposed to all the Dangers of Invasion from without, and Convulsions within.

He has endeavoured to prevent the Population of these States; for that Purpose obstructing the Laws for Naturalization of Foreigners; refusing to pass others to encourage their Migrations hither, and raising the Conditions of new Appropriations of Lands.

He has obstructed the Administration of Justice, by refusing his Assent to Laws for establishing Judiciary Powers.

He has made Judges dependent on his Will alone, for the Tenure of their Offices, and the Amount and payment of their Salaries.

He has erected a Multitude of New Offices, and sent hither Swarms of Officers to harass our People, and eat out their Substance.

He has kept among us, in Times of Peace, Standing Armies without the consent of our Legislatures.

He has affected to render the Military independent of, and superior to the Civil Power.

He has combined with others to subject us to a Jurisdiction foreign to our Constitution and unacknowledged by our Laws; giving his Assent to their Acts of pretended Legislation:

For quartering large Bodies of Armed Troops among us:

For protecting them, by a mock Trial, from punishment for any Murders which they should commit on the Inhabitants of these States:

For cutting off our Trade with all Parts of the World:

For imposing Taxes on us without our Consent:

For depriving us, in many Cases, of the Benefits of Trial by Jury:

For transporting us beyond Seas to be tried for pretended offences:

For abolishing the free System of English Laws in a neighbouring Province, establishing therein an arbitrary Government, and enlarging its Boundaries so as to render it at once an Example and fit Instrument for introducing the same absolute Rule into these Colonies:

For taking away our Charters, abolishing our most valuable Laws, and altering fundamentally the Forms of our Governments:

For suspending our own Legislatures, and declaring themselves invested with Power to legislate for us in all Cases whatsoever.

He has abdicated Government here, by declaring us out of his Protection and waging War against us.

He has plundered our seas, ravaged our Coasts, burnt our towns, and destroyed the Lives of our People.

He is at this Time transporting large Armies of foreign Mercenaries to compleat the works of Death, Desolation and Tyranny, already begun with circumstances of Cruelty and Perfidy scarcely paralleled in the most barbarous Ages, and totally unworthy the Head of a civilized Nation.

He has constrained our fellow Citizens taken Captive on the high Seas to bear Arms against their Country, to become the Executioners of their Friends and Brethren, or to fall themselves by their Hands.

He has excited domestic Insurrections amongst us, and has endeavoured to bring on the Inhabitants of our Frontiers, the merciless Indian Savages, whose known Rule of Warfare, is an undistinguished Destruction of all Ages, Sexes and Conditions.

In every stage of these Oppressions we have Petitioned for Redress in the most humble Terms: Our repeated Petitions have been answered only by repeated Injury. A Prince, whose character is thus marked by every act which may define a Tyrant, is unfit to be the Ruler of a free People.

Nor have we been wanting in Attentions to our British Brethren. We have warned them from Time to Time of Attempts by their Legislature to extend an unwarrantable jurisdiction over us. We have reminded them of the Circumstances of our Emigration and Settlement here. We have appealed to their native Justice and Magnanimity, and we have conjured them by the Ties of our common Kindred to disavow these Usurpations, which, would inevitably interrupt our Connections and Correspondence. They too have been deaf to the Voice of Justice and of Consanguinity. We must, therefore, acquiesce in the Necessity, which denounces our Separation, and hold them, as we hold the rest of Mankind, Enemies in War, in Peace, Friends.

We, therefore, the Representatives of the UNITED STATES OF AMERICA, in General Congress, Assembled, appealing to the Supreme Judge of the World for the Rectitude of our Intentions, do, in the Name, and by the Authority of the good People of these Colonies, solemnly Publish and Declare, That these United Colonies are, and of Right ought to be, Free and Independent States; that they are absolved from all Allegiance to the British Crown, and that all political Connection between them and the State of Great Britain, is and ought to be totally dissolved; and that as Free and Independent States, they have full Power to levy War, conclude Peace, contract Alliances, establish Commerce, and to do all other Acts and Things which Independent States may of right do. And for the support of this declaration, with a firm Reliance on the Protection of Divine Providence, we mutually pledge to each other our lives, our Fortunes and our sacred Honor.

The Constitution of the United States

We the People of the United States, in Order to form a more perfect Union, establish Justice, insure domestic Tranquility, provide for the common defence, promote the general Welfare, and secure the Blessngs of Liberty to ourselves and our Posterity, do ordain and establish this Constitution for the United States of America.

ARTICLE I

Section 1

All legislative Powers herein granted shall be vested in a Congress of the United States, which shall consist of a Senate and House of Representatives.

Section 2

The House of Representatives shall be composed of Members chosen every second Year by the People of the several States, and the Electors in each State shall have the Qualifications requisite for Electors of the most numerous Branch of the State Legislature.

No Person shall be a Representative who shall not have attained to the Age of twenty five Years, and been seven Years a Citizen of the United States, and who shall not, when elected, be an Inhabitant of that State in which he shall be chosen.

[Representatives and direct Taxes shall be apportioned among the several States which may be included within this Union, according to their respective Numbers, which shall be determined by adding to the whole Number of free Persons, including those bound to Service for a Term of Years, and excluding Indians not taxed, three fifths of all other Persons.] The actual Enumeration shall be made within three Years after the first Meeting of the Congress of the United States, and within every subsequent Term of ten Years, in such Manner as they shall by Law direct. The Number of Representatives shall not exceed one for every thirty Thousand, but each State shall have at Least one Representative; and until such enumeration shall be made, the State of New Hampshire shall be entitled to chuse three, Massachusetts eight, Rhode Island and Providence Plantations one, Connecticut five, New York six, New Jersey four, Pennsylvania eight, Delaware one, Maryland six, Virginia ten, North Carolina five, South Carolina five and Georgia three.

When vacancies happen in the Representation from any State, the Executive Authority thereof shall issue Writs of Election to fill such Vacancies.

The House of Representatives shall chuse their Speaker and other Officers; and shall have the sole Power of Impeachment.

Section 3

The Senate of the United States shall be composed of two Senators from each State, chosen by the Legislature thereof, for six Years; and each Senator shall have one Vote.

Immediately after they shall be assembled in Consequence of the first Election, they shall be divided as equally as may be into three Classes. The Seats of the Senators of the first Class shall be vacated at the Expiration of the second Year, of the second Class at the Expiration of the fourth Year, and of the third Class at the Expiration of the sixth Year, so that one third may be chosen every second Year; and if Vacancies happen by Resignation, or otherwise, during the Recess of the Legislature of any State, the Executive thereof may make temporary Appointments until the next Meeting of the Legislature, which shall then fill such Vacancies.

No person shall be a Senator who shall not have attained to the Age of thirty Years, and been nine Years a Citizen of the United States, and who shall not, when elected, be an Inhabitant of that State for which he shall be chosen.

The Vice President of the United States shall be President of the Senate, but shall have no Vote, unless they be equally divided.

The Senate shall chuse their other Officers, and also a President pro tempore, in the absence of the Vice President, or when he shall exercise the Office of President of the United States.

The Senate shall have the sole Power to try all Impeachments. When sitting for that Purpose, they shall be on Oath or Affirmation. When the President of the United States is tried, the Chief Justice shall preside: And no Person shall be convicted without the Concurrence of two thirds of the Members present.

Judgment in Cases of Impeachment shall not extend further than to removal from Office, and disqualification to hold and enjoy any Office of honor, Trust or Profit under the United States: but the Party convicted shall nevertheless be liable and subject to Indictment, Trial, Judgment and Punishment, according to Law.

Section 4

The Times, Places and Manner of holding Elections for Senators and Representatives, shall be prescribed in each State by the Legislature thereof; but the Congress may at any time by Law make or alter such Regulations, except as to the Place of Chusing Senators.

The Congress shall assemble at least once in every Year, and such Meeting shall be on the first Monday in December, unless they shall by Law appoint a different Day.

Section 5

Each House shall be the Judge of the Elections, Returns and Qualifications of its own Members, and a Majority of each shall constitute a Quorum to do Business; but a smaller number may adjourn from day to day, and may be authorized to compel the Attendance of absent Members, in such Manner, and under such Penalties as each House may provide.

Each House may determine the Rules of its Proceedings, punish its Members for disorderly Behavior, and, with the Concurrence of two-thirds, expel a Member.

Each House shall keep a Journal of its Proceedings, and from time to time publish the same, excepting such Parts as may in their Judgment require Secrecy; and the Yeas and Nays of the Members of either House on any question shall, at the Desire of one fifth of those Present, be entered on the Journal.

Neither House, during the Session of Congress, shall, without the Consent of the other, adjourn for more than three days, nor to any other Place than that in which the two Houses shall be sitting.

Section 6

The Senators and Representatives shall receive a Compensation for their Services, to be ascertained by Law, and paid out of the Treasury of the United States. They shall in all Cases, except Treason, Felony and Breach of the Peace, be privileged from Arrest during their Attendance at the Session of their respective Houses, and in going to and returning from the same; and for any Speech or Debate in either House, they shall not be questioned in any other Place.

No Senator or Representative shall, during the Time for which he was elected, be appointed to any civil Office under the Authority of the United States which shall have been created, or the Emoluments whereof shall have been increased during such time; and no Person holding any Office under the United States, shall be a Member of either House during his Continuance in Office.

Section 7

All bills for raising Revenue shall originate in the House of Representatives; but the Senate may propose or concur with Amendments as on other Bills.

Every Bill which shall have passed the House of Representatives and the Senate, shall, before it become a Law, be presented to the President of the United States; If he approve he shall sign it, but if not he shall return it, with his Objections to that House in which it shall have originated, who shall enter the Objections at large on their Journal, and proceed to reconsider it. If after such Reconsideration two thirds of that House shall agree to pass the Bill, it shall be sent, together with the Objections, to the other House, by which it shall likewise be reconsidered, and if approved by two thirds of that House, it shall become a Law. But in all such Cases the Votes of both Houses shall be determined by Yeas and Nays, and the Names of the Persons voting for and against the Bill shall be entered on the Journal of each House respectively. If any Bill shall not be returned by the President within ten Days (Sundays excepted) after it shall have been presented to him, the Same shall be a Law, in like Manner as if he had signed it, unless the Congress by their Adjournment prevent its Return, in which Case it shall not be a Law.

Every Order, Resolution, or Vote to which the Concurrence of the Senate and House of Representatives may be necessary (except on a question of Adjournment) shall be presented to the President of the United States; and before the Same shall take Effect, shall be approved by him, or being disapproved by him, shall be repassed by two thirds of the Senate and House of Representatives, according to the Rules and Limitations prescribed in the Case of a Bill.

Section 8

The Congress shall have Power To lay and collect Taxes, Duties, Imposts and Excises, to pay the Debts and provide for the common Defence and general Welfare of the United States; but all Duties, Imposts and Excises shall be uniform throughout the United States;

To borrow money on the credit of the United States;

To regulate Commerce with foreign Nations, and among the several States, and with the Indian Tribes;

To establish an uniform Rule of Naturalization, and uniform Laws on the subject of Bankruptcies throughout the United States;

To coin Money, regulate the Value thereof, and of foreign Coin, and fix the Standard of Weights and Measures;

To provide for the Punishment of counterfeiting the Securities and current Coin of the United States;

To establish Post Offices and Post Roads;

To promote the Progress of Science and useful Arts, by securing for limited Times to Authors and Inventors the exclusive Right to their respective Writings and Discoveries;

To constitute Tribunals inferior to the supreme Court;

To define and punish Piracies and Felonies committed on the high Seas, and Offenses against the Law of Nations;

To declare War, grant Letters of Marque and Reprisal, and make Rules concerning Captures on Land and Water;

To raise and support Armies, but no Appropriation of Money to that Use shall be for a longer Term than two Years;

To provide and maintain a Navy;

To make Rules for the Government and Regulation of the land and naval Forces;

To provide for calling forth the Militia to execute the Laws of the Union, suppress Insurrections and repel Invasions;

To provide for organizing, arming, and disciplining the Militia, and for governing such Part of them as may be employed in the Service of the United States, reserving to the States respectively, the Appointment of the Officers, and the Authority of training the Militia according to the discipline prescribed by Congress;

To exercise exclusive Legislation in all Cases whatsoever, over such District (not exceeding ten Miles square) as may, by Cession of particular States, and the acceptance of Congress, become the Seat of the Government of the United States, and to exercise like Authority over all Places purchased by the Consent of the Legislature of the State in which the Same shall be, for the Erection of Forts, Magazines, Arsenals, dock-Yards, and other needful Buildings;—And

To make all Laws which shall be necessary and proper for carrying into Execution the foregoing Powers, and all other Powers vested by this Constitution in the Government of the United States, or in any Department or Officer thereof.

Section 9

The Migration or Importation of such Persons as any of the States now existing shall think proper to admit, shall not be prohibited by the Congress prior to the Year one thousand eight hundred and eight, but a tax or duty may be imposed on such Importation, not exceeding ten dollars for each Person.

The privilege of the Writ of Habeas Corpus shall not be suspended, unless when in Cases of Rebellion or Invasion the public Safety may require it.

No Bill of Attainder or ex post facto Law shall be passed.

No capitation, or other direct, Tax shall be laid, unless in Proportion to the Census or Enumeration herein before directed to be taken.

No Tax or Duty shall be laid on Articles exported from any State.

No Preference shall be given by any Regulation of Commerce or Revenue to the Ports of one State over those of another: nor shall Vessels bound to, or from, one State, be obliged to enter, clear, or pay Duties in another.

No Money shall be drawn from the Treasury, but in Consequence of Appropriations made by Law; and a regular Statement and Account of the Receipts and Expenditures of all public Money shall be published from time to time.

No Title of Nobility shall be granted by the United States: And no Person holding any Office of Profit or Trust under them, shall, without the Consent of the Congress, accept of any present, Emolument, Office, or Title, of any kind whatever, from any King, Prince or foreign State.

Section 10

No State shall enter into any Treaty, Alliance, or Confederation; grant Letters of Marque and Reprisal; coin Money; emit Bills of Credit; make any Thing but gold and silver Coin a Tender in Payment of Debts; pass any Bill of Attainder, ex post facto Law, or Law impairing the Obligation of Contracts, or grant any Title of Nobility.

No State shall, without the Consent of the Congress, lay any Imposts or Duties on Imports or Exports, except what may be absolutely necessary for executing it's inspection Laws: and the net Produce of all Duties and Imposts, laid by any State on Imports or Exports, shall be for the Use of the Treasury of the United States; and all such Laws shall be subject to the Revision and Controul of the Congress.

No State shall, without the Consent of Congress, lay any duty of Tonnage, keep Troops, or Ships of War in time of Peace, enter into any Agreement or Compact with another State, or with a foreign Power, or engage in War, unless actually invaded, or in such imminent Danger as will not admit of delay.

ARTICLE II

Section 1

The executive Power shall be vested in a President of the United States of America. He shall hold his Office during the Term of four Years, and, together with the Vice-President chosen for the same Term, be elected, as follows:

Each State shall appoint, in such Manner as the Legislature thereof may direct, a Number of Electors, equal to the whole Number of Senators and Representatives to which the State may be entitled in the Congress: but no Senator or Representative, or Person holding an Office of Trust or Profit under the United States, shall be appointed an Elector.

The Electors shall meet in their respective States, and vote by Ballot for two persons, of whom one at least shall not lie an Inhabitant of the same State with themselves. And they shall make a List of all the Persons voted for, and of the Number of Votes for each; which List they shall sign and certify, and transmit sealed to the Seat of the Government of the United States, directed to the President of the Senate. The President of the Senate shall, in the Presence of the Senate and House of Representatives, open all the Certificates, and the Votes shall then be counted. The Person having the greatest Number of Votes shall be the President, if such Number be a Majority of the whole Number of Electors appointed; and if there be more than one who have such Majority, and have an equal Number of Votes, then the House of Representatives shall immediately chuse by Ballot one of them for President; and if no Person have a Majority, then from the five highest on the List the said House shall in like Manner chuse the President. But in chusing the President, the Votes shall be taken by States, the Representation from each State having one Vote; a quorum for this Purpose shall consist of a Member or Members from two-thirds of the States, and a Majority of all the States shall be necessary to a Choice. In every Case, after the Choice of the President, the Person having the greatest Number of Votes of the Electors shall be the Vice President. But if there should remain two or more who have equal Votes, the Senate shall chuse from them by Ballot the Vice-President.

The Congress may determine the Time of chusing the Electors, and the Day on which they shall give their Votes; which Day shall be the same throughout the United States.

No person except a natural born Citizen, or a Citizen of the United States, at the time of the Adoption of this Constitution, shall be eligible to the Office of President; neither shall any Person be eligible to that Office who shall not have attained to the Age of thirty-five Years, and been fourteen Years a Resident within the United States.

In Case of the Removal of the President from Office, or of his Death, Resignation, or Inability to discharge the Powers and Duties of the said Office, the same shall devolve on the Vice President, and the Congress may by Law provide for the Case of Removal, Death, Resignation or Inability, both of the President and Vice President, declaring what Officer shall then act as President, and such Officer shall act accordingly, until the Disability be removed, or a President shall be elected.

The President shall, at stated Times, receive for his Services, a Compensation, which shall neither be increased nor diminished during the Period for which he shall have been elected, and he shall not receive within that Period any other Emolument from the United States, or any of them.

Before he enter on the Execution of his Office, he shall take the following Oath or Affirmation:—"I do solemnly swear (or affirm) that I will faithfully execute the Office of President of the United States, and will to the best of my Ability, preserve, protect and defend the Constitution of the United States."

Section 2

The President shall be Commander in Chief of the Army and Navy of the United States, and of the Militia of the several States, when called into the actual Service of the United States; he may require the Opinion, in writing, of the principal Officer in each of the executive Departments, upon any subject relating to the Duties of their respective Offices, and he shall have Power to Grant Reprieves and Pardons for Offenses against the United States, except in Cases of Impeachment.

He shall have Power, by and with the Advice and Consent of the Senate, to make Treaties, provided two thirds of the Senators present concur; and he shall nominate, and by and with the Advice and Consent of the Senate, shall appoint Ambassadors, other public Ministers and Consuls, Judges of the supreme Court, and all other Officers of the United States, whose Appointments are not herein otherwise provided for, and which shall be established by Law: but the Congress may by Law vest the Appointment of such inferior Officers, as they think proper, in the President alone, in the Courts of Law, or in the Heads of Departments.

The President shall have Power to fill up all Vacancies that may happen during the Recess of the Senate, by granting Commissions which shall expire at the End of their next Session.

Section 3

He shall from time to time give to the Congress Information of the State of the Union, and recommend to their Consideration such Measures as he shall judge necessary and expedient; he may, on extraordinary Occasions, convene both Houses, or either of them, and in Case of Disagreement between them, with Respect to the Time of Adjournment, he may adjourn them to such Time as he shall think proper; he shall receive Ambassadors and other public Ministers; he shall take Care that the Laws be faithfully executed, and shall Commission all the Officers of the United States.

Section 4

The President, Vice President and all civil Officers of the United States, shall be removed from Office on Impeachment for, and Conviction of, Treason, Bribery, or other high Crimes and Misdemeanors.

ARTICLE III

Section 1

The judicial Power of the United States, shall be vested in one supreme Court, and in such inferior Courts as the Congress may from time to time ordain and establish. The Judges, both of the supreme and inferior Courts, shall hold their Offices during good Behavior, and shall, at stated Times, receive for their Services a Compensation which shall not be diminished during their Continuance in Office.

Section 2

The judicial Power shall extend to all Cases, in Law and Equity, arising under this Constitution, the Laws of the United States, and Treaties made, or which shall be made, under their Authority; to all Cases affecting Ambassadors, other public Ministers and Consuls; to all Cases of admiralty and maritime Jurisdiction; to Controversies to which the United States shall be a Party; to Controversies between two or more States; between a State and

Citizens of another State; between Citizens of different States; between Citizens of the same State claiming Lands under Grants of different States, and between a State, or the Citizens thereof, and foreign States, Citizens or Subjects.

In all Cases affecting Ambassadors, other public Ministers and Consuls, and those in which a State shall be Party, the supreme Court shall have original Jurisdiction. In all the other Cases before mentioned, the supreme Court shall have appellate Jurisdiction, both as to Law and Fact, with such Exceptions, and under such Regulations as the Congress shall make.

The Trial of all Crimes, except in Cases of Impeachment, shall be by Jury; and such Trial shall be held in the State where the said Crimes shall have been committed; but when not committed within any State, the Trial shall be at such Place or Places as the Congress may by Law have directed.

Section 3

Treason against the United States, shall consist only in levying War against them, or in adhering to their Enemies, giving them Aid and Comfort. No Person shall be convicted of Treason unless on the Testimony of two Witnesses to the same overt Act, or on Confession in open Court.

The Congress shall have power to declare the Punishment of Treason, but no Attainder of Treason shall work Corruption of Blood, or Forfeiture except during the Life of the Person attainted.

ARTICLE IV

Section 1

Full Faith and Credit shall be given in each State to the public Acts, Records, and judicial Proceedings of every other State. And the Congress may by general Laws prescribe the Manner in which such Acts, Records and Proceedings shall be proved, and the Effect thereof.

Section 2

The Citizens of each State shall be entitled to all Privileges and Immunities of Citizens in the several States.

A Person charged in any State with Treason, Felony, or other Crime, who shall flee from Justice, and be found in another State, shall on demand of the executive Authority of the State from which he fled, be delivered up, to be removed to the State having Jurisdiction of the Crime.

No Person held to Service or Labour in one State, under the Laws thereof, escaping into another, shall, in Consequence of any Law or Regulation therein, be discharged from such Service or Labour, But shall be delivered up on Claim of the Party to whom such Service or Labour may be due.

Section 3

New States may be admitted by the Congress into this Union; but no new States shall be formed or erected within the Jurisdiction of any other State; nor any State be formed by the Junction of two or more States, or parts of States, without the Consent of the Legislatures of the States concerned as well as of the Congress.

The Congress shall have Power to dispose of and make all needful Rules and Regulations respecting the Territory or other Property belonging to the United States; and nothing in this Constitution shall be so construed as to Prejudice any Claims of the United States, or of any particular State.

Section 4

The United States shall guarantee to every State in this Union a Republican Form of Government, and shall protect each of them against Invasion; and on Application of the Legislature, or of the Executive (when the Legislature cannot be convened) against domestic Violence.

ARTICLE V

The Congress, whenever two thirds of both Houses shall deem it necessary, shall propose Amendments to this Constitution, or, on the Application of the Legislatures of two thirds of the several States, shall call a Convention for proposing Amendments, which, in either Case, shall be valid to all Intents and Purposes, as part of this Constitution, when ratified by the Legislatures of three fourths of the several States, or by Conventions in three fourths thereof, as the one or the other Mode of Ratification may be proposed by the Congress; Provided that no Amendment which may be made prior to the Year One thousand eight hundred and eight shall in any Manner affect the first and fourth Clauses in the Ninth Section of the first Article; and that no State, without its Consent, shall be deprived of its equal Suffrage in the Senate.

ARTICLE VI

All Debts contracted and Engagements entered into, before the Adoption of this Constitution, shall be as valid against the United States under this Constitution, as under the Confederation.

This Constitution, and the Laws of the United States which shall be made in Pursuance thereof; and all Treaties made, or which shall be made, under the Authority of the United States, shall be the supreme Law of the Land; and the Judges in every State shall be bound thereby, any Thing in the Constitution or Laws of any State to the Contrary notwithstanding.

The Senators and Representatives before mentioned, and the Members of the several State Legislatures, and all executive and judicial Officers, both of the United States and of the several States, shall be bound by Oath or Affirmation, to support this Constitution; but no religious Test shall ever be required as a Qualification to any Office or public Trust under the United States.

ARTICLE VII

The Ratification of the Conventions of nine States, shall be sufficient for the Establishment of this Constitution between the States so ratifying the Same.

Done in Convention by the Unanimous Consent of the States present the Seventeenth Day of September in the Year of our Lord one thousand seven hundred and Eighty seven and of the Independence of the United States of America the Twelfth. In Witness whereof We have hereunto subscribed our Names.

GO WASHINGTON-Presidt. and deputy from Virginia

New Hampshire—John Langdon, Nicholas Gilman

Massachusetts—Nathaniel Gorham, Rufus King

Connecticut—Wm: Saml. Johnson, Roger Sherman

New York—Alexander Hamilton

New Jersey—Wil: Livingston, David Brearley, Wm. Paterson, Jona: Dayton

Pennsylvania—B Franklin, Thomas Mifflin, Robt. Morris, Geo. Clymer, Thos. FitzSimons, Jared Ingersoll, James Wilson, Gouv Morris

Delaware—Geo: Read, Gunning Bedford jun, John Dickinson, Richard Bassett, Jaco: Broom

Maryland—James McHenry, Dan of St Thos. Jenifer, Danl Carroll

Virginia—John Blair, James Madison Jr.

North Carolina—Wm. Blount, Richd. Dobbs Spaight, Hu Williamson

South Carolina—J. Rutledge, Charles Cotesworth Pinckney, Charles Pinckney, Pierce Butler

Georgia—William Few, Abr Baldwin

Attest: William Jackson, Secretary

AMENDMENT I

Congress shall make no law respecting an establishment of religion, or prohibiting the free exercise thereof; or abridging the freedom of speech, or of the press; or the right of the people peaceably to assemble, and to petition the Government for a redress of grievances.

AMENDMENT II

A well regulated Militia, being necessary to the security of a free State, the right of the people to keep and bear Arms, shall not be infringed.

AMENDMENT III

No Soldier shall, in time of peace be quartered in any house, without the consent of the Owner, nor in time of war, but in a manner to be prescribed by law.

AMENDMENT IV

The right of the people to be secure in their persons, houses, papers, and effects, against unreasonable searches and seizures, shall not be violated, and no Warrants shall issue, but upon probable cause, supported by Oath or affirmation, and particularly describing the place to be searched, and the persons or things to be seized.

AMENDMENT V

No person shall be held to answer for a capital, or otherwise infamous crime, unless on a presentment or indictment of a Grand Jury, except in cases arising in the land or naval forces, or in the Militia, when in actual service in time of War or public danger; nor shall any person be subject for the same offense to be twice put in jeopardy of life or limb; nor shall be compelled in any criminal case to be a witness against himself, nor be deprived of life, liberty, or property, without due process of law; nor shall private property be taken for public use, without just compensation.

AMENDMENT VI

In all criminal prosecutions, the accused shall enjoy the right to a speedy and public trial, by an impartial jury of the State and district wherein the crime shall have been committed, which district shall have been previously ascertained by law, and to be informed of the nature and cause of the accusation; to be confronted with the witnesses against him; to have compulsory process for obtaining witnesses in his favor, and to have the Assistance of Counsel for his defence.

AMENDMENT VII

In Suits at common law, where the value in controversy shall exceed twenty dollars, the right of trial by jury shall be preserved, and no fact tried by a jury, shall be otherwise re-examined in any Court of the United States, than according to the rules of the common law.

AMENDMENT VIII

Excessive bail shall not be required, nor excessive fines imposed, nor cruel and unusual punishments inflicted.

AMENDMENT IX

The enumeration in the Constitution, of certain rights, shall not be construed to deny or disparage others retained by the people.

AMENDMENT X

The powers not delegated to the United States by the Constitution, nor prohibited by it to the States, are reserved to the States respectively, or to the people.

AMENDMENT XI

The Judicial power of the United States shall not be construed to extend to any suit in law or equity, commenced or prosecuted against one of the United States by Citizens of another State, or by Citizens or Subjects of any Foreign State.

AMENDMENT XII

The Electors shall meet in their respective states, and vote by ballot for President and Vice-President, one of whom, at least, shall not be an inhabitant of the same state with themselves; they shall name in their ballots the person voted for as President, and in distinct ballots the person voted for as Vice-President, and they shall make distinct lists of all persons voted for as President, and of all persons voted for as Vice-President and of the number of votes for each, which lists they shall sign and certify, and transmit sealed to the seat of the government of the United States, directed to the President of the Senate;—The President of the Senate shall, in the presence of the Senate and House of Representatives, open all the certificates and the votes shall then be counted;—The person having the greatest Number of votes for President, shall be the President, if such number be a majority of the whole number of Electors appointed; and if no person have such majority, then from the persons having the highest numbers not exceeding three on the list of those voted for as President, the House of Representatives shall choose immediately, by ballot, the President. But in choosing the President, the votes shall be taken by states, the representation from each state having one vote; a quorum for this purpose shall consist of a member or members from two-thirds of the states, and a majority of all the states shall be necessary to a choice. And if the House of Representatives shall not choose a President whenever the right of choice shall devolve upon them, before the fourth day of March next following, then the Vice-President shall act as President, as in the case of the death or other constitutional disability of the President.—The person having the greatest number of votes as Vice-President, shall be the Vice-President, if such number be a majority of the whole number of Electors appointed, and if no person have a majority, then from the two highest numbers on the list, the Senate shall choose the Vice-President; a quorum for the purpose shall consist of two-thirds of the whole number of Senators, and a majority of the whole number shall be necessary to a choice. But no person constitutionally ineligible to the office of President shall be eligible to that of Vice-President of the United States.

AMENDMENT XIII

Section 1

Neither slavery nor involuntary servitude, except as a punishment for crime whereof the party shall have been duly convicted, shall exist within the United States, or any place subject to their jurisdiction.

Section 2

Congress shall have power to enforce this article by appropriate legislation.

AMENDMENT XIV

Section 1

All persons born or naturalized in the United States, and subject to the jurisdiction thereof, are citizens of the United States and of the State wherein they reside. No State shall make or enforce any law which shall abridge the privileges or immunities of citizens of the United

States; nor shall any State deprive any person of life, liberty, or property, without due process of law; nor deny to any person within its jurisdiction the equal protection of the laws.

Section 2

Representatives shall be apportioned among the several States according to their respective numbers, counting the whole number of persons in each State, excluding Indians not taxed. But when the right to vote at any election for the choice of electors for President and Vice-President of the United States, Representatives in Congress, the Executive and Judicial officers of a State, or the members of the Legislature thereof, is denied to any of the male inhabitants of such State, being twenty-one years of age, and citizens of the United States, or in any way abridged, except for participation in rebellion, or other crime, the basis of representation therein shall be reduced in the proportion which the number of such male citizens shall bear to the whole number of male citizens twenty-one years of age in such State.

Section 3

No person shall be a Senator or Representative in Congress, or elector of President and Vice-President, or hold any office, civil or military, under the United States, or under any State, who, having previously taken an oath, as a member of Congress, or as an officer of the United States, or as a member of any State legislature, or as an executive or judicial officer of any State, to support the Constitution of the United States, shall have engaged in insurrection or rebellion against the same, or given aid or comfort to the enemies thereof. But Congress may by a vote of two-thirds of each House, remove such disability.

Section 4

The validity of the public debt of the United States, authorized by law, including debts incurred for payment of pensions and bounties for services in suppressing insurrection or rebellion, shall not be questioned. But neither the United States nor any State shall assume or pay any debt or obligation incurred in aid of insurrection or rebellion against the United States, or any claim for the loss or emancipation of any slave; but all such debts, obligations and claims shall be held illegal and void.

Section 5

The Congress shall have power to enforce, by appropriate legislation, the provisions of this article.

AMENDMENT XV

Section 1

The right of citizens of the United States to vote shall not be denied or abridged by the United States or by any State on account of race, color, or previous condition of servitude.

Section 2

The Congress shall have power to enforce this article by appropriate legislation.

AMENDMENT XVI

The Congress shall have power to lay and collect taxes on incomes, from whatever source derived, without apportionment among the several States, and without regard to any census or enumeration.

AMENDMENT XVII

The Senate of the United States shall be composed of two Senators from each State, elected by the people thereof, for six years; and each Senator shall have one vote. The electors in each State shall have the qualifications requisite for electors of the most numerous branch of the State legislatures. When vacancies happen in the representation of any State in the Senate, the executive authority of such State shall issue writs of election to fill such vacancies: Provided, That the legislature of any State may empower the executive thereof to make temporary appointments until the people fill the vacancies by election as the legislature may direct.

This amendment shall not be so construed as to affect the election or term of any Senator chosen before it becomes valid as part of the Constitution.

AMENDMENT XVIII

Section 1

After one year from the ratification of this article the manufacture, sale, or transportation of intoxicating liquors within, the importation thereof into, or the exportation thereof from the United States and all territory subject to the jurisdiction thereof for beverage purposes is hereby prohibited.

Section 2

The Congress and the several States shall have concurrent power to enforce this article by appropriate legislation.

Section 3

This article shall be inoperative unless it shall have been ratified as an amendment to the Constitution by the legislatures of the several States, as provided in the Constitution, within seven years from the date of the submission hereof to the States by the Congress.

AMENDMENT XIX

The right of citizens of the United States to vote shall not be denied or abridged by the United States or by any State on account of sex.

Congress shall have power to enforce this article by appropriate legislation.

AMENDMENT XX

Section 1

The terms of the President and Vice President shall end at noon on the 20th day of January, and the terms of Senators and Representatives at noon on the 3d day of January, of the years in which such terms would have ended if this article had not been ratified; and the terms of their successors shall then begin.

Section 2

The Congress shall assemble at least once in every year, and such meeting shall begin at noon on the 3d day of January, unless they shall by law appoint a different day.

Section 3

If, at the time fixed for the beginning of the term of the President, the President elect shall have died, the Vice President elect shall become President. If a President shall not have been chosen before the time fixed for the beginning of his term, or if the President elect shall have failed to qualify, then the Vice President elect shall act as President until a President shall have qualified; and the Congress may by law provide for the case wherein neither a President elect nor a Vice President elect shall have qualified, declaring who shall then act as President, or the manner in which one who is to act shall be selected, and such person shall act accordingly until a President or Vice President shall have qualified.

Section 4

The Congress may by law provide for the case of the death of any of the persons from whom the House of Representatives may choose a President whenever the right of choice shall have devolved upon them, and for the case of the death of any of the persons from whom the Senate may choose a Vice President whenever the right of choice shall have devolved upon them.

Section 5

Sections 1 and 2 shall take effect on the 15th day of October following the ratification of this article.

Section 6

This article shall be inoperative unless it shall have been ratified as an amendment to the Constitution by the legislatures of three-fourths of the several States within seven years from the date of its submission.

AMENDMENT XXI

Section 1

The eighteenth article of amendment to the Constitution of the United States is hereby repealed.

Section 2

The transportation or importation into any State, Territory, or possession of the United States for delivery or use therein of intoxicating liquors, in violation of the laws thereof, is hereby prohibited.

Section 3

The article shall be inoperative unless it shall have been ratified as an amendment to the Constitution by conventions in the several States, as provided in the Constitution, within seven years from the date of the submission hereof to the States by the Congress.

AMENDMENT XXII

Section 1

No person shall be elected to the office of the President more than twice, and no person who has held the office of President, or acted as President, for more than two years of a term to which some other person was elected President shall be elected to the office of the President more than once. But this Article shall not apply to any person holding the office of President, when this Article was proposed by the Congress, and shall not prevent any person who may be holding the office of President, or acting as President, during the term within which this Article becomes operative from holding the office of President or acting as President during the remainder of such term.

Section 2

This article shall be inoperative unless it shall have been ratified as an amendment to the Constitution by the legislatures of three-fourths of the several States within seven years from the date of its submission to the States by the Congress.

AMENDMENT XXIII

Section 1

The District constituting the seat of Government of the United States shall appoint in such manner as the Congress may direct: A number of electors of President and Vice President equal to the whole number of Senators and Representatives in Congress to which the District would be entitled if it were a State, but in no event more than the least populous State; they shall be in addition to those appointed by the States, but they shall be considered, for the purposes of the election of President and Vice President, to be electors appointed by a State; and they shall meet in the District and perform such duties as provided by the twelfth article of amendment.

Section 2

The Congress shall have power to enforce this article by appropriate legislation.

AMENDMENT XXIV

Section 1

The right of citizens of the United States to vote in any primary or other election for President or Vice President, for electors for President or Vice President, or for Senator or Representative in Congress, shall not be denied or abridged by the United States or any State by reason of failure to pay any poll tax or other tax.

Section 2

The Congress shall have power to enforce this article by appropriate legislation.

AMENDMENT XXV

Section 1

In case of the removal of the President from office or of his death or resignation, the Vice-President shall become President.

Section 2

Whenever there is a vacancy in the office of the Vice President, the President shall nominate a Vice President who shall take office upon confirmation by a majority vote of both Houses of Congress.

Section 3

Whenever the President transmits to the President pro tempore of the Senate and the Speaker of the House of Representatives his written declaration that he is unable to discharge the powers and duties of his office, and until he transmits to them a written declaration to the contrary, such powers and duties shall be discharged by the Vice President as Acting President.

Section 4

Whenever the Vice President and a majority of either the principal officers of the executive departments or of such other body as Congress may by law provide, transmit to the President pro tempore of the Senate and the Speaker of the House of Representatives their written declaration that the President is unable to discharge the powers and duties of his office, the Vice President shall immediately assume the powers and duties of the office as Acting President.

Thereafter, when the President transmits to the President pro tempore of the Senate and the Speaker of the House of Representatives his written declaration that no inability exists, he shall resume the powers and duties of his office unless the Vice President and a majority of either the principal officers of the executive department or of such other body as Congress may by law provide, transmit within four days to the President pro tempore of the Senate and the Speaker of the House of Representatives their written declaration that the President is unable to discharge the powers and duties of his office. Thereupon Congress shall decide the issue, assembling within forty eight hours for that purpose if not in session. If the Congress, within twenty one days after receipt of the latter written declaration, or, if Congress is not in session, within twenty one days after Congress is required to assemble, determines by two thirds vote of both Houses that the President is unable to discharge the powers and duties of his office, the Vice President shall continue to discharge the same as Acting President; otherwise, the President shall resume the powers and duties of his office.

AMENDMENT XXVI

Section 1

The right of citizens of the United States, who are eighteen years of age or older, to vote shall not be denied or abridged by the United States or by any State on account of age.

Section 2

The Congress shall have power to enforce this article by appropriate legislation.

AMENDMENT XXVII

No law, varying the compensation for the services of the Senators and Representatives, shall take effect, until an election of Representatives shall have intervened.

Federalist No. 10

The Same Subject Continued: The Union as a Safeguard Against Domestic Faction and Insurrection

From the New York Packet.
Friday, November 23, 1787.

Author: **James Madison**

To the People of the State of New York:

Among the numerous advantages promised by a well constructed Union, none deserves to be more accurately developed than its tendency to break and control the violence of faction. The friend of popular governments never finds himself so much alarmed for their character and fate, as when he contemplates their propensity to this dangerous vice. He will not fail, therefore, to set a due value on any plan which, without violating the principles to which he is attached, provides a proper cure for it. The instability, injustice, and confusion introduced into the public councils, have, in truth, been the mortal diseases under which popular governments have everywhere perished; as they continue to be the favorite and fruitful topics from which the adversaries to liberty derive their most specious declamations. The valuable improvements made by the American constitutions on the popular models, both ancient and modern, cannot certainly be too much admired; but it would be an unwarrantable partiality, to contend that they have as effectually obviated the danger on this side, as was wished and expected. Complaints are everywhere heard from our most considerate and virtuous citizens, equally the friends of public and private faith, and of public and personal liberty, that our governments are too unstable, that the public good is disregarded in the conflicts of rival parties, and that measures are too often decided, not according to the rules of justice and the rights of the minor party, but by the superior force of an interested and overbearing majority. However anxiously we may wish that these complaints had no foundation, the evidence, of known facts will not permit us to deny that they are in some degree true. It will be found, indeed, on a candid review of our situation, that some of the distresses under which we labor have been erroneously charged on the operation of our governments; but it will be found, at the same time, that other causes will not alone account for many of our heaviest misfortunes; and, particularly, for that prevailing and increasing distrust of public engagements, and alarm for private rights, which are echoed from one end of the continent to the other. These must be chiefly, if not wholly, effects of the unsteadiness and injustice with which a factious spirit has tainted our public administrations.

By a faction, I understand a number of citizens, whether amounting to a majority or a minority of the whole, who are united and actuated by some common impulse of passion, or of interest, adversed to the rights of other citizens, or to the permanent and aggregate interests of the community.

There are two methods of curing the mischiefs of faction: the one, by removing its causes; the other, by controlling its effects.

There are again two methods of removing the causes of faction: the one, by destroying the liberty which is essential to its existence; the other, by giving to every citizen the same opinions, the same passions, and the same interests.

It could never be more truly said than of the first remedy, that it was worse than the disease. Liberty is to faction what air is to fire, an aliment without which it instantly expires. But it could not be less folly to abolish liberty, which is essential to political life, because it nourishes faction, than it would be to wish the annihilation of air, which is essential to animal life, because it imparts to fire its destructive agency.

The second expedient is as impracticable as the first would be unwise. As long as the reason of man continues fallible, and he is at liberty to exercise it, different opinions will be formed. As long as the connection subsists between his reason and his self-love, his opinions and his passions will have a reciprocal influence on each other; and the former will be objects to which the latter will attach themselves. The diversity in the faculties of men, from which the rights of property originate, is not less an insuperable obstacle to a uniformity of interests. The protection of these faculties is the first object of government. From the protection of different and unequal faculties of acquiring property, the possession of different degrees and kinds of property immediately results; and from the influence of these on the sentiments and views of the respective proprietors, ensues a division of the society into different interests and parties.

The latent causes of faction are thus sown in the nature of man; and we see them everywhere brought into different degrees of activity, according to the different circumstances of civil society. A zeal for different opinions concerning religion, concerning government, and many other points, as well of speculation as of practice; an attachment to different leaders ambitiously contending for pre-eminence and power; or to persons of other descriptions whose fortunes have been interesting to the human passions, have, in turn, divided mankind into parties, inflamed them with mutual animosity, and rendered them much more disposed to vex and oppress each other than to co-operate for their common good. So strong is this propensity of mankind to fall into mutual animosities, that where no substantial occasion presents itself, the most frivolous and fanciful distinctions have been sufficient to kindle their unfriendly passions and excite their most violent conflicts. But the most common and durable source of factions has been the various and unequal distribution of property. Those who hold and those who are without property have ever formed distinct interests in society. Those who are creditors, and those who are debtors, fall under a like discrimination. A landed interest, a manufacturing interest, a mercantile interest, a moneyed interest, with many lesser interests, grow up of necessity in civilized nations, and divide them into different classes, actuated by different sentiments and views. The regulation of these various and interfering interests forms the principal task of modern legislation, and involves the spirit of party and faction in the necessary and ordinary operations of the government.

No man is allowed to be a judge in his own cause, because his interest would certainly bias his judgment, and, not improbably, corrupt his integrity. With equal, nay with greater reason, a body of men are unfit to be both judges and parties at the same time; yet what are many of the most important acts of legislation, but so many judicial determinations, not indeed concerning the rights of single persons, but concerning the rights of large bodies of citizens? And what are the different classes of legislators but advocates and parties to the causes which they determine? Is a law proposed concerning private debts? It is a question to which the creditors are parties on one side and the debtors on the other. Justice ought to hold the balance between them. Yet the parties are, and must be, themselves the judges; and the most numerous party, or, in other words, the most powerful faction must be expected to prevail. Shall domestic manufactures be encouraged, and in what degree, by restrictions on foreign manufactures? are questions which would be differently decided by the landed and the manufacturing classes, and probably by neither with a sole regard to justice and the public good. The apportionment of taxes on the various descriptions of property is an act which seems to require the most exact impartiality; yet there is, perhaps, no legislative act in which greater opportunity and temptation are given to a predominant party to trample on the rules of justice. Every shilling with which they overburden the inferior number, is a shilling saved to their own pockets.

It is in vain to say that enlightened statesmen will be able to adjust these clashing interests, and render them all subservient to the public good. Enlightened statesmen will not always be at the helm. Nor, in many cases, can such an adjustment be made at all without taking into view indirect and remote considerations, which will rarely prevail over the immediate interest which one party may find in disregarding the rights of another or the good of the whole.

The inference to which we are brought is, that the CAUSES of faction cannot be removed, and that relief is only to be sought in the means of controlling its EFFECTS.

If a faction consists of less than a majority, relief is supplied by the republican principle, which enables the majority to defeat its sinister views by regular vote. It may clog the administration, it may convulse the society; but it will be unable to execute and mask its violence under the forms of the Constitution. When a majority is included in a faction, the form of popular government, on the other hand, enables it to sacrifice to its ruling passion or interest both the public good and the rights of other citizens. To secure the public good and private rights against the danger of such a faction, and at the same time to preserve the spirit and the form of popular government, is then the great object to which our inquiries are directed. Let me add that it is the great desideratum by which this form of government can be rescued from the opprobrium under which it has so long labored, and be recommended to the esteem and adoption of mankind.

By what means is this object attainable? Evidently by one of two only. Either the existence of the same passion or interest in a majority at the same time must be prevented, or the majority, having such coexistent passion or interest, must be rendered, by their number and local situation, unable to concert and carry into effect schemes of oppression. If the impulse and the opportunity be suffered to coincide, we well know that neither moral nor religious motives can be relied on as an adequate control. They are not found to be such on the injustice and violence of individuals, and lose their efficacy in proportion to the number combined together, that is, in proportion as their efficacy becomes needful.

From this view of the subject it may be concluded that a pure democracy, by which I mean a society consisting of a small number of citizens, who assemble and administer the government in person, can admit of no cure for the mischiefs of faction. A common passion or interest will, in almost every case, be felt by a majority of the whole; a communication and concert result from the form of government itself; and there is nothing to check the inducements to sacrifice the weaker party or an obnoxious individual. Hence it is that such democracies have ever been spectacles of turbulence and contention; have ever been found incompatible with personal security or the rights of property; and have in general been as short in their lives as they have been violent in their deaths. Theoretic politicians, who have patronized this species of government, have erroneously supposed that by reducing mankind to a perfect equality in their political rights, they would, at the same time, be perfectly equalized and assimilated in their possessions, their opinions, and their passions.

A republic, by which I mean a government in which the scheme of representation takes place, opens a different prospect, and promises the cure for which we are seeking. Let us examine the points in which it varies from pure democracy, and we shall comprehend both the nature of the cure and the efficacy which it must derive from the Union.

The two great points of difference between a democracy and a republic are: first, the delegation of the government, in the latter, to a small number of citizens elected by the rest; secondly, the greater number of citizens, and greater sphere of country, over which the latter may be extended.

The effect of the first difference is, on the one hand, to refine and enlarge the public views, by passing them through the medium of a chosen body of citizens, whose wisdom may best discern the true interest of their country, and whose patriotism and love of justice will be least likely to sacrifice it to temporary or partial considerations. Under such a regulation, it may well happen that the public voice, pronounced by the representatives of the people, will be more consonant to the public good than if pronounced by the people themselves, convened for the purpose. On the other hand, the effect may be inverted. Men of factious tempers, of local prejudices, or of sinister designs, may, by intrigue, by corruption, or by other means, first obtain the suffrages, and then betray the interests, of the people. The question resulting is, whether small or extensive republics are more favorable to the election of proper guardians of the public weal; and it is clearly decided in favor of the latter by two obvious considerations:

In the first place, it is to be remarked that, however small the republic may be, the representatives must be raised to a certain number, in order to guard against the cabals of a few; and that, however large it may be, they must be limited to a certain number, in order to guard against the confusion of a multitude. Hence, the number of representatives in the two cases not being in proportion to that of the two constituents, and being proportionally greater in the small republic, it follows that, if the proportion of fit characters be not less in the large than in the small republic, the former will present a greater option, and consequently a greater probability of a fit choice.

In the next place, as each representative will be chosen by a greater number of citizens in the large than in the small republic, it will be more difficult for unworthy candidates to practice with success the vicious arts by which elections are too often carried; and the suffrages of the people being more free, will be more likely to centre in men who possess the most attractive merit and the most diffusive and established characters.

It must be confessed that in this, as in most other cases, there is a mean, on both sides of which inconveniences will be found to lie. By enlarging too much the number of electors, you render the representatives too little acquainted with all their local circumstances and lesser interests; as by reducing it too much, you render him unduly attached to these, and too little fit to comprehend and pursue great and national objects. The federal Constitution forms a happy combination in this respect; the great and aggregate interests being referred to the national, the local and particular to the State legislatures.

The other point of difference is, the greater number of citizens and extent of territory which may be brought within the compass of republican than of democratic government; and it is this circumstance principally which renders factious combinations less to be dreaded in the former than in the latter. The smaller the society, the fewer probably will be the distinct parties and interests composing it; the fewer the distinct parties and interests, the more frequently will a majority be found of the same party; and the smaller the number of individuals composing a majority, and the smaller the compass within which they are placed, the more easily will they concert and execute their plans of oppression. Extend the sphere, and you take in a greater variety of parties and interests; you make it less probable that a majority of the whole will have a common motive to invade the rights of other citizens; or if such a common motive exists, it will be more difficult for all who feel it to discover their own strength, and to act in unison with each other. Besides other impediments, it may be remarked that, where there is a consciousness of unjust or dishonorable purposes, communication is always checked by distrust in proportion to the number whose concurrence is necessary.

Hence, it clearly appears, that the same advantage which a republic has over a democracy, in controlling the effects of faction, is enjoyed by a large over a small republic,—is enjoyed by the Union over the States composing it. Does the advantage consist in the substitution of representatives whose enlightened views and virtuous sentiments render them superior to local prejudices and schemes of injustice? It will not be denied that the representation of the Union will be most likely to possess these requisite endowments. Does it consist in the greater security afforded by a greater variety of parties, against the event of any one party being able to outnumber and oppress the rest? In an equal degree does the increased variety of parties comprised within the Union, increase this security. Does it, in fine, consist in the greater obstacles opposed to the concert and accomplishment of the secret wishes of an unjust and interested majority? Here, again, the extent of the Union gives it the most palpable advantage.

The influence of factious leaders may kindle a flame within their particular States, but will be unable to spread a general conflagration through the other States. A religious sect may degenerate into a political faction in a part of the Confederacy; but the variety of sects dispersed over the entire face of it must secure the national councils against any danger from that source. A rage for paper money, for an abolition of debts, for an equal division of property, or for any other improper or wicked project, will be less apt to pervade the whole body of the Union than a particular member of it; in the same proportion as such a malady is more likely to taint a particular county or district, than an entire State.

In the extent and proper structure of the Union, therefore, we behold a republican remedy for the diseases most incident to republican government. And according to the degree of pleasure and pride we feel in being republicans, ought to be our zeal in cherishing the spirit and supporting the character of Federalists.

Publius

Federalist No. 51

The Structure of the Government Must Furnish the Proper Checks and Balances Between the Different Departments

From the New York Packet.
Friday, February 8, 1788.

Author: **Alexander Hamilton** or **James Madison**

To the People of the State of New York:

To what expedient, then, shall we finally resort, for maintaining in practice the necessary partition of power among the several departments, as laid down in the Constitution? The only answer that can be given is, that as all these exterior provisions are found to be inadequate, the defect must be supplied, by so contriving the interior structure of the government as that its several constituent parts may, by their mutual relations, be the means of keeping each other in their proper places. Without presuming to undertake a full development of this important idea, I will hazard a few general observations, which may perhaps place it in a clearer light, and enable us to form a more correct judgment of the principles and structure of the government planned by the convention. In order to lay a due foundation for that separate and distinct exercise of the different powers of government, which to a certain extent is admitted on all hands to be essential to the preservation of liberty, it is evident that each department should have a will of its own; and consequently should be so constituted that the members of each should have as little agency as possible in the appointment of the members of the others. Were this principle rigorously adhered to, it would require that all the appointments for the supreme executive, legislative, and judiciary magistracies should be drawn from the same fountain of authority, the people, through channels having no communication whatever with one another. Perhaps such a plan of constructing the several departments would be less difficult in practice than it may in contemplation appear. Some difficulties, however, and some additional expense would attend the execution of it. Some deviations, therefore, from the principle must be admitted. In the constitution of the judiciary department in particular, it might be inexpedient to insist rigorously on the principle: first, because peculiar qualifications being essential in the members, the primary consideration ought to be to select that mode of choice which best secures these qualifications; secondly, because the permanent tenure by which the appointments are held in that department, must soon destroy all sense of dependence on the authority conferring them. It is equally evident, that the members of each department should be as little dependent as possible on those of the others, for the emoluments annexed to their offices. Were the executive magistrate, or the judges, not independent of the legislature in this particular, their independence in every other would be merely nominal. But the great security against a gradual concentration of the several powers in the same department, consists in giving to those who administer each department the necessary constitutional means and personal motives to resist encroachments of the others. The provision for defense must in this, as in all other cases, be made commensurate to the danger of attack. Ambition must be made to counteract ambition. The interest of the man must be connected with the constitutional rights of the place. It may be a reflection on human nature, that such devices should be necessary to control the abuses of government. But what is government itself, but the greatest of all reflections on human nature? If men were angels, no government would be necessary. If angels were to govern men, neither external nor internal controls on government would be necessary. In framing a government which is to be administered by men over men, the great difficulty lies in this: you must first enable the government to control the governed; and in the next place oblige it to control itself. A dependence on the people is, no doubt, the primary control on the government; but experience has taught mankind the necessity of auxiliary precautions. This policy of supplying, by opposite and rival interests, the defect of better motives, might be traced through the whole system of human affairs, private as well as public. We see it particularly displayed in all the subordinate distributions of power, where the constant aim is to divide and arrange the several offices in such a manner as that each may be a check on the other that the private interest of every individual may be a sentinel over the public rights. These inventions of prudence cannot be less requisite in the distribution of the supreme powers of the State. But it is not possible to give to each department an equal power of self-defense. In republican government, the legislative authority necessarily predominates. The remedy for this inconveniency is to divide the legislature into different branches; and to render them, by different modes of election and different principles of action, as little connected with each other as the nature of their common functions and their common dependence on the society will admit. It may even be necessary to guard against dangerous encroachments by still further precautions. As the weight of the legislative authority requires that it should be thus divided, the weakness of the executive may require, on the other hand, that it should be fortified. An absolute negative on the legislature appears, at first view, to be the natural defense with which the executive magistrate should be armed. But perhaps it would be neither altogether safe nor alone sufficient. On ordinary occasions it might not be exerted with the requisite firmness, and on extraordinary occasions it might be perfidiously abused. May not this defect of an absolute negative be supplied by some qualified connection between this weaker department and the weaker branch of the stronger department, by which the latter may be led to support the constitutional rights of the former, without being too much detached from the rights of its own department? If the principles on which these observations are founded be just, as I persuade myself they are, and they be applied as a criterion to the several State constitutions, and to the federal Constitution it will be found that if the latter does not perfectly correspond with them, the former are infinitely less able to bear such a test. There are, moreover, two considerations particularly applicable to the federal system of America, which place that system in a very interesting point of view. First. In a single republic, all the power surrendered by the people is submitted to the administration of a single government; and the usurpations are guarded against by a division of the government into distinct and separate departments. In the compound republic of America, the power surrendered by the people is first divided between two distinct governments, and then the portion allotted to each subdivided among distinct and separate departments. Hence a double security arises to the rights of the people. The different governments will control each other, at the same time that each will be controlled by itself. Second. It is of great importance in a republic not only to guard the society against the oppression of its rulers, but to guard one part of the society against the injustice of the other part. Different interests necessarily exist in different classes of citizens. If a majority be united by a common interest, the rights of the minority will be insecure. There are but two methods of providing against this evil: the one by creating a will in the community independent of the majority that is, of the society itself; the other, by comprehending in the society so many separate descriptions of citizens as will render an unjust combination of a majority of the whole very improbable, if not impracticable. The first method prevails in all governments possessing an hereditary or self-appointed authority. This, at best, is but a precarious security; because a power independent of the society may as well espouse the unjust views of the major, as the rightful interests of the minor party, and may possibly be turned against both parties. The second method will be exemplified in the federal republic of the United States. Whilst all authority in it will be derived from and dependent on the society, the society itself will be broken into so many parts, interests, and classes of citizens, that the rights of individuals, or of the minority, will be in little danger from interested combinations of the majority. In a free government the security for civil rights must be the same as that for religious rights. It consists in the one case in the multiplicity of interests, and in the other in the multiplicity of sects. The degree of security in both cases will depend on the number of interests and sects; and this may be presumed to depend on the extent of country and number of people comprehended under the same government. This view of the subject must particularly recommend a proper federal system to all the sincere and considerate friends of republican government, since it shows that in exact proportion as the territory of the Union may be formed into more circumscribed Confederacies, or States oppressive combinations of a majority will be facilitated: the best security, under the republican forms, for the rights of every class of citizens, will be diminished: and consequently the stability and independence of some member of the government, the only other security, must be proportionately increased. Justice is the end of government. It is the end of civil society. It ever has been and ever will be pursued until it be obtained, or until liberty be lost in the pursuit. In a society under the forms of which the stronger faction can readily unite and oppress the weaker, anarchy may as truly be said to reign as in a state of nature, where the weaker individual is not secured against the violence of the stronger; and as, in the latter state, even the stronger individuals are prompted, by the uncertainty of their condition, to submit to a government which may protect the weak as well as themselves; so, in the former state, will the more powerful factions or parties be gradnally induced, by a like motive, to wish for a government which will protect all parties, the weaker as well as the more powerful. It can be little doubted that if the State of Rhode Island was separated from the Confederacy and left to itself, the insecurity of rights under the popular form of government within such narrow limits would be displayed by such reiterated oppressions of factious majorities that some power altogether independent of the people would soon be called for by the voice of the very factions whose misrule had proved the necessity of it. In the extended republic of the United States, and among the great variety of interests, parties, and sects which it embraces, a coalition of a majority of the whole society could seldom take place on any other principles than those of justice and the general good; whilst there being thus less danger to a minor from the will of a major party, there must be less pretext, also, to provide for the security of the former, by introducing into the government a will not dependent on the latter, or, in other words, a will independent of the society itself. It is no less certain than it is important, notwithstanding the contrary opinions which have been entertained, that the larger the society, provided it lie within a practical sphere, the more duly capable it will be of self-government. And happily for the REPUBLICAN CAUSE, the practicable sphere may be carried to a very great extent, by a judicious modification and mixture of the FEDERAL PRINCIPLE.

PUBLIUS

How to Write a Critical Analysis

Each analysis will summarize and evaluate a text assigned by the instructor.

A critical analysis summarizes and evaluates a text. An analysis states a text's thesis, explains its logic, and summarizes its conclusions. Additionally, a critical digest evaluates a text's style, organization, logic, conclusions, and usefulness.

The purpose of a critical analysis differs from an abstract. Both give readers a sense of a text's main idea. However, a critical analysis fully describes a text's scope, method, and analysis, as well as indicates whether, in the digester's view, a text achieves its objectives and offers value to readers.

Content Standards for Critical Analysis: Each analysis shall include four sections with the following headings, content, and length:

- **Title:** Using APA style, this section states the complete author, title, and publication data of the text that the digest critiques.
- **Summary:** This section states the assigned text's thesis, explains its logic, and summarizes its conclusions. Do not merely paraphrase, especially when describing the logic of the text (350–450 words).
- **Evaluation:** This section evaluates, in light of other authoritative research or persuasive experience, the text's style, organization, logic, conclusions, and usefulness. State your reasons. Be critical (250–350 words).
- **References:** This is a list of the sources cited in the body of the analysis. It must contain at least one reference to another source.

Example Critical Analysis Paper

Title

Landsbergen, D. & Wolken, G. (2001). Realizing the promise: Government information systems and the fourth generation of information technology. Public Administration Review, 61(2), 206–221. Retrieved January 11, 2004, from EBSCO Business Source Premier database.

Summary

Interoperability is the sharing of information between people and agencies. Landsbergen and Wolken (2001) suggest the development of interoperable systems results in a more effective and efficient organization that can respond to the needs of citizens. As a result, reduced paperwork and improved policy decisions are made, which are in line with government reinvention efforts. Benefits and barriers to the implementation of interoperability were gleaned from a literature review. Criteria to base case studies and interviews on were gathered from the review of the literature. In the study information was gathered from agencies. The point of view projected throughout the study was from the government agency rather than the citizen.

 Landsbergen and Wolken (2001) conclude that information needs to be shared between departments, specific mechanisms to share information need to be implemented, such as the use of meta-data. However, there is no state or federal support in the law to create cooperation among agencies. Management teams need to coordinate legal, policy, and managerial issues between agencies. The creation of a "formbook" could expedite the coordination effort. The formbook would serve as a storing place for inoperability agreements so that agencies would have resources to draw upon when creating agreements. The formbook would also create a standard practice for inoperability agreements. The technical standards that are implemented between agencies become public law.

States need to partner with the federal government early in the development in order for the coordination to work. States would rather work cooperatively with the federal government than be told what to do and how to do it. Due to the cost involved, states prefer to imitate a model that is proven to be effective, a pilot project. States would support a clearinghouse of best practices with a proven track record of implementation.

The privacy problems created through interoperability are seen by agencies as unfounded. The fear of information sharing by the public, however, is very different (Toregas, 2001). The conclusion by the agencies is that "more information corrects distortion" (Landsbergen & Wolken, 2001, p. 6). By providing substantial information the public will be able to make more informed and better decisions about government interactions.

Evaluation

This article sets the reader up to think that a new idea is being proposed, interoperability. The word interoperability, however, is just a fancy word that the authors introduced for information sharing. The concept of interoperability is discussed in the e-government literature as a shift in thinking about government, making government more accessible to citizens (Cornfield, Rainie, & Horrigan, 2003; Holmes, 2001; Weare, 2002).

The methodology used in this article, a qualitative study based on case studies and interviews of leaders in the information technology field is a valid way to measure the barriers and benefits to the implementation of interoperability. The sampling method used was the snowball method where one expert referred the interviewer to another expert that could answer the same set of questions. The sampling technique was a way to ensure that the information gathered was from the best in the field.

The article examines the theory of interoperability, but also applies the theory to application. Interoperability is a theory that has a long way to go before it can be placed into practical use. Organizations need to make the best practices standard practices. Then vertically align standards across the agencies and horizontally throughout the levels of government. The legal and policy standards need to correlate before agencies can effectively work together. The statutes may need to be changed to allow agencies to work together. Greater efficiency and effectiveness will result through interoperability, thus allowing the government to reap the benefits and save the stakeholders revenue.

References

Cornfield, M., Rainie, L., & Horrigan, J. B. (2003, March 20). Untuned keyboards: Online campaigners, citizens, and portals in the 2002 elections. Pew Research Center. Retrieved on December 29, 2003, from http://www.pewinternet.org/reports/toc.asp? Report=85

Holmes, D. (2001). Egov: Ebusiness strategies for government. London: Nicholas Brealey Publishing.

Toregas, C. (2001). The politics of e-gov: The upcoming struggle for redefining civic engagement. National Civic Review, 90(3), 235–240. Retrieved December 20, 2003, from EBSCO Business Premier database.

Weare, C. (2002). The internet and democracy: The causal links between technology and politics. International Journal of Public Administration, 25(5), 659–691.

How to Write a Research Paper

The goal of a research paper is to find out what research has to say about the topic. It is a compilation of what other authors believe. The paper needs to be written in third person; personal opinions (I) should not be in the body of the paper. When compiling the work of other authors, it is important to first paraphrase what the author wrote and then give credit to the author by citing the authors last name and year of publication (see APA manual for more citations). In the conclusion, the opinion of the writer can be highlighted and compared to the opinions of researchers.

1. Determine a broad topic to study.
   Examples:
   E-government
   High School Dropout

2. Background research
   Read material (books, journals, newspapers, magazine articles) on the topic and narrow your focus
   Examples:

Big Topic	Focus
E-government	Local government impact
High school dropout	Interventions that work

3. Write a research question.
   Examples:
   What impact has e-government had on local governments?
   What are the interventions that affect the dropout rate the most?

4. Library search
   Search for journal articles related to the topic at the Eastfield Library or on the Eastfield Library website. If using the electronic library, use the EBSCO Academic Premier or Business Premier databases to locate full text articles on the topic.

5. Reference list
   Type the reference list using American Psychological Association Style (APA).

6. Note-taking

Read the articles and take notes in your own words. Use direct quotes sparingly.
Two note-taking strategies

- Use index cards

    One colored set for sources—cut and paste from reference list
    White index cards for notes—number the white index cards to match the source the information is being taken.
    Take notes from the article on white index cards.

- Computer method

    Enter notes in a word-processing program after reading an article. After entering the paragraph(s) or sentence, cite the (author, year) so that the next step will be easier.

7. Categorize notes

Read through all the notes, look for similar parts and parts that can be put into subheadings.

- Index card method
- Put. index cards in piles as to similarities and give each pile a label (subheading for paper).

    Enter notes into the computer.

- Computer method

    Print out all notes from the computer

    Read the notes

    Find similarities and subheading topics, then label the paragraphs or sentences

    Go to the file on the computer and cut and paste ideas under the headings created

8. Revise three steps.

- Fixing Gaps

    Read through the paper and look for areas where more information may be needed.
    Look up additional articles and add information where needed.

- Combining authors

    Read through paper and look for redundancy. Are two authors saying the same thing? Combine the authors statements and cite both examples (Thomas, 2004; Newman, 2003). See APA manual for more information on multiple citations.

further	consequently	as a result	finally
in addition	likewise	however	in contrast
in conclusion	for instance	subsequently	specifically
finally	otherwise	since	therefore

(Maimon & Peritz, 2003)

- Transitions

    Add transition words and sentences to make the paper flow.
    Examples of transition words:

9. Write the introduction and conclusion.

10. Edit your paper.

Check the paper for capitalization, punctuation, spelling, English usage, and sentence structure.

This is a suggested method of research for Eastfield College students. Developed by Glynn Newman, MPA.

REFERENCES

American Psychological Association. (2001). *Publication manual of the American Psychological Association* (5th ed.). Washington, DC: APA.

Maimon E. P. & Peritz, J. H. (2003). *A writers resource: A handbook for writing and research.* Boston, MA: McGraw-Hill Higher Education.

How to Create a Reference Page

The references listed here are some example of the American Psychological Association style (APA). The examples are a starting point for students to use; the how- to sheet is not intended to replace the APA manual (APA, 2001). Students will need to refer to the APA manual for examples not included.

Rules for reference pages

- Reference page needs to contain all the sources cited in the paper, no more, no less.
- References need to be double-spaced.
- References must be in alphabetical order.
- Double-space all references.
- Start the Reference page on a new page at the end of the paper.

Sample references

- BOOK, TWO AUTHORS
  Shafritz J. M. & Russell, E. W. (1999). *Introducing public administration.* New York: Longman, Inc.
- Journal article, one author
  Van Slyke, D. M. (2003). The mythology of privatization in contracting for social services. *Public Administration Review,* 63(3), 296–315.
- Journal article, more than one author
  Kaylor, C., Deshazo, R. & Eck, D. V. (2001). Gauging e-government: A report on implementing services among American cities. *Government Information Quarterly,* 18(4), 293–307.
- Magazine article, one author, no pages
  Drucker, P. F. (1995, February). Really reinventing government. *The Atlantic Monthly.*
- Newspaper article
  Barr, S. & McAllister B. (1997, July 11). Downsizing cuts federal union representation: More postal employees covered. *The Washington Post,* p. B2.

- Government document
  National Performance Review. (1996). The best kept secrets in government. Washington: U.S. Government Printing Office.

- Newspaper article, no author
  Study finds free care used more. (1982, April 3). *Wall Street Journal,* pp. A1, A25

- Article retrieved from an electronic database
  Tillman, B. (2002). The changing political landscape. *Information Management Journal,* 36(1), 14–17. Retrieved October 1, 2003, from EBSCO Business Premier database.

- Web page with private organization as author
  Midwest League. (2003). Pitching, individual records. Retrieved October 1, 2003, from http://www.midwestleague.com/indivpitching.html

- Web page, government author
  Wisconsin Department of Natural Resources. (2001). Glacial habitat restoration areas. Retrieved September 18, 2001, from http://www.dnr.state.wi.us/org/land/wildlife/hunt/hra.htm

  Adapted from, Williams, O. (2003). *American Psychological Association (APA) format* (5th ed.). University of Minnesota, Crookston. Retrieved on April 12, 2004, from http://www.crk.umn.edu/ library/links/apa5th.htm

REFERENCE

American Psychological Association. (2001). *Publication manual of the American Psychological Association* (5th ed.). Washington, DC: APA.

Example Research Paper

E-Government and Strategic Management

Glynn E. Newman

Unknown University

Abstract

The emergence of technological advances has caused government to conduct business through a new medium of communication. The Internet revolution has changed the way in which business takes place. Government is being challenged to provide electronic services to citizens. Each governmental unit is at a different stage in the implementation of e-government. There are many successful models of government providing more services through the Internet. However, the challenges become barriers to governments implementing electronic delivery systems.

This paper discusses the factors in the implementation of e-government. A common definition of e-government will be proposed. A benchmarking model of implementation that focuses on the successes and problems will be examined. Finally, implications for governments implementing e-government will be presented.

E-Government

Information technology has changed numerous aspects of American society. These technological advances challenge governments. The Department of Defense in the 1960s developed the Internet as a tool for communication (Ho, 2002). The results of the invention have transformed the way people conduct business. In 1993, the government began using online services (Shi, 2002). Computer usage has increased and e-government has moved into high gear because of citizens familiarity with other electronic service deliveries by the private sector. The use of e-commerce and e-business has created a greater demand on governments to deliver services electronically. E-government has caused more citizens to request government documents, services, and information without entering a library, government office or even leaving their home. Communication between governmental officials and citizens has been revolutionized, by the ability of citizens to transmit and access information 24 hours a day. E-government is creating a transformation in the way families, businesses, entertainment, and government interact with one another (Menzel, 1998).

In the year 2000 the federal government spent $1.5 billion on Internet activities and forecasters predict that by the year 2005, $6.2 billion will be spent on Internet activities (Layne & Lee, 2001). The increased spending is not only assisting with the relationship between the citizens and government, but it is also increasing the efficiency and effectiveness of government. E-government has the potential to transform the way in which government performs business. The purpose of this paper is to establish a common definition of e-government, discuss the stages of e-government implementation, highlight the successes and problems, and address the implications for governments.

Definition

A U.S. Commerce report states that the digital revolution has arrived, the number of people using the Internet has risen astronomically, from three million users in 1994 to three hundred million users in the year 2000 (Fletcher, 2002). Private sector innovations with e-commerce have brought about pressure for the public sector to adopt technology as a way to make government more efficient and effective (Koh & Prybutok, 2003). The term e-government stems from the private term e-commerce (Lenk & Traunmuller, 2002). The major difference between e-commerce and e-governments is that government involvement can be mandatory, while e-commerce is voluntary. Citizens can be forced legally to use electronic services, giving the government legitimate powers. Taxes must be filed if you are a law-abiding citizen. Given the fact that the speed of the Internet and the reliability of the technology, it would be to the governments advantage to have citizens file taxes electronically. On the other hand, when transacting business with private companies, choice is always an option for citizens to determine whether to buy goods and services online or to conduct their business face to face. While the efficiency may be improved for the government with the use of e-government, instead of using force the government tries educating the citizen about the benefits of online services. However, even though e-government holds enormous potential, many citizens have not embraced electronic government (Rose, 2002). The e-commerce business started out with some of the same problems e-government is facing today. As the younger generation gets older and is used to using electronic transactions in other areas of their lives, the generation will come to demand the same types of services from the government, rather than wasting time standing in long lines (Seifert & Petersen, 2002).

E-government is defined as the use of all communications technologies to improve citizen access, participation, and satisfaction with government. The goal is to provide citizens effective, efficient delivery of services and knowledge to improve the relationship between the government and the citizen and the government and other entities. New patterns of relationship will be forged (Layne & Lee, 2001; Marche & McNiven, 2003; Moon, 2002; Seifert & Petersen, 2002). Information technology (IT) is embedded into the e-government service delivery model. IT is defined as the mechanical organizational components that function to store or transmit data using digital devices. It is the infrastructure for making the transactions of e-government a reality (danziger & andersen, 2002).

E-government is about increasing government efficiency and effectiveness (Marche & McNiven, 2003; Moon, 2002). The speed of service delivery to citizens is improved so citizens needs can be responded to in a much more efficient and effective manner through technological advances (Marche & McNiven, 2003). The shift to e-government could result in a qualitative change in the way government and the citizen conduct business together. The long lines and the limited hours of government operation would not serve as barriers to citizens. It would help to break down the stereotypes of government inefficiency by decreasing the red tape involved with transactions. The improved quality and accessibility to services could create a very positive relationship (Seifert & Petersen, 2002).

Public administrators have an opportunity to benefit through the use of Internet and information technology as it transforms the way citizen conduct business. Services that required citizens to visit city hall can now be conducted online. With the use of technology many of the human errors have been eliminated and greater efficiency can be achieved. An example of human error would be the presidential election of 2000, which could have used electronic governance to improve public governance (Rose, 2002).

Since many governments are examining ways to restructure and save money, e-government is often used as a solution (Seifert & Petersen, 2003; Moon, 2002). To assist with changes, state and local governments are used as a focus for the implementation of e-government projects due to the direct role in delivering services to the public. The population served in state and local agencies is more compact and therefore easier to study in order to generalize to the larger population (Seifert & Petersen, 2002).

As the development of e-government takes place, the citizenry needs to be informed about governmental issues. Fletcher (2002) describes the citizens as "a crucial ingredient in the rich and complex recipe for the setting of policy and the ensuing administration of government" (p. 724). Policy engagement can be influenced by the amount of e-government experience found in the citizenry (Marche & McNiven, 2003).

The vision for e-government is to create a system that is fast, free, friendly, available 24-7, that provides information and services that include active participation in government processes (Fletcher, 2002). E-government goals are increased efficiency and information technology resource management. As a result, the increase in the speed of transactions and reduction in personnel will produce a cost savings to governments. Automation of standardized tasks will reduce errors and improve the consistency of the task. Streamlining operating procedures will assist in reducing the layers in the organization. The reduction of the time employees spend on repetitive tasks will give them opportunities to develop new skills (Seifert & Petersen, 2002). According to the Government Paperwork Elimination Act (GPEA) of 1998, by the year 2003 the government is supposed to use electronic forms, applications, and signatures when applicable. This act is the push for the federal government to offer electronic transactions to citizens. Subsequently, the reality of e-government as a vital role for government is emerging more clearly (Fletcher, 2002).

Stages of Implementation

Surrounding the advent of e-government, each government entity is at a different place when it comes to implementation. Private corporations are familiar with benchmarking to determine progress and growth in e-commerce. Web delivery services by the private and public sector are experiencing problems with benchmarking results. There is not a research model that is considered standard in either industry. The only measurable data is content and usage of Web pages. Given the nature of business and its customer base it would be more difficult to benchmark. On the other hand, e-government for the public sector offers fewer services and should find it easier to benchmark (Kaylor, Deshazo & Van Eck, 2001).

Subsequently, Seifert and Peterson (2002) offer a four-stage benchmarking process that governments need to evolve through to reach this goal of transforming the government structure from an agency-centric organization to a citizen-centric agency that is capable of providing government access twenty-four hours a day, seven days a week. The government may not follow a linear path through the stages. The stages, however, can be used as a benchmarking system for governments (Moon, 2002).

The first stage is presence, where citizens gather information (Seifert & Petersen, 2002). The government houses a Web site that gives information such as hours of operation, mailing address, and phone numbers, but there are no interactions with the citizen. The information is limited to the presentation of government information (Koh & Prybutok, 2003; Layne & Lee, 2001, Moon, 2002; Schelin, 2003; Seifert & Petersen, 2002;Wimmer, 2002). This level can also be called the brochureware level, where the information on the site is equivalent to what might be in a brochure (Schelin, 2003; Seifert & Peterson, 2002). One-way communication takes place at this stage. Basic web technology is used on this type of site (Moon, 2002).

The second stage is the interaction stage (Seifert & Petersen, 2002). E-mail contact and obtaining and printing forms to be mailed in are types of services available on these sites. Simple informational transactions exist at this stage (Seifert & Petersen, 2002). Moon (2002) calls this stage the request and response stage where customers request and receive information from the agency. Data interchange takes place trough the use of e-mail links on sites. Data-transfer technologies are also used (Moon, 2002; Schelin, 2003). An example of an interaction stage Web site is the Social Security Administration. The agency receives requests for Medicare applications, then processes them and responds to the request. (Moon, 2002). Layne and Lee (2001) combine stage one and stage two and call it the cataloguing stage. This is where the government is getting their information organized in order to present it to the public.

The third stage is the transaction stage. Citizens are able to complete many tasks at any time of the day, such as license renewals, submitting bids for contracts, and paying fees and taxes (Koh & Prybutok, 2003; Layne & Lee, 2001; Moon, 2002; Seifert & Petersen, 2002; Wimmer, 2002). The government is shifting to a "citizen-centric realm" (Schelin, 2003, p. 130). Moon (2002) describes this stage as the service and financial transaction stage. This is achieved by "putting live database links to on-line interfaces" (Layne & Lee, 2001, p. 125). The technological pieces that need to be in place are an electronic data interchange, electronic filing system, and digital signature (Moon,

2002). The web transactions should not have to be handled by government personnel. The transactions should be posted directly to the government systems (Layne & Lee, 2001). A group in the community that perhaps favors the online transactions the most is private business. Businesses need to be able to access permits and licenses in an efficient manner. Through e-government, businesses are able to avoid wasteful time standing in long lines, losing the business money. As a result when businesses are making decisions on where to relocate, the ability to complete regular transactions online may be viewed as a benefit if moving to the community (Moulder, 2001).

During stage three, the goal of e-government is to provide a single stop for citizens to conduct various businesses. Government administrators have discussed a one-stop shop model, which would grant customers access to government from a single point of entry. This concept takes into account a shift from public service to customer orientation (Wimmer, 2002). The shift must take into account various customer situations and provide a clear path that meets customers needs. In order for a smooth transition to occur there must be two distinct and separate values recognized, the external customer and the internal public administrators perspective (Wimmer, 2002). The government makes information "transparent" to the citizen, where the information is accessible and in language that can be easily understood. The ability of the government to hide the complexity of transactions and inner workings of the technical side are important in the development of "one-stop shopping" for citizens (Marche & McNiven, 2003). A one-stop shop is, "the ability to obtain diverse services in a timely, convenient and user-friendly manner from a single source" (Ho, 2002, p. 436). The private sector has used one stop shopping for years. The one-stop shop operates like an umbrella over the governmental agencies used to increase integration of services (Ho, 2002).

In order to develop a stage three, one-stop shop, it would require several key features of administrative tasks. First, the government would need to be able to move from traditional business to electronic business smoothly. The infrastructure and personnel training would need to be in place. Second, services that are provided by different departments are linked to a single point of entry. This would require a vertical teaming across departments. Third, to insure authenticity and privacy, there is a need for security across the Internet and the ability to handle highly sensitive and personal data. Again the infrastructure would need to be in place to ensure that encryption software was being used effectively. A fourth key administrative task would be to ensure the internal and external transfer of information between citizens and business customers. Fifth, customers need to have clear instructions on the Web site in order to fill out information according to standards. Sixth, be sure that the Web site has support to bridge the language between citizen, business, and administrative legal terminology. Customers need to be able to link to definitions of terms. Once all of these services are provided, then the reality of a one-stop government is complete (Wimmer, 2002).

An example of a one-stop shop is the federal government Web site. In 2000 the federal government launched a new initiative for one-stop government access. The site is www.firstgov.gov. It provided a user-friendly portal to all the federal governments Web sites. This increased the push for local governments to improve their web-based services (Fletcher, 2002; Moon, 2002).

The fourth stage in the Seifert and Petersen (2002) benchmarking model is transformation. There should be collaborative decision-making that transforms the organization into customer-centric relations. There are not many examples of this stage, due to the financial and administrative constraints (Seifert & Petersen, 2002). Moon (2002) calls this stage the political participation stage. If e-government is at this stage, citizens are able to vote online or file comments online. The policy-making process becomes visible to the citizens, because the processes are available to them without leaving home. Thus, the result is an increase in the participative nature of government through electronic means (Marche & McNiven, 2003).

Layne and Lee (2001) propose two additional stages that need to occur to bring the governments to the highest level of complexity with the e-government solutions—vertical and horizontal integration. Vertical integration refers to agencies at the federal, state, and local levels working together to provide citizens with efficient services. For example, if a citizen filed at the local level for a business permit, the information would be sent to the state government for a state license and then to the federal government for the employer identification number. Horizontal integration of services is the coordination across functions and services, for example, if a business needed to pay unemployment insurance and business taxes at the same time to different agencies. The agencies would transfer the money to the proper agency and the payment would be credited to both departments. Vertical integration is less complex than horizontal integration (Layne & Lee, 2001).

Accordingly, Kaylor, Deshazo, and Van Eck (2001) conducted a study, which looked at implementation as opposed to end-users. The city council of Ann Arbor, Michigan was determined to provide services to their citizens more efficiently than it currently was doing and charged Kaylor, Deshazo, and Van Eck (2001) to help them develop a more efficient form of service delivery. The study considered functions and services provided by other cities, and a rubric was developed to determine cities that were considering having e-government and the important pieces that needed to be in place to have an effective service for citizens. The rubric consisted of twelve functional areas including payments, registration, permits, customer service, communication, licenses, images, audio/video/documents, applications, e-procurement, and miscellaneous. Once all information was gathered the results were tallied into what the authors called the municipality's e-score.

The findings concluded that some cities did not provide e-government services at all. Cities that tended not to provide e-government services were smaller. In addition, the number of cities that did not have an electronic presence indicated that cost played a significant role. Cities with larger budgets tended to have electronic presence. The cities that received a significant e-score seemed to have many similar functions though not in any particular order. Some of the functions that made for good e-scores are: e-commerce, registration and permits, customer service, communication documents, and information and participation (Kaylor, Deshazo, and Van Eck, 2001).

Wimmer (2002) concludes by stating electronic service delivery could be enhanced if there was a level of cooperation between e-government solutions. Online customers could use their local service provider to connect them to an e-government Web site if there was a single point of contact. One-stop government has made gains, but for the most part is still in the early stages of development. In order for e-government to be complete there must be an integration of information technology from a single source, whereby citizens are active in the utilization of technology. A citizens participation may be to gain information, apply for a permit, get in contact with a public official and use the Internet to get those things done. The citizen should determine how far he is willing to use electronic media (Wimmer, 2002).

E-Government Successes

While many e-government initiatives are still evolving, there have been many promising findings from research on the actual implementation and best practices for implementation. Moon (2002) conducted an examination of data from a survey conducted by the International City/County Management Association and Public Technology Incorporated on the adoption of e-government. The survey showed that 85.3 percent of local governments have their own Web sites and 57.4 percent of them had an intranet. Five years ago 46 cities had their own Web sites. The development of Web sites is a new phenomenon. Of the responding governments only 8.2 percent of them had a comprehensive plan of e-government. Many local governments do not have long-term strategic plans in place to advance e-government. The types of services offered by these sites are often in stage one or two. Only ten cities offer property registration online.

Moon (2002) concluded that larger organizations are more likely to adopt e-government. Cities with a politically active public and more money are more likely to adopt, due to the increased pressures to be efficient. For larger governments it was easier to afford the new technologies. Cities with a council-manager form of government are more likely to have an e-government plan, due to the fact that city managers have professional values versus political values of a mayor-council form of government, innovations were taken on more seriously. Council manager forms of government have an easier time implementing e-government reinvention (Moon, 2002).

Similarly, Shi (2002) investigated the success of e-commerce and the factors related to the success, specifically transformational leadership and strategic planning. The evolution of e-government has caused changes in the way people work and challenged government to improve the service delivery models. The public expects to be able to access government information at anytime and be able to conduct government business over secure connections at anytime. Shi (2002) studied the effects of transformational leadership and strategic planning on an organization. He found a positive correlation between the development of both strategic planning and transformational leadership and the success of the e-government. Shis (2002) findings about strategic planning having a direct effect on the development of e-government were in direct correlation with Moon's (2002) findings about the development of e-government plans by the council-manager forms of government. The plan and the leader determined the success of the initiative.

While Shi (2002) conducted survey research on the managerial aspects of e-government, Danzinger and Andersen (2002) conducted an analysis of empirical research studies and grouped the results by categories. As far as the capabilities of technology, the areas that showed the most positive interactions with the organization were efficiency and productivity. The three specific highest scoring items were time-saving, citizen-to citizen interaction, and structuring of problems that were found in all of the studies. Ninety-four percent of the studies found that management control was improved through the IT influx. This study confirms the findings of Shi (2002) as far as the role of the managers changing; however a discussion as to how the managers role changed was not discussed by Danzinger and Andersen (2002). The negative impacts on the development of IT were in the areas of citizens legal issues and citizens interactions with government. The findings of this study in relation to the negative impact of e- government on the citizen-to-government relationship are in direct contrast to the vision for e-government (Layne & Lee, 2001; Marche & McNiven, 2003; Moon, 2002; Seifert & Petersen, 2002).

In a very different type of study focused on demonstrating the efficiency of e-government, Thurman and Davis (2001) described the transformation to e-government services at the Department of Energy. The initial investment in the project was $15 million; the cost per customer was $18.55. In 2000, the cost was $8.6 million and the cost per customer transaction was $2.59. In the long term the investments paid off in customer satisfaction. The way the Department of Energy determines the success of the products, which are the scientific documents, is through counting the number of transactions occurring on the site. The investment saves researchers time and provides useful information. The initial investment was a large sum of money. However, with the number of customers to the site increasing because of the ease of use of the site and the type of information catalogued on the site, the costs are decreasing and benefits of scientist-to-scientist sharing of information is paying off. The number of transactions occurring determines success.

Another department in the federal government implementing e-government effectively is the Internal Revenue Service (IRS). The IRS is implementing electronic tax filing to improve efficiency and effectiveness in its internal operations. The agency partnered with Adobe and used Adobe Portable Document Format, which allows citizens to print forms. Forty million United States taxpayers filed their 2000 taxes electronically (Moon, 2002). The results were phenomenal with a decrease in call volume and millions of dollars saved. The IRS has developed forms that assist citizens with filing taxes online. The traditional method costs the IRS three dollars to mail out forms, but online that cost is one penny for a thousand electronic files. The effectiveness of the e-government service delivery for the IRS is apparently due to the cost savings and with the increased number of citizens who filed taxes electronically in the year 2000 (Rose, 2002).

Internal services for all government agencies also improve by being able to transfer money electronically between agencies and provide information to the employees through the intranet. The ability of the agency to store and organize data also improves through the use of technology. Routine tasks can be conducted quickly, such as responding to employees need for insurance statements (Moon, 2002).

With the increase in the number of citizens conducting business online an important aspect to e-government is the easy access to areas on the government Web sites. Citizens need to be able to find the area they are looking for, take care of the business and log out as quickly as possible. However, government agencies have a need to promote their existence, which means the needs of the government and the needs of the citizen are conflicting. It is difficult to promote the agency on the Web site and provide citizens with quick and easy access to a wide range of services (Marche & McNiven, 2003). Web pages need to be developed with attention to the standard of accessibility. Each individual site and the overall site design need to be consistent, reliable, and attractive in their presentation (Fletcher, 2002).

In a specific study to determine the best features of Web sites, Fagan and Fagan (2001) examined Web sites to determine the ease in locating state legislative documents. After viewing fifty state sites they concluded that the states might want to focus on usability of the site rather than with many graphics and animation. A description of the ideal Web site is as follows, on the first page citizens access is stated in text-based format what documents are on line and where they are found. Adobe PDF versions of the documents are available for the printing of a more official document. A thesaurus and hyperlinks to a glossary of legislative terms is provided for citizens to access.

A different perspective was taken by Westerback (2000) to determine the best practices in the federal e-government plan. Westerback (2000) examined the General Accounting Offices 11 strategic management plans and the evidence of implementation of the 11 plans. Of the 11 plans three were found to have strong support for implementation of the policies. The first one is making sure that strategic planning was embedded with customer needs. Strategic planning was a strong predictor of success for e-government, not only in the federal government, but also in the local and state governments (Moon, 2002; Shi, 2002). The second factor where there was strong support for implementation was measuring the performance of key processes (Westerback, 2000). This is apparent with the Department of Energy Web site tracking of visits to the site and determining costs per user (Thurmon & Davis, 2001). Third, managing information technology as investments to insure that infrastructure is accounted for in the strategic plan. E-government can only be as good as the infrastructure that houses the service delivery model, so in the strategic plan managing the infrastructure component is as important as oil to a car (Moulder, 2001; Westerback, 2000).

E-Government Problems

Consequently, there are also many problems associated with e-government. Some of the barriers stated by governments are security and privacy issues, lack of citizen resources, lack of technology staff, and administrative issues such as lack of financial resources (Moon, 2002).

Privacy

The concern of the public about the privacy of information shared through the Internet is a large issue when shifting to e-government (Fletcher, 2003; Koh & Prybutok, 2003; Layne & Lee, 2001). In a survey conducted, more than half of the people surveyed mentioned security as the utmost concern when shifting to e-government platforms. Fewer than 35 percent of the people who use the Internet trusted the government with their personal information (Fletcher, 2003; Layne & Lee, 2001). Only 28 percent of people felt comfortable submitting personal information electronically to the government (Fletcher, 2002). The government telling citizens that information is secure is not enough. Government agencies need to hire independent auditing firms with citizen input to help the public retain confidence in the method of delivery (Layne & Lee, 2001). After all, most economic and social interactions involve trust. Trust is a major concern of electronic government and public administrators must work hard to engender trust (Rose, 2002; Toregas, 2001). A way to help build trust might be to start with a target audience for e-government. E-government services many times do not have a specific audience; the audience is the community as a whole. The government will establish a core group of users to build upon. With the core group of users trusting the government services on the Internet, the citizen-to-citizen contact will build more trust and the growth will continue (Lenk & Traunmuller, 2002).

The growth of Internet surveillance technologies has increased dramatically. The paths of users track on the Internet can be recorded, which leaves open the question of privacy. One of the major concerns with the use of the Internet is the use of surfing monitoring devices called cookies. Cookies that are placed on the users computer so the Web site can track the places that the user goes to on the site. The government needs to establish guidelines for privacy, openness, and accountability (Marche & McNiven, 2003; Seifert & Petersen, 2002). Another concern is the sharing of private information with other agencies. The General Accounting Office stated that 23 out of 70 agencies shared personal information with other agencies. At the present time, with the concern of terrorism, there seems to be a lesser focus on citizen privacy rights, but it remains to be seen if the shift remains the same (Seifert & Petersen, 2002).

With the tightening of privacy policies due to the September 11 attack, the privacy legislation is in a state of flux. At this time the Federal Trade Commission (FTC) is calling for enforcement of current privacy laws rather than the creation of new legislation. However, the legislature sees the need for more detailed privacy legislation and is pushing bills to the floor. The president will ultimately be the one to determine the focus for the nation (Tillman, 2002).

The Computer Security Act of 1987 (P.L. 100-235) established that any agency that contains a Federal information system must have a security and privacy plan in place. The law states that the plans must contain conditions for risk of misuse, unauthorized access, or loss of information. Federal Web sites must prominently display the privacy policies of the agency as of December 1999 (Fletcher, 2002). "Online forms should have a clear and specific purpose and be specifically directed to specifically authorized authorities" (Layne & Lee, 2001, p. 132).

Computer security is another challenge for governments. In order to build citizen confidence and trust, organizations need to ensure that the risks of fraud or improper use of data is not an issue (Seifert & Petersen, 2002). Governments are political units and must comply with the Freedom of Information Act that allows public information to be released to journalists, lawyers and law enforcement (Rose, 2002). Seifert and Petersen (2002) list six areas that governments need to address when it comes to security issues: "Security program management, access controls, software development and change controls, segregation of duties, operating systems controls, and service continuity" (p. 205). When promoting the use of online services for citizens, preventing the disclosure of private information that is stored in government databases should be a primary concern for governments. If government officials can ensure the citizen that the information provided by electronic delivery will be protected, a better relationship can be fostered (Menzel, 1998; Rose, 2002).

Digital divide

Certainly an issue that the government will need to address is the digital divide. Not all citizens have equal access to the technology. "This digital divide is a detriment to the wholesale embrace of e-gov as a truly democratic technology" (Toregas, 2001, p. 236). The access to the Internet, technology skills, and literacy skills need to be available for e-government use. Assumptions of literacy and digital divide arise as issues of e-government (Marche & McNiven, 2003). These groups of people are more likely to be left behind in the access to information. Often times, government services are needed by the poor, less-educated, limited English proficient, and elderly, and these are the groups many times that do not have access to computers or the necessary skills to be able to understand how it works (Seifert & Petersen, 2002). Governments must respond to the citizens needs for access to information in order to decrease the divide created between those with advantages and those without (Marche & McNiven, 2003).

In order for e-government systems to be determined as effective, one hundred percent of the citizens need to be able to access them at all times. As far as participation the government also needs to look at the access to computers for all. Other avenues should also be considered such as automated phone services, public Internet access facilities, and service facilities in order to reach the entire population (Layne & Lee, 2001; Seifert & Petersen, 2002).

Toregas (2001) suggests that one way to assist those without access to computers is to place computer terminals in libraries and shopping malls. In order to assist in the development of literacy skills the suggestion is to develop literacy centers in neighborhoods to assist with literacy skills and computer skills.

Retention of workers

Recruitment and retention of government information technology workers is a challenge faced by governments. The salary structure and the inability to offer the same types of benefits workers could receive in the private sector are reasons that government has to outsource projects or delay implementation (Seifert & Petersen, 2002). The structure of cyber workplaces is much different from the bureaucratic structure of government. In cyber work environments democratic and decentralized forms of communication happen. A shift will need to take place in the government in order for the cyber agencies within the bureaucratic organization to be successful. The financial commitment needs to be made in order to retain the IT workers in government positions (Menzel, 1998).

Administrative concerns

Government administrators are faced with tremendous challenges over implementing new technologies in governments. Financial concerns are always on the mind of administrators and limited resources play a significant role when it is time to invest in implementing new technology (Kaylor, Deshazo & Van Eck, 2001). E-government is providing new services and improved efficiency; however with the increased efficiency greater funding and increased accountability are needed. (Seifert & Petersen, 2002).

When governments are faced with tight budgets the temptation may be there to sell Web site space for ads or offer links to businesses. Menzel (1997) poses the question, "How far should governments go in commercializing governments?"

There are considerations to take into account before moving forward on a technology project, but of those considerations none is considered standard for e-government. Something to consider before implementation is your ability to evaluate e-government. When looking at governmental Web sites there is no standard design to consider, thus causing all sites to be different. Some standard features could be navigation systems, sufficient help features, and appropriate general information. Governments do not need to reinvent the wheel, given there are numerous private sector businesses that have already paved the way. Even though others have paved the way, governments need access to comprehensive benchmarks of progress made by other cities (Kaylor, Deshazo & Van Eck, 2001).

Implications for Government Entities

Public administration will be transformed through e-government. Current governmental systems are based on the bureaucratic structure that emphasizes the vertical divisions in power (Seifert & Petersen, 2002). The emphasis in the traditional structure focuses on departmentalization and making tasks routine to improve efficiency. Government workers become experts in one job and there is one best way to do the task. The departments report to a central manager that is in charge of coordination and control of all the departments. The problem in the bureaucratic model is the inability to focus on the client. The focus is on procedures rather than responding to the human element, whichproduces rigidity in workers. As a result, the department becomes inefficient (Ho, 2002). On the other hand with the advent of e-government, the departmental agencies work together to develop the one-stop shop approach. The barriers between agencies will begin to be removed through the development of a horizontal structure rather than a vertical structure. The lines of authority in the organization will begin to not be as clear. As a result, the accountability will suffer because the origination of responsibility and credit will not be clear-cut (Seifert & Petersen, 2002). The focus of the government is on the citizen rather than the work (Ho, 2002). Layne and Lee (2001) explain further by stating.

In our view, these emerging trends will turn public administration both inside out and upside down. Public management will be turned inside out as the largely internal focus of management in the past is replaced by an external focus, specifically a focus on citizens and citizenship. Public management will be turned upside down as the traditional top-down orientation of the field is replaced not necessarily by a bottom-up approach, but by a system of shared leadership (p. 133).

E-government not only will have an impact on citizens, but on the structure of the government interactions internally and externally (Ho, 2002; Seifert & Petersen, 2002). The public manager will focus on customer satisfaction, service delivery flexibility, and managing the IT network in contrast to the traditional bureaucratic managers focus of the work processes. The outcomes, ability to support the innovations, and citizen impact become the central focus (Ho, 2002).

The focus of a governmental entity can be viewed simply by viewing the Web site. Ho (2002) examined the Internet Web sites of several cities to determine the orientation of the cities. He proposes that a city's Web site can inform the user of the orientation of the city management. If departments construct the Web site like the organizational structure of the city, such as, then the city is more bureaucratic in nature. However, if the Web site is more user-oriented with large amounts of information located on the first page allowing the user to determine what to look at. An analysis of fifty-five Web sites was conducted and each city was rated on a three-pronged scale. The results showed that larger cities were more customer-friendly and innovative. Cities that had been using a Web page for longer periods of time were more user-friendly.

However, one area that was a concern to the author was the administrative focus of Web sites in cities where the population was largely minority-based and of a lower average income. The new shift in Internet services for cities focuses on shifting from the customer service realm to a participatory democracy where users will be able to give input and hold discussion groups on line. A suggestion of the author would be to include accountability pieces to insure consumer awareness of city customer service and finances. Web sites that contain accountability would help address some of the issues of distrust for the government and create citizens that are empowered.

E-government is making it easier to express individual opinions. Citizens can form political opposition groups and communicate very easily through the use of the Internet. There has been increased lobbying to different groups. However, with the increase in the volume of information from the public, the voices may not be heard because of the number of them. More efficient systems will need to be developed to handle the volume of responses from the pubic (Marche & McNiven, 2003).

Despite the big push from the federal government toward e-government, the implementation of e-government initiatives are at an infant stage (Layne & Lee, 2001). Layne and Lee (2001) contend that it will take at least another decade to fully implement e-government due to the infrastructures that need to be built and the policy issues that need to be figured out. Governments need to take time to develop Web pages with attention to the standards of accessibility, availability, usability, privacy, and maintenance. The Web sites need to be consistent, reliable, and attractive in their presentation (Fletcher, 2002).

Government adoption of e-government is more rhetoric than implementation. The implementation is still at an early level. The age of the Internet for governments is still a work in progress. Local governments are still in the process of getting basic information on to Web pages and securing methods for the transfer of data securely. Local governments need to develop and implement a plan for short term and long-term growth. The plan needs to include technology infrastructure and implementation strategies (Moulder, 2001). The future is positive, but more technical, personnel, and financial commitments will need to be made by governments and supported by citizens in order for the advancement of e-government (Moon, 2003).

Conclusion

In conclusion, the improvement of efficiency and effectiveness in government is needed. E-government not only can assist in increasing efficiency and effectiveness in government, e-government holds a promising future to increase the involvement of citizens in government. However, not all citizens are able to access the Internet to be involved. The voices of many will be left unheard if the government does not provide avenues to assist those that do not have access or skills to use e-government. Several authors (Layne & Lee, 2001; Marche & McNiven, 2003; Seifert & Petersen, 2002; Toregas, 2001) discussed the problem of the digital divide, however, only one author (Toregas, 2001) provided concrete suggestions to assist governments in the implementation. More research is needed in how governments can effectively deal with the populations that are a product of the digital divide.

Governments need to take time and develop strategic plans for e-government. The portals for citizens to use should be secure and private. Governments should have clear standards written into their plan that address security and privacy. Again, just as with the digital divide, the authors stated the problems (Lenk & Traunmuller, 2002; Marche & McNiven, 2003; Seifert & Petersen, 2002), but were unable to offer any solutions. Research needs to be conducted that focuses on the security and privacy issues.

The shifts required in the government organizational structure will take time to evolve. The bureaucratic structure of government is entrenched in the organization. Citizens views of government are marred by images of the red tape, inefficiency, and impersonal interactions. Trust will need to be built between the citizens and the government. Through the change in the structure of government, the controlled hierarchical structure of the government with the focus on the work and how the work is performed will shift to a focus on the interactions with citizens. Only time will tell if structural changes will occur in government to produce the milieu needed to support the full development of e-government.

References

Danziger, J. N. & Andersen, K. V. (2002). The impacts of information technology on public administration: An analysis of empirical research from the "golden age" of transformation. *International Journal of Public Administration,* 25(5), 591–627. Retrieved October 1, 2003, from EBSCO Business Premier database.

Fagan, J. C. & Fagan, B. D. (2001). Citizens access to on-line state legislative documents. *Government Information Quarterly,* 18(2), 105–121. Retrieved October 1, 2003, from EBSCO Business Premier database.

Fletcher, P. D. (2002). The government paperwork elimination act: Operating instructions for an electronic government. *International Journal of Public Administration,* 25(5), 723–736. Retrieved October 1, 2003, from EBSCO Business Premier database.

Ho, A. (2002). Reinventing local governments and the e-government initiative. *Public Administration Review,* 62(4), 434–444. Retrieved October 1, 2003, from EBSCO database.

Kaylor, C., Deshazo, R. & Eck, D. V. (2001). Gauging e-government: A report on implementing services among American cities. *Government Information Quarterly,* 18(4), 293–307. Retrieved October 1, 2003, from EBSCO Business Premier database.

Koh, C. E. & Prybutok, V. R. (2003). The three ring model and development of an instrument for measuring dimensions of e-government functions. *Journal of Computer Information Systems,* 43(3), 34–39. Retrieved October 1, 2003, from EBSCO Business Premier database.

Layne, K. & Lee, J. (2001). Developing fully functional e-government: A four-stage model. *Government Information Quarterly,* 18(2), 122–136. Retrieved October 1, 2003, from EBSCO Business Premier database.

Lenk, K. & Traunmuller, R. (2002). Preface to the focus theme on e-government. *Electronic Markets,* 12(3), 147–148. Retrieved October 1, 2003, from EBSCO Business Premier database.

Marche, S. & McNiven, J. D. (2003). E-government and e-governance: The future isn't what it used to be. *Canadian Journal of Administrative Sciences,* 20(1), 74–86. Retrieved October 1, 2003, from EBSCO Business Premier database.

Menzel, D. C. (1998). www.ethics.gov: Issues and Challenges facing public managers. *Public Administration Review,* 58(5), 445–452. Retrieved October 1, 2003, from EBSCO Business Premier database.

Moon, M. J. (2002). The evolution of e-government among municipalities: Rhetoric or reality? *Public Administration Review,* 62(4), 424–433. Retrieved October 1, 2003, from EBSCO Business Premier database.

Moulder, E. (2001). E-government . . . If you build it, will they come? *Public Management,* 83(8), 10–14. Retrieved October 1, 2003, from EBSCO Business Premier database.

Rose, G. M. (2002). Encouraging citizen adoption of e-government by building trust. *Electronic Markets,* 12(3), 157–162. Retrieved October 1, 2003, from EBSCO Business Premier database.

Schelin, S. H. (2003). E-government: An overview. In G. D. Garson (Eds.), Public information technology: *Policy and management issues* (pp. 120–137). Hershey, PA: Idea Group Publishing.

Seifert, J. W. & Peterson R. E. (2002). The promise of all things? Expectation and challenges of emergent electronic government. *Perspectives on Global Development and Technology,* 1(2), 193–212. Retrieved October 1, 2003, from EBSCO Business Premier database.

Shi, W. (2002). The contribution of organizational factors in the success of electronic government commerce. *International Journal of Public Administration,* 25(5), 629–657. Retrieved October 1, 2003, from EBSCO Business Premier database.

Tillman, B. (2002). The changing political landscape. *Information Management Journal,* 36(1), 14–17. Retrieved October 1, 2003, from EBSCO Business Premier database.

Toregas, C. (2001). The politics of e-gov: The upcoming struggle for redefining civic engagement. *National Civic Review,* 90(3), 235–240. Retrieved October 1, 2003, from EBSCO Business Premier database.

Traunmuller, R. (2002). Preface to the focus theme on e-government. *Electronic Markets,* 12(3), 147–148. Retrieved October 1, 2003, from EBSCO Business Premier database.

Wimmer, M. A. (2002). Integrated service modeling for online one-stop government. *Electronic Markets,* 12(3), 149–156. Retrieved October 1, 2003, from EBSCO Business Premier database.

Westerback, L. K. (2000). Toward best practices for strategic information technology management. *Government Information Quarterly,* 17(1), 27–41. Retrieved October 1, 2003, from EBSCO Business Premier database.

Leadership Failures of Hurricane Katrina

Glynn E. Newman

Abstract

Hurricane Katrina was the worst natural disaster in American history. There were many lives lost and many people displaced by the storm. The government response to the storm was slow and inept. The systems in place were not used effectively to meet the needs of the situation. This paper will examine the leadership failures of Hurricane Katrina and offer some lessons that were learned from the catastrophe.

Hurricane Katrina made landfall on August 29, 2005. It struck the Gulf Coast region of the United States and impacted the city of New Orleans the most. One of the reasons the storm impacted New Orleans most is because New Orleans has 350 miles of levees surrounding the city. The storm caused the levees to break, which resulted in a city that was mostly submerged under water (Menzel, 2006; US House, 2006). The impact of the storms was great. There were:

- 770,000 people displaced (Halton, 2006)
- 1,330 lives claimed (estimated), 80 percent of the lives claimed were people living in the New Orleans area (Menzel, 2006)
- 3,000 people left unaccounted for (as of the 2006 US House report)(US House, 2006).
- $96 billion in property damage
- 1.1 million evacuees (Menzel, 2006)

It was by far the worst natural disaster in American history (Halton, 2006; Menzel, 2006; US House, 2006). This paper will examine the government response to Hurricane Katrina, analyze the leadership failures, and offer lessons learned so that an emergency response of this nature is not repeated.

Government Framework

Emergency management is the overall plan to prevent and prepare for disasters (Waugh & Streib, 2006). Emergency management includes the following:

1. hazard mitigation to prevent disaster
2. disaster preparedness
3. disaster response activities
4. disaster recovery (Waugh & Streib, 2006)

The government had an emergency plan in place. The plan will be outlined here.

The Department of Homeland Security had an emergency management plan as required by the Homeland Security Act of 2002. The National Incident Management System (NIMS), which was introduced in 2004, provided a framework for incidents at all levels of government. NIMS defines roles and responsibilities in a standard format and helps agencies work together through a framework. The development of a common language and management system so that different disciplines and jurisdictions could communicate and collaborate during disasters (GAO, 2006; Miller, 2007). The structure that is used within the NIMS is the Incident Command (IC) system. This is the command structure for NIMS. There are five command areas that NIMS/IC addresses: command, operations, planning, logistics, and finance administration. Each commander manages their agency, however the same objectives are set for each (GAO, 2006a; Miller, 2007).

In order for NIMS to work effectively, training is needed. Responders must participate in realistic exercises to improve response. People must be trained for their role and for being a back up for other roles, in case someone is unable to complete their role. Cross-training people is also another important aspect so that they are able to gain other perspectives (Miller, 2007).

Under the NIMS framework the DHS developed the National Response Plan (NRP) which was designed "to be an all-discipline, all-hazards plan establishing a single, comprehensive framework for the management of domestic incidents where federal involvement is necessary (GAO, 2006a, p. 14). The NRP is only used when the federal government is needed to help support state and local areas in a disaster situation. Within the NRP there is a Catastrophic Incident Annex (CIA), which "describes an accelerated, proactive national response to catastrophic incidents" (GAO, 2006a, p. 14). At the time of Hurricane Katrina this CIA plan was not complete, it lacked detail.

Discounted Warnings of Impending Disaster

The leaders at all levels of government failed to recognize the type of trouble New Orleans was in even before Hurricane Katrina hit. There were numerous studies and simulations conducted of the result of a category 3 or 4 hurricane hitting New Orleans. For instance, in July 2004, a tabletop exercise, called Hurricane Pam, was conducted based upon a category 3 hurricane hitting New Orleans. FEMA funded the tabletop exercise in which 300 government officials and the American Red Cross gathered to identify and analyze the problems of such a large hurricane. The result of this exercise revealed many shortfalls in the emergency plans. One of these was they found that as many as 100,000 household did not have a car to evacuate the area (Wise, 2006; Menzel, 2006; Wheatley, 2006). Follow-up workshops did not meet until July 2005 and no action plan was developed before Katrina hit. On FEMA'S potential catastrophe list, New Orleans was number three (Wheatley, 2006).

Subsequently, government officials did not heed the warnings that were given by the National Weather Service (NWS) days before the catastrophe. They thought, "it can't happen here" (Wheatley, 2006, p. 18). The National Weather Service released storm track projections 56 hours before the Hurricane hit land. The NWS director, Max Mayfield spoke by telephone with governors of Mississippi and Louisiana two days before the hurricane hit to warn them of what was coming. He also gave them daily storm briefings. The day before Katrina hit the NWS issued this warning, "Most of the area will be uninhabitable for weeks.

Perhaps longer, human suffering incredible by modern standards" (US House, 2006, p. 3). The mitigation and preparedness aspect of emergency management was not deployed.

There was also confusion over who was in charge of the efforts (Wise, 2006). There were warnings of the scale of the hurricane 56 hours before landfall. However, a mandatory evacuation order did not come until 19 hours before the storm hit. Instead of evacuating all people from the city, the decision was made by Mayor Ray Nagin to house the remaining people in the city. "The incomplete pre-landfall evacuation led to deaths, thousands of dangerous rescues, and horrible conditions for those who remained" (Wise, 2006, p. 305). In the NRP there are elements for the federal government to supersede the state and local government; it is called the Catastrophic Incident Annex (CIA), however in this case it was not used. The House Katrina Investigation Committee considered this as a leadership failure on the part of Secretary Chertoff, which will be discussed later in the paper (Wise, 2006)

Communication Failures

Hurricane Katrina paralyzed the communication networks that were in place in the Gulf Coast region. The communication systems were inoperable. In emergency management interoperability is discussed so that agencies can communicate with one another; however the basic operation of communication was lost during Hurricane Katrina so that within agencies communication did not exist. This is an area that needs to be addressed by leaders (Halton, 2006).

The ability of people to communicate during a response is vital. The first line is to keep basic communication within agencies going. Back up systems need to be in place, that can be pulled off of the shelf if cell phone towers fall, which they did in the storm. "Simple activities such as exchanging radios, sharing operational planning, and attending briefings of interagency partners were often cited as alleviating much of the technological barriers" (Halton, 2006, p. 222). Decision makers at all levels of the government need to have solid information on which to base their decisions and determine the next course of action.

Hurricane Katrina Leadership Failures

The National Emergency System was deemed inept at responding to the needs of the community and unable to coordinate the relief effort in the aftermath of Hurricane Katrina. The criticisms fell upon the leadership in the responding agencies. The emergency management system that was in place in the Federal government was not followed and therefore was deemed ineffective (Waugh & Streib, 2006).

"Failures at all levels of government that significantly undermined and detracted from the heroic efforts of first responders, private individuals, and organizations, faith-based groups, and others" (Waugh & Streib, 2006, p. 135). Leadership was the element that was missing in response to Katrina; therefore improving leadership needs to be the focus rather than organizational change.

As a result of the lack of preparation for the catastrophe, many people were unable to leave the city due to lack of resources. Many remained in their homes or evacuated to the Superdome and the Convention Center, which are not places where people are supposed to have to live. They were subjected to "limited light, air, and sewage facilities in the Superdome, the blistering heat of the sun, and in many cases limited food and water. They feared for their safety and survival" (US House, 2006, p. 1).

The established processes for responding to natural disasters is to start at the local level, then go to the state level and then to the federal level. With Hurricane Katrina responses at all levels to the disaster was slow and uncoordinated (Schneider, 2005). The local officials were overwhelmed with the demands of the disaster and they were unable to take the first steps to help mitigate the situation. At the state level the Governor Kathleen Babineaux Blanco did not declare martial law or a state of emergency, however she did request the assistance of the federal government. At the federal level the response was too slow to meet the demands of the people. "The delays, hesitation, and confusion exhibited by government officials at all level exacerbated the pain, suffering, and frustration of disaster victims" (Schneider, 2005, p. 515).

The House report on Katrina named failures of leadership. Examples are as follows:

- Secretary Chertoff acted "late, ineffectively, or not at all" in carrying out his responsibilities to designate Katrina an "incident of national significance," "convene the Interagency Incident Management Group," designate the principal federal official and order the "invocation of the national response plan's catastrophic incident annex" (US House, 2006, p. 131)
- "The White House failed to de-conflict varying damage assessments and discounted information ultimately proved accurate" (US House, 2006, p. 140)
- "Despite adequate warning 56 hours before landfall, Governor Blanco and Mayor Nagin delayed ordering a mandatory evacuation in New Orleans until 19 hours before landfall" (US House, 2006, p. 2)
- "The failure to order a timely mandatory evacuation, Mayor Nagin's decision to shelter but not evacuate the remaining population, and decisions of individuals let to an incomplete evacuation" that, in turn, resulted in preventable deaths, great suffering, and further delays in relief" (US House, 2006, p. 2)

Another agency that did not respond appropriately in the disaster was the Federal Emergency Management Agency (FEMA). One of the main problems with the leadership of the FEMA is the lack of expertise in handling natural disasters. Michael Brown who was appointed to the position by President Bush in 2003 had no previous experience in crisis management. The agency also had several of the department heads in an acting role, so not only was Brown inexperienced, but so was his team (Schneider, 2005).

FEMA's director showed that he was out of touch with the situation through many of the statements he made. For instance, Brown attributed the high numbers of people that died in New Orleans to "people who did not heed evacuation warnings" (p. 516), making the statement without any understanding of the people or situation at hand. The people that remained in New Orleans had no resources to leave; they had no money, and no transportation (Schneider, 2005).

Hurricane Katrina was also the first large-scale catastrophe where NIMS and the NRP were deployed; it was the first test of the system. Secretary of Homeland Security stated that planning for the disaster was insufficient. The organizations did not know their roles in the process. He stated, "I think 80 percent or more of the problem lies with planning. And that goes to the evacuation issue. It goes to how well we work with the military when the military has large numbers of assets they can bring to bear on the problem, and how fluid we are with them" (Wise, 2006, p. 303). The confusion over procedures of the NRP and roles, contributed to the late, ineffective response. Under the NRP each agency is supposed to develop more detailed response plans. There was no clear understanding of the roles of each agency. The more detailed plans were nonexistent when Katrina hit (Wise, 2006).

Two GAO (2006a; 2006b) reports on Hurricane Katrina show that there needed to be improved leadership and clearly defined and well understood roles, responsibilities, and lines of authority at all levels of government. At the federal level the DHS is responsible for reporting to the President and managing incidents of national significance. There was a lack of clearly defined roles. For example, "the Secretary of Homeland Security initially designated the head of FEMA as the Principal Federal Officer (PFO), who appointed separate Federal Coordinating Officer's (FCO's) for Alabama, Louisiana, and Mississippi. It was not, however, clear who was responsible for coordinating the overall federal effort at a strategic level" (GAO, 2006a, p. 20). The Secretary of Homeland Security was to take the lead in the catastrophe because he reports directly to the President, however, he deferred it to the director of FEMA and therefore he lines of communication and responsibility were not clear. Who was reporting to the President? (GAO, 2006a; GAO, 2006b).

The leadership at the federal, state, and local level during Katrina faltered. At the federal level in charge there were poorly trained political appointees unable to respond to the disaster as needed. The warning signs of earlier exercises were not heeded. Agencies within the federal government did not know how to work together and cooperate to solve problems. They did not know how to follow the very system that they put into place (Halton, 2006).

The disaster showed the disconnect between the situation and the decision makers and "how blind high-ranking federal officials were to the multitude of efforts made by personnel within and among agencies to aid in the rescue and recovery" (Menzel, 2006, p. 808). The federal government was not equipped to deal with a catastrophic crisis of this magnitude.

Another perspective on the leadership failure is that senior leaders many times are bound by formal operating procedures and legal policies of the organization and are unable to act as they think they should. The bureaucracy of government sometimes gets in the way of acting in a situation. An excellent example of this inability to act in a situation is the following story:

> As flames blazed 400 miles away in New Orleans on Labor Day, about 600 firefighters from across the nation sat in an Atlanta hotel listening to a FEMA lecture on equal opportunity, sexual harassment, and customer service. Your job is going to be community relations," a FEMA official told them. . . "You'll be passing out FEMA pamphlets and out phone number.

The room, filled with many fire fighters who, at FEMA's request, had arrived equipped with rescue gear, erupted in anger. "This is ridiculous," one yelled back. "Our fire departments and mayors sent us down here to save people, and you've got us doing this?" The FEMA official climbed atop a chair, and tried to restore order. "You are now employees of FEMA, ad you will follow orders and do what you're told," he said, sounding more like the leader of an invading army than a rescue squad. . . [The firefighters] got tired of hanging around their hotel and returned home (Wheatley, 2006, p. 17).

This story shows the inability of the government to take control for fear of reprisals. What was needed was action, helping save people and property, not rules and regulations.

During the Katrina response, "every level of government was uncertain about who was in charge at crucial moments. Leaders were afraid to actually lead, reluctant to cost businesses money, break jurisdictional rules, or spawn lawsuits" (Wheatley, 2006, p. 18).

When a quick response is needed leadership needs to be able to make decisions based upon the situation not based upon the rules of the organization. The leader needs to make sure that the needed resources reach the areas that need them as fast as possible (Wheatley, 2006).

In conclusion, the House Select Committee report concludes "we are left scratching our heads at the range of ineffectiveness that characterized government behavior right before and after this storm. . . Too many leaders failed to lead" (US House, 2006, p. 359-360).

Lessons Learned

Since the events of 911 and Hurricane Katrina, there have been strong pressures to move to command and control approaches to emergency management. Waugh and Streib (2006) argue that command and control systems of emergency management are not able to account for all the aspects of catastrophic disasters. During catastrophic disasters "authority is shared, responsibility is dispersed, resources scattered, and collaborative processes are essential" (p. 131). In a hierarchical command control structure the ability to approve and dispatch the necessary personnel may be delayed depending upon where the leader is in response to the disaster (Waugh & Strieb, 2006).

In emergency management it is necessary to collaborate with other agencies. An effective emergency manager is defined as "one who could interact effectively with other government officials and with the broader disaster relief community" (Waugh & Strieb, 2006, p. 132). Linkages between agencies need to be maintained in order to deal with catastrophes. Leaders need to build networks with other agencies and take part in frequent training and planning exercises with them. Waugh & Strieb (2006) recommend using a unified command structure rather than a command control structure. With a unified command there is more sharing of information and coordination of effort. The focus of management needs to be on mitigation first. "One dollar spent on mitigation saves two (or several) dollars in recovery" (Waugh & Strieb, 2006, p. 135).

Leaders need to develop a flexible approach to leadership. "Flexibility needs to be a key requirement for leaders in catastrophic disasters and hierarchical decision processes are neither flexible nor speedy in rapidly changing circumstances" (Waugh & Strieb, 2006, p. 136). "Emergency managers need to be able to innovate, adapt, and improvise because plans, regardless of how well done, seldom fit circumstances" (Waugh & Strieb, 2006, p. 132).

Wise (2006) calls this flexible approach adaptive management. He states that adaptive management will assist in emergency management situations. Adaptive management is the ability to change the management approach as new information arrives. The policies and procedures are not the guidelines that are followed, but the feedback from the situation is what guides the response. The ICS remains in place as the protocol and system; however adaptive management provides a framework for a manager to make decisions. Managers listen to stakeholders and modify plans to meet their needs.

On the other hand, some of the failures of the senior leadership in the country resulted in "spontaneous action" of communities and organizations (p. 18). For example, West Virginia responded by sending 130 cargo planes from the National Guard filled with supplies and intended to be returned filled with displaced people. FEMA only allowed three of the

130 planes to be loaded with people. Four hundred people benefited from the efforts of the West Virginia Governor. This act was a spontaneous response to the situation at hand. West Virginia is one of the poorest states, but did more than many other states to help support the people of New Orleans (Wheatley, 2006).

In order to maintain effective collaboration between agencies the following needs to occur (Wise, 2006):

1. Define and articulate common outcomes
2. Establish joint strategies to achieve outcomes
3. Identify and address needs by sharing resources
4. Agree upon roles and responsibilities
5. Establish similar policies and procedures
6. Develop ways to monitor, evaluate, and report collaborative efforts
7. Involve nonfederal partners and stakeholders in decision making

Formal frameworks need to be put in place to facilitate the "interpersonal interaction across the agency, intergovernmental, and intersectorial boundaries and at multiple levels" (Wise, 2006, p. 315).

The GAO (2006a) made several critical leadership recommendations in order to mitigate the damage of another hurricane. All of the recommendations made the Department of Homeland Security is responsible for implementation. They are as follows:

- Ensure co-location of relevant federal, state, and local decision-makers, including leaders of state National Guards, to enhance unity of effort
- For events preceded by warning, ensure preparations to pre-position a fully resourced and integrated interagency Federal Joint Field Office (JFO) to coordinate and, if necessary, direct federal support to the disaster
- Co-locate a single Department of Defense point of contact at the JFO and current FEMA regional offices to enhance coordination of military resourced supporting the response
- Identify and develop rosters of federal, state, and local government personnel who are prepared to assist in disaster relief
- Enhance ongoing review of state evacuation plans and incorporate planning for continuity of government to ensure continuation of essential and emergency services (GAO, 2006, p. 33).
- When there are warnings of an impending disaster such a Hurricane Katrina the GAO (2006) recommends that Congress give federal agencies the authority to act and do what is necessary to prepare for the disaster.

In addition to these suggestions there are some recommendations that FEMA needs to be its own cabinet level position as it was prior to the development of the DHS. However, the GAO (2006a; 2006b) suggests that no matter what the location of FEMA is a cabinet level post, or under the DHS their needs to be better leadership and training within FEMA. "Conditions underlying FEMA's performance during Hurricane Katrina involved the experience and training of DHS or FEMA leadership; the clarity of FEMA's mission and related responsibilities and authorities to achieve mission performance expectation; the adequacy of its human financial, and technological resource;

and the effectiveness of planning exercises, and related partnerships. These issues must be addressed whether or not FEMA remains in DHS" (GAO, 2006a, p. 34). Another recommendation is that Congress should add professional qualifications to the FEMA leadership positions. This would ensure that the FEMA director had the experience to do the job.

Conclusion

In conclusion, the government had structures in place, the emergency management plan to respond to Hurricane Katrina. These were NIMS, ICS, and the National Response Plan. Several federal agencies, including DHS were unfamiliar with their roles in responsibilities in NIMS and the NPR (US House, 2006). Training on the roles and responsibilities of each person during a catastrophe needs to happen. All people in the organization need to know the plan and need to be able to know their role in it. This was not the case during Hurricane Katrina.

Within the federal government there were many inexperienced people that were making decisions based on faulty data. The National responsibility in catastrophic events needs to be better defined in the NRP (Menzel, 2006), so that there can be a quicker response to the needs of people. What we have seen from Katrina is the Federal government needs to step in and be the lead in the situation. They have the resources and ability to call to action many more departments than the state or local officials.

In addition, more preplanning needs to take place in order to prevent the catastrophic nature of Katrina. The warnings were there from the FEMA exercise. Plans should have been made from this exercise so that more lives would have been saved. The data was there, but no one took it seriously or felt the urgency to make the plans for disaster.

The federal government tested out their emergency management system on a large scale and it failed. The government needs to revisit the system to ensure that a botched emergency response such as Katrina does not happen again.

REFERENCES

Government Accountability Office. (2006a). Catastrophic disasters: Enhanced leadership, capabilities, and accountability controls will improve the effectiveness of the Nation's preparedness, response, and recovery system. Retrieved on August 1, 2007, from http://www.pogo.org/p/contracts/katrina/GAO.html

Government Accountability Office. (2006b). Expedited Assistance for Victims of Hurricanes Katrina and Rita: FEMA's Control Weaknesses Exposed the Government to Significant Fraud and Abuse. Retrieved on August 1, 2007, from http://www.pogo.org/p/contracts/katrina/GAO.html

Halton, B. (2006). Katrina: Size, scope, and significance. *Fire Engineering,* 159(5), pp. 220–224. Retrieved on August 1, 2007, from Academic Search Premier database.

Menzel, D. C. (2006). The Katrina aftermath: A failure of federalism or leadership? *Public Administration Review,* 66, (6), pp. 808–818. Retrieved on August 1, 2007, from Wilson First Search database.

Miller, T. (2007). All together Now: The National Incident Management System is unifying multi-agency emergency response. *American City and County,* 122(1), pp. 34–37. Retrieved on August 1, 2007, from Wilson First Search database.

Schneider, S. K. (2005). Administrative breakdowns in the governmental; response to Hurricane Katrina. *Public Administration Review,* 65(5), pp. 515–516. Retrieved on August 1, 2007, from Wilson First Search database.

United States House of Representatives. (2006). A Failure of initiative: A final report of the select bipartisan committee to investigate the preparation for and response to Hurricane Katrina. Retrieved on August 1, 2007, from http://katrina.house.gov/

Waugh, W. L. (2006). Collaboration and leadership for effective emergency management. *Public Administration Review,* 66(6), pp. 131–140. Retrieved on August 1, 2007, from Wilson First Search database.

Wheatley, M. (2006). Leadership: Lessons from the *real world. Leader to Leader,* 41, pp. 16–20. Retrieved on August 1, 2007, from Wilson First Search database.

Wise, C. R. (2006). Organizing for homeland security after Katrina: Is adaptive management what's missing? Public Administration Review, 66(3), pp. 302–318. Retrieved on August 1, 2007, from Wilson First Search database.

Study Guide

CHAPTER 1

Democracy in America

CHAPTER OUTLINE

I. Evolution of American Democracy
   A. Democracy must contain the following:
      1. Dignity of individuals
      2. Equal protection under the law
      3. Decisions made by majority rule
      4. Opportunity for each individual to participate in decision-making
      5. One person, one vote
   B. Natural Law—a doctrine that says society should be governed by certain ethical principles that are a part of nature
      1. Introduced by Aristotle in 384 BC
   C. Newton introduced self-government in 1642, based on science and reason
   D. Locke and Hobbes developed social contract theory
      1. People are free and equal by God-given rights and each person is required to give consent to be governed
   E. Hobbes believed that a single ruler would be better than no ruler. Locke disagreed.
   F. Locke believed that the government's job was to preserve the private property of the citizens
   G. Locke's work was used by Thomas Jefferson to draft the Constitution
II. Politics in America
   A. Politics—who gets what, when, where, and how
   B. Government—legitimately uses force to carry out decisions
III. A Land of Law, Not of People
   A. Constitution limits government intervention
      1. First Amendment guarantees freedom of speech beyond the reach of government
IV. A Foreign Eye on Democracy
   A. Alexis de Tocqueville, French philosopher visited America
      1. Wrote a book, Democracy in America
      2. America sets an example for the world in how a democracy should work

V. Direct and Representative Democracy
  A. Direct democracy
      1. People govern themselves, vote on policies and laws and live by majority rule
      2. America is not a direct democracy
  B. Representative democracy
      1. Elected representatives make decisions for the people
      2. America is a representative democracy
VI. The Majority or Power Elite

Key Terms

Democracy—system of government in which the people rule

Natural Law—doctrine that states that society should be governed by certain ethical principles

Social Contract Theory—people are free and equal by God-given rights and people give their consent to be governed

Politics—determining who gets what, when, where, and how in society

Government—organization that extends to the entire society that legitimately uses force to carry out its decisions

Direct democracy—type of government where people govern themselves, vote on policies and laws and live by majority rule

Representative democracy—elected representatives make decisions on behalf of the people

CHAPTER 2

The U.S. Constitution

CHAPTER OUTLINE

I. The Constitution Defined
   A. Constitutional government ruled by laws
   B. Establishes individual liberties
   C. Governmental bodies are established, authority established, rules determined, how members chosen
      1. House of Representatives
      2. Senate
      3. Presidency
      4. Supreme Court
   D. Can only be changed by general popular consent—majority needs to agree upon the change
II. Constitutional Beginnings
   A. Two parts to be included by settlers
      1. Individual security
      2. Rule of law—laws made to govern the land
   B. New England Colonies set up compacts
      1. A compact is an agreement that binds two or more parties to enforceable rules
   C. Charter companies were created
      1. The English king controlled the charter companies for the purpose of gathering natural resources from the new world
   D. Proprietary Colonies created
      1. Colonies set up like the British government—kings, parliament
III. Five Precedents to the Constitution
   A. Five important events that led to the Constitution
      1. Magna Carta of 1215—a written document that stated that the powers of the English King were not absolute
      2. Mayflower Compact of 1620—prior to landing at Plymouth the Pilgrims wrote a social contract to ensure the success of the community
      3. Colonial Charters of 1630–1732

       4. Declaration of Independence of 1776
         a. Unity began to develop between the states
         b. Thomas Jefferson wrote the first draft
       5. Articles of Confederation of 1781–1789
         a. The first Constitution
         b. Formed a loose league of friendship between the states
         c. Called the "Articles of Confusion"

IV. Problems Facing a New Nation
   A. Lack of national unity
   B. National debt was increasing
   C. The national government could not tax the citizens
   D. Inflation—a rise in the general price levels of the economy due to the government raising prices
   E. No national army

V. Constitutional Convention 1787
   A. Purpose—revise the Articles of Confederation—ended up writing the Constitution
   B. Fifty-five delegates attended
      1. National commitment
      2. Wide viewpoints
      3. Well-educated men
      4. Unified in thinking about economics, military, and politics
      5. Distinguished gentlemen
   C. All states represented, but Rhode Island
   D. Decided on a republic form of government where the power lies in the vote of the citizens
   E. Determined the three branches executive, legislative, and judicial
   F. Determined that there would be taxes on imports but not exported goods
   G. Representation in Congress was the most serious debate
      1. Two houses would be created in the Legislature—called the Great Compromise
         a. House of Representatives—based on population
         b. Senate—number based on number of states
   H. Three-fifths compromise developed—three-fifths of slaves would be counted in apportioning seats
   I. Only thirty-nine of the fifty-five signed the new Constitution
      1. Those who did not sign claimed that the government was given too much authority
      2. The supporters of the Constitution were the Federalists

Key Terms

Constitutional—a government of laws
General Popular Consent—majority of Americans vote to determine the change
Rule of law—laws that govern the land
Compact—agreement that legally binds two or more parties
Bicameral Legislature—consisting of two chambers or houses
Magna Carta—document that stated that powers of the king were not absolute
Feudal—individual

Natural rights—people were born free and society was formed to protect their rights

Mayflower compact—written contract made by the Pilgrims

Proprietary—royal colonies

Minutemen—the colonial troops

Articles of Confusion—another name for the Articles of Confederation

Inflation—rise in the price levels in the economy because the government printed too much money

Federalists—supported the Constitution

Anti-federalists—against the Constitution

CHAPTER 3

Federalism

CHAPTER OUTLINE

   I. Federalism—dividing power between two separate governments
      A. 40% of people live in federalist counties
  II. Why Federalism?
      A. Protect minorities from unjust majorities
      B. Dividing power between national and local governments
      C. Division of power creates competition
      D. Large group of leaders rather than one
      E. Increase participation in the political process
      F. Allows states to try different policies that may meet the needs best
 III. Recipe for Federalism
      A. Constitution provides structure—strong national government
         1. National government needed the power to tax and regulate interstate commerce
         2. Congress needs to carry out laws that are "necessary and proper" to carry out national government powers, also called the implied powers clause.
         3. States cannot interfere with the national government
         4. States cannot make war, create an army, or coin money
  IV. The 10th Amendment and the States
      A. Reserves powers to the states or people
         1. States rights to marriage, divorce, maintain control of property, criminal law, contract law, highways, educational systems, and social welfare
         2. State has concurrent power—state and national government are able to tax and spend, establish court system, and make and enforce laws
         3. White separatists used states rights to deny equal opportunity to African Americans
   V. The Federal System Evolves
         1. State centered federalism, 1787–1868—states were independent and did not share power. States in control of slave issue
         2. Dual federalism, 1868–1913—National and state government powers were separate

3. Cooperative federalism, 1913–1964—National economy created, federal government had power over states, can be compared to goulash or a marble cake, relationship established to solve policy problems
   a. Gulf Oil Spill—example of Cooperative federalism
4. Centralized federalism, 1964–1980—National government had vision and goals, national government takes primary responsibility and directs state and local laws, compared to a pineapple upside-down cake
5. Representational federalism, 1985–1995—States retain their constitutional role by electing the president and members of congress

VI. Federalism and the Federal Courts
   A. Judges of federalism
      1. McCulloch v. Maryland (1819)—State of Maryland taxed the Baltimore branch bank, which was established by Congress, refused to pay the taxes. Doctrine of national supremacy established. National law is superior to any other laws
      2. Brown v. Board of Education (1954)—power of the states to segregate ended by the national government
      3. State poll tax was found unconstitutional in 1966
   B. Federal Grants
      1. Purposes
         a. Supply state and local governments with money
         b. Establish minimum standards
         c. Equalize resources
         d. Minimize growth of federal agencies
      2. Types
         a. Categorical formula grants—funds set aside for specific purposes (school lunch, welfare)
         b. Block grants—broad grants for education, social services, and healthcare. Can be sued by the states with flexibility
         c. Revenue Sharing—terminated in the states and local governments by 1987
         d. Project grants—a certain amount of money is put toward a specific project, such as the National Science Foundation

VII. Tomorrow's Federalism
   A. More complex
   B. States are more organized and have taken on greater responsibilities
   C. Preemption exists
   D. Citizens are concerned with efficiency

Key Terms

Federalism—dividing power between national and state governments

Tyranny—one leader in control

Necessary and proper clause—"necessary and proper" to carry out national government powers, also called the implied powers clause.

Dual Federalism—National and state government powers were separate

Cooperative federalism—National economy created, federal government had power over states, can be compared to goulash or a marble cake, relationship established to solve policy problems

Centralized federalism—national government assumes primary responsibility in all policy decisions, pineapple upside-down cake

Representational federalism—states retain their constitutional role by selecting the president and congress

National supremacy—national law superior to any other laws

***Brown v. Board of Education* (1954)**—ended segregation in education, "separate was not equal"

Categorical Formula Grant—funds set aside for specific purposes (school lunch, welfare)

Block Grant—broad grants for education, social services, and healthcare. Can be sued by the states with flexibility

Revenue Sharing Grant—terminated in the states and local governments by 1987

Project Grants—a certain amount of money is put toward a specific project, such as the National Science Foundation

Preemption—the right of a federal law to preclude enforcement of a state or local law

CHAPTER 4

Legislative Branch

CHAPTER OUTLINE

I. Legislative Branch Constitutional Roots
   A. Checks and balances created
   B. Article I created bicameral legislature or Congress—two parts
      1. House of Representatives—lower house
         a. Membership based on population of the state
         b. membership total 435
         c. Requirements
            • Age: 25 years
            • lived in the U.S. for seven years
            • legal resident of the state represented
         d. Length of term
            • Elected every two years
            • Keep in touch with constituents
            • More democratic because it changes more frequently
            • Small districts
            • Redistricting based on the population every 10 years
   C. Senate—upper house
      a. Two members per state, total 100 members
      b. Requirements
         • Age: 30 years
         • lived in U.S. for nine years
         • legal resident of the state represented
      c. Length of term
         • Six-year term
         • Powerful position
         • Statewide election
         • Name recognition
II. The Powers of Congress
   A. Most important duty is to make laws
      1. Bills, proposed laws, must be approved by both the House and Senate
   B. Impose taxes
   C. Regulate interstate commerce

     D. Establish a national bank

     E. Establish a post office

     F. Declare war

     G. Raise and support an army and navy

     H. Establish a court system

     I. Borrow and spend money

     J. Propose amendments to the Constitution

     K. House of Representatives

        1. Select the president if Electoral College cannot

        2. Initiate impeachment of the government official

     L. Senate

        1. Confirms the presidential cabinet and judiciary

        2. Tries impeached government official

III. Congressional Duties

     A. Work has to please constituents

     B. 15-hour days

     C. Time spent between Washington and home state

     D. Casework—assisting constituents with their problems

     E. Large offices with large numbers of staff

     F. Salary of $174,000 per year

     G. Cannot be paid for speeches or public appearances

IV. Incumbency Advantages

     A. Incumbent—person who is currently holding office

        1. For the most part win

        2. Senate—70 percent chance that incumbent will win

        3. House—90 percent chance that incumbent will win

        4. Resources

           a. Franking privilege—free use of U.S. mail

           b. Travel expenses paid by the taxpayers

           c. Name recognition

           d. Campaign funding from interest groups and individuals

V. Membership in Congress

     A. More educated

     B. More white

     C. More male

     D. Wealthier

     E. Senate called "millionaires club"

VI. Organization of Congress

     A. Senate

        1. Majority Leader is the head

        2. Not many rules to follow

        3. Vice President is the tie breaker in voting

     B. House of Representatives

        1. Speaker of the House is the leader

           a. Determines committees

           b. Appoints members to the Rules Committee

           c. Determines who will speak

           d. Elected by the membership

VII. Committee System
  A. Screen and write legislation
  B. Work done in committees
  C. Experts developed
  D. Standing committees—permanent committees
    1. Bills must pass through standing committees
    2. Committees chaired by majority party
    3. Committee may rewrite bills or write their own bills
    4. Less than 10 percent of the bills make it to the floor of the House or Senate
    5. Membership and leadership based on length of time in office—seniority system
VIII. A Bill Becomes Law
  A. Steps to a law
    1. Member of Congress must introduce bill
    2. Bill is given a number and sent to committee
    3. Committee sends the bill for research
    4. Bill moves to standing committee
    5. Bill sent to the House or Senate floor for approval
    6. Both the House and Senate approve
    7. Given to the president for signature

Key Terms

Bicameral—Congress is made up of two houses, the House of Representatives and the Senate

Legislature—House of Representatives and the Senate

Congress—made up of two parts—the House of Representatives and Senate

House of Representatives—lower house

Senate—upper house

Redistricting—changing the districts after every ten years

Bill—proposed law

Casework—helping constituents deal with problems

Incumbents—the people who hold the office during the election

Franking privilege—the free use of U.S. mail services

Majority leader—leader of the Senate

Speaker of the House—leader of the House of Representatives

Standing committees—permanent committees that specialize in certain areas

Seniority system—longest serving members receive privileges

Filibuster—when long speeches are made in the Senate to prevent the bill from being acted upon

CHAPTER 5

Executive Branch

CHAPTER OUTLINE

I. The President
   A. President of the U.S. is one of the most powerful people in the world
   B. President—elected leader with authority equal and independent of the legislature
   C. Chief executive officer
   D. Overseer of laws passed by Congress
   E. Chief of the Armed forces
   F. Constitutional Convention created the three branches
   G. George Washington—first president

II. Qualifications
   A. Natural born citizen of the U.S.
   B. Age: 35 years
   C. Resident of the U.S. for 14 years

III. Term of Office
   A. Did not want a monarchy
   B. Term limits established after Washington's presidency—four years
   C. 1951—Congress passed law that limited presidential terms to two four-year terms

IV. Removal
   A. President not above the law
   B. Can be removed due to treason, bribery, or other high crimes and misdemeanors
   C. House of Representatives determines whether or not to pursue impeachment offenses
   D. Impeachment has been used on two presidents

V. Benefits
   A. Compensation package—president's pay
      1. $400,000 per year
      2. $50,000 for expenses
      3. $100,000 for travel
      4. White House residence

        5. Retreat at Camp David

        6. Best medical treatment

        7. Automobiles

        8. Aircraft

        9. Pension after leaving office

      10. Security for the family

VI. Succession

    A. Constitution

        1. If president cannot perform duties—vice president takes over

        2. Presidential Succession Act of 1947 (Amended)

           a. Succession as it is today

           b. The Vice President

           c. Speaker of the House

           d. President pro tempore of the Senate

           e. Secretary of State

           f. Secretary of the Treasury

           g. Secretary of Defense

           h. Attorney General

           i. Secretary of the Interior

           j. Secretary of Agriculture

           k. Secretary of Commerce

           l. Secretary of Labor

           m. Secretary of Health and Human Services

           n. Secretary of Housing and Urban Development

           o. Secretary of Transportation

           p. Secretary of Energy

           q. Secretary of Education

           r. Secretary of Veterans Affairs

           s. Secretary of Homeland Security

VII. Duties and Powers of the president

    A. Founders were distrustful of a strong president

    B. There is not a list of powers that are trusted to the president

VIII. Chief Executive

    A. President administers the policy that the legislature creates

    B. Can demand written reports from governmental entities

    C. Appoints government officials

    D. Restructure agencies

    E. Propose budgets

IX. Appointments

    A. Appoints 1,300 people to jobs—ambassadors, Supreme Court members, attorney general, and counsels

    B. Policy decisions made by the Congress

    C. Judges—key appointments

    D. Selects people that are loyal and like minded

    E. Nominees for appointments are confirmed by the Senate

X. Removing Officials

    A. Constitution does not give the president power to remove appointees from office

    B. Many presidents have removed officials without question

XI. Line Item Veto
   A. Enacted in 1997
   B. Certain items in a bill could be vetoed without vetoing the entire bill
   C. In 1998—*Clinton v City of New York*—court held the line item veto as unconstitutional
XII. Budget Making
   A. Congress responsible for the budget
   B. After WWI better management needed passed Budgeting and Accounting Act of 1921
      1. President given more of a role in fiscal planning
      2. President predicts how much money it will take to run the government for one fiscal year
      3. Budget cycle starts October 1 and goes to September 30
      4. President determines department expenditures
      5. Office of Management and Budget (OMB) assists the president with the budget
XIII. Pardoning Power
   A. President can grant reprieve or pardon for offenses against the U.S.
XIV. Office of the Vice President
   A. Vice president now an important role

Key Terms

President—an elected leader with authority equal to and independent of a national legislature

Royal governor—appointed by the King of England and given some powers

Compensation—the pay

FBI—Federal Bureau of Investigations

CIA—Central Intelligence Agency

Fiscal Year—period of time relating to expenditures, revenues, and debt

Budget—itemized summary of the estimated expenditures with proposals for financing them

Budget Cycle—begins October 1

Office of Management and Budget—helps the president formulate the budget

CHAPTER 6
The Federal Bureaucracy

CHAPTER OUTLINE

I. The Federal Bureaucracy
   A. Bureaucracy—management or administration marked by hierarchical authority among numerous offices and nonelected officials
   B. Max Weber—six components of a bureaucracy
      1. chain of command—authority flows from top to bottom
      2. division of labor—work is specialized
      3. specification of authority—clear lines of authority
      4. goal orientation—clear structure, authority, and rules
      5. impersonality—all employees treated equally
      6. productivity—evaluation based on rules
   C. Distributed Intelligence—distributes information throughout the organization workers make decisions to help productivity
   D. Waste basket theory—inefficient areas of government can be eliminated
   E. Bureaucrats—career government employees
II. Evolution of the Federal Bureaucracy
   A. Elites originated the federal government
   B. Elites—group or class of persons enjoying superior status
   C. Andrew Jackson—concerned about the lack of involvement of middle and lower class people—developed the spoils system
      1. Spoils system—rewarding party loyalists and friends with employment
   D. Spoils system unacceptable due to the abuse of power
   E. Civil service employment created in 1877
   F. The Pendleton Act classified federal jobs and set up Civil Service Commission to oversee actions
III. Merit System
   A. A system based on the competence, neutrality, and nonpartisan
   B. Schedule of workers created from a GS–1 to GS–15—highest level college degree needed
   C. 905 of federal employees fall under the general salary schedule
   D. Difficult to remove civil service employees

IV. Policy Implementation
  A. Bureaucracy carries out the laws that Congress passes
  B. Make rules and activities for the policy
V. Red Tape and Complexity
  A. Big government associated with unresponsiveness
  B. Biggest criticism—government employees have a job for life

Key Terms

Bureaucracy—management or administration marked by hierarchical authority
Distributed intelligence—Information is disseminated throughout the organization
Bureaucrats—career government employees
Elites—group or class of people who enjoy superior status
Spoils system—system of public employment based on rewarding party loyalists and friends
Pendleton Act—classified jobs and set up a merit system of employment
Policy implementation—making the rules and activities for the policy

CHAPTER 7

The Judicial Branch

CHAPTER OUTLINE

I. Judicial Power
   A. Judges must remain independent of a political party
   B. Determine which acts are not constitutional
   C. Power of judicial review—to view the laws of the land and determine their constitutionality

II. Structure of the Courts
   A. Three Levels of Federal Court
      1. Supreme Court
         a. Highest court
         b. Only hears a few cases each year
         c. Cases are on appeal from a lower court
         d. If states are in disagreements the Supreme Court will hear the case for the first time
         e. Nine justices
         f. Appointed by the president and approved by the Senate
         g. Lifetime terms
         h. Session is from October to June
         i. Current justices
            • Chief Justice John Roberts
            • Antonin Scalia
            • Samuel Alito
            • Anthony Kennedy
            • Elena Kagan
            • Stephen Breyer
            • Sonia Sotomayor
            • Ruth Bader Ginsburg
            • Clarence Thomas
   B. Court of Appeals
      a. Another name—circuit courts
      b. Twelve courts
      c. Appellate court
      d. No new evidence can be submitted
      e. Judges are appointed for life by the president and confirmed by the Senate

    C. District Courts
- a. Trial courts
- b. Hear cases for the first time
- c. Every state has one court large states more
- d. Texas has four
- e. Judges are appointed for life by the president and confirmed by the Senate
- f. Criminal and civil cases
- g. Grand juries determine if the case will be brought to trial

III. Supreme Court Justice Selection Criteria
- A. Many hold common backgrounds
    1. Law degree and judicial experience
        - a. Law degree
        - b. Attended prestigious law schools
        - c. Federal judgeship experience
    2. Age
        - a. Average—50 years
    3. Race and Gender
        - a. First female—Sandra Day O'Connor in 1981
        - b. First African American—Thurgood Marshall in 1971
    4. Ideology or policy preference
        - a. Presidents appoint people with similar views

IV. Supreme Court Process
- A. Steps in the process
    1. Select a case to review
    2. Filing briefs
        - a. Both sides submit briefs that outline facts and arguments
    3. Oral argument
        - a. Each side has 30 minutes to speak
        - b. Justices can interrupt at any time to ask questions
        - c. Costs up to $500,000 to bring a case to the Supreme Court
    4. Conference
        - a. Cases are discussed Wednesday/Friday and a preliminary vote is taken
    5. Assignment of opinions
        - a. Determine who will write the majority opinion for the case
        - b. Chief justice assigns
        - c. Dissenting opinion written by opposition

V. Supreme Court Checks and Balances
- A. Internal checks
    1. Supreme Court relies on the executive branch to enforce the decisions
- B. Presidential influence
    1. President influences the balance of power
- C. Congressional checks
    1. Congress cannot reverse a decision
    2. Congress can pass a similar bill
    3. Can impeach judges

VI. Checks on Inferior Courts
- A. Supreme Court can change rulings of lower courts
- B. Courts do not want verdicts changed—careful to comply with constitutional law

Key Terms

Judicial review—Power to review laws of local, state, and congress to determine their Constitutionality.

Appellate jurisdiction—cases have been ruled upon by a lower court, but appealed to a higher court to hear arguments

Original jurisdiction—the court hears a case for the first time

Grand jury—district court hears the case for the first time to determine whether or not it should go to trial

Jury trial—determines guilt or innocence

Majority opinion—court decision in written form

Dissenting opinion—a judge's written opinion when disagreeing with majority decision

Judicial restraint—decisions of a lower court are allowed to stand because they are in line with the Constitution

Judicial activism— judges use their power to further justice

CHAPTER 8
Political Culture and Participation

CHAPTER OUTLINE

I. Political Culture—widely shared belief concerning the relationship of citizens to the government and to one another
   - A. Values—shared ideas about what is good
     1. Individualism
     2. Equality
     3. Justice
     4. Nationalism
   - B. Beliefs—shared ideas about what is true
II. Eighteenth Century Classical Liberalism
   - A. Europeans
     1. Concerned with government of aristocracy
     2. Creation of inequalities
     3. Class system developed
   - B. Natural rights introduced
     1. Rights of all people to dignity and worth
     2. Government cannot interfere with rights of people
III. Individual Liberty—right to act, believe or express oneself as you wish
   - A. Most widely held political value
   - B. Individual has rights and responsibilities
IV. Political Liberty
   - A. Thomas Jefferson, John Locke, Adam Smith, Jean-Jacques Rousseau
   - B. Attack on the monarchy
   - C. Government should protect the people
V. Economic Freedom
   - A. Capitalist—individual can make economic decisions without government intervention
   - B. Allows people to create businesses
   - C. Government needs to promote private enterprise and provide services that the private sector cannot afford
VII. The Plight of Equality
   - A. Thomas Jefferson wrote in the Declaration of Independence, "all men are created equal"

IV. Political Equality
  A. Laws should apply equally to all
  B. One person is not better than another
VIII. Equality of Opportunity
  A. Eliminating the artificial barriers to success in life
  B. Accepted value in America
IX. Equality of Results
  A. Equal sharing of all income and material possessions, regardless of one's ability, talent, or life's work
  B. Robin Hood model
  C. Viewed as morally wrong
  D. Fairness for all—equality of opportunity versus equality of results
X. Fairness
  A. Should be a minimum income level that no one should go below
  B. Americans do not want to set an upper level of income cap on the amount that can be made
XI. Political Influence
  A. Income and wealth
    1. Concerned with the distribution of income
    2. Conflicts when one group seems to be getting more than another
  B. New inequality
    1. Income differences have declined yet have begun to increase in the past few years
    2. Wage losses attributed to foreign competition, technological changes, immigration, subcontracting
  C. What does social mobility mean?
    1. The extent to which people move upward or downward in income and status over a lifetime
    2. Class conflict—when upper and lower social classes conflict over wealth and power
    3. Class consciousness—an awareness of one's class position and a feeling of political solidarity with others within the same class in opposition to other classes
    4. America—middle class values are the focus
XII. Public Opinion
  A. Politicians need to have the pulse of the people
  B. Expressed by Americans through
    1. protest
    2. voting in elections
    3. running for office
    4. writing letters
    5. demonstrations
XIII. What is Public Opinion?
  A. Distribution of individual preferences or evaluations of a given issue, candidate or institution
XIV. How Do People Feel?
  A. Random choice—giving each individual the opportunity to be involved in the survey

   B. Question Selection important
      1. Pretest questions
      2. Order of questions important
      3. Consensus—large number of people agree on the same issue
      4. Polarized issue—when a large number of people are divided over an issue
 XV. Measuring Public Opinion
      A. First attempts—straw poll—nonscientific measure of public opinion
         1. Difficult to gather a representative sample of the population
         2. Sample must be representative of entire population
         3. *Literary Digest* poll stated that Alfred Landon would beat Franklin
             D. Roosevelt. This was wrong
 XVI. What Happened?
      A. Used cross sectional techniques for sampling no method to sample selection
      B. Sample was taken from phone books and from automobile owners—upper
          middle class were selected that thought very differently
      C. Timing—conducted too early—people undecided
      D. Self-selection—received responses back only from those who were highly
          motivated
 XVII. Polling Perfected
      A. Late 1940s polling techniques were reliable
      B. Used for marketing goods and political campaigns
XVIII. Agents of Political Socialization
      A. Process through which an individual acquires political orientation
      B. Three agents
         1. Family
            a. First social agent
            b. Parents pass views on to child
            c. You are likely to align with the political view of your parent
         2. Schools
            a. Respect for nations symbols taught at school
            b. Pledge of Allegiance
            c. High schools reinforce what is taught in elementary
            d. More education one receives more likely to vote
            e. College helps students think critically about their beliefs
            f. The longer in school the more liberal one becomes
         3. The mass media
            a. Television takes up much time 30 hours each week
            b. More than 20 percent learn of presidential candidates from the late-
                night TV comedians
 XIX. Social Variables and Opinion Influence
      A. Class and income
         1. The less income one has the more one favors liberal candidates
         2. The more wealthy and educated tend to vote more often
         3. Poor people vote Democratic
         4. Rich people vote Republican
         5. Middle class split the vote
      B. Race and ethnicity
         1. African Americans vote Democratic
         2. Whites vote Republican

      3. Hispanics vote Democratic

      4. As minorities rise in social status the more conservative they are

  C. Religion

      1. Less religious you are the more liberal

      2. Religious minority groups tend to be more democratic

      3. Republican party gaining support from white Protestant and right-to-life supporters

Key Terms

Political Culture—widely shared belief concerning the relationship of citizens to the government and to one another

Values—shared ideas about what is good

Beliefs—shared ideas about what is true

Natural rights—rights of all people to dignity and worth

Liberty—right to act, believe or express oneself how you want

Capitalist—individual can make economic decisions without government intervention

Equality of opportunity—eliminating the artificial barriers to success in life

Equality of results—Equal sharing of all income and material possessions, regardless of one's ability, talent, or life's work

Public Opinion—distribution of individual preferences or evaluations of a given issue, candidate or institution

Straw Poll—nonscientific measure of public opinion

Political Socialization—process through which an individual acquires political orientation

CHAPTER 9

Campaigns and Voting

CHAPTER OUTLINE

I. Introduction
  A. People decide during elections the way they feel the country should go
  B. Problem people do not know the campaign process

II. The Art of Campaigning
  A. Requirements for office
    1. Each office has requirements that are stated in the Constitution
    2. President
      a. Natural-born citizen of the U.S.
      b. Resident of the country for 14 years
      c. Age: 35 years
    3. U.S. House of Representatives
      a. Representation based on state population
      b. California—52 people
      c. Resident of the state
      d. Citizen of the U.S. seven years
      e. Age: 25 years
    4. U.S. Senate
      f. Two from each state
      g. Resident of the state
      h. Citizen of the U.S. for 9 years
      i. Age: 30 years
  B. Political salesperson
    1. Needs to be able to sell self to others
    2. Be proficient in raising money
    3. Organizational skills
  C. Communication skills
    1. Communicate in different settings with compassion
      a. Press conferences
      b. Phone interviews
      c. Small audiences
      d. Large audiences
      e. Debate and answer questions

D. Politics in the blood
   1. Passion for politics
      a. Handshaking
      b. Meetings
      c. Speeches
      d. Consensus on issues
      e. Collaboration
III. Campaign Structure
   A. Primary election or caucus—determines the candidate for the party
      1. Caucus is held before voting to discuss issues, then vote on the candidate
   B. General election
      1. Where the person who receives the most votes wins the office
      2. Presidential Election 1st Tuesday in November every 4 years
   C. Presidential elections
      1. Same structure as above—two differences
         a. Delegates from all 50 states meet at the convention to determine the platform of the party
         b. After general election or popular vote the person who wins the office must win in the Electoral College
         c. Electoral College chooses the president based on electoral votes
         d. Each state has electoral votes based on the number of members in Congress
         e. Texas has 34 Electoral College votes
         f. Bush and Gore election of 2002 was decided in the Electoral College, not by the popular vote
IV. Campaign Incumbents
   A. People who currently hold the office
   B. Sources of funding
      1. Public money—income tax money divided equally between the 2 parties
      2. Small donations—given directly to the candidate
      3. Hard money—donations limited to $1,000 per donor
      4. Soft money—no limits, money raised by the party
   C. Political Action Committee (PACs)
      1. Most reliable source of income
      2. Corporations and unions give money to PACs
      3. Most often supports the incumbent
   D. Self-financing
      1. No limits to personal money
   E. Issue ads
      1. Interest groups run ads
      2. Ads do not specifically name the candidate
      3. Not regulated by the FEC
V. Voter decisions
   A. Income
      1. Higher incomes more likely to vote
   B. Age
      1. Older Americans vote more often
   C. Gender
      1. Women better voter turnout than men

    D. Political affiliation
       1. Vote for the party rather than the candidate
    E. Race
       1. Whites vote more regularly than African-Americans

VI. Voter Turnout
    A. Voter registration
       1. Discourages people to vote
       2. Required to fill out a form 30 days before voting
       3. People uninformed
       4. New locations to register to vote
    B. Number of elections
       1. Year-round elections
       2. Burn-out
       3. Hard to keep track
    C. Absentee voting
       1. Early voting when planning to be absent on election day

VII. Political Parties
    A. Anti-Federalists—Thomas Jefferson
       1. Did not want the growth of a strong national government
       2. Fought against the Constitution
       3. Thomas Jefferson—candidate for president
    B. Federalists—Alexander Hamilton
       1. Supported the Constitution
       2. Supported John Adams for president
    C. John Adams elected President in 1796—support for the Constitution
       1. First election where political parties played a role
    D. Birth of the Democratic Party
       1. Jefferson renamed the Anti-Federalist Party the Democratic-Republican Party
       2. Organized people to vote—first in history
       3. Election of 1800—Thomas Jefferson won
       4. House determined the election
       5. First peaceful transfer of power—Adams left office
    E. Jacksonian Democrats
       1. Election of 1824—popular vote counts
       2. Jackson won majority in popular vote, but not in the electoral college
       3. John Quincy Adams won in the Electoral College and with the House of Representatives—became the 10th president of the U.S.
       4. Jackson organized for the election of 1828—Democratic-Republican Party now changed name to Jacksonian Democrats
       5. Jackson won the election of 1828 with the support of Westerners, urban workers, and non-slave holding southerners. Served for two terms
       6. 1832—first party convention
       7. Whig party formed in opposition to Jackson
       8. During the period of 1830–1850, Whig party and Democrats were the two-party system
    F. Birth of the Republican Party
       1. Election of 1860—Republicans began
       2. Abraham Lincoln—candidate represented industrial base

      3. Democrats represented rural America

      4. 1860–1884—Republicans were in the White House

    G. The pendulum swings

      1. The Great Depression began in 1929

      2. End of Republican domination

      3. Franklin D. Roosevelt's "New Deal" emerged for Democrats

      4. New Deal Coalition formed urban working class, poor, southerners, and liberal intellectuals

      5. White House in Democratic control from 1932–1968 except during 1952–1960

    H. The pendulum swings again

      1. 1968—trend toward Republican leadership—Democrats lost 5 of the last 9 elections

      2. Conservative shift in the country

VIII. Political Party Structure

    A. National committees

      1. Democratic National Committee

      2. Republican National Committee

      3. National Chair selected by each party

      4. Chair is spokesperson for the party

      5. Hold national conventions every 4 years

    B. State and local parties

      1. Local level most important

      2. Increase in political activity at the local level

IX. Role of Political Parties

    A. Assist in resolving political differences

    B. Promote change

    C. Gather power

      1. The more elected officials in your party, the more influence you have

    D. Stability

      1. Promote stability in the electorate

    E. Services

      1. Organize elections money, staff

    F. Policy formulation

      1. National party platform—explains stance on issues

X. Political Parties After the Election

    A. Legislative branch

      1. Each political party elects a leader

      2. The majority leaders in the House and the Senate are from the party that is control

      3. Party leaders select the leaders of committees and select office locations

      4. Each person running for office needs the support of his/her party

    B. Executive branch

      1. President makes appointments

    C. Judicial branch

      1. Should be nonpartisan, but is not

      2. Judges are appointed to their positions and views align with the president who appoints them

XI. Third Party Role
   A. Help major parties change
   B. Not a major effect on elections
   C. Never won a presidential election
   D. Green Party, Reform Party

Key Terms

Primary election—the first step in a campaign where the party determines the candidate through voting

Caucus—the party gathers to meet and discuss issues and determine the candidate for the party

General election—where there is a contest between two parties or more on a ballot and the majority winner fills the political office

Electoral college—ensures that the president was selected with intelligent input from all the states. After the popular vote the Electoral vote is taken and this determines who will be president

PACs—Political Action Committees

Absentee voting—used when you are out of the area on Election Day

Incumbents—people currently holding office while seeking re-election

Political party—a group with common vision that comes together to elect officials to public office

Anti-Federalist Party—did not want the growth of a strong national government, against the Constitution

Federalists—supported the Constitution

Democratic-Republican Party—Jefferson renamed the Anti-Federalist Party the Democratic-Republican Party

Majority—over 50 percent

Jacksonian Democrats—Jackson organized for the election of 1828 Democratic-Republican Party now changed name to Jacksonian Democrats, won the election

Whig Party—business owners and slaveholders in the south who were against abolishing the national bank began this party

New Deal coalition—urban working class, Catholics, Jews, poor southerners, and liberal intellectuals pulling together to elect Roosevelt

Democratic National Committee—(DNC) runs the Democratic party

Republican National Committee—(RNC) runs the Republican party

National party platform—a document that explains the party's stance on issues

Speaker of the House—leader of the House of Representatives

Reform Party—led by Ross Perot in 1992 and 1996

Green Party—led by Ralph Nader in 2000

CHAPTER 10

The News Media

CHAPTER OUTLINE

    I. Forms of News Media
        A. Newspapers
            1. First printed in 1690s
            2. Way to inform and mobilize the public
            3. Way to educate the public
            4. Now newspapers are not as political
            5. 1980s people using TV as the way to get political information
            6. Two Journalistic styles
                a. Yellow journalism—sensationalized stories not based on fact—reserved for tabloids
                b. Muckracking investigative journalism to bring out the injustices that are done to people—still done today
        B. Magazines
            1. Wide variety of subjects
            2. Most highly-read magazine—Time
        C. Radio
            1. Used in the 1920s for political information
            2. Fireside chats by Franklin D. Roosevelt created confidence
      D. Television
        A. Introduced in 1940s
        B. Most influential form for disseminating political information
        C. Entertains and informs
        E. Cyber Media
        F. Social Networking
   III. The News Medias Sources of Power
        A. Agenda setting—power to create a national focus for the country
            1. News media has the power to determine what is seen by the public and what is not
            2. "Out of sight, out of mind"

    B. Interpreting the news
       1. Provide only a small section of a larger story
       2. Whole story is never told to the viewer
    C. Persuasion
       1. Advertisements sell merchandise
       2. Politicians try to change view on politics
       3. President influences public opinion through radio and TV broadcasts
    D. Socialization
       1. Shapes the cultures and values of society

IV. Media and Elections
    A. Media link between the candidate and the voter
    B. Candidates need to be able to communicate well
    C. Voters get candidate information from the media
    D. Negative campaigning works—voters say they do not like it, decline in voter turn-out may be the result

V. Government Regulation
    A. Newspapers and magazines not regulated by the government
    B. Federal Communication Commission oversees radio and television
       1. Fairness doctrine—different viewpoints must be represented on programs, repealed in 1987 by the Reagan administration
       2. Equal-time rule—TV and radio stations give equal time to the opposing candidate for equal price
          a. Does not apply to newscasts or talk shows
       3. Right of rebuttal—if someone is attacked on TV or radio the person who was attacked needs equal time to respond
       4. Government cannot place prior restraint on broadcasts before they are aired—cannot censor stories

VI. Libel and Slander
    A. Cannot tell untruths about people that damage credibility
    B. When a person is written about falsely and malicious words have been said about them it is called libel
    C. Slander—when a person has been spoken about falsely and malicious words have been used
    D. D. New York Times v. Sullivan (1964)—person has to prove that the media published the document with "malicious intent"—control is given to the media

VII. The Black Press

Key Terms

Freedom of press—the freedom of the media to criticize action or inaction of the government without being closed down or arrested

Mass media—the way in which information is distributed to the public

Yellow journalism—sensationalized stories not based on fact—reserved for tabloids

Muckracking—investigative journalism to bring out the injustices that are done to people

Agenda setting—power to create a national focus for the country

Socialization—process through which an individual acquires political orientation

Fairness Doctrine—different viewpoints must be represented on programs repealed in 1987 by the Reagan administration

Equal-time rule—TV and radio stations need to give equal time to the opposing candidate for an equal price

Right of rebuttal—if someone is attacked on TV or radio the person who was attacked needs to get equal time to respond

Prior restraint—government cannot censor stories before they are broadcast or printed

Libel—when a person is written about falsely and malicious words have been said about them

Slander—when a person has been spoken about falsely and malicious words have been used

CHAPTER 11
Civil Liberties and Civil Rights

CHAPTER OUTLINE

I. Civil Liberties—individual rights and freedoms that are guaranteed by the federal government
    A. Civil liberties cannot be violated
    B. Freedom from dictation by the government or anyone else as to what you do
    C. When violations occur, courts are involved in resolving disputes

II. The Bill of Rights—first ten amendments to the Constitution
    A. Approved in 1791
    B. Courts applied to cases became powerful
    C. Individual freedoms stated
    D. *Barron v. Baltimore* (1833)—Barron denied money from the state, Bill of Rights was not extended to the states
    E. Incorporation doctrine
        1. After the Civil War, Bill of Rights was still not accepted by all the states.
        2. By 1920 the Supreme Court's ruling on many cases resulted in most of the Bill of Rights being applied by the states
        3. 14th Amendment was the problem if states adopted the Bill of Rights then the slaves would need to be freed

III. First Amendment—Freedom of speech and press
    A. Government cannot rule what you think
    B. Regulation of what you say and do through court cases
        1. Alien and Sedition Acts—1798—publication of any anti-government writing was a criminal offense
        2. Anti-government speech
            a. *Schenck v. United States* (1919) Clear and Present Danger test
            b. Direct Incitement test (1969)
        3. Obscenity and pornography
            a. *Chaplinsky v. New Hampshire* (1942)—obsecenity, lewdness, and fighting words are not protected by the First Amendment
            b. *Roth v. United States* (1957)—Roth test, social importance
            c. *Miller v. California* (1973)—community standards defined to local area
            d. Supreme Court strict on child pornography cases

    C. Freedom of religion

        1. Colonists did not want an established religion for the colonies

    D. Two parts

        a. Establishment Clause—Congress will not establish a state-sponsored religion

          • Separation of church and state

          • *Lemon v. Kurtzman* (1971)—Lemon Test established

        b. Free Exercise Clause government cannot prohibit people from exercising their own religion

  IV. Second Amendment

    A. Right to bear arms—right to protect

    B. 1993—Brady Bill enacted—waiting period of five days on handguns

    C. 1994—Violent Crime Control and Law Enforcement Act—banning 19 semi-automatic weapons

  V. Due process

    A. Fourth Amendment

        1. Search and Seizure—warrant needed

        2. Police can search under these circumstances:

          a. Cars suspected of criminal activity

          b. If items are in plain view

          c. Consent of person or roommate

          d. If under arrest

    B. Fifth Amendment

        1. Self-incrimination—Miranda warning

    C. Sixth Amendment—right to counsel

    D. Eighth Amendment—Cruel and unusual punishment

        1. 1960—death penalty in question by NAACP

        2. *Furman v. Georgia* (1972)—death penalty fair punishment

        3. *Gregg v. Georgia* (1976)—Georgia death penalty constitutional

        4. States without the death penalty—Alaska, North Dakota, Minnesota, Wisconsin, Michigan, West Virginia, Massachusetts, Rhode Island, Vermont, and Hawaii

  VI. Public Privacy Rights—not stated clearly in Bill of Rights

    A. Abortion rights—*Roe v. Wade* (1973)—abortion rights

        1. 24-hour waiting period

        2. Parental consent needed

    B. Homosexuality

        1. *Bowers v. Hardwick* (1986) ruled in favor of the state—outlawing hetero- or homosexual oral or anal sex in Georgia—Hardwick not prosecuted.

    C. Right to die

        1. Supreme Court—1997—terminally ill people cannot commit suicide

        2. Public view—61% believe doctors should be able to assist in suicide

  VII. Slavery

    A. Governmental acts

    B. Article I of the 1787 Constitution

        1. Slaves counted as three-fifths of a person for taxation and representation purposes

        2. No regulation of the slave trade

      C. Article IV guaranteed escaped slaves would be returned to their master

      D. 1808 slave trade was banned

      E. *Dred Scott v. Sanford* (1857)—African Americans are not citizens of the United States.

      F. Abolitionists—people who fought against slavery

          1. William Lloyd Garrison—founded the Anti-Slavery Society in 1833

VIII. Civil War

      A. North against slavery, South needed slavery to keep the economy thriving

          1. South needed cheap labor

          2. North was more industrialized

          3. Most tragic war to this date

          4. North won

      B. 1883 Emancipation Proclamation

          1. Lincoln stated all slaves in the Confederacy would be freed

IX. Civil War Amendments

      A. Three Amendments

          1. 13th Amendment to the Constitution

             a. Slavery was banned

             b. Southern states that wanted to be admitted into the Union needed to ban slavery

             c. Laws called black codes were adopted to keep the African Americans from realizing their freedom. Examples:

                • Arresting unemployed for vagrancy

                • Roots of the Jim Crow laws

          2. 14th Amendment to the Constitution

             a. Due process amendment

          3. 15th Amendment to the Constitution

             a. Right to vote

             b. Between 1865 and 1880 African Americans voted and held political offices

X. Segregation

      A. Civil rights cases—Supreme court found that segregation in government buildings was illegal, but in private establishments discrimination could not be prohibited

      B. Jim Crow laws established as a result of the cases

          1. African Americans second class citizens

          2. Separate facilities

          3. Poll taxes and literacy tests enacted to keep from voting

          4. Grandfather clause—whites who could not read could exempt out of the literacy test so that they could vote

          5. *Plessy v. Ferguson* (1896)—separate but equal was acceptable—segregation upheld

XI. Equal Protection Fight

          1. *Brown v. Board* (1954)

             a. NAACP with Thurgood Marshall as the head of a team of lawyers fought for equal treatment in education

             b. White and African American schools were not equal

  c. Supreme Court overturned *Plessy* (1896) stating that separate is not equal

  d. Took time for the change to be implemented—civil rights movement began at this point

XII. Civil Rights—positive acts that government has taken to protect people against discrimination on the basis of race, sex, national origin, age, or sexual orientation

 A. One year after Brown (1954), the killing of Emmitt Till occurred

 B. Men found not guilty in his killing

 C. 1955 Rosa Parks refused to give up her seat to a white person on a bus in Montgomery, Alabama

  1. Nonviolent bus boycott was planned

 D. Martin Luther King Jr. led nonviolent demonstrations

  1. March on Washington—"I Have a Dream" speech

 E. Civil Rights Act of 1964

  1. Discrimination and segregation abolished

XIII. Gender Equality

 A. Women's rights

  1. As a result of women not being able to own property

  2. 1900 women demanding same right to vote as men

   a. 19th Amendment passed in 1920

  3. *Reed v. Reed* (1971) sexual classifications must be reasonable, not arbitrary

  4. Women must have the same legal adult age

  5. Women cannot be locked out of police and fire employment

  6. Insurance and retirement plans must be the same

  7. Schools must pay female coaches the same amount as male coaches

  8. First female secretary of state—Madeline Albright

XIX. Affirmative Action—attempt to improve the chances of minority applicants

 A. 1965—Lyndon Baines Johnson increased minorities in the construction business

 B. Opponents did not want quotas

 C. *Regents of the University of California v. Bakke* (1978)—reverse discrimination, setting aside a certain number of seats for admission to college, unconstitutional

 D. *United Steelworkers v. Weber* (1979) plant systematic plan to increase the number of minorities was constitutional—righting the wrongs of the past

 E. *Grutter v. Lee Bollinger* (2003)—Law school admission race can be one determining factor in admission decisions

 F. *Gratz v. Lee Bollinger* (2003)—undergraduate admissions—point system was unconstitutional, look at the applicant as an individual

XX. Immigration Policy

Key Terms

Civil liberties—personal rights and freedoms guaranteed by the government

Bill of Rights—First ten amendments to the Constitution

Incorporation—application of the Bill of Rights to the states

Establishment clause—First Amendment—freedom of religion—creates separation of church and state

Free Exercise clause—First Amendment—freedom of religion—right to choose and practice religion of choice

Lemon Test—three pronged test—secular purpose, cannot advance or prohibit religion, and must not have excessive government entanglement

Probable cause—reason to suspect criminal activity

Miranda warning—when arrested statement of rights

Civil rights—positive acts that government has taken to protect people against discrimination on the basis of race, sex, national origin, age, or sexual orientation

Abolitionists—people who fought against slavery

Emancipation Proclamation—issued by President Lincoln in 1863, stated that all slaves who lived in the Confederacy would be freed

13th Amendment—Banned slavery

14th Amendment—Due process

15th Amendment—voting rights regardless of race

Jim Crow laws—Laws that supported separation of the races

Grandfather clause—whites able to vote based on their family lineage

Plessy v. Ferguson (**1896**)—"separate but equal"

Brown v. Board of Education (**1954**)—"separate is not equal"

Nonviolent—without violence

Affirmative action—Programs that attempt to improve the chances of minorities

CHAPTER 12

Social Welfare

CHAPTER OUTLINE

I. Social Welfare Policy
    A. Government program designed to help people live more quality lives
    B. Educational support
    C. Economic support
    D. Healthcare support
II. The Evolution of Social Welfare Policy
    A. New Deal programs
        1. Franklin D. Roosevelt
        2. 1930 reaction to Great Depression
        3. State resources not enough to combat poverty
        4. 1933 unemployment rate—25%
        5. Bank issues
            a. In 1933 new legislation for the banking industry proposed
            b. Emergency Banking Act allowed Secretary of Treasury to oversee bank transactions—banks remained closed until they were financially sound
            c. President Roosevelt explained the banking situation to the American people and deposits became greater than withdrawals
        6. Unemployment Issues
            a. Civil Works Administration—began November 1933
                • Jobs program paid $15 per week
                • Four million people employed
                • Corruption and wages too high
                • 1934—program ended
            b. Works Progress Administration (WPA)
                • Earned $55 per month
                • Improved hospitals, airfields and playgrounds
                • hired 30% of the unemployed
                • Ended in 1942
            c. Social Security
                • Insurance program for older Americans started in 1935
                • Payroll tax on all workers except government workers, farmers, and domestic labor workers

        d. Unemployment Insurance and Compensation evolves
- Insurance fund for unemployed workers contained in the Social Security Act of 1935
- Payroll taxes deducted from paychecks and placed in a fund for unemployed workers
- When workers are laid off collect money from the fund until another job is found

        e. Aid to Families with Dependent Children (AFDC)
- Welfare
- Set up to help widowed mothers and mothers with disabled husbands
- Money not originally meant for unwed mothers

III. The Great Society

  A. 1960—Lyndon Baines Johnson fought poverty and racial injustice
1. Premised on a better life for all
2. Congress passed 78 programs
3. Expanded Social Security

  B. Social Welfare Policies Evolve
1. Welfare Reforms of 1996
    a. Welfare recipients not encouraged to work
    b. Twenty-seven percent of the women were on the program for six to nine years
    c. Name changed to Temporary Aid to Needy Families (TANF)
- Goal promote nuclear family
- Job preparation
- Work
- Marriage
- Two years of receiving money—person required to work
- Lifetime maximum of services five years
- Decline in the numbers of people receiving welfare

    d. Healthcare
- Medicare and Medicaid passed in the 1960s
- Medicare is the public health insurance program used by the elderly and disabled
  - Pays for hospital visits and doctor visits
  - Expensive monthly premiums
- Medicaid assists the poor and elderly to pay medical bills
  - States set the standards
- Problems with the healthcare system
  - High cost of health care
  - Uninsured people 40 million
  - High cost of malpractice

    e. Education
- State and local governments oversee 90 percent of funding comes from these sources
- Federal government role—low
- Texas—current funding system called Robin Hood—districts with property wealth give back to the state large amounts of money to equalize wealth throughout the state

I. Fiscal Policy—the taxing and spending of money

  A. Government spends one dollar of every four

  B. Ways the government receives money
1. Individual income taxes
    a. Due every April 15
    b. 48% of federal tax money
2. Corporate income taxes

        a. 10% of tax revenue

        b. collected from large and small businesses

     3. Excise tax

        a. 4% of taxes

        b. "Sin Tax"

        c. Tax on liquor, telephones, gasoline, air travel, and other luxury items

     4. Social Security receipts

        a. Second largest source of income

        b. Payroll deductions

        c. Lower income workers pay more—regressive tax

     5. Duties and tariffs

        a. Collect money on people bringing in items from other countries

II. Federal Spending

    A. 50% goes to entitlement programs

        a. Social Security

        b. Unemployment

        c. Medicare & Medicaid

    B. 15% of federal spending goes to interest on the national debt

    C. 15% for defense—since September 11, 2001 this has increased

    D. 15% grants to states

    E. 5% other operations

III. The Budget Process

    A. Executive Branch—Office of Management and Budget (OMB) create budget and send to Congress

    B. Fiscal year begins October 1

    C. Executive Branch Role

     1. Office of Management and Budget works for two years ahead on budget projections

     2. Budgets from departments are aligned with President's vision

     3. December revisions take place

     4. Budget brought before a committee to approve

     5. Budget given to the President

     6. President submits budget to Congress between the first Monday in January and the first Monday in February

    D. Legislative Branch Role

     1. President submits budget to Congressional Budget Office (CBO)

     2. CBO prepares reports for Congress by February 15

     3. Congress has from March to September to approve

    E. General Accounting Office (GAO) Role

     1. Comptroller General—appointed by president to 15 year term

        a. David Walker appointed in 1998

     2. GAO audits departments to assure money is being spent appropriately

IV. Monetary Policy

    A. Federal Reserve

     1. Regulate interest rates

     2. President appoints to 14-year terms

     3. Six members and a chairperson (four year term)

     4. Buying and selling of securities

     5. Regulate 12 federal banks

     6. Oversees foreign currency

     7. Alan Greenspan—chairperson—fourth four-year term

V. Deficit

    A. When the federal governments revenues are less than the expenditures

    B. 1985—Gramm-Rudman-Hollings Act—cap on the amount of money in the deficit and a pay back plan

VI. Debt

    A. 6 trillion dollars

    B. Accumulation of the deficits over a period of years

    C. Reasons for large debt

      1. tax cuts without spending cuts

      2. healthcare costs rising

      3. unforeseen problems arise

    D. Ways to reduce debt

      1. Require balanced budgets

      2. Not allow the Treasury to borrow money—government shut down without money

      3. Congress could print more money—causing inflationary problems

VII. Trade Policy

    A. Trade deficit—values of imports greater than goods leaving the country

    B. First trade deficit in 1971

    C. Trade problems

      1. U.S. not producing enough goods

      2. Certain goods are not accepted

      3. High taxes on certain items in other countries

    D. Barriers to trade

      1. Protectionism—creating high tariffs on importing certain products, encouraging selling of the product in another market

VIII. Government Regulation

    A. Competitive market economy—U.S.

    B. Government intervention protects citizens

    C. Two types of regulation used

      1. Economic—government controls the behavior of businesses

        a. Federal Communications Commission

      2. Social—consumer and worker safety

        a. Equal Employment Opportunity Commission

        b. Environmental Protection Agency

        c. Occupational Safety and Health Administration

Key Terms

Social welfare policy—a government program designed to help people live more quality lives

New Deal programs—started by President Franklin D. Roosevelt in response to the hard times of the depression in the 1930s

Civil Works Administration (CWA)—a program to put people to work on public works projects pay was too high only in operation from 1933–1934

Works Progress Administration (WPA)—a work program started in 1935, workers improved hospitals, airfields and playgrounds

Social Security—an insurance program for older Americans

Unemployment—insurance fund for unemployed workers

Aid to Families with Dependent Children (AFDC)—welfare for widowed mothers or mothers with disabled husbands

Temporary Aid to Needy Families—revised version of AFDC implemented in 1996 to replace AFDC

Medicare—public health insurance program used by the elderly and disabled

Medicaid—federal and state partnership that help the elderly and poor pay medical bills

Fiscal policy—government controlling taxing and spending

Monetary policy—Controlling the money supply and interest rates

Income taxes—taxes collected from individuals each year, due April 15

Corporate taxes—taxes collected from large and small companies

Excise taxes—"sin tax" taxes on luxury items, gasoline, liquor, telephones

Regressive tax—when low income workers end up paying more into the system than upper income people

Office of Management and Budget (OMB)—create the budget for the executive branch

Congressional Budget Office (CBO)—after receiving the budget from the OMB, prepares the budget for Congress to view

General Accounting Office (GAO)—conducts audits of agencies and programs

Deficits—amount of money in revenues less than expenditures

Revenues—money received through taxes

Expenditures—money spent

Debt—the accumulation of all budget deficits over the years

Trade deficit—when value of imports is greater than value of exports

Protectionism—high tariffs on importing certain products, encouraging the selling of the products in another market

Competitive market economy—economy based on the law of supply and demand

Economic regulation—government controls the behavior of businesses

Social regulation—government regulation concerned with consumer safety

CHAPTER 13

Foreign and Military Policy

CHAPTER OUTLINE

I. The Evolution of the United Nations
  A. Early 1900s unstable world
  B. Russia, England, France, and the U.S. fought Germany, Austria-Hungary, and Japan—deadliest wars—killed 10 million
  C. All nations brought together to guarantee security
  D. League of Nations—1919—Treaty of Versailles
  E. January 1, 1942—declaration of United Nations by Franklin D. Roosevelt
  F. Principal Organs
    1. General Assembly—created to handle any matters affecting world peace
    2. Security Council—maintain international peace and security
    3. Economic and Social Council
    4. Trusteeship Council
    5. International Court of Justice
    6. Secretariat
  G. Every nation has one vote—no veto power for any nation
  H. Majority vote passes resolutions
II. Will the UN Survive?
  A. President George W. Bush asked for support war in Iraq
  B. Without the U.S. the UN will not survive
III. The Evolution of the Cold War
  A. Conflict between the U.S. and Russia
  B. After World War II & the fall of communism in 1991
  C. U.S. and Russia—banded together to fight against Hitler
  D. Pledge made by the U.S. to support free people who are dissatisfied with pressure—Truman Doctrine
IV. Containment
  A. America's policy of containment 1947
    1. Communism "malignant parasite"
    2. U.S. foreign policy should focus on building independent areas
    3. Containment—stop the advancement of communism

     V. Marshall Plan

       A. Program to rebuild the nations of Western Europe after World War II

       B. Build strong economies to stop the spread of communism

     VI. North Korea

       A. Conflict in North Korea—U.S. took North Korea

       B. China stepped in to protect North Korea

       C. U.S. retaliated, but lost 40,000 men

     VII. The Vietnam War

     VIII. Nuclear Freeze

       A. Increase nuclear military powers in the U.S., Britain, France, Germany

       B. Carter began intense military spending

       C. Reagan continued to spend on weapons

       D. Gorbachev and Reagan began weapon reduction talks

     IX. Reducing Nuclear Weapons

       A. Cold war between the U.S. and Russia

       B. Deterrence used by U.S. and Russia—second strike capability

       C. Series of Arms talks

          1. SALT I

          2. SALT II

          3. START I

          4. START II

     X. Osama bin Laden

Key Terms

Balance of power—bring order to international relations by creating a system of friendship between nations where relative strength could balance that of others

Collective security—bring all nations together to guarantee each other's territorial integrity and independence against external aggression

New World Order—secret movement aimed to place the world under a global totalitarian dictatorship

One World Government—creation of the New World Order

Truman Doctrine—called for support of free people who are being pressured by armed minorities

Cold War—political and military struggle between the U.S. and Soviet Union

Containment—strategy to oppose the expansion of Soviet power through the use of military power, economic assistance, and political influence

Marshall Plan—program to rebuild the nations of Western Europe in the aftermath of WWII in order to stop communist takeover

Deterrence—setting up second strike capabilities

Mutual Assured Destruction—assuring the death of each other's country

SALT I—treaty to limit ABMs

SALT II—treaty to limit strategic launch vehicles

START I—1991, reduction of nuclear weapons

START II—1993, first strike capability reduced

CHAPTER 14
The Texas Constitution Yesterday and Today

CHAPTER OUTLINE

I. The Purpose of the Texas Constitution
   A. State made of laws, not people
   B. Legal document
   C. Legitimacy
      1. People value the Constitution—it is legitimate
      2. Constitutional amendments allow changes to be made
   D. Establishment
      1. Constitution organizes and establishes the government
      2. One state government
      3. Framework described
      4. Texas Constitution is long and very specific
   E. The Power to Operate
      1. Social contract theory—people are free and they need to give their consent to be governed
      2. Police powers
      3. Power of taxation
      4. State is the source of protection
   F. Limitations
      1. Constitutions tell the government what it cannot do
      2. Texas Bill of Rights—first ten amendments
      3. Texas Bill of Rights provides maximum standards
II. Texas Constitution Yesteryear and Beyond
   A. Seven Constitutions
      1. First—1827
      2. Second—1836—Republic of Texas established
      3. Third—1845—Admitted into the Union—Statehood Constitution
         a. Created biennial legislative session
         b. Permanent school fund
         c. Homestead Act
      4. Fourth—1861—after succession from Union slavery added to the Constitution
      5. Fifth—1866—line item veto added

6. Sixth—1869—conform to radical reconstructionists
   a. Contained annual legislative sessions, appointed judiciary
   b. Big salaries for state officials
   c. E.J. Davis Governor
      - Threatening administration—using power to control
7. Seventh—1876—Constitution
   a. Highly restrictive
   b. Anti-governmental due to E.J. Davis

Key Terms

Tacit consent—implied consent from actions or statements

Social contract theory—belief that people are free and equal by God-given right and that this requires all people give their consent to be governed

Biennial—once every two years

Community property—any property gained by one spouse during a marriage is equally the property of the other spouse

Militia—voluntary force to protect the homeland

CHAPTER 15

Why Texas Politics?

CHAPTER OUTLINE

I. Understanding Government and Politics in Texas
  A. Texas history of individualism and traditionalism
  B. State legislature requires 6 hours of government or political science in college
  C. Grades six and seven—civics or history
  D. Political awareness
II. Texas Politics and Government
  A. Politics—the art or science of government or governing
  B. Politics is involved when goods need to be distributed
  C. Government—the act or process of governing
  D. Public Policy—any government decision
III. Ideas in America and Texas
  A. Five basic ideas
    1. Individualism
    2. Liberty
    3. Equality
    4. Constitutionalism
    5. Democracy
IV. Three Ideas Relevant to Political Analysis
  A. Individualism
    1. Most important value for Texans
    2. There is no authority over a person's absolute freedom
    3. High priority placed on the individual in Texas—open shop law
  B. Liberty
    1. Allowed to make own choices
    2. Interference in order to maintain control
  C. Equality
    1. Does not mean the same to everyone
    2. Political equality—one person one vote
    3. Economic equality—each person should have the same wealth
    4. Equality of opportunity—everyone should have the same chances in life no barriers to success

    D. Democracy
      1. People rule
      2. Participation in government decisions
  V. Conditions of Democracy
    A. Political equality—no matter my preference, it is counted equally
    B. Participation—majority engaged in political process
    C. Nontyranny—rights of citizens will not be violated
    D. Deliberation—citizens are able to talk about issues with candidates
  VI. Forms of Democracy
    A. Classical democracy
      1. Individual most important
      2. Individual given the opportunity to participate
      3. Participation is valued
      4. System does not exclude anyone from participation
      5. Impossible model in a large city
    B. Majoritarian democracy
      1. Majority rule
      2. Majority is not always correct
      3. Minority rights must be considered
      4. One person one vote
      5. Majority cannot take away rights of the minority
    C. Pluralist democracy
      1. Divide the power among many
      2. Minority and majority rights are protected
      3. Texas divided into different levels—representatives elected to speak for citizens
  VII. Elitist Challenge
    A. Small number of people control decisions
    B. Elite run for political office and are involved in the political process
    C. Person running for office needs to be able to afford the campaign

Key Terms

Politics—the art or science of government or governing

Government—the act or process of governing

Public Policy—any government decision

Political equality—no matter what my preference it is counted equally

Economic equality—each person should have the same wealth

Equality of opportunity—everyone should have the same chances in life no barriers to success

Democracy—people rule

Participation—majority engaged in political process

Nontyranny—rights of citizens will not be violated

Deliberation—citizens have the ability to talk about issues or candidates

Classical democracy—individual most important

Majoritarian democracy—majority rule

Pluralist democracy—divide power

Elitism—those who participate in the political process economically

CHAPTER 16

Local Government: Texas Cities, Counties, and Special Districts

CHAPTER OUTLINE

I. Local Governments in Texas
   A. Created by the state
   B. State did not provide resources
   C. 1990s jail facilities needed, no money from State
   D. Carry out state responsibilities—Dillon Rule
   E. Home rule status—allows cities to have authority over decisions and policies
II. Types of Cities
   A. Diversity
   B. 1800s rural and agrarian
   C. Two types of cities—Constitution of 1876
      1. General law city—a city is only allowed to exercise powers specifically granted by the legislature
         a. Fewer than 5,000 residents
         b. Many restrictions
      2. Home rule city
         a. Population of 5,000 or more
         b. Can adopt any form of government that does not conflict with the state Constitution
         c. Charter—city's constitution
III. Forms of Governments in Texas
   A. Mayor-Council
      1. Legislative function to the council
      2. Executive function to the mayor
      3. Mayor elected by the people
         a. Weak mayor—most Texas cities support this, top ten cities have weak mayor system
            • Do not have the power to appoint or remove city officials
            • Minimal budget authority

        b. Strong mayor
- Appoints city officials with approval of the city council
- El Paso and Houston

        c. City charter will determine the mayor's powers

    4. City Commission

        a. 1900 Galveston

        b. Citizens proposed a more responsive city government due to Galveston hurricane

        c. Elected commissioners collectively serve as a policy-making body and administrative heads of departments

        d. Ennis, Texas uses this form

  B. Council-Manager

        a. Policy if set by elected council members, but a professional manager is hired to carry out the day to day duties

        b. Very popular in Texas

        c. Policy and administration are separate

        d. Mayor is figurehead

        e. Council hires the city manager

        f. Turn public policy into action

        g. Create the budget

        h. Need excellent financial skills

        i. Average salary $183,000—tenure on average 3–5 years in a city

IV. County Government in Texas

  A. Administrative subunit of the state—authority comes from state

  B. 3,066 counties in U.S.—254 in Texas

  C. Los Angeles County—largest population

  D. Deliberation—citizens are able to talk about issues with candidates

  E. Collection of state taxes, enforcing state laws

V. Metropolitan Challenge

  A. Metropolitan Statistical Area (MSA)—official designation of a metropolitan region in the U.S.

  B. Problems

        a. Air pollution

        b. Crime control

        c. Housing

        d. Education

        e. Transportation

        f. Racial Discrimination

Key Terms

General law city—a city is only allowed to exercise powers specifically granted by the legislature

Home rule city—allows cities to have authority over decisions and policies

Strong mayor—appoints city officials with approval of the city council with political power

Weak mayor—do not have the power to appoint or remove city officials, minimal budget authority

Council manager—policy if set by elected council members, but a professional manager is hired to carry out the day to day duties

City Commission—elected commissioners collectively serve as a policy making body and administrative heads of departments

Metropolitan Statistical Area—official designation of a metropolitan region in the U.S.

CHAPTER 17

Texas Political Culture

CHAPTER OUTLINE

I. Texas Terrain
   A. Big Bend Country
   B. Panhandle Plains
   C. Hill Country
   D. Prairies and Lakes
   E. Piney Woods
   F. South Texas Plains
   G. Gulf Coast Region
II. Demographics of Texas
III. Political Culture—Political values and beliefs of a people about their political system
   A. Individualistic Political Culture—focuses on the individual without government interference
   B. Moralistic Political Culture—focuses on government doing good for the people
   C. Traditionalistic Political Culture—Government controled by societies elite

Key Terms

Aquifer—underground layer of rock or sand that captures and holds water
Political Culture—the political valuses and beliefs of a people about their political system
Individualistic Politcal Culture—focuses on the individual without government interference
Morlaistic Political Culture—focuses on government doing good for the people
Traditionalistic Political Culture—government controlled by societies elite

CHAPTER 18

Texas Political Participation

CHAPTER OUTLINE

I. African American Right to Vote in Texas
II. Hispanic Right to Vote
III. Women's Right to Vote
IV. Participation in the Texas Voting Process

Key Terms

Political Participation—when you take an active part in influencing government decisions
Poll Taxes—paying money to vote
Tejanos—Hispanics

CHAPTER 19

Texas Elections and Voting

CHAPTER OUTLINE

I. Types of Elections
    A. Primary Elections
    B. General Elections
    C. Special Elections
II. Texas Electorate

Key Terms

Secretary of State—person in charge of all election activities
Primary Election—first step in choosing one Democratic candidate and one Republican candidate
General Election—Republican candidate for office runs against the Democratic candidate
Special Election—takes place at carious times throughout the year
Run off Election—if one candidate did not win the majority of the vote this election is conducted

CHAPTER 20

Political Parties

CHAPTER OUTLINE

Key Terms

Political Parties—organizations that assist candidate in being elected to a government post

Republican—one of the mainstream political parties symbolized by an elephant

Democrat—one of the mainstream political parties symbolized by an donkey

Party Platform—expresses the values and beliefs in and will vote and fight for in their positions

Temporary Party Organization—Takes place on the even numbered years

Permanent Organizational Structure—the structure of the Texas political parties

Parlimentary Procedure—used in meetings as a way to be equitable and fair

CHAPTER 21

Interest Groups: Attaining Their Share and More

CHAPTER OUTLINE

I. Introduction
  A. Interest Groups—groups try to achieve their goals with government assistance
  B. Lobbying—making contact with public officials
  C. Founders warned of selfishness of interest groups
II. A Nation of Joiners
  A. Alexis de Tocqueville—French
    1. Noticed the tendency of Americans to join groups
    2. Americans are open to the idea of groups
    3. More diverse country than many—need an avenue to express views and opinions
    4. Constitution allows groups to be formed without being persecuted
III. Why Develop Interest Groups?
  A. Social stresses
    1. During times of war people unite in support or against the war
    2. Protect citizens' rights
    3. Protection against large companies polluting the environment
  B. Economic stresses
  C. Immigration
  D. Urbanization
  E. Industrialization
IV. The Purpose of Joining
  A. Economic and social reasons
    1. Group members receive perks
V. Who Joins?
  A. Wealthy and educated
    1. Can afford the dues
    2. Free time to participate
    3. Interest groups target these people with advertisements
    4. Largest group are whites because of higher incomes and education

VI. Types of Groups
    A. Single issue
        1. Focus on one issue
        2. NRA
        3. MADD
    B. Multi-issue Groups—must be prepared to operate on the local state and national levels
        1. AFL-CIO, NOW
    C. Economic interest groups
        1. Concerned with the economic welfare of their members
VII. Function of Interest Groups
    A. Lobbyists
    B. Provide money for congressional campaigns
    C. Provide political and substantive information to Congress and members
VIII. Interest Group Success
    A. Success depends on the amount of money that can be raised
    B. When a member gets elected to office
    C. Leadership
    D. Patrons
    E. Solid membership base

Key Terms

Interest groups—groups try to achieve their goals with government assistance
Lobbying—making contact with public officials
Substantive work—conducting impact studies on a proposed law

CHAPTER 22

The Texas Legislature

CHAPTER OUTLINE

I. Texas Legislative Structure
   A. Bicameral—it has two chambers, the House of Representatives and the Senate
   B. House of Representatives
      1. 150 members
      2. Raises money for the state
      3. Can impeach government officials
   C. State Senate
      1. 31 members
      2. Confirms governor's appointments
      3. Directs the trial for impeachment
   D. Sessions
      1. Biennial—meets every two years
      2. Meets for 140 days
      3. Special sessions can be called by the governor—they last for 30 days only
   E. Qualifications and Terms
      1. House of Representatives
         a. Need to be a citizen of the U.S.
         b. Qualified voter
         c. At least 21 years old
         d. State resident for two years before the election
         e. Resident of the district elected to for at least one year
         f. Serve two-year terms
      2. State Senate
         a. Citizen of the U.S.
         b. Qualified voter
         c. Resident of the state for five years
         d. One year resident of the district
         e. At least 26 years old
         f. Four-year term
   F. Leaders
      1. House of Representatives
         a. House Speaker

          b. Two-year term

          c. Appoints committee chairs

          d. Appoints all members of committees

          e. Recognizes those who want to speak on the House floor

          f. Assigns bills to committees

       2. State Senate

          a. Lieutenant Governor is the head of the Senate—elected through statewide elections

          b. Appoints all committee chairs

          c. Appoints all committee members

          d. Recognizes senators who want to speak on the floor

          e. Votes to break a tie

          f. Assigns bills to committees

    G. Committees

       1. Make the organization more efficient

       2. Focus on areas of specialty

       3. Draft and revise bills

       4. Conduct hearings

    H. Pay and Compensation

       1. $600 per month or $7,200 per year

       2. $118 per day for expenses while the legislature is in session

       3. Mileage rates same as all state workers

II. Personal Characteristics

    A. Occupation

       1. Low pay legislature leads to many business people and lawyers as representatives

       2. Job needs flexibility

    B. Gender and Party Affiliation

III. Legislative Process

    A. A Bill becomes a law

       1. Bill is drafted—needs to be sponsored by a member of the legislature

       2. Bill must be read on three consecutive days in House and Senate

       3. Bill is brought to committees

       4. Committees might hold public hearings or meetings

       5. Committees determine what happens to a bill

       6. Bill is brought to the House Calendar Committee or Senate Procedural Committee

       7. House Calendar Committee

          a. Daily calendar

          b. Sends notice to all members 36 hours before a bill will be heard

          c. Votes are taken to determine bills that are placed on the calendar

       8. Senate Procedural Committee

          a. Sets the calendar for the Senate

       9. Bill Reaches the House or Senate floor

          a. Bill is read by the sponsor—20 minutes

          b. Questions are asked

          c. All members can speak about the bill and offer changes—(10 minutes is the limit in the House, no time limits in the Senate)

d. Sponsor closes the debate (20 minutes in the House, no time limits in the Senate)
e. Vote is taken
f. During the next session the third reading of the bill is done
g. When both the House and Senate have approved a bill it is given to the governor
h. Governor can sign or veto the bill

Key Terms

Bicameral—two chambers, House and State Senate

Biennial legislature—meets every two years

House Speaker—House of Representatives leader, elected by the House

Senate President—Lieutenant governor, elected by statewide vote

Pro-tempore—elected by the members of the Senate, head of the Senate when the lieutenant governor is not there

Legislative process—the process that is followed in order for a bill to become law

CHAPTER 23

The Texas Executive Branch

CHAPTER OUTLINE

I. Texas Executive Structure
   A. Plural executive branch—each of the members of the executive branch are elected—not appointed
   B. Secretary of state is appointed by the governor
   C. No one person to control everything
   D. 43 states have a cabinet system
II. The Governor
   A. Qualifications
      1. Term of four years
      2. Age: 30 years—minimum
      3. Lives in Texas for five years
      4. Two women and three Republican, the rest Democrat
III. Powers
   A. Appointment powers
      1. Appoint people to 150 boards and commissions to six year terms
   B. Budgetary Powers
      1. Governor only makes recommendations to the legislature
      2. Legislative Budget Board—lieutenant governor, speaker of the house and 8 other legislative members write the budget
      3. Can make emergency transfers from agencies to agencies
      4. Reports to the state on the budget situation at the beginning of each session
   C. Military powers
      1. Governor cannot declare war
      2. Governor can call the National Guard, Texas Rangers, or DPS into action when natural disasters or riots break out
   D. Clemency powers
      1. Governor appoints the Board of Pardons and Paroles
      2. Board makes recommendations to the governor and the governor makes the final decisions
      3. Governor can only issue a 30-day reprieve on a death row case
   E. Veto power
      1. Governor can veto any bill

        2. Governor can ignore a bill—if he/she does, it will automatically become law

   F. Special session power

        1. Governor can call special sessions—30 days at a time

        2. No time limit as to how many are called in a row

        3. Governor sets the agenda for the special session

   G. Compensations

        1. Salary $115,345 per year

        2. Mansion to live in

        3. Travel expenses

        4. Security team

        5. Access to state owned planes, cars, helicopters

        6. Governor cannot work in another job

IV. Lieutenant Governor

   A. One of the most powerful officials in Texas

   B. Elected and serves four years

   C. Power over the Senate and influence over legislation

   D. Will move into the governorship if something happened to the governor

   E. Control over the budget—chair of the Legislative Budget Board

   F. David Dewhurst—elected in 2002

   G. Salary $7,200 per year

V. Attorney General

   A. State lawyer

   B. Collects child support payments

   C. Enforces consumer protection laws

   D. Defends state laws

   E. Civil law cases

   F. Salary $150,000 per year

   G. Four-year terms

   H. Greg Abbott—current attorney general

VI. Comptroller of Public Accounts

   A. Comptroller—tax collector and chief accountant

   B. Must have enough revenue in order to pass a bill—pay-as-you-go system

   C. Conducts audits of school districts and state agencies

   D. Salary $150,000

   E. Current comptroller is Susan Combs

VII. Commissioner of the General Land Office

   A. Land Commissioner manages state-held land and mineral rights

   B. The state owns 22 million acres of land

   C. Provides loans on land to veterans

   D. Jerry Patterson—current Land Commissioner

VIII. Commissioner of Agriculture

   A. Responsible for ensuring there is support for agricultural research and education

   B. Inspections of scales, pumps and meters

   C. Salary $92,217 per year

   D. Todd Staples—current commissioner of agriculture

IX. Secretary of State
    A. Carries out election laws
    B. Appointed by the governor
    C. John Steen—current secretary of state
    D. Salary $125,880

Key Terms

Plural executive branch—each of the members of the executive branch are elected to positions rather than appointed

Legislative budget board—lieutenant governor, speaker of the house and eight other legislative members write the budget

Lieutenant Governor—elected to a four-year term, power over the senate and influence over legislation

Attorney General—state's lawyer

Comptroller—tax collector and chief accountant for the state

Land Commissioner—manages the state-held land and mineral rights

Agricultural Commissioner—responsible for education and research in the area of agriculture

Secretary of State—election activities and laws

CHAPTER 24

The Texas Judiciary

CHAPTER OUTLINE

I. Laws based on Constitution
- A. Two types of law
  1. Civil—non-criminal legal disputes
  2. Criminal

II. Structure of the Judicial Branch
- A. Five levels
  1. Municipal courts
     - a. Lowest ranking
     - b. Traffic tickets
     - c. City ordinance cases
     - d. Constables deliver warrants
  2. Justice of the Peace
     - a. "Small claims" court
     - b. Civil cases no more than $200
     - c. Constables deliver warrants
  3. County Courts
     - a. Assist in rural areas
     - b. Three courts at this level
       - Constitutional County Courts
         - 254 exist, one in each county
         - Civil cases amounts from $200–$5,000
         - Class A and B Misdemeanor criminal cases
       - Statutory Probate Courts
         - Six largest cities
         - Probate matters—guardianship, mental health
       - County Courts at Law
         - Relieve the burden of the other courts
         - Appellate jurisdiction from lower courts
  4. District courts
     - a. Trial courts
     - b. One in each county
     - c. Criminal and civil cases

      5. Court of Appeals
        a. Only hears cases that have been ruled on by lower courts—appellate jurisdiction
        b. 14 courts
        c. Chief justice and two other justices
        d. Dallas has 13 justice positions
      6. Court of Criminal Appeals
        a. Highest state court for criminal cases
        b. Eight judges
        c. Cases can only be appealed to the U.S. Supreme court from here
      7. Texas Supreme Court
        a. Highest civil court
        b. Final jurisdiction on civil and juvenile cases
        c. Chief justice and eight other judges

III. How to Become a Judge
    A. Municipal judge
      1. Local areas decide qualifications
      2. Most are appointed by the city council
    B. Justice of the Peace
      1. Elected
      2. Four-year terms
      3. Does not need to be a licensed attorney
    C. Constitutional County Court
      1. Elected to four-year term
      2. Not required to be a lawyer
      3. Salary of $56,000 per year
    D. Statutory County Courts and Court-at-Law
      1. Judges must have a law degree
      2. Elected to four-year terms
      3. $56,000 per year salary
    E. District Courts
      1. Citizen of the U.S.
      2. Licensed to practice law in Texas
      3. Resided in area for two years
      4. Elected to four-year term
      5. Salary $57,300 per year
    F. Court of Appeals/Court of Criminal Appeals/Texas Supreme Court
      1. Court of Appeals—four-year terms—elected in district in which they live
      2. Court of Criminal Appeals and Texas Supreme Court—six-year terms—statewide election
      3. Licensed to practice law in Texas
      4. Citizen of the U.S. and Texas
      5. Age: 35 years
      6. Practicing attorney or judge for at least 10 years

IV. Is the Judiciary for Sale?
    A. Texas one of only eight states electing judges
    B. Candidates launch statewide elections
    C. Money is needed for elections

Key Terms

Civil cases—non-criminal legal disputes

Original jurisdiction—cases heard for the first time

Appellate jurisdiction—cases ruled on in a lower court and are sent to another level to determine if legal procedures were followed correctly

Municipal Courts—Limited jurisdiction, lowest level

Justice of Peace—elected position, cases under $200

District Courts—each county has one, criminal and civil cases

Constitutional County Courts—Civil cases between $200–$5,000

Statutory Probate Courts—hear probate cases

County Courts at Law—relieve burden of other county courts, civil jurisdiction

Court of Appeals—hears cases ruled on in the lower courts, 14 in Texas

Court of Criminal Appeals—highest court in Texas for criminal cases

Supreme Court—highest civil court in Texas